.

"Lest We Be Marshall'd"

SERIES ON LAW, POLITICS, AND SOCIETY

JUDICIAL POWERS AND POLITICS
IN OHIO, 1806–1812

Donald F. Melhorn Jr.

The University of Akron Press
Akron, Ohio

FIRST EDITION 2003

07 06 05 04 03   5 4 3 2 1

LIBRARY OF CONGRESS CATALOGING-IN-PUBLICATION DATA

Melhorn, Donald F., 1935–
    Lest we be marshall'd : judicial powers and politics in Ohio,
1806–1812 / Donald F. Melhorn, Jr.
        p. cm.
    ISBN 1-931968-01-2 (hardcover : alk. paper)
    1. Judicial power—Ohio—History.   2. Judicial review—Ohio—
History. 3. Political questions and judicial power—Ohio—History.
I. Title.
KFO525 .M45 2003
347.771'012—dc21

                                                 2003005510

The paper used in this publication meets the minimum requirements of

American National Standard for Information Sciences—Permanence of Pa-

per for Printed Library Materials, ANSI Z 39.48—1984. ∞

To Marshall & Melhorn and its people

The judiciary—but not to remain so independent
as to place it without control or responsibility,
lest we again be *Marshall'd*.

One gun, three cheers!

—A Fourth of July toast, drunk in Cincinnati in 1808

Contents

Illustrations   xi

Preface   xiii

INTRODUCTION   A Question for President Jefferson   1

1   Judicial Review and the Constitution   7

2   The First Ohio Decision: *The Cost Award Cases*   19

3   The Ohio Supreme Court Hears *Rutherford v. M'Faddon*   35

4   A Moot Court Argument   47

5   Judicial Review Challenged: *". . . lest we again be Marshall'd"*   61

6   Charles Hammond and *The Rights of the Judiciary*   77

7   The Judges Impeached: The Opposing Contentions   88

8   The Judges Tried: Proceedings in the Ohio Senate   106

9   The Judges Deprived: The *Sweeping Resolution*   119

10   The Judges Defiant: Tod and Sprigg   136

11   Greene County's Subversives: Snowden and Huston   149

12   The Resolution Repealed   164

13   A New Constitutional Equilibrium   179

Appendix

A. *The Cost Award Cases*   193

B. Charles Hammond, *The Rights of the Judiciary*, with appended text of Sloan's speech in the Ohio House of Representatives   197

C. Article of Impeachment, George Tod   237

D. Circular Letter of Members of the Ohio Bar   239

E. *Resolution on the Subject of Filling Vacancies
in Office* [the "Sweeping Resolution"]   241
F. James Snowden, "To the Resolution Judges of the State of Ohio"   242

Abbreviations   247

Notes   249

Bibliography   271

Index   281

Illustrations

Samuel Huntington 43

The Litchfield Law School, Litchfield Connecticut 48

Tapping Reeve lecturing to students 49

Charles Hammond 83

Article of Impeachment against George Tod 97

George Tod 103

The Old Statehouse, Chillicothe 109

The Borders Cabin 151

Tod's tally sheet of Ohio Senate roll call votes on repeal
of the Sweeping Resolution 173

Calvin Pease 185

George Tod 190

Preface

Dame Veronica Wedgwood, a historian of the English Revolution and a superb storyteller, once observed that an "experiment in reconstructing as accurately and fully as possible a detached incident or character *without attempting to prove any general point or demonstrate any theory whatsoever* is a useful exercise" from which, sometimes, "unexpected clues are found to far more important matters."[1] Such an experiment began for me with the discovery that during the first decade after Ohio's admission to the Union in 1803, two of the state's judges had been put on trial by impeachment for claiming the power to pass on the constitutionality of laws enacted by the state legislature. While the incident was addressed by political historians and briefly mentioned in comprehensive histories of the Ohio legal profession, no lawyer had ever attempted to reconstruct it. I thought this might be done in an article-length piece which a law review might publish. I little expected that recounting this seemingly aberrational episode would implicate any general point or theory about the power of courts to pass on the constitutionality of laws—the "power of judicial review"—a distinctive feature of American jurisprudence which has fascinated legal historians and constitutional scholars. This book exhibits the fate of that expectation.

My adventures in pursuing the story left me with a profound sense of gratitude for the privileges of access to some of the nation's great libraries, and of appreciation for the courtesy and assistance invariably extended by their research librarians. I regret that preoccupation with the objects of my searches kept me from recalling many of their names, but that has taken nothing from the sincerity of my thanks to them. They include those who staff research desks at libraries of the Ohio State Historical Society in Columbus, the Western Reserve Historical Society in Cleveland, the Harlan Hatcher Graduate Library at the University of Michigan, and the Sterling Memorial Library and especially its Manuscripts and Archives Division, at Yale. The law libraries where I was generously assisted in much of my legal research are those of the University of

Michigan and the University of Toledo. Among staff members in pubic and county libraries I have particularly to thank the Toledo-Lucas County Public Library's James Marshall and Michael Lora, Gillian Marsham Hill of the Greene County Records and Archives Center, and the Muskingum Genealogical Society's Don Atkinson. And I owe large debts of gratitude to Catherine Keene Fields, Director of the Litchfield Historical Society, to the members of her staff, and to Lynne Templeton Brickley whose research endeavors together with those of earlier volunteers have contributed greatly to the society's incomparably rich repository of information about early American legal education.

Andrew R. L. Cayton, Professor of History at Ohio's Miami University and a distinguished historian of early Ohio and the Old Northwest, was kind enough to join me some years ago in giving a Continuing Legal Education seminar at a convention of the Ohio State Bar Association, which provided opportunities both to attempt my first telling of the story of the impeachment trials and, in Professor Cayton's part of the session, to hear his assessment of the trials' setting in a broader historical context. Professor Suzanna Sherry, then of the University of Minnesota Law School and an editor of *Constitutional Commentary*, was helpful in regard to publication in that journal of an article I had written, recounting a moot court argument over judicial review by the students at Litchfield Law School. And my publisher the University of Akron Press, its Director Michael Jabara Carley, its Production Coordinator Amy Petersen, and the two referees who anonymously reviewed earlier drafts to provide criticisms and suggestions I found immensely valuable, all deserve special thanks.

The law firm of Marshall & Melhorn, to whose people this book is dedicated, was founded in Toledo by Edwin J. Marshall in 1895. A relic of his legal scholarship is the remnant of Marshall's great collection of law books still in the firm's library—all that it has space to retain. Among this remnant are the foundation works of Ohio's legal history: the session laws going back to territorial times, the earliest works of statutory codification, the first law journals, and all the case reports. The practical benefit of having these works ready at hand was enormous, for significant parts of the story, never previously recounted, did not become apparent to me until, in the course of writing, I began to assemble disconnected bits of information, much of it from these sources.

The privilege of conducting a seminar course on the history of the American legal profession at the University of Toledo College of Law has given me the advantage of teaching about some of the events here described, and my students have helped me to perceive, and in at least one case to find, things that I would otherwise have missed. In that case a seminar paper by Jonathan H. Cable, a descendant of Ohio lawyers in almost every generation back to the first settlers, provided biographical information concerning his ancestor Philip Cabell, one of the judges of the Jefferson County Court of Common Pleas, who cast a decisive vote for the ruling by which that court became the first in Ohio to claim and exercise the power of judicial review.

Colleagues, two of their spouses, and others who read parts of my draft manuscript for clarity provided valuable suggestions and insights. I am indebted for these contributions to Roman Arce, John F. Bodie Jr., Stephen P. Evans, James and Cindy Irmen, Paul and Carol Kraus, Kenneth J. Mauer, Ruth A. Meacham, Amy M. Natyshak, Thomas W. Palmer and Michael S. Scalzo, all of Marshall & Melhorn, along with Judge Richard W. Knepper of the Ohio Sixth District Court of Appeals, and my neighbor Ryan L. Schoen.

The assistance and expertise of the firm's librarian Barbara Avery, its information systems manager Devon A. Gordon, mailroom supervisor Sylvester Jackson, and my secretary Kimberly K. Tippin were always cheerfully provided, and are particularly appreciated when I reflect on what, in each case, being without that help would have meant.

"Lest We Be Marshall'd"

SERIES ON LAW, POLITICS, AND SOCIETY

A Question for President Jefferson

"You will probably think it very extraordinary, in an individual unknown to you, to take the Liberty of addressing you," wrote Leonard Jewett to Thomas Jefferson in July 1809, a few months after Jefferson's completion of his second presidential term. Jewett was a freshman member of the Ohio House of Representatives. "The subject on which I crave your Opinion," his letter continued, "is simply this:

Have the judges of our high Judicial Courts the right of declaring a Law Unconstitutional Null and Void, whenever the Law is manifestly at Variance with the Constitution?

"This question," Jewett reported, "has agitated our State for two or three years and still threatens us with unpleasant forebodings."[1]

Jewett's letter is not a recent find; it is included in one of the earliest published collections of Jefferson's correspondence. But the events in Ohio to which it refers have been passed over, up to now, in works of American legal history. Had it been a legislator from New York, say, or Massachusetts, or Virginia who had written in 1809, six years after *Marbury v. Madison*,[2] to report that a disruptive public controversy over the power of courts to pass on the constitutionality of laws had broken out in one of those states, that news would have gotten considerable attention. Scholars have taken great interest in the establishment of such a power—now called "the power of judicial review."[3] It is a distinctive feature of American constitutional jurisprudence.

Parts of the story have been recounted capably in modern works of political history. Andrew R. L. Cayton's *The Frontier Republic: Ideology and Politics in the Ohio Country, 1780–1825*, and Donald J. Ratcliffe's *Party Spirit in a Frontier Republic: Democratic Politics in Ohio, 1793–1821* both include in their comprehensive accounts of political life in early Ohio some of the occurrences Jewett referred to. William T.

Utter's "Judicial Review in Early Ohio," an article published in the *Mississippi Valley Historical Review* in 1927, is the first scholarly work on the subject, but it does not address the occurrences' setting in constitutional history, or in the history of the Ohio legal profession. The context of related contemporary happenings outside Ohio is well covered in Richard E. Ellis's *The Jeffersonian Crisis: Courts and Politics in the Young Republic.* An article by William E. Nelson on the evolution of constitutional theory in the states, published in 1972, examines the exercise of judicial review by state courts prior to the Civil War, but its conclusions are subject to the limitation of a research base which includes little about Ohio. The same limitation afflicts Nelson's recent work, *Marbury v. Madison: The Origins and Legacy of Judicial Review,* where, in a summary applicable as well to the states, he declares that "neither the doctrine of judicial review nor the cases decided under it aroused significant controversy during the decades from 1790 to 1820." Leonard Jewett and his fellow citizens of Ohio's frontier republic would have disagreed warmly with that assertion.[4]

The author of this present work is a lawyer, and a teacher of a law school course on the history of the American legal profession. Published during the bicentennial year of Ohio statehood, the work is intended for a readership that, it is hoped, will include fellow members of the bar and lay persons interested in the early history of the state, as well as scholars of American constitutional history. Readers in each of these constituencies will find the book's topical coverage broader than expected in some respects, in others perhaps narrower than might be desired. The author's affection for the profession in which he and his paternal ancestors have gained their livelihood will be evident in a more comprehensive portrayal of the legal system, greater attention to biographical detail, and considerably more anecdotal content than would be typical of a work of legal history focusing entirely on judicial review—here a principal, but not the sole subject of the narrative.

Jefferson did not reply to Jewett's letter. He had refrained from expressing his view of the judiciary's constitutional powers on a previous occasion when he thought that might embarrass fellow Republicans, and "furnish something for the opposition to make a handle of."[5] He might have known or suspected that Republican political friends in Ohio were involved in this controversy. Whether or not he identified Jewett with the "opposition" (Jewett was a Federalist), Jefferson was certainly alert to the danger of embarrassing allies in the new state with a frank discussion of the power of courts to pass on the constitutionality of laws.

Jefferson believed in the separation of governmental powers, and in the balance of powers thus separated. Throughout his public life he decried whatever he perceived to threaten that balance, and supported whatever he thought would safeguard it. But as the nature of that threat changed during his lifetime, so did Jefferson's views on judicial review. In his *Notes on the State of Virginia,* written in 1781–82 and published in 1787, he urged that "the powers of government should be so divided and balanced among the several [branches], as that no one could transcend their legal limits without being effectually checked and restrained by the others," and criticized the constitution his home state of Virginia had adopted in 1776, for establishing the legislature's primacy over both the governor and the state's courts. Later writings confirm Jefferson's expectation that the "effectual check" would be administered by courts as they passed on challenges to the constitutionality of legislative acts in cases coming before them. Writing to Madison in 1789 Jefferson cited as an argument favoring addition of a Bill of Rights to the U.S. Constitution, "the legal check which it puts into the hands of the judiciary."[6]

By the time he took office as president, however, Jefferson was wary of a federal judiciary which had become, as he called it, a "stronghold" of the Federalist Party.[7] He began then to give thought to what has since become known as "concurrent review," conceiving the power to interpret and apply the constitution as being held equally by the three government branches, each judging constitutional questions for itself as they applied within its sphere of responsibility. But Jefferson never developed either a fully articulated theory of concurrent review or a comprehensive explanation of how it would work in practice. He gave a simple example in a letter to Abigail Adams, explaining his actions soon after taking office to dismiss pending prosecutions and pardon offenders convicted under the Sedition Act. Adopted during the administration of his Federalist predecessor John Adams, Abigail's husband, the act had been condemned as unconstitutional by Jefferson and his fellow Republicans, but upheld by the federal courts in prosecutions under the act. Jefferson wrote: "The judges, believing the law constitutional, had a right to pass sentence . . . because that power was placed in their hands by the constitution. But the Executive, believing the law to be unconstitutional, was bound to remit the execution of it, because that power has been confided to him by the constitution."[8]

In this case, where the two branches are in disagreement over a law's constitutionality, each appears to be exercising acknowledged constitutional powers—

the courts to try and sentence violators of a law, the president to pardon those convicted. But what constitutional authority might Congress or a state legislature exercise when it disagrees with a court's decision that one of its statutory enactments is unconstitutional? If the legislative body resorts to the process for amending a constitution, it concedes—at least it does not dispute—the decision's correctness under the constitution presently in effect. Nor can it directly challenge the decision by an impeachment prosecution of the judges who rendered it, for their ouster would not overturn the decision as a judgment; only the judicial branch could do that.

Jefferson was asked about judicial review by another correspondent, W. H. Torrance, who wrote to him from Georgia in 1815. This time he replied, reaffirming his view that the executive and legislative branches had equal rights with the judiciary to determine constitutional questions in matters within their respective competence. "In general," Jefferson wrote, "that branch which is to act ultimately, and without appeal, on any law, is the rightful expositor of the validity of the law, uncontrolled by the opinions of the other co-ordinate authorities." But the explanation and examples he provided for this formula are not very illuminating. As to laws involving property, "character" (i.e., defamation) and crime, all of which come before courts "through a definite course of legal proceeding," Jefferson acknowledged that courts might decide constitutional questions but, he added cryptically, "they of course decide for themselves." As to laws prescribing executive action "to be administered by that branch ultimately and without appeal," the executive would have the final say as to constitutionality. The legislature would have the same power over "laws governing [its own] proceedings." Jefferson admitted the inadequacy of this "branch which is to act ultimately and without appeal" test, where more than one branch has significant interests or responsibility in relation to the subject matter of a law of disputed constitutionality. "It may be said that contrary decisions may arise in such case[s], and produce inconvenience," he wrote. "This is possible, and is a necessary failing in all human proceedings." But if Jefferson did not provide a theoretical answer as to which branch's decision should prevail, he was optimistic that "the prudence of the public functionaries, and the authority of public opinion, will generally produce accommodation." "This," Jefferson wrote, "is what I believe myself to be sound."[9]

But belief in "accommodation" depended on faith; Jefferson did not find it logically defensible. "There is another opinion," he continued, "entertained by some men of such judgment and information as to lessen my confidence in my own. That is, that the legislature alone is the exclusive expounder of the constitution, in every part of it whatever." This view, Jefferson told Torrance, "merits respect for its safety, there being in the body of the nation a control over [the legislature]" by means of a "subsequent exercise of [the] elective franchise." "Safety" for Jefferson was not in the legislature's power over the judiciary, but in the electorate's more remotely exercised power over both branches: in a democratic society the people, he thought, are the ultimate guardians of the constitution. Jefferson even foresaw elections in which the branches' conflicting interpretation of the constitution as it applied to a legislative enactment would be an issue on which the judiciary might "enlist public opinion" *against* the legislature. He saw that possibility as one which "encourages a judge or executive . . . to adhere to their former opinion" contrary to the legislature's. This prediction invoked a fundamental tenet Jefferson articulated in the same letter to Torrance, addressing conflicts that might arise if, as he urged, all three branches were equally empowered to interpret and apply the constitution. A constitution's vitality ultimately depended on "the prudence of the public functionaries, and the authority of public opinion."[10]

This book tells of the testing of such prudence and the exercise of that authority, in a conflict over judicial review in a newly-established American midwestern state, a conflict which lasted for nearly six years. The issue, which Jewett aptly described as one which "has agitated our State . . . and still threatens us with unpleasant forebodings," implicated virtually all arguably legitimate constitutional response options where a claim to the power of judicial review is seriously questioned. Might judges who assert that claim be removed from office? If such removal were by legislative process of impeachment, might it be accomplished solely on political grounds, or would it require a showing of legally sufficient cause? To what might such cause extend, apart from official corruption or acts of serious personal misconduct? Might it include a judge's undertaking to pass on the constitutionality of a law, if the legislature held such an undertaking to be a usurpation of a power not granted to the judicial branch by the constitution? Which branch is to determine whether laws are constitutional, when the constitution itself does not explicitly address the question?

Other questions involved the exercise of the power of judicial review, by a court's determining a particular statute to be unconstitutional. Suppose the legislature, or a substantial segment of the public, disagrees with such a determination. Are there constitutional means of resisting it, other than impeaching the judges or amending the constitution? What if the legislature defiantly reenacts the statute? What if people continue to comply with it? What if the decision invalidating the statute is deliberately ignored by prominent members of the legal profession?

Nowhere else in nineteenth-century America were all these questions presented so explicitly.

CHAPTER ONE

Judicial Review and the Constitution

Jewett's news is more surprising to us than it was to Jefferson. Wasn't the power of courts to pass on the constitutionality of laws, the power of "judicial review" as it later came to be called, settled forever by *Marbury v. Madison* and Chief Justice John Marshall's celebrated opinion in that case, decided in 1803, the year Ohio was admitted to the Union? That was six years before Jewett's letter, reporting the "agitation" in Ohio he found so ominous. And wasn't judicial review a power that state courts had exercised before the delegates met in Philadelphia to frame the U.S. Constitution? Didn't the framers all understand and expect that the "judicial power" the Constitution's Article III conferred on federal courts would include passing on the constitutionality of acts of Congress, even though the Constitution made no express mention of such a power? And wasn't that understanding spelled out and confirmed in the Federalist Papers, the essays of Hamilton, Madison, and Jay which explained the Constitution while it was pending for ratification?

Legal historians are divided on the assumptions behind these leading questions. Some have challenged pre-1787 state court cases cited as precedents for judicial review, suggesting that some were decided on a basis other than the court's holding a law unconstitutional. William Crosskey, among the most skeptical of the readers, has found only two cases that he would accept as such precedents. And against David Engdahl's conclusions that "the delegates to the Constitutional Convention in Philadelphia evidently assumed that courts as a matter of course would disregard unconstitutional acts," and that such a prospect "was discussed favorably at several ratifying conventions," are Professor J. M. Sosin's findings from virtually the same evidence that "the extant records of the constitutional convention do not reveal a consensus among the delegates for judicial review of acts of Congress, nor that even a majority of them positively favored

such power"; that "in no state convention was judicial review a conspicuous issue"; and that "not all men assumed that it [judicial review] would flow auto-
matically from a written constitution or was part of the ordinary judicial function as understood in the Anglo-American legal experience" as it was in 1787.
Professor Larry Kramer has plausibly suggested that Constitutional Convention
delegates who favored judicial review deliberately refrained from moving to have
it included in the Constitution, believing that "any effort to add such a provision would fail, presumably defeated by a combination of delegates opposed to
judicial review and delegates who did not want to invite needless controversy in
getting the new Constitution ratified."[1]

There is also, as Jefferson discerned, a difference between courts passing on
the constitutionality of laws as part of their "ordinary judicial function," and
insisting that whenever in the exercise of that function courts determine a law to
be unconstitutional, that determination not only concludes the rights of the
parties to the case and stands as a precedent to be followed in future judicial
cases, but is binding as well upon the legislative and executive branches of government. That consequence is sometimes distinguished by the term "judicial supremacy," in contrast to Jefferson's doctrine of "concurrent review," which holds
that courts only "decide for themselves" as to the constitutionality of legislative
acts. Nowadays judicial supremacy is widely accepted as a "matter of course,"
and many scholars have dismissed former Attorney General Edwin Meese's suggestion that decisions of the U.S. Supreme Court are constitutionally binding
only on parties to a case.[2] The distinction has added significance for constitutional adjudication in a federal system, where federal courts may be called upon
not only to pass on the constitutionality of acts of the federal legislature but to
determine the scope of the federal government's powers and the limits of federal versus state governmental authority. As Mr. Justice Holmes once remarked
more than a hundred years after *Marbury,* "I do not think the United States
would end if we [the U.S. Supreme Court] lost our power to declare an Act of
Congress void. I do think the Union would be imperiled if we could not make
that declaration as to the laws of the several states."[3]

The prospect that a federal judiciary led by the U.S. Supreme Court would
claim and exercise judicial supremacy over a whole range of questions arising
under the Constitution, not only passing on the constitutionality of acts of
Congress but making decisions binding on state governments that would en-

large the federal government's powers and curtail those of the states, was clearly identified by the Anti-Federalists, opponents of the Constitution's ratification. They predicted that the federal courts would

not confine themselves to any fixed or established rules, but will determine, according to what appear to them the reason and spirit of the constitution. The opinions of the supreme court, whatever they may be, will have the force of law; because there is no power provided in the constitution, that can correct their errors, or controul [*sic*] their adjudications. From this court there is no appeal.[4]

The author of this criticism is believed to have been Robert Yates, a New York lawyer whose letters published in New York newspapers under the pseudonym "Brutus" were taken so seriously by supporters of the Constitution that three of them, Alexander Hamilton, James Madison, and John Jay, were moved to respond in the eighty-five essays originally published in the same media, which became known as the Federalist Papers. In *The Federalist, No. 78* Hamilton came out strongly, not only for the power of federal courts to pass on the constitutionality of laws, but for the supremacy of their judgments in the exercise of that power. Hamilton's arguments eventually become the basis of Chief Justice Marshall's claim to the power of judicial review in *Marbury*. They are the orthodox Federalist justification for that claim.[5]

Hamilton began by asserting what no one disputed, that "no legislative act . . . contrary to the Constitution can be valid," for "the Constitution is, in fact . . . a fundamental law." But constitutional supremacy does not necessarily imply the power of judicial review. Why should the branch of government which applies and enforces laws, not the branch which enacts them, be responsible for resolving questions as to a statute's constitutionality? Hamilton responded to this question with a peculiar construct. "The courts," he wrote, "were designed to be an intermediate body between the people and the legislature, in order, among other things, to keep the latter within the limits assigned to their authority." But he does not explain why the legislature, whose members are directly (or at first, in the case of the U.S. Senate, indirectly) elected for limited terms, should not be seen to have the better claim to act for the people in enforcing constitutional limitations, than unelected judges over whose selection the people have comparatively little control, and over whose tenure as lifetime appointees they have no control at all. Would it not have been at least as plausible to argue that it was Congress, the legislative branch, that was "designed to be the intermediate body" between the people and the courts in matters of constitutional interpretation? This was the view Jefferson cited as an alternative to judicial review—a view which he said "merits respect for its safety."[6]

The same problem of question-begging afflicts Hamilton's response to the anticipated charge that power to invalidate congressional statutes would make the federal judiciary superior to the legislative branch. "The power of the people," he declared, "is superior to both." Marshall would emphasize this point in *Marbury*, declaring that "the people have an original right" to establish the Constitution, that enactments which violate it are void, and not "law," and that "it is emphatically the province and duty of the judicial department to say what the law is." But how far does this judicial "say" extend? If responsibility for determining the constitutionality of statutes were solely the legislature's, then judges' "saying what the law is" would be limited to their determining other problems that afflict legislation, such as ambiguity, or conflict with other enactments. Why is it that the legislature's, not the courts', having ultimate power to determine the constitutionality of laws is a proposition "too extravagant to be maintained," as Marshall asserted in *Marbury*? Professor Sosin has expressed it succinctly: "John Marshall assumed what he had to prove, that the Constitution of 1787 gave this power to the judiciary."[7]

Hamilton's best argument was one in which Marshall must have concurred privately, but would have found awkward to put forward himself. The judiciary, Hamilton believed, is the branch best suited to determine constitutional questions because its members, by and large, are learned in such matters, and are trustworthy. "Few men," Hamilton said, "will have sufficient skill in the laws to qualify them for the stations of judges," and "the number must still be smaller of those who unite the requisite integrity with the requisite knowledge." Uncorrupted by powers exercised by legislative and executive branch officeholders over the purse or the sword, the judiciary, he asserted, "will always be the least dangerous to the political rights of the Constitution." This argument carried substantial weight in Hamilton's time, as it does today. But some of Hamilton's contemporaries who would subsequently come to experience the federal judiciary's performance in the 1790s would find reason to question his reassurance that it was "least dangerous" to constitutional rights.

There is little historical support for the assumption upon which the Federalist Papers are typically cited in modern constitutional litigation, that they were taken as a sort of official explanation of the Constitution's text, considered by state ratifying conventions in the way that draftsmen's comments to a comprehensive modern statute such as the Uniform Commercial Code are laid before enacting bodies to be considered along with the proposed statutory text itself. *The Federalist* did not circulate outside New York until mid-1788, by which time a sufficient number of states had already ratified, assuring that the Constitution would take effect. As Professor Jack Rakove has concluded in a work just published, there is "little evidence that [the Federalist Papers] exerted any influence over the public debate" with respect to ratification. Concurring, Professor Kramer characterizes *The Federalist*'s "canonical status" as "most definitely . . . a post-Ratification phenomenon." It would not have a second edition until 1799.[8]

In the meantime judicial review was challenged by Zephaniah Swift, whose *System of the Laws of the State of Connecticut* was published in two volumes in 1795 and 1796. Although it was based on Sir William Blackstone's *Commentaries on the Laws of England*, Swift's *System* had enough Connecticut content to give it a plausible claim to be the first comprehensive American legal treatise. Swift directly challenged Hamilton's thesis that the judiciary represented the people as guardians of a constitution. To the contrary, he said, "the majesty of the people, and the supremacy of the government" are concentrated in the legislature, whose members "stand in the place of the people, and are vested with all their power, under the constitution." Since in the course of adopting each law, legislators "must consider and determine whether it be compatible with the constitution," it would be a "manifest absurdity, and . . . degrading to the legislature to admit the idea that the judiciary may rejudge the same question which they have decided." Nor did Swift agree that judges were more likely than legislators to make correct decisions on the constitutionality of laws. "It is as probable that the judiciary will declare laws unconstitutional which are not," he said, "as it is that the legislature will exceed their constitutional authority."[9]

Swift's view of the constitutional primacy of the legislative branch was widely held in postrevolutionary America. In early state governmental structures the three branches were by no means equal. State court judges were typically appointed by the legislature to serve for a term of years; the advent of popular election of judges was a mid–nineteenth century phenomenon. Connecticut's judges were appointed for annual terms when Swift wrote, although such appointments were customarily renewed. The constitutionally superior status implied by a legislature's power over judicial selection made the claim of state-court power to invalidate legislative acts seem incongruous. A Vermont lawyer, Daniel Chipman, wrote in his preface to the first published volume of that state's court decisions that the "powers [originally] exercised by the Legislature with the approbation of a majority of the people naturally confirmed the idea that the power of the Legislature was unlimited and supreme." No one, Chipman continued, at first believed "that the judiciary had any power to inquire into the constitutionality of acts of the legislature, or pronounce them void for any cause." It was widely assumed, as Professor Kramer has found, that constitutional restrictions on legislative power were addressed to the legislative branch, and that "it was the legislature's delegated responsibility to decide whether a proposed law was constitutionally authorized, subject to oversight by the people."[10]

Both bodies of opinion on judicial review—the Federalist orthodoxy which Hamilton expounded in *The Federalist, No. 78* and Marshall would reassert in *Marbury v. Madison*, as well as the doctrine of legislative responsibility which Swift espoused—emigrated to Ohio where, during the first decade after statehood was achieved in 1803, they became the doctrinal bases of opposing positions in the controversy over the powers and status of the state's judiciary.

The political elements of that controversy also originated in the East, with the advent of party alignments during the presidency of John Adams. Although the Republicans, opponents of Adams and supporters of Thomas Jefferson, were united by common distrust of Federalist policies, their own ideological makeup was diverse as to a number of matters, including the constitutional role of the judiciary. We have seen that Jefferson himself accepted judicial review as a proper function of courts, with qualifications he did not fully articulate as to how far the binding effect of their decisions should extend. "Old" Republicans, especially strong in the South, who idealized agrarian society, advocated states' rights and held a correspondingly restrictive view of federal government powers and responsibilities, mistrusted the federal judiciary and sought to curtail its powers and independence. "Radical" Republicans in middle and northern states advocated legal reforms which typically included replacing the common law with an entirely statutory regime, simplifying legal procedures, diminishing the role of a professional bar and judiciary, and making state court judges politically accountable. High on their agenda in Pennsylvania and eventually, as we will see, in Ohio, were demands to expand the small-claims jurisdiction of justices of the peace—lay magistrates before whom parties could represent themselves in proceedings conducted informally. Both "old" and "radical" Republicans were opposed by others within Republican ranks known as "moderate" or "independent" Republicans. Historians often use such labels with disclaimers, pointing out that they describe largely unorganized, issue-oriented political group-ings. A principal one of those issues, as to which "moderate" or "independent" Republicans often concurred with Federalists, was the status, composition, and powers of federal and state judiciaries.

In 1798, midway through the single term of John Adams's presidency, the Federalist-dominated Congress attempted to use the law of seditious libel to si-lence Republican press criticism, much of it strident, some of it scurrilous. The Sedition Act adopted in 1798 criminalized publication of "false, scandalous and malicious" writings critical of the federal government or its officials. In ensuing prosecutions of journalists, including a Republican congressman, Matthew Lyon of Vermont (whose offense was to publish in his newspaper that President Adams had "an unbounded thirst for ridiculous pomp"), federal judges not only rejected defendants' objections that the law was unconstitutional, but cut short counsel's attempts to raise such objections in argument and refused to allow them to be considered by jurors. Juror nullification of oppressive British laws had been a treasured feature of American colonial jurisprudence, and the power of the juries to determine the law as well as the facts of a case still had substan-tial, albeit declining, recognition. John Adams once called it an "absurdity" to insist that jurors had to accede to a judge's view of the law "against their own opinion." The jury's exclusion from decision making where the law of the Con-stitution was in question was troubling. Even more troubling were the pro-pros-ecution bias and undisguised political partisanship with which federal judges presided over Sedition Act trials. Notorious in that regard was the conduct of two members of the U.S. Supreme Court, William Paterson and Samuel Chase, who tried Sedition Act cases as judges of federal circuit courts in which they sat. Service in such courts was then a collateral duty of all Supreme Court justices.[11]

Sedition Act prosecutions polarized opinion on judicial review. Among Fed-eralists the controversy tended to "harden convictions" that constitutional inter-pretation was solely the province of the judiciary. But Republicans saw the pow-er of judicial review exercised by a judiciary dominated by their political opponents and corrupted by partisanship, as especially dangerous. Jefferson and Madison experimented with different means of enforcing constitutional limita-tions when they drafted resolutions for the Virginia and Kentucky legislatures advocating state action to declare the Sedition Act unconstitutional. To objec-tions from other states that "the judicial authority is to be regarded as the sole expositor of the Constitution," Madison replied that in "great and extraordinary cases, in which all the forms of the Constitution may prove ineffectual against infractions," the right of "parties to the Constitution" (i.e., the states) to judge whether it has been violated "must extend to violations . . . by the judiciary as well as by the executive, or the legislature."[12]

National elections in 1800 turned the political tide, bringing Jefferson to the presidency and Republican majorities to both houses of Congress. The Republicans' first move against the Federalist judiciary was the repeal of the Judiciary Act of 1801, a lame-duck Adams administration measure which had created badly needed additional federal judgeships. Republicans mistrusted the appointees to these judgeships, all identified as Federalists. But whether they could be ousted by repeal of the law which created their positions, notwithstanding the Constitution's having given federal judges lifetime tenure, was warmly disputed. With the repeal measure expected to come into question before the Supreme Court under newly appointed chief justice John Marshall, congressional debate extended to whether the constitutionality of that or any other federal statute could be determined by the federal courts. But Marshall and his fellow justices avoided the issue, and so declined the invitation it presented for a ruling which might have led to confrontation with Congress and the president.[13]

Meanwhile the Court faced another challenge, in a proceeding brought by William Marbury whose lame-duck appointment as a District of Columbia justice of the peace had been made and confirmed by the Senate during the waning days of the Adams administration. The commission which would enable Marbury to exercise the functions of that position had been duly signed, but not delivered, when the Adams administration left office. When James Madison, secretary of state in Jefferson's administration, who had the routine duty of delivering federal officeholders' commissions, refused to deliver Marbury's, Marbury brought an action of *mandamus* in the U.S. Supreme Court. *Mandamus* is a common law remedy, employed to order a public official to perform an official act within the scope of his duties, as to which he had no discretion. The likely prospect of Madison's refusing to obey any such order issued for Marbury seemed to provide an opportunity to test the Court's authority over the executive branch. Professor Charles Warren thus called *Marbury v. Madison* "the mandamus case." But Chief Justice Marshall adroitly made it a case of judicial review. Marshall's ruling, dismissing Marbury's claim, was that a provision of the 1789 Judiciary Act which purported to grant the Court jurisdiction to entertain suits for *mandamus* was unconstitutional.

The manner in which Marshall came to that ruling was unusual. Whenever there is doubt as to its jurisdiction, a court will almost always dispose of that question first, dismissing the case if it finds jurisdiction lacking, and not addressing any other issue. In *Marbury*, where jurisdiction was purportedly conferred by a law of questionable constitutionality, the Supreme Court might have been expected first to address the question whether it had the power to pass on the constitutionality of laws, the power of judicial review. If it decided that it possessed such a power, the Court would then determine the constitutionality of the provision of the 1789 Judiciary Act on which its jurisdiction in Marbury's case depended. If it held that provision unconstitutional the Court would then dismiss the case, without ruling on the merits of Marbury's claims that he had a right to delivery of his commission and that *mandamus* was the proper legal remedy for vindicating that right.

But Marshall addressed these questions in a different order, engaging in what Jefferson would later call the "very censurable" practice of "traveling out of his case to prescribe what the law would be in a moot case, not before the court." Dealing first with the merits of issues on which the Court could not properly have ruled *after* it found that it lacked jurisdiction, Marshall concluded that Marbury had a right to his commission and that *mandamus* was a proper remedy for obtaining it. Only then did he address the provision of the Judiciary Act of 1789 which purported to allow suits for *mandamus* to be brought in the Supreme Court, and hold that provision unconstitutional. This holding was based on Marshall's conclusion that *mandamus* pertained to the exercise of the Court's *original* as opposed to its *appellate* jurisdiction, the Constitution having given the Court only appellate jurisdiction in cases like Marbury's. Then, having pronounced the act unconstitutional, Marshall finally came to the question whether the Court was empowered to pass on the constitutionality of laws. His conclusion that it was so empowered is the celebrated doctrine of *Marbury v. Madison.* Marshall's arguments for this conclusion were essentially those which Hamilton had urged in *The Federalist, No. 78* for the doctrine of judicial supremacy.[14]

In the meantime both state and federal judges had become targets of Republican-inspired impeachment prosecutions. In January 1803 Alexander Addison, an insolent and overbearing presiding judge of a Pennsylvania trial court who often injected his Federalist political opinions into court proceedings, was convicted by the state senate on a charge of having refused to allow a colleague of Republican persuasion who sat on his court as an associate judge, to address the jury. In March 1804, encouraged by Addison's conviction, the Pennsylvania House brought impeachment charges against three state supreme court judges. The accusation against them was ludicrous—the judges were charged with having ordered a party in a case before them to apologize for calling his adversary "a liar, a rascal and a coward." Radical Republicans backed the prosecution to promote their agenda for legal reforms which included revising state laws to remove Latin and technical terms, referring small claims to arbitration, and expanding the monetary jurisdiction of lay magistrates. The same years, 1803 through 1805, saw Republican-initiated impeachment prosecutions of federal judges. John Pickering, a New Hampshire district court judge whose drunkenness and insanity had made him unfit to perform his judicial duties, was tried by the U.S. Senate in March 1804. In November of that year, after national elections had returned Jefferson for a second term and strengthened Republican congressional majorities, U.S. Supreme Court Justice Samuel Chase was indicted on charges primarily relating to his oppressive and partisan conduct in two trials of Republican journalists over which he had presided while hearing cases on circuit in Pennsylvania and Virginia.[15]

The Pennsylvania and U.S. constitutions both provided for impeachment for "Treason, Bribery, or other high Crimes and Misdemeanors," but none of the accused judges was charged with conduct amounting to a crime. Federalists, in the minority in the Pennsylvania legislature as well as in Congress, maintained that only criminal conduct could be grounds for impeachment, and accordingly they voted solidly against the judges' indictments by the lower houses, and in favor of acquittal when they were tried by the state or U.S. senates. Republicans who supported the prosecutions countered with a theory of "dangerous tendency," derived from the British law of treason. That law held that conduct which threatened public order could be treasonous if it could be said to have a tendency to threaten the king, aid his enemies or destabilize his government. Accordingly, in these impeachment cases the radicals urged a claimed tendency of the judicial conduct that was the subject of charges to produce evil consequences, maintaining that the accused had behaved in a way which deprived litigants of constitutional rights and denied them equal justice. The charges against Judge Pickering thus attacked only his courtroom behavior, and avoided mention of the intemperance and insanity which had caused it.[16]

Both Addison and Pickering were convicted and deprived of office. But the three Pennsylvania supreme court judges and U.S. Supreme Court Justice Chase were acquitted, by votes greater than a majority for conviction, but less than the constitutionally required two-thirds. Moderate Republicans who voted with Federalists for acquittal were the keys to these results. Thus while the Addison and Pickering cases stand as precedents for blatant politicking and mental incapacity as grounds for impeachment, at least where performance in office is seriously affected, the verdicts in the other cases were inconclusive as to the doctrines partisans on each side had put forward: impeachment warranted only for crime, versus impeachment permitted for any misbehavior having a "dangerous tendency."[17]

Commenting on the Chase verdict, Chief Justice of the United States William H. Rehnquist has opined that had Chase been convicted, "it would have been a relatively short step, though by no means an inevitable one, for Congress to use impeachment as a means of curbing judges whose rulings did not please the dominant viewpoint of that body." How short and how inevitable that step would have been might be questioned in retrospect, but at the time it certainly was perceived as a possibility. A speech by one of the federal judiciary's most determined foes, Virginia senator William Branch Giles, especially alarmed the judges' supporters. Introducing a set of rules he had drafted for the Senate's conduct of the Chase trial, Giles asserted that impeachment prosecutions "need imply no criminality or corruption," and that a Senate vote for removal from office was "nothing more than a notice to the impeached officer that he held opinions dangerous to the State, and that his office must be put in better hands." Members of the federal judiciary, Giles said, were subject to removal for any cause which Congress might find sufficient. The Constitution's granting them lifetime tenure "during good behavior" was "merely to shield the judges from the power of the *Executive*"; it had nothing to do with "the power of the *Legislature* over the courts." "Many of the State Legislatures," Giles observed, "exercised a power nearly similar."[18]

Giles went on in that speech to address Chief Justice Marshall's rulings in *Marbury v. Madison.* "If the Judges of the Supreme Court should dare, *as they had done,* to declare an act of Congress unconstitutional, or to send a mandamus to the Secretary of State," he declared, "it was the undoubted right of the House [of Representatives] to impeach them, and of the Senate to remove them for giving such opinions, however honest or sincere they may have been in entertaining them." There are indications that Marshall would have been next in line for prosecution had Chase been convicted. Such a prosecution would certainly have challenged the *Marbury* doctrine, but Chase's acquittal ended that threat. Marshall would continue to lead the Court as it made important and controversial constitutional decisions concerning federal-state relations and the scope of the federal government's authority. But the Court did not again undertake to pass on the constitutionality of an act of Congress until, more than two decades after Marshall's death, its 1857 *Dred Scott* decision invalidated Missouri Compromise legislation which excluded slavery from some of the territories.[19]

Voting with Giles on all of the charges of which Giles would have found Chase guilty was Thomas Worthington, elected to the U.S. Senate from the new state of Ohio upon its admission to the Union in 1803. A native Virginian, Worthington was the acknowledged leader of Ohio's Republicans, and his political stance was vigorously partisan. John Quincy Adams described him sourly as "a man of plausible, insinuating address, and of indefatigable activity in the pursuit of his purposes" with "a sort of polish in his manner, and a kind of worldly wisdom, which may perhaps more properly be called cunning." An ardent proponent of statehood, Worthington had previously come to Washington to lobby Congress to reject a Federalist scheme to divide the Ohio portion of the Northwest Territory with a view to future admission of the divisions as separate states. With support from congressional Republicans including Giles, Worthington convinced Congress to direct the immediate convening of a convention to adopt a constitution for an undivided Ohio, with statehood to follow. The convention was held at Chillicothe in November 1802; the constitution it adopted was approved by Congress; and state government began operation in March of the ensuing year.[20]

After he left the U.S. Senate in 1807 Worthington became an advocate of the positions Giles had taken, against judicial review, against judicial independence, and for the legislature's exercising control over the judiciary by use of a broadly interpreted impeachment power. From Adena, his stately country home near Chillicothe which now belongs to the Ohio State Historical Society, Worthington led a Republican faction in state politics for whom, during the first decade of statehood, the Ohio judiciary's subordination to the General Assembly was the unifying tenet.

CHAPTER TWO

The First Ohio Decision: "The Cost Award Cases"

The first published decision of an Ohio court was carried under the headline "Important Law Intelligence" in the December 25, 1806 issue of the Chillicothe *Scioto Gazette.* Chillicothe was Ohio's first state capital. The court was the Common Pleas Court of Jefferson County, which sat in the Ohio River town of Steubenville. It decided that Ohio courts were competent to pass on the constitutionality of laws enacted by the state legislature, and that a law in question, a measure known as the Fifty Dollar Act which expanded the monetary limit of the small-claims jurisdiction of Ohio justices of the peace, was unconstitutional. Expounded in opinions separately written by the court's four judges, the decision applied to an unspecified number of recent cases, none identified with parties' names. Newspapers—the *Gazette* was then one of five in Ohio, all weeklies—were the only medium in which the opinions could have been published. The advent of a regular system for reporting Ohio judicial opinions was still years away.[1]

Justices of the peace, magistrates elected in each township, were at the foundation level of the state's judicial hierarchy. They were almost always lay citizens without formal legal training; their honorary title was "Squire." Many were men of substantial standing in their communities, reputed for integrity, fairness and good sense. Their judicial proceedings were conducted informally. Hearings took place in justices' homes or in other places. Until 1819 they could hold court in taverns. A traveler passing through Adams County in 1807 "found Squire Ellis seated on a bench under the shade of two locust trees, with a table, pen and ink, and several papers, holding a Justice's Court" on the bank of the Ohio River. The session's business completed, the squire, the parties and spectators joined in a "libation to peace and justice." "There was something in the scene," the traveler observed, "so primitive and so simple, that I could not help enjoying it with much satisfaction." Our traveler must have joined in the libation.[2]

Like other legal institutions, justices' courts were variously perceived. That their procedures were informal and parties could represent themselves suggested that they were tribunals in which people in modest circumstances might have the facts of their cases fully presented and obtain fair and sympathetic hearings. This vision of justices' justice was held by George Turner, a judge of the Northwest Territory's highest court and a member of its legislative council, who debated with territorial governor Arthur St. Clair over a proposal Turner made in 1790 to expand the civil jurisdiction of magistrates who were the justices' predecessors in the territory's legal system. Turner urged an increase to twenty dollars in the magistrates' monetary limit, equating that amount to "the medium value of a cow and a calf"—the domestic animals on which families depended for subsistence, taking that value as a standard for the minimum of property needed to sustain an independent livelihood.

Turner argued that debtors should have an effective opportunity for judicial hearing before even that minimum could be taken by a creditor on execution. A "cheap and summary remedy [must] be provided," he said, "as well to accommodate the time [when a defendant would be able to attend] as the means [the court procedure] to a class of people almost wholly agricultural." Responding to the governor's objection that lay magistrates would be "illiterate and ignorant of law," Turner cited their "plain good sense and integrity." St. Clair did not disagree with Turner's vision of how proceedings before the magistrates would be conducted, but he did not like what he saw. Judicial tribunals, St. Clair asserted, should operate at a higher level of sophistication, and with predictable results. "Arbitrary decisions of single justices often entirely ignorant of law" would lack consistency, with "one justice deciding one way today, another justice another way tomorrow, and a third in a manner different from both." St. Clair despised as undignified the informality of lay magistrates' proceedings. And he argued that making access to courts easy and inexpensive would tend to promote lawsuits, spreading the "litigious spirit . . . like a devouring pestilence."[3]

Sharply contrasting with this vision of a people's tribunal hospitable to defendants' self-representation is Timothy Walker's description of justices' courts in his "Letters from Ohio," describing the legal system he found when he arrived in Cincinnati from Massachusetts in 1831 to begin what would be a highly productive legal career. Walker reported that justices acted summarily, with little

consideration for defendants. "In order to encourage the bringing of suits before him," Walker wrote, "he [a justice of the peace] makes it almost a uniform
principle to decide for the plaintiff. This very simple rule of decision enables
the magistrate to despatch business in a most summary manner. . . . Produce
your claim, swear stiffly to it, and you have judgment in ten minutes." Cincinnati
had become an important commercial center by the time of Walker's arrival in
1831, and his portrayal of collection practice before that city's justices might be
inapplicable to earlier times or other places in Ohio. But there is no question as
to the typicality of Ohio justices of the peace in respect to their interest in max-
imizing caseloads from which they derived substantial income from assessments
of costs and fees. Walker reported that the "large amount of collecting business" attracted to justices' courts made their position "a profitable office, and
there is great competition for obtaining it." The justices enjoyed great political
power. Besides being men of influence and standing in their own communities,
many also served in the legislature. Always substantial, their numbers in both
the Ohio House and Senate sometimes approached near majorities.[4]

The monetary limit of justices' small-claims jurisdiction was continually increased. Starting at five dollars for magistrates in the Northwest Territory, it was
raised by territorial legislation first to twelve, then to twenty dollars—on both
occasions as compromises with Governor St. Clair, who could enforce his opposition with a veto. The limit stood at twenty dollars when Ohio's first state constitution was adopted in 1802, and when state government began operation in
the following year. In December 1803 the new state legislature, the Ohio General
Assembly, increased the limit to thirty-five dollars. The Fifty Dollar Act provided for the further increase to that amount; it was adopted at the end of the next
session, in February 1805.[5]

Expansion of the justices' small-claims jurisdiction affected another group
for whose members collection work provided a significant source of income, the
state's lawyers. Many were opposed to such expansion. But whether, as was popularly supposed, their opposition was based on fear of losing business to parties'
self-representation, may well be doubted. It was, of course, at least theoretically
true that as the jurisdictional limit was increased, parties whose cases fell within
the margin of the increase who formerly had to hire a lawyer to represent them
in the court of common pleas might now represent themselves before a justice.
But lawyers also practiced in justices' courts, and it seems quite plausible that expansion of the justices' jurisdiction brought them more business, at least in

those courts, than they lost to self-representation. Even a law which for the four years from 1820 to 1824 largely excluded lawyers from appearing before justices of the peace seems to have produced little increase in parties' self-representation. During that time lawyers were simply replaced by paid nonlawyer advocates—the pettifoggers, some of whom were famously successful.[6]

It was the comparative efficiency of county courts of common pleas in rendering and collecting judgments for small amounts, that more plausibly accounts for the preference many lawyers had for those courts over justices of the peace in small-claims cases. Convened three times a year and typically lasting no more than a week, common pleas court sessions (sometimes called "terms") brought together in the county seat all the functionaries who were official participants in the judicial process—lawyers, judges, jurors, sheriff, and court clerk. With parties and witnesses also in attendance, everyone whose participation was necessary to move cases along—to trial if need be, then to judgment and execution—was likely either to be present or available to be summoned. Lawyers attending the sessions could work productively, handling several collection cases simultaneously along with other court business.

After statehood, debate over the policy and desirability of increasing the monetary limit of small-claims jurisdiction was overtaken by a constitutional objection. It was claimed that increasing the limit would infringe the right of trial by jury, a mode of trial not available before a justice of the peace. It was argued that, in providing that "the right of trial by jury shall be inviolate," the 1802 Ohio Constitution incorporated the monetary limit on small claims triable by single magistrates, which had applied under territorial law when the Ohio Constitution was framed. Although that limit, twenty dollars, was coincidentally the same as under the U.S. Constitution's Seventh Amendment, which guaranteed jury trial "in suits at common law, where the value in question shall exceed twenty dollars," the Seventh Amendment's guarantee applied only to federal courts. (Other, more fundamental provisions of the U.S. Constitution's Bill of Rights became applicable to the states after adoption in 1868 of the Fourteenth Amendment, which made "due process of law" a requirement of state jurisprudence.) The Seventh Amendment was sometimes cited in Ohio, however, as an indication of the wisdom or reasonableness of that amount as a claimed state constitutional standard. Thus the Fifty Dollar Act was challenged as unconstitutional to the extent that it allowed justices of the peace to hear cases where recovery of more than twenty dollars was sought, cases which at the time of statehood would have had to be brought in a court of common pleas where the mode of trial was to a jury.[7]

There were two defenses to this attack. One was that claiming twenty dollars as a constitutional limitation gave "inviolate" too narrow a reading. "Inviolate," it might have been argued, incorporated the entire legal regime which governed the right of jury trial when the 1802 constitution was adopted, including the authority which the territorial legislature had exercised to increase from time to time the monetary limit of small claims which single magistrates could determine without juries. We will find one instance in which this argument was made, but it was not made often. The more frequently asserted defense of the Fifty Dollar Act was that there simply *was* no denial of jury trial in cases to which it applied, since any party dissatisfied with the outcome before a justice of the peace could bring the case before a jury by appealing it to the court of common pleas.

That opportunity would surprise a modern lawyer. Appeals nowadays only address contentions that a lower court erred on a point of law: it is axiomatic that an appellate court will not retry the facts of the case, with or without a jury. But in the early nineteenth century in Ohio and other states, a dissatisfied litigant had a choice with respect to appellate remedies. By "certiorari" or "writ or error" (the former for a justice's, the latter for a common pleas court judgment) he could obtain review of claimed legal errors shown by the record. Alternatively, by taking an "appeal" to the same higher court he could secure a complete retrial of the case there. "Appeal" had a broader meaning then; one scholar has described it as "an equitable rehearing in front of a superior authority." In early nineteenth-century practice common pleas courts routinely retried cases brought on appeal from justices of the peace, and the Ohio Supreme Court retried cases appealed from common pleas courts. Such retrials were conducted with juries in all cases involving claims for a money judgment. The Fifty Dollar Act itself provided for retrials on appeal from a justice of the peace, directing that "the parties shall proceed [in the court of common pleas] in all respects, in the same manner as though the suit had originally been instituted in said court." But there was a catch. In order to secure a retrial a defendant had to post a bond covering payment of the judgment as well as court costs, in the event the appeal were unsuccessful. Opponents of the Fifty Dollar Act cited this requirement, arguing that it made jury trial available only to defendants who could and would post security for payment of the claim they wished to contest before a jury, and so unconstitutionally burdened the exercise of the right to jury trial.[8]

The Jefferson County Common Pleas Court which confronted this constitutional challenge to the Fifty Dollar Act was constituted quite differently from Ohio courts of common pleas as we know them today. The model of a professional judiciary whose members are educated in the law, follow it as a career, and typically come to the bench after practicing for a time as lawyers, took several decades after the Revolution to be implemented fully in state legal systems. Framers of Ohio's 1802 constitution gave the state's common pleas judiciary a hybrid composition with both professional and lay members, adopting a similar feature of Pennsylvania's judicial system. Each Ohio county's common pleas court consisted of a presiding judge, sometimes called the "president," and either two or three associate judges. There were no constitutional qualifications for judicial office apart from residency—presidents to reside within their circuits, associates within their respective counties. But the understanding reflected in elections to the Ohio common pleas bench was that presiding judges should be lawyers, and associate judges lay citizens. Presiding judges each rode a circuit comprised of the common pleas courts of several adjacent counties, while associate judges sat only in the common pleas court of the county where each resided. Originally three, the number of Ohio common pleas circuits increased as new counties were established. Each court in a circuit held its three yearly sessions during the eight months or so when travel was possible; dates for the sessions were set by the legislature; each typically lasted no more than a week. Court sessions were also known as court "terms," and we will sometimes refer to them as such.[9]

All common pleas presidents and associates as well as judges of the Ohio Supreme Court were elected by members of the legislature to serve for seven years. Members of the two houses met together at least once during each General Assembly session, pursuant to a joint resolution which specified the time of the meeting and the offices to be filled. Each representative or senator cast one vote, with a majority required to elect a candidate. Although the 1802 constitution spoke of judges as being thus "appointed," in this work we will take the liberty of describing them as their contemporaries often did, as being "elected." Besides indicating that their selection was by vote, "elected" serves to distinguish the constitutional process for the filling vacancies occurring while the legislature was in recess, when the governor could issue commissions good until the end of the next legislative session. That power of interim selection, which we will call "appointment," was one of the few executive powers Ohio governors then possessed. It was much used during the first decade of statehood, when many judges did not complete their terms and the General Assembly was in recess most of the time. The Assembly's annual sessions began on the first Monday in December and typically ran no later than the end of February.[10]

Besides the vocational distinction which set presiding judges apart as members of the legal profession, there was, in practice, substantial social separation between common pleas presidents on the one hand, and their associates in each county. Presidents rode and lodged with lawyers who followed their circuits, and with whom they typically developed close personal relationships. Associates lived at home; the setting in which their judicial duties were performed was community-based. But having the same judicial powers as their president, whose decisions were always made subject to their concurrence, associates could overrule him, and they could even hold court in his absence. The implications of these powers are especially striking as we try to imagine what American trial courts would be like today, if the judge sat with a panel of lay citizens, poised to overturn any ruling they disagreed with.

Anecdotal evidence suggests that there were wide variations in associates' assertiveness in court proceedings. Some allowed their presidents to take complete charge. One citizen declared that the number of judges on his county's common pleas bench was "one hundred—a *one* and two ciphers [zeroes]." Benjamin Tappan, known for his brashness as a young lawyer, once dismissed an objection that the temporary absence of one of the associates deprived the court of a quorum, by stating that he would address his remarks to the saddle bags the absentee had left at his seat. On the other hand was a long remembered incident in Hamilton County involving Cincinnati lawyer James Gazlay, one of the Ohio bar's first members of Irish heritage. He was fined for contempt when, exasperated over receiving successive but directly contrary rulings on the same question—both rulings made with the associates and the president voting in opposition, but with each reversing his position from one ruling to the next—Gazlay declared that he was appearing before "one mule and three jackasses."[11]

There were better moments. The associates gave each county common pleas court a distinctively intimate connection with the community it served. Their acquaintance, personally or by reputation, with local inhabitants who came before the court as civil litigants or criminal defendants informed discretionary rulings on such matters as granting continuances, giving security, setting bail, and sentencing. In nonjury cases where they and the presiding judge made findings of fact, their "good common sense business knowledge . . . aided in making the findings of the court much more satisfactory to litigants than the verdicts of a jury." Associates also had administrative duties. Remaining in session after their president departed for the next county on his circuit, they settled the prosecutor's compensation and other expenses of the court's operation. One of their local governmental functions was the granting of tavern licenses.[12]

But it was what the best of these citizen judges stood for that contributed most to the value of their service in early Ohio. They were the nexus between locally nuanced commonsense precepts and the "learned law" itinerant professionals brought. To proceedings of county courts of common pleas, at first conducted in temporary facilities so primitive—or so profane when the setting was a tavern—as even then to seem ridiculous, associate judges lent rectitude of character and dignity of bearing. When the first purpose-built courthouse was constructed, usually in the initial decade of a county's existence, the associates often had a hand in the project. They were upholders of the law, deacons of its temples, and, as the Ohio Constitution said, "conservators of the peace in their respective counties."[13]

At its December 1805 term, a year before the *Scioto Gazette*'s publication of their opinions in the group of unnamed cases involving the Fifty Dollar Act, some of the Jefferson County Court of Common Pleas judges had another case involving the same law. More is known of the facts of this case. In August 1804, Daniel M'Faddon brought an action before Benjamin Hough, a justice of the peace in Jefferson County, to collect a debt of $32.50. When the defendant Benjamin Rutherford did not contest the claim Squire Hough gave judgment for the sum demanded. But Rutherford thereupon took the case to the common pleas court by a writ of *certiorari*. The record does not indicate the basis on which he sought review, but *certiorari* would have been the appropriate procedural vehicle for claiming that the law purporting to give justices of the peace jurisdiction of claims greater than twenty dollars was unconstitutional. Actually that law was the Fifty Dollar Act's predecessor, which set the thirty-five dollar limit in effect in 1804 when Squire Hough heard the action. But for a $32.50 judgment the difference between the thirty-five and fifty-dollar limits was immaterial, and the case was subsequently, and in substance correctly taken as a challenge to the Fifty Dollar Act. It became known as *Rutherford v. M'Faddon* after it left the justice's court, in accordance with a practice of making the party seeking review the first to be named in case captions.[14]

The name of Rutherford's opponent is variously spelled. Court records of the case also refer to him as "McPhaddin," "McFaddin," and "M'Fadden," the "-en" spelling being used in the caption in the record of the Ohio Supreme Court where, as we will learn, the action was finally concluded. Still another spelling, "M'Faddon," appeared in a contemporary newspaper report, and although it is unofficial is has been used in almost all subsequent references to the case. We will conform to that usage and settle on "M'Faddon."[15]

Rutherford, the defendant against whom Squire Hough had entered the $32.50 judgment, was represented in the common pleas court by Charles Hammond, a young attorney embarked on a brilliant legal career. When the case came up in August 1805 it was put over for further argument at the next term of court in December. At that term, however, only the court's three associate judges, Jacob Martin, Philip Cabell, and Thomas Patton were present. But they were a quorum, and they proceeded to rule, finding no error and affirming the judgment below. Although the record does not indicate the basis on which Hammond argued for reversal, a subsequent remark by one of the associates indicates that he challenged the constitutionality of the law which granted jurisdiction to justices of the peace of claims in excess of twenty dollars, and that the court by its three associate judges rejected that challenge, disclaiming any power to determine objections to a legislative act's constitutionality. Thus, as of December 1805, judicial review had lost in Jefferson County. But by December of the following year, as indicated by the opinions published in the *Scioto Gazette*, two of the associates had changed their minds.[16]

Unlike *Rutherford v. M'Faddon*, none of the cases which together were the subject of these opinions originated before a justice of the peace. All were brought as original actions in the Jefferson County common pleas court, and would have been tried by a jury had any party sought that mode of trial. Thus the issue in respect to the Fifty Dollar Act's constitutionality was not, as one would be inclined to expect, raised by defendants in a justice court, protesting that their cases were not heard by a jury. Here the issue was raised by plaintiffs in a court of common pleas, complaining of a provision of the act which denied their entitlement to be awarded court costs. Since these cases are not identified with parties' names we will call them *"The Cost Award Cases."*

Ohio law gave common pleas courts jurisdiction in cases "where the amount in dispute exceeds the jurisdiction of a Justice of the Peace." The "amount in dispute" was the amount claimed, not the amount awarded. But the Fifty Dollar

Act provided that where the amount awarded in any common pleas court action was less than fifty dollars, the plaintiff would be denied costs unless he declared under oath that he "did truly believe the debt or damages sustained amounted to fifty dollars or more." But there is no suggestion in the common pleas judges' opinions that such a declaration was offered in any of the Jefferson County cases. If creditors' attorneys got collection cases into common pleas court by routinely overclaiming amounts due, even at the risk of losing their entitlement to recover costs, that would be consistent with our hypothesis concerning the attractiveness of the more efficient common pleas collection process.[17]

Set forth in appendix A, the opinions are published here for the first time since their original publication in the *Scioto Gazette.* For the reader it may be helpful to restate the issues with which Presiding Judge Pease and his three associates dealt:

(a) Did their common pleas court have the power of judicial review—that is to say, was it competent to pass on the constitutionality of acts of the legislature? If so,

(b) Was the Fifty Dollar Act unconstitutional, to the extent that it empowered Justices to hear cases where the amount claimed exceeded twenty dollars? If so,

(c) Where a plaintiff sued in common pleas for more than fifty dollars but obtained a judgment for less, and failed to declare under oath that he had believed himself entitled to more, should the Fifty Dollar Act's denial of costs without such a declaration be invalidated?

The *Scioto Gazette*'s report indicates that the case was "argued at length, upon different days, by Jenings and King, in favor of giving costs, and Paul and Hammond, against it." The argument for awarding costs was that the Fifty Dollar Act was unconstitutional in respect to its monetary limit for the civil-claims jurisdiction granted to Justices of the Peace, and accordingly, that the act's denial of costs in common pleas courts, in cases which properly belonged there, should be disregarded as being "part of the same [constitutionally objectionable] system." The defendants' counsel, one of whom was Charles Hammond, responded narrowly. Conceding plaintiffs' contention that the fifty dollar limit was unconstitutional, they maintained that the act's denial of costs in common pleas should be upheld notwithstanding, as a matter ordinarily within the legistature's purview, there being no common law right to costs. In modern legal parlance the argument was that the cost-denial provision was "severable."

Judge Pease, who wrote the lengthiest opinion, had no difficulty deciding that the court was competent to rule on constitutional questions affecting the validity of legislation. Nor did he hesitate to pronounce the Fifty Dollar Act unconstitutional as infringing a right of jury trial where more than twenty dollars was claimed. "When the constitution speaks of the right of trial by jury," Pease declared, "we must understand it as speaking of the right of trial by jury as it existed under the laws in force when the constitution was formed." He did not address the argument that the right, as it then existed, was subject to the legislature's power to adjust the small-claims limit from time to time as the territorial legislature had done before statehood. He denied, moreover, that the right was adequately assured by the opportunity to obtain a jury trial on appeal.

As to the last question—whether or not the Fifty Dollar Act's denial of costs in common pleas actions was valid—Pease admitted having difficulty. He acknowledged that there was no common law right to recover costs, and that the matter was customarily dealt with by legislation. But he held that the close connection of the denial of costs in common pleas with the constitutionally invalid grant of jurisdiction to the justices made the cost denial unconstitutional as well.

The written opinions of Judge Pease's three Jefferson County associates are great rarities. They are among the very few—if not the only—opinions of associate judges published during the first five decades of statehood while such judges were members of the Ohio common pleas bench. Judge Pease must have encouraged his lay colleagues to write on this occasion, for their opinions would be valuable as public declarations of support against the attack he must have known would come in the next legislature. Two of the associates, judges Philip Cabell and Jacob Martin, joined with Pease to provide the overall three-to-one majority essential for the court to act. Judge Thomas Patton, dissenting, did not deny the power of judicial review, but he argued cogently for the constitutionality of the Fifty Dollar Act. Patton maintained that the requirement for posting bond in order to gain access to a jury on appeal did not amount to denial of the right of jury trial. In coming to this conclusion Patton weighed the "mischiefs and confusion" he expected to result from the court's holding the act invalid.

The other associates, judges Cabell and Martin, acknowledged having been persuaded by Presiding Judge Pease's arguments. Martin wrote that "the reasons he has advanced seem to me conclusive on the subject, and unanswerable." Cabell, in what we may take to be a reference to the associates' previous rejection of a challenge to the Fifty Dollar Act's constitutionality in *Rutherford v. M'Faddon*, admitted having changed his mind. "Upon a former occasion," he wrote, "I conceived the court could not inquire into the constitutionality of an act of the legislature. I was then under the mistaken impression that it was suspending a law. I am now satisfied of the mistake, and concur in the opinion with my brother judges."

For Philip Cabell, lay judicial service was a heritage. His father, Abraham Cabell, had served for decades as a justice of the peace in western Pennsylvania. Neighbors who petitioned for Abraham's appointment in 1771 described him as "a person in whom they have confidence . . . a man of proper reputation who understands both [German and English] languages." Father and son soldiered together in the Revolution as officers in Washington's army. Then Philip moved west, settling in what would become Jefferson County in 1785, two years before the Northwest Territory's establishment. In 1797 Philip was appointed one of the lay judges of a territorial court of quarter sessions. A record identifies him as one of the officials who in 1792 acquired the land for Steubenville's first courthouse, a one-room log building where the Jefferson County Court of Common Pleas sat when it heard *Rutherford v. M'Faddon* and *The Cost Award Cases*. Philip Cabell's service as an associate judge of that court began with its establishment at the time of statehood.[18]

Presiding Judge Calvin Pease was the epitome of a frontier jurist. Born in Suffield, Connecticut, he studied law with his uncle before he emigrated in 1800 to what was then the Connecticut Western Reserve. He was admitted to the bar of the Northwest Territory later that year. When state government was organized in 1803 Pease was elected presiding judge of the common pleas circuit which included Jefferson County. He was then twenty-five years of age. Tall and robust, he endured better and longer than most of his contemporaries the rigors of circuit travel in Ohio's forested wilderness, where county seats were at first no more than hamlets occupying clearings connected by pathways, and rivers without bridges were formidable barriers. Pease was an accomplished horseman; his longtime mount, Pompey, was widely admired. His gift of humor was reflected in stories lawyers who accompanied him on circuit liked to tell about him. Once while being ferried across a river on an overloaded barge, Pompey fell overboard and swam alongside to the other bank, where he and his owner were reunited. Squeezing the water out of the change of linen he carried in his saddlebags, Pease was overheard saying to Pompey, "Are you not ashamed of yourself—awkward, stupid animal that you are—to fall into the water, spoil my clothes, and give me a wet seat for the next ten miles?" Then they rode off, Pompey at a fast trot, leaving Pease's companions far behind. Pease later explained that Pompey was "very much ashamed" of the mishap, and "feared the other horses would laugh at him." On another occasion, after Pease had carefully rehearsed a newly elected justice of the peace in performance of the marriage ceremony, he rode twenty-five miles to Ravenna, the site of the wedding, in time to hear the Justice bless the couple by intoning the words Pease had supplied—*"and may God have mercy on your souls"*—taken from the traditional form of the death sentence. But Pease took his own judicial duties seriously. On the bench he was dignified and decisive, dealing firmly with lawyers who appeared before him, including, it was especially noted, those older than he. The ability to deal effectively with elders might have contributed to Pease's success in persuading his Jefferson County colleague Judge Cabell, who was twenty-four years his senior, to change his mind about judicial review.[19]

Pease was undoubtedly the "very intelligent correspondent" the *Scioto Gazette* credited for having "politely communicated" the Jefferson County judges' decision. But the manner he chose for communicating it to members of the Ohio General Assembly was anything but polite: indeed his choice to publish it in a Chillicothe newspaper a few weeks after they began their session seems deliberately provocative. In the same December 25, 1806 issue the *Gazette* reported that a similar ruling had been made by the common pleas court of Belmont, the next county on Pease's circuit. Losing no time in responding to his challenge, the Ohio House resolved on Monday, December 29, 1806 to appoint a committee to inquire into Pease's "official conduct."

The same resolution charged the committee with an unrelated inquiry into the behavior of Judge Robert F. Slaughter, president of the second, or middle common pleas circuit. The two cases present an interesting comparison. Slaughter was faulted for failing to appear at scheduled sessions of the courts on his circuit. His excuses, pleaded in his ensuing impeachment prosecution, cited a litany of misfortunes—his horse went lame; he couldn't afford to buy another; the owner of a horse he borrowed wouldn't allow it to be ridden to the next county. Illness, another occupational hazard, was Slaughter's excuse for missing other sessions. He had "pleurisy, which is in some measure periodical, happening in the spring of the year"; and he considered it "imprudent and unsafe for him in that situation, to make the whole tour of the circuit—it was the most unpleasant season of the year, and the waters were high, [and] he knows that he would of necessity [have] been compelled to swim some and ford others," and so on, at length. But the Ohio Senate rejected Slaughter's excuses, voted him guilty of the impeachment charges and removed him from office.[20]

The Slaughter case exemplifies a legislature's use of the impeachment power as a broad grant of authority to discipline the judiciary, as Senator Giles, citing the practice of states, had advocated in proposing rules for U.S. Supreme Court Justice Samuel Chase's trial. That practice was already established in Ohio. Dr. William Irwin, a Fairfield County physician who served as an associate judge, had been impeached and removed from office in the previous session for unexcused absences from court, having declared himself "at liberty to neglect his duties whenever they interfered with his private concerns." But Ohio legislators did not regard the impeachment process as limited to neglect-of-duty or other cases of personal misconduct, whether or not criminal. Impeachment appears to have taken as a constitutionally proper response to a judge's *usurpation* of power—his exercise of authority beyond the scope of "the judicial power of the state" conferred on the courts by the 1802 Ohio Constitution. No Ohio legislator appears ever to have questioned the appropriateness of the impeachment process for testing a judge's *claim* to the power of judicial review, to determine whether that power was conferred on courts by the constitution. On the other hand, if the courts had such a power, the question whether an erroneous exercise of it was grounds for impeachment would, as we will see, find Ohio legislators far from unanimous. Legislators in other states who disagreed with state-court rulings invalidating legislative acts had threatened judges with impeachment, but no such threat had materialized in prosecution. In this case the Ohio House committee's inquiry into the Jefferson and Belmont common pleas decisions was regarded from the start as an investigation into potential impeachment charges, with Pease the target.[21]

No record of the committee's deliberations has been found. It would be especially interesting to know whether it was aware of rulings of other American courts which might have been taken as precedents. From subsequent indications that *Marbury v. Madison* was widely known in Ohio we may suppose that the committee members were familiar with that decision. But there is nothing to suggest that they were aware of cases in which state courts had claimed the power of judicial review, or that they were cognizant of two such cases in which legislated increases in the monetary limits of magistrates' small-claims jurisdiction had similarly been challenged as violating constitutional rights of jury trial. In 1786 when New Hampshire's legislature confronted a judicial ruling that its increase of the monetary limit for claims triable before justices of the peace was unconstitutional, there were demands to "impeach the obstinate [judges]." But at their next session the legislators chose instead to repeal the law in question.[22]

In Pennsylvania a legislative enactment increasing the monetary limit of justices' jurisdiction was met by a constitutional challenge in *Emerick v. Harris*, a case appealed to the Pennsylvania Supreme Court. As in Ohio, that case presented the issue of the legitimacy of judicial review as well as the question whether the increase violated a constitutional right of jury trial. But after the court heard argument in 1803 and took the case under advisement, its decision was delayed by the impeachment prosecution of three of its judges, recounted in the preceding chapter. Although all three were acquitted in 1805 the Pennsylvania court had still not decided *Emerick v. Harris* by the time, in January 1807, the Ohio House conducted its inquiry into Judge Pease's rulings.[23]

It is more likely that committee members were aware of *Rutherford v. M'Faddon*, the case involving Squire Hough's judgment for $32.50 in which the Jefferson County Court of Common Pleas by its associate judges had earlier rejected a challenge to the Fifty Dollar Act's constitutionality. The possibility of that case's reaching the Ohio Supreme Court was still open, for Ohio law imposed no time limit for issuance of the process, a writ of error, by which an appeal to that court might have been taken.[24]

Chaired by Representative Philip Lewis, the committee charged with the inquiry was geographically and politically diverse, with at least one member from each of the state's three common pleas circuits. Proceeding expeditiously, they reported within a few days. As to Judge Pease's rulings, they concluded that "the law [the Fifty Dollar Act] is constitutional," and accordingly that his judgments to the contrary were "erroneous." But what they added surprised many House members. "Your committee further report, that notwithstanding they consider the law to be constitutional, yet [they] are of opinion, that courts have the right to judge the constitutionality of our statutes."

House debate on the Lewis committee's report lasted an entire day, as motions from the floor separately challenging the committee's conclusions were each defeated by narrow majorities. Tallies of the floor votes revealed that the committee members themselves were divided—three to two in favor of recognizing the power of judicial review, and in a different combination three to two for affirming the Fifty Dollar Act's constitutionality. Further House floor debate then focused solely on judicial review. Forming themselves into a committee of the whole, the House members voted by an unreported but undoubtedly narrow margin in favor of a proposed resolution that the House has "no right to interfere with the court in giving an opinion as to the constitutionality of a law, unless it appears that they [the judges] have acted through corrupt motives; and further . . . that there was no evidence before them of the president of the third circuit [Judge Pease] and his associates having acted through improper motives." But when this resolution came to a final vote for passage, it lost on a fifteen-to-fifteen tie. On that vote the matter was dead for the session.[25]

To their leader Thomas Worthington, still in the U.S. Senate, his political lieutenants back home reported this frustrating outcome. Lawyer Wyllys Silliman wrote ruefully that "the charge against Judge Pease has fallen to the ground." But Governor Edward Tiffin, Worthington's brother-in-law, hinted at revival. "Part [of the House] were for impeaching [Pease]," he wrote, "but not quite a majority—so the affair rests so."[26]

It was with the judiciary that the affair would rest for the time being. Rulings invalidating the Fifty Dollar Act had been made only in cases initiated in common pleas courts; no judgment of a justice of the peace had yet been struck down. And Pease and his associates in Jefferson and Belmont counties were only common pleas judges; they did not have the final judicial say. Some members of the General Assembly might have been reluctant to take legislative action against a legal ruling which the state's highest court might reverse.

On March 31, 1807, after the session ended, a writ of error was issued to bring *Rutherford v. M'Faddon* before the Ohio Supreme Court when it sat in Jefferson County in August of that year.[27]

CHAPTER THREE

The Ohio Supreme Court Hears "Rutherford v. M'Faddon"

The 1802 constitution required the Ohio Supreme Court to hold one session a year in each Ohio county. The court's members were called "judges," the senior was "chief judge." Dates for sessions were set by the legislature, usually in the same act which scheduled thrice-yearly common pleas court terms. For the first five years after statehood the supreme court had three judges, and the constitution provided that they could act with a quorum of two. That allowed the duties of the supreme court's annual circuit to be divided up, so that each judge sat in approximately two-thirds of the counties. The constitution permitted the legislature to add another judge to the court at any time after a five-year period, which ran until 1808. With the two-judge quorum provision still in effect the four judges could then divide the state into two supreme court circuits, each served by two of their number. But the resulting reduction in each judge's attendance requirement from two-thirds to half the counties was more than offset by the legislature's continual establishment of new counties as the state was populated.[1]

The absence of any constitutional provision for resolving disagreements on legal questions between members of a two-judge panel, or between the two circuit panels of a four-judge court, reflected the framers' expectation that the conduct of trials, not the development of a body of case law through its appellate decisions, would be the supreme court's principal business. Its trials involved cases in which the court had original jurisdiction as well as cases being retried on appeal. The scope of the court's original jurisdiction was at first quite broad, extending to actions where title to land was in question or where the amount in controversy exceeded a thousand dollars, to suits for divorce or alimony, and to all criminal prosecutions. Such original jurisdiction was exercised concurrently with the common pleas courts, except for divorce and alimony and prosecutions for capital offenses, of which the supreme court had exclusive cognizance.[2]

The court's establishment as an itinerant tribunal also reflected the vision of the 1802 constitution's Republican framers, of what the state's judiciary ought to be and how it should serve. Federalists, on the other hand, were appalled by what they saw. Writing to Paul Fearing, the territory's Federalist delegate in Congress who would lose that position after statehood, Marietta lawyer Levin Belt reported that instead of making the supreme court judges "as respectable and independent as the situation of the State would admit of," they would be compelled "to travel, like peddlers, into every County in the State." Thus, Belt continued, "for the sake of carrying justice to the doors of the people, the Judges are to risk their lives from bad accommodations to live meanly sparing, to make their wages equal to their traveling expense, and give their time and trouble to boot." Comparing Pennsylvania's judicial system which the Ohio Constitution's framers had taken as a structural model, Belt noted that "in that State the Judges are well paid, well accommodated and their task made practicable from their number and from having roads from one County to another, and Taverns and Court Houses when they get there." Belt believed that it was not conducive "to the prosperity or respectability of a Society" to make its judges "the Waiters, rather than the Waited-upon." "What a truly desirable object of ambition," he exclaimed sarcastically, "will be a Judgeship in the State of Ohio."[3]

The Ohio Supreme Court's original members were Chief Judge Samuel Huntington and Judges Return Jonathan Meigs Jr. and William Sprigg. Meigs resigned the following year and was replaced by Daniel Symmes. Sprigg's resignation early in 1806 created another vacancy, which Governor Edward Tiffin endeavored to fill by exercise of his power to make interim appointments while the legislature was in recess. The appointment would be effective until the end of the ensuing 1806–07 session, when members of the General Assembly would elect someone, not necessarily the interim appointee, to fill the seat.

The designation "1806–07" exemplifies the convention used to date sessions of the legislature which form much of the chronological framework of events recounted in this book. The Ohio General Assembly met annually on the first Monday of December, and its sessions ran into the following year (here 1807). Elections for legislative seats were held annually on the second Tuesday of October. House members had a one-year term, senators two years. Senate terms were staggered, with approximately half the seats up for election each year. The governor's term was two years. Members of the House and Senate might resolve to meet at any time during a legislative session to elect common pleas and supreme court judges, and they often did so near the end of a session.[4]

In March 1806, Tiffin offered the interim appointment to Judge Pease, who declined it, citing the legislature's recent rejections of other interim appointees. Failure to gain election to the supreme court after resigning his common pleas seat to take the interim appointment would present "a very unpleasant situation," Pease wrote, "having a family dependent on me for support, without property to render me in the least independent, and being hitherto prevented from establishing myself in the profession of the law." Pease's seven-year term on the common pleas bench would run until 1810.[5]

When Pease declined insecure promotion Governor Tiffin chose George Tod, who served on the Ohio Supreme Court as an interim appointee during the 1806 judicial season. Ohio House and Senate members subsequently confirmed Tod's appointment, electing him to the seat at the 1806–07 General Assembly session by a one-vote majority over a rival candidate. The election was held January 1, 1807, just a few days before the House voted inconclusively on Judge Pease's decisions invalidating the Fifty Dollar Act. There is no indication that any of the legislators sought to elicit Tod's views on questions addressed by those decisions. The absence of any procedure for committee hearings or other inquiry into a candidate's judicial philosophy is another reflection of the prevailing perception of judges as hearing officers, not lawmakers.[6]

Tod was a pioneer settler in the Connecticut Western Reserve. After spending the summer of 1800 there with a party of Connecticut Land Company surveyors he emigrated with his wife and two infant children, becoming one of the first inhabitants of Youngstown. Tod was then twenty-seven years old. He had an elite legal education, having completed the eighteen-month course of study at Tapping Reeve's law school in Litchfield, Connecticut. Before that he attended Yale, graduating in the Class of 1795. Ohio Supreme Court Chief Judge Samuel Huntington was another Yale graduate. Senior to Tod in social standing as well as age, Huntington was the adopted son and namesake of a Connecticut signer of the Declaration of Independence.[7]

How did they and other aspiring lawyers who emigrated to Ohio after attending eastern institutions of higher learning, see themselves and (a different question) present themselves, in respect to their educational backgrounds? A modern lawyer inured to the degree snobbery which nowadays pervades American learned professions would be surprised to find almost no mention in any early nineteenth-century Ohio lawyer's writings, of where he was educated. That is not to say that institutional education was little valued. Tod kept his Litchfield Law School notebooks long after they were useful in his practice, and gave them to his son along with his Yale undergraduate copybooks to keep as heirlooms. But if many other first-generation Ohio lawyers had no institutional education beyond what they received in schools attended as children, and obtained their basic legal knowledge by "reading law" with practitioners or by independent self-study, there is no indication of any widely held belief that either of these last-mentioned means of preparation was inferior, if diligently pursued. The statutory educational requirement for admission to the Ohio bar during the first decade of statehood was simply that applicants have "regularly and attentively studied law." The requirement was tested by examination, but if some passed who were unqualified, their shortcomings were not typical of those who made the law their profession. It is a fallacy to equate what might seem to be lenient educational requirements for admission to the bar with the general level of *practicing* lawyers' legal learning—mistakenly supposing, as another writer has asserted, that Ohio's first lawyers were "doubtless men of little education and less legal knowledge." Practicing in settings where direct observations of their performance superseded formal educational attainments as indicators of competence, their professional abilities were continually tested and evaluated.[8]

The egalitarianism which pervaded frontier Ohio minimized the importance attached to academic degrees from eastern institutions. In "Letters from Ohio" published in the *New England Magazine* in 1831 shortly after his arrival in Cincinnati from the Harvard Law School, Timothy Walker reported that "diplomas and titles are treated with a most unreverential levity. The question is not, where or how a man was educated, but what he is." Ohioans, Walker wrote, "hold to the doctrine of equality most pertinaciously." Thus, "if you ask who among us are *lions,* I shall be obliged to answer, 'all or none.' We have few trees towering much above the rest."[9]

The Litchfield Law School conferred no degrees, issued no diplomas, and held no formal commencement exercises. Students left when they completed Reeve's course of lectures, as Tod did in 1797. In October of that year he and Sally Isaacs were married in New Haven, where he was admitted to the bar and practiced for the next two years. Minutes of the Yale chapter of Phi Beta Kappa record that in September 1799 Tod gave an "elegant oration" at one of the society's public exercises in New Haven, on "The Causes of the Low State of Literature in the United States." Departing this seat of learning and culture for life in the Connecticut Western Reserve cannot have been easy.[10]

With the cession in 1800 of the State of Connecticut's claims of sovereignty, the Western Reserve, "New Connecticut," came under the government of the Northwest Territory, and lands in the reserve became subject to territorial taxation. Tod, Pease, and Huntington were all sent out by the Connecticut Land Company to represent landowners' interests, particularly in protecting against foreclosure for tax delinquencies. The three were admitted together to the territorial bar at a session of the General Court in Marietta, in October 1800. Tod gained early recognition for his service as prosecutor for Trumbull County, the political subdivision into which the settled portion of the Western Reserve was organized. His determined but unsuccessful attempt to convict a white settler for the murder of an Indian impressed territorial governor Arthur St. Clair.[11]

Tod and Sally came out with their two-year-old daughter and infant son in 1801, traveling across New York State by horse-drawn wagon. From John Young, proprietor of what was still a mostly notional Youngstown, they purchased a two-and-a-half acre parcel that would become the first of three homesteads they would occupy. Tod acquired the second the following year, an eighty-acre parcel purchased from Huntington after the latter decided to move to Cleveland. Among Tod's papers in the Western Reserve Historical Society archives is a note listing "Expenses of Building My House, Sept. 1802," apparently pertaining to the dwelling he built on this second homestead. Totaling less than twenty dollars, the expenses all relate to the dwelling's foundation, for which he hired workers and paid them partly in whiskey. It is likely that Tod himself erected the log superstructure with assistance from neighbors. Visitors from Connecticut who traveled to the reserve all remarked on the extreme primitiveness of settlers' dwellings. Even "titled men," as one of them called those who were officeholders, lived in one-room cabins "in which all of the family, with their guests, eat, sleep and perform all domestic operations." There is no reason to suppose that any of Tod's Youngstown homes were more commodious. His third, on eighty acres which he purchased on land contract about the year 1805 and named "Brier Hill," was also a log cabin. There he and Sally raised their family, eventually of seven children. They were never prosperous. Sally prepared meals over an open hearth for almost four decades.[12]

Besides its employment as a medium of exchange, whiskey was consumed in quantity on the Ohio frontier, often intemperately. Jacob Burnet, a pioneer of the territorial bar who came to Cincinnati in 1796, recalled that many of the town's first lawyers succumbed to drink. But most lawyers who established themselves to the extent of making at least part of their living from the profession were moderate imbibers. Recounting jovial evenings spent in wilderness taverns with lawyers of Tod's generation including Tod himself, Henry B. Curtis noted that "it would be a mistake to suppose that these convivial scenes were inspired by drinking." With only one, unspecified exception Curtis "could not recall a single instance of drunkenness on these occasions, or excess of indulgence in that vice."[13]

But even those lawyers who came to the Ohio frontier who did not fall victim to drink found it difficult to maintain the intellectual acuity and mental discipline formerly nourished by eastern educational and cultural resources. Young men who went out as sojourners and returned to homes in the East recalled what one of Tod's friends sarcastically called the "paradise" of Ohio, "whose charms for me are now, alas, no more." Written upon arriving back in Massachusetts from a visit in 1804, his letter went on in mock regret to bid adieu to the Ohio country's "endless forests hung with eternal gloom," to "roads of mud . . . where horses mire," to "plains where scrub oaks thrive and horrid serpents dwell," to "streams, with filth & ague stored—and those o' whiskey, too." More than time and distance separated Tod as an immigrant to the Western Reserve, struggling to provide for his family by meagerly remunerative professional employment, from the confident young Yale and Litchfield graduate who delivered an "elegant" Phi Beta Kappa oration at the New Haven State House in 1799. The "low state of literature" he deplored in that speech was nowhere lower than what he would find in the culture of frontier Ohio.[14]

Although the State of Connecticut was overwhelmingly Federalist, the political sympathies of Connecticut emigrants to the reserve were largely Republican. Many joined with Worthington and his followers in southwestern Ohio to become enthusiastic supporters of the statehood movement. Political demographics made it seem inevitable that, if constituted with boundaries as specified in the Ordinance of 1787, the new state would be predominantly Republican. The territorial governor Arthur St. Clair and other Ohio Federalists were, accordingly, opposed to immediate statehood on the basis of those boundaries. They favored a territorial division along the line of the Scioto River, creating two new states to be admitted later when each separately attained a population of sixty thousand free inhabitants, specified in the Ordinance as a requirement for statehood. New Englanders who had settled in Marietta and on other Ohio Company lands in southeastern Ohio were Federalist in sympathy, and they were expected to form a majority in *Erie*, as the eastern state was to be called. A collateral effect of the Scioto boundary would be to deprive Chillicothe of the centrality of its location, eliminating any possibility of its becoming the western state's capital, and improving that prospect for Cincinnati. Thus it was a coalition of Federalist and Cincinnati interests that got a "division act" through the territorial legislature in 1801. The assent of Congress being necessary for the measure to take effect, Worthington and a colleague immediately left for Washington to lobby against it. The territory's congressional delegate Paul Fearing, a Federalist, called for help, urging St. Clair to send emissaries, preferably with Republican credentials, to counter Worthington's efforts and lobby for the division. Tod was to be one of those emissaries, but before he could leave Congress acted, directing the holding of the constitutional convention which met in Chillicothe and adopted the 1802 constitution which took effect the following year.[15]

Tod's being on the losing side of the struggle over statehood eclipsed what had begun as a promising political career. On journeys to southwestern Ohio in 1801 and 1802 he had effectively represented interests of reserve landowners before the territorial legislature. Huntington, writing to Moses Cleaveland who directed the Connecticut Land Company's affairs from its home state, called Tod "the most influential man in our county over the [territorial] legislature." Huntington, Tod, and Pease all then considered themselves Republicans, and maintained Republican political ties both with their native Connecticut and with the Jefferson administration in which Pease's uncle, Gideon Granger, was postmaster general. Huntington and Pease supported immediate statehood, taking Worthington's side on that issue. But Tod having chosen to follow Governor St. Clair, the defeat of the division scheme and St. Clair's ensuing dismissal by President Jefferson left Tod in poor standing with statehood's victorious proponents. Huntington, a delegate to the constitutional convention in Chillicothe, wrote from there to report conversations with Worthington and other southern Ohio Republican leaders concerning Tod's prospects. "They have been very polite, especially Col. Worthington," Huntington told Tod, [but] "they will not allow you to be a Republican. You must convince them of their mistake."[16]

The convincing took time. Elected from Trumbull County to the Ohio Senate in October 1804, Tod gained recognition for his efforts to revise and expand the body of statutory law inherited from the territorial regime. The product of that work occupies the notably fat third volume of Ohio's session laws. When the bill which became the Fifty Dollar Act was debated in the 1804–05 session Tod steadfastly opposed raising the monetary limit for cases heard by justices of the peace, voting against all proposals for limits greater than twenty dollars. Sally gave birth to their fourth child, David, while Tod was in Chillicothe attending that session. Chronically short of money, and needing the modest salary a judicial position would provide, Tod began during the 1805–06 session to campaign for a Supreme Court seat. Whether Sprigg timed his resignation to occur after the legislature had adjourned in order to allow his successor to be seated by interim appointment, and whether Tod also knew that Pease would decline such an appointment, are conjectural. The three were not close friends, but it is plausible to suppose that Sprigg and Pease would have favored Tod's candidacy.[17]

The Ohio Supreme Court's annual circuit ran clockwise, beginning in northeast Ohio early in the month of August, then proceeding south and west through the counties along the Ohio River, turning north through western border counties, and finally east through counties in the middle of the state, reached by mid-December. No courts were held in yet-to-be settled north central, northwest, or west central Ohio during the first decade of statehood. Since both Tod and Chief Judge Huntington resided in the northeast and their colleague Judge Daniel Symmes lived in Cincinnati, the 1806 and 1807 supreme court circuits commenced with Huntington and Tod sitting in the northeastern counties, then alternating as one or the other sat with Symmes in the Ohio River counties. As a rule sessions were conducted with a two-judge quorum. In June 1807, before that year's circuit began, Symmes wrote to Huntington advising that "it will be impossible for me to ride into your quarter this year," and "promising myself the pleasure of meeting you and brother Tod at Steubenville," the seat of Jefferson County, the fourth county on the circuit. In the same letter Symmes remarked that "if any division or difficulty should present, the point of cause can be reserved with the Bench (as usual) until the Court is full." The remark is interesting, for it suggests an early understanding that the entire bench should be responsible for rulings on important and novel questions of law, an understanding later formalized in a practice of holding *en banc* sessions attended by all of the judges. In any event, whether by happenstance or design, the court was "full" for

Samuel Huntington (1765–1817)
Judge, Ohio Supreme Court, 1803–1808
Governor of Ohio, 1808–1810

the session in Jefferson County that year, with all three judges present when *Rutherford v. M'Faddon* came to be heard.[18]

The case was brought up on writ of error, a procedure which, like *certiorari* in respect to judgments of justices of the peace, allowed only legal errors demonstrated by the record to be addressed. The record certified to the Ohio Supreme Court in this case included copies of records in proceedings below, before Justice of the Peace Benjamin Hough and in the Jefferson County Court of Common Pleas. From Hough's record it appears that the action was brought on a "due bill" for $32.50, and began with his issuing a writ of *capias*—an order to seize the person of the defendant Rutherford, which required his giving bail to secure his appearance. Whether Rutherford actually did appear is unclear. The record states that he "confess'd a judgment for the above sum of $32.50," but the confession might have been pursuant to a provision in the due bill that authorized judgment for the amount due to be entered in Rutherford's absence. In any event he did not contest M'Faddon's claim before the justice. There is no indication of his demanding a jury trial, or objecting to the lack of one. Nor, it will be recalled, did Rutherford seek a jury trial before the common pleas court, having elected to bring the case there by *certiorari* rather than by *appeal*.

Charles Hammond again appeared for Rutherford when the case came before the Ohio Supreme Court. Largely self-taught, he had struggled to gain first a literary, then a legal education. As a precocious teenager he contributed as "The Plough Boy" to the columns of the western Pennsylvania *Telegraph*; the following year at age nineteen he began the study of law with Philip Doddridge, a respected attorney in what is now West Virginia. In 1801, his twenty-first year, Hammond crossed the Ohio River to gain admission to the bar of the Northwest Territory, and was appointed prosecuting attorney for Belmont County. For the next several years and while he represented Rutherford he maintained his residence on the Virginia side of the river, but regularly practiced before courts in southeast Ohio. Brilliant, articulate, sometimes abrasive, he was known for his Federalist political views. His opponent before the Ohio Supreme Court in the Rutherford case was Obadiah Jennings, counsel for Benjamin M'Faddon. Jennings was also capable. Jacob Burnet, the pioneer Cincinnati lawyer who was one of the bar examiners when Hammond and Jennings appeared together before the Northwest Territory's General Court at Marietta to seek admission, retained for almost fifty years "a distinct recollection of the very satisfactory manner in which they passed the ordeal."[19]

The Ohio Supreme Court began its Jefferson County session as scheduled, on August 17, 1807, a Monday. Its decision in *Rutherford v. M'Faddon* was announced from the bench on Friday August 21, the date in the court record being confirmed by the Steubenville *Western Herald* in its weekly issue published the following day. Dating of entries of other judgments rendered at that session suggests that the arguments in the Rutherford case began on Thursday and extended into Friday, the day the decision was announced. It is likely that this was the last case heard at this session, for the judges had to be in neighboring Belmont County, next on the circuit, the following Monday. As entered by the clerk the judgment was simply that "the Court are of Opinion that there is error in the said proceedings, And therefore it is considered by this Court, that the proceedings aforesaid be reversed, annulled and held for nought—each party to pay his own costs."

No record of Hammond's or Jennings's arguments to the court has been found, and the formal statements of position noted in the record—for Rutherford, that "the judgment aforesaid [for $32.50] was rendered for the said Daniel, when according to the law of the land, the said judgment ought to have been rendered for him the said Benjamin," and for M'Faddon, a general denial: *"in nulla est erratum"*—are uninformative. The decision immediately attracted attention. The Fifty Dollar Act was well known and popular; Squire Hough was a person of substantial local standing, and the *Western Herald*'s reporting indicates that its editor regarded the case as an important story. In an article headed "Important Law Intelligence" and signed "Edit.," the paper informed its readers that, with Judge Symmes dissenting, the court had held the Fifty Dollar Act "unconstitutional and therefore not law," and further, that "We are assured that the Judges of this Court as soon as they can gain leisure for the purpose will commit their opinions on this constitutional question, and their reasons therefor, to writing, and that we shall be furnished with a copy." "Edit." and "We are assured" suggest that the *Western Herald*'s editor was either present at the hearing or spoke with the judges soon afterward. Even with type having to be set by hand, the article made the next day's edition. That it ran again the following week is another indication that its content was believed to be especially newsworthy.[20]

Judge Symmes, who resigned from the court after completing the 1807 circuit to take up a federal appointment in the government land office in Cincinnati, never explained his dissent. Huntington's and Tod's separate opinions were published six weeks later, beginning with Huntington's which ran in the *Western Herald* on October 3, 1807. In subsequent weeks the opinions were carried in the Chillicothe *Scioto Gazette* and then in the Cincinnati *Liberty Hall and Cincinnati Mercury.* Marietta also had a weekly newspaper, but its issues for the period in question are lost. Many collections of early Ohio newspapers have issues missing, a problem which vexes researchers.

Continuing circuit duties left Huntington and Tod little in the way of what the *Herald's* editor called "leisure" to write what they certainly understood would be works of considerable constitutional and political import, with consequences for their own careers. Initial public response to their decision confirmed the assessment of the Ohio House the previous winter, that the legitimacy of judicial review, not whether the Fifty Dollar Act was constitutional, was the question of primary interest. The *Scioto Gazette's* announcement on October 8 that the following week it would begin publication of the judges' opinions, "by many thought extremely problematical," previewed them by recalling that "a right to decide upon the constitutionality of acts of the state legislature was last winter assumed" by the Jefferson County court of common pleas. Letters from Ohio newspaper readers likewise focused on the Ohio Supreme Court's claim to the power of judicial review.[21]

Fortunately for whatever prospects that claim might have had for gaining acceptance in Ohio, its opponents never learned that one of their supreme court's judges had previously addressed it, in another court.

CHAPTER FOUR

A Moot Court Argument

Spared the industrial development that came to New England mill towns situat-
ed along rivers and streams, Litchfield, on a northwest Connecticut hilltop, has
retained the beauty and serenity and much of the outward appearance it had
when the law school established by Tapping Reeve flourished there from the
1780s to 1833. Reeve enjoyed teaching young men who came to study in his
Litchfield law office; one of his first pupils was his brother-in-law, Aaron Burr.
The transformation of that office teaching practice into a law school may be
dated either from 1782, when Reeve began giving a formal course of lectures, or
from 1784 when he erected a small frame building next to his house to serve as a
lecture hall. Only twenty by twenty-two feet in size, without basement or fire-
place, the building was moved away and put to another use after the school
closed in 1833. Reeve's house had a succession of later owners and occupants. In
1914, after it had been acquired by the Litchfield Historical Society, U.S. Chief
Justice William Howard Taft led a campaign to raise funds for restoration. The
lecture building was returned to its original location beside the house in 1930.
"There is nothing about it to catch the eye," James Barr Ames of Harvard once
wrote, "but it has a peculiar interest for the lawyer, as the birthplace of the
American law school." In 1998 the house and lecture building were reopened to
the public after additional restoration work on the structures, and their transformation by the society into an interpretive museum.[1]

Meanwhile, in a monumental effort of biographical research conducted in
the 1930s after his retirement from New York law practice, Samuel H. Fisher
identified approximately one thousand of the students who had attended the
Litchfield Law School during the five decades of its existence, and compiled
summaries of their subsequent careers. Enhanced by research contributions of
other volunteers and members of its curatorial staff, the Litchfield Historical

The Litchfield Law School (c. 1782–1833). Tapping Reeve's house and lecture building.
(Courtesy Litchfield Historical Society, Litchfield, Connecticut)

Society's extensive archival holdings of Litchfield Law School records, its students' notes and their letters home, have become an incomparably rich source of information about what the late Professor Arthur Sutherland, a historian of the Harvard Law School, aptly described as "the best professional instruction available in the United States" during the American Republic's first half-century. Except for classes which George Wythe and St. George Tucker taught at William and Mary for a few years beginning in 1779 the Litchfield school antedated university-based American legal education, and it enjoyed a uniquely national reputation and following. Harvard's law school was founded in 1817, but did not begin to thrive until Joseph Story was appointed to head its faculty in 1829. Litchfield closed four years later, its demise brought about by declining enrollment and the ill health of James Gould, who had succeeded Reeve as professor and proprietor.[2]

Tapping Reeve Instructing Law Students by James Calvert Smith. The student standing to recite is John C. Calhoun. (Courtesy Litchfield Historical Society, Litchfield, Connecticut)

The number of Litchfield law students who gained distinction in later life is extraordinary. Of the approximately one thousand whom Fisher identified as having attended the school, three became U.S. Supreme Court justices (Henry Baldwin, appointed in 1830, Levi Woodbury in 1845, Ward Hunt in 1873); thirty-four including George Tod were members of highest state courts; sixteen were chief justices of such courts. Fourteen state governors, six U.S. cabinet members, and two U.S. vice presidents—John C. Calhoun in addition to Burr—were educated at Litchfield, along with twenty-eight U.S. senators and a hundred and one members of Congress. Other Litchfield alumni are remembered for contributions to education. John C. Wright and Edward King were cofounders with Timothy Walker of the law school which is now the University of Cincinnati College of Law. Jessup W. Scott, lawyer and sometime editor of the *Toledo Blade*, founded the University of Toledo. Scott's Litchfield classmate Horace

Mann, for whom schools throughout the nation have been named to commemorate his contributions to the development of state-supported public education, served in Ohio during the 1850s as president of Antioch College. Two of Tod's Litchfield classmates who emigrated to Ohio as pioneers had their promising potential careers tragically cut short. John Starke Edwards, who had ambitious plans for raising Merino sheep on Lake Erie's South Bass Island, fell victim to sudden illness in 1813 shortly after his election to Congress. Epaphras Bull, a leader of a group of emigrants from Danbury, Connecticut whose lake shore settlement on the Catawba Peninsula was raided by Indians in the aftermath of the British capture of Detroit in the War of 1812, fled with other survivors to Cleveland where he died, apparently of shock and exhaustion.[3]

Contemporary accounts of the Litchfield educational experience describe a distinctive learning routine. Reeve lectured for an hour and a half each morning. A painting by James Calvert Smith shows him in his austerely furnished lecture hall, bandy-legged in frock coat and breeches, grasping papers in one hand and gesturing with the other which holds his spectacles. All of the students depicted are absorbed in note taking, except one, John C. Calhoun, who stands to recite or ask a question. During afternoons students used the law library in Reeve's home to read cases and other legal works cited in the lectures.

On Saturdays there were oral quizzes administered by local attorneys, similar to the examinations students would soon face when they applied for admission to the bar. The final step in their learning process was to transcribe their lecture notes into neatly written copies. Many were elaborately indexed and annotated. Subsequently bound into volumes, the notes became foundation works of the students' own law libraries as they entered practice. Passed to succeeding generations as heirlooms, more than sixty sets of Litchfield students' notes are now held in public archives, where as a unique record of the teaching of American law during the first fifty years of the nation's existence they are just beginning to be discovered by legal historians. Tod's Litchfield notebooks, inscribed as a gift to his son David, are now held by the Western Reserve Historical Society in Cleveland.

At a time when lawyers depended more on formal oral communication than is typical of most professional practice today, development of forensic skills had correspondingly greater importance in legal education. Even those who prepared for the bar by self-study or by "reading" law in a lawyer's office eagerly sought out opportunities to practice courtroom speech. "Exercise yourself . . .

in preparing orations on feigned cases," was Thomas Jefferson's exhortation to a young man who had sought his advice on study for a legal career, and "suit your arguments to the audience before whom it is supposed to be spoken." Young men who apprenticed in urban law offices sometimes formed moot court societies solely to gain practice experience. New Jersey's *Institutio Legalis,* one of the most durable of these organizations, provided forensic training to aspirants to that state's bar for more than a generation after the American Revolution. Shorter-lived but remarkably innovative in its teaching method was the proprietary law school Creed Taylor taught in Needham, Virginia in 1821 and 1822, where there were no classroom lectures at all, and learning exercises consisted solely of moot court cases over which Taylor presided as judge.[4]

Moot courts in early American legal education were only remotely related to the "moots" in the Inns of Court, a significant component of English legal education until the mid-seventeenth century. American *moot courts* were fundamentally different. Conducted as contests with advocates representing opposing parties disputing over a single legal issue, they were more like modern appellate arguments. In English moots, by contrast, "the exercise lay principally in drawing the pleadings, and only incidently in arguing points of substance," and hypothetical cases were sometimes of stupendous complexity. American moot court practice was at least partly derived from the debate tradition of early American higher education, a legacy of European scholasticism. *Syllogistic disputations,* exercises conducted in Latin with dialogue strictly governed by the logical form of the syllogism, were a feature of the Harvard College curriculum in the seventeenth century. By the mid–eighteenth century a new debate form, *forensic disputation,* conducted in the English language with a broader range of topics and without the strictures of syllogistic logic, had taken over. At Yale, when Tod was a student, forensic disputations were the "keystone of [college president Ezra] Stiles' curriculum." They were an important means of bringing the college into the nineteenth century, as Stiles transformed Yale's mission from the training of Connecticut clergymen and schoolmasters to the preparation of young Americans for productive careers in all fields of learning and lives of service to the new nation. For debates conducted twice weekly on questions he assigned, juniors and seniors each prepared a written argument, pro or con, which they were in turn called upon to deliver orally. Stiles would then announce his own decision, which always addressed the merits of the question. The topics he selected for debate included many that were provocative as well as challenging. Some were moral conundrums: "Is virtue its own reward in life?" and "Is a coerced promise binding?" Others raised political and social questions. For a disputation held on June 19, 1787 as the delegates to the Constitutional Convention were beginning their deliberations, Stiles had Yale students debate "Whether the States acted wisely in sending Delegates to the General Convention now sitting in Philadelphia?" And when college reconvened in November after the convention had completed its work, Stiles assigned: "Whether it is expedient for the States to adopt the new Constitution?" Other topics were remarkably forward-looking. "Whether Females ought to be admitted to public civil Government?" was debated as early as 1782, and questions concerning the social and political status of women appeared regularly thereafter. Copybooks in which Tod transcribed some of his Yale undergraduate debate arguments are also preserved in the Western Reserve Historical Society's archives along with his Litchfield Law School lecture notes. Tod's Yale arguments include a passionate submission for the affirmative of a question Stiles put in 1794: "Would it be politic for the State of Connecticut to free suddenly its slaves?"[5]

Before the advent of organized athletics in American colleges forensic activities, debate and to a lesser extent, oratory, were outlets for students' competitiveness. Apart from faculty administered exercises such as those over which Ezra Stiles presided were extensive programs of debate and public speaking which students themselves conducted in their own organizations. Generally known as literary societies, these organizations had names with classical allusions: *Zelothean* was the first in Ohio, founded in 1812 at Ohio University. During the next three decades the *Philozetian* and *Adelphic* societies were established at Western Reserve College; Oberlin had the *Dialectic,* Dennison the *Calliopean.* At Yale Tod served for a time as president of *Linonia,* and he was also among the approximately one-third of his class elected to *Phi Beta Kappa,* whose Yale chapter conducted its own extensive debate and oratorical activities.[6]

Literary society debate styles were both *forensic,* with arguments delivered from written-out versions prepared in advance, and *ex tempore,* in which advocates spoke without written notes. Society members typically took turns arguing and presiding, all voting on the merits of the question at the conclusion of each debate. Choices students themselves made of the questions they would argue were wide-ranging. Some were reprises of issues already encountered in faculty-run debates. Others presented imaginative political hypotheses: "Whether it would be sound policy for the United States to dissolve the state governments and unite in one grand indivisible body?" Still others were whimsical: "Should old bachelors be taxed for the support of old maids?" was a *Linonia* topic. But most striking is the persistence and prescience of student interest in questions which would become great issues in the nation's future, but were not yet subjects of public controversy. Two of those questions, women's equality and slavery, were argued in the 1790s in student organizations to which Tod belonged.[7]

Brought to Litchfield by Yale graduates who retained their enthusiasm for debating, the organization and procedures of college literary societies and the imaginativeness of members' topical choices were readily translated to the law school's moot court. On July 28, 1796 Tod and sixteen Litchfield classmates who were members of "the Debating Society in Mr. Reeve's Office," half of them Yale graduates, signed their names to a constitution modeled closely on the college societies' organization and practices. Court sessions were to be held weekly on Thursday evenings; the moot court society's president and two other student members were to serve as the judges; other students would take turns as counsel, two on a side. Legal issues for argument were to be framed with "writs, pleadings, etc., in the same manner as a suit or the like Question would be bro't before a regular Court." The choice of the issue for each session was left to the counsel who were to argue, but other members would specify it for them if they could not agree. One member, elected as clerk, had the important duty of making a record of each case, a record which included the arguments of counsel as well as summaries of the judges' opinions. As to arguments, this record was probably compiled from submissions counsel had written out in advance and used as notes for oral delivery, as many had learned to do from college exercises in forensic disputation. The judges' opinions were delivered extemporaneously at the conclusion of each case, and were summarized for the record by the moot court reporter. The Litchfield moot court constitution further provided that "if the President [sitting as the moot court's chief justice] so direct," the clerk might show the record of a case to Mr. Reeve, "and request his opinion thereon." On occasions when this was done the record indicates whether or not Reeve concurred with the student judges' decision. But he had no other involvement in their proceedings. Like the college literary societies the moot court at Litchfield during Reeve's time was entirely student-run.[8]

On August 31, 1797, six years before Chief Justice John Marshall's decision in *Marbury v. Madison*, judicial review was argued in the Litchfield Law School moot court. The students voted to suspend their constitution's requirement for framing the issue with "writs, pleadings, etc." as in an actual case, in order to permit judicial review to be debated as an abstract question: "Have the judiciary a right to declare laws—which are unconstitutional—void?" This avoided having a "two-issue" argument, presenting a challenge to the constitutionality of a particular law in addition to the fundamental question whether courts were competent to hear and determine such challenges. The question was debated as a matter of state, not federal constitutional law, but it was framed in general terms, without focus on any particular state's legal system.

The advocates who participated in this argument were among the most able of Reeve's students. Presumably, in accordance with their moot court constitution, they chose the issue for themselves. That constitution also prescribed a method for assigning arguments by alphabetical order, but its application in this case is unclear. The counsels' agreement on the issue to be argued would almost necessarily have included an understanding as to which side each would take. Tod's Yale classmate Stephen Twining made the argument for the affirmative, in favor of judicial review. Twining had taught school before entering Yale. Tod and Thomas Scott Williams argued for the negative. Williams was only twenty years old, seventeen when he graduated from Yale in the Class of 1794. In later life he served for many years on the Connecticut Supreme Court, the last thirteen as its chief justice. He was an exceptionally brilliant student; Reeve would call him "the best scholar ever sent out from Litchfield."[9]

One should always be cautious about claiming any happening to be unique in history, especially in legal history. But so far as this author is aware the Litchfield moot court case is the only proceeding before an American court (albeit a law students' practice court) in which judicial review was argued as a disputed issue of constitutional law prior to *Marbury v. Madison,* and as to which there is a substantial and informative record of what was said by advocates on both sides. If not thus unique the Litchfield moot court argument is at least rare, for there appear to have been few instances when the power of judicial review was disputed before federal or state courts during the 1790s, as they ruled on objections to the constitutionality of laws with "no serious traverse as to the propriety of judicial action," as Professor Goebel put it. In 1795, when a federal circuit court sitting in Richmond heard a case in which the constitutionality of a federal excise tax on carriages was disputed, John Wickham, the attorney representing the United States, stated that although "the power of the court by a judicial decision to declare an act of the federal legislature null and void" was a "point of much delicacy," he would not address it in view of "information I have received from the bench, that, although never solemnly decided by the supreme court, it has come before each of the judges in their different circuits, and they have all concurred" in recognizing the power. The circuit court cases to which Wickham referred arose under the so-called Pension Act, which purported to make federal judges administrators of Revolutionary War veterans' disability pension claims. When two Pension Act cases subsequently reached the Supreme Court it disposed of them without opinion, the rulings being at least consistent with the conclusion some of the justices had reached as members of circuit court panels, that in its delegation to the federal judiciary of duties not judicial in character, the Pension Act was unconstitutional. And when the carriage tax case, *U.S. v. Hylton*, came up on appeal the Supreme Court rejected the challenge to the tax law's constitutionality without comment on its capacity to rule on such questions.[10]

Arguments over judicial review in state court cases prior to *Marbury* are not well reported, especially as to submissions against recognition of the power. In the Rhode Island case of *Trevett v. Weeden* where the court dismissed a prosecution for failing to accept state-issued paper money on the ground that the statute requiring such acceptance was unconstitutional, prevailing counsel James Varnum later published an account of the case which included his argument in favor of judicial review, a preview of points Hamilton would assert two years later in *The Federalist, No. 78*. Varnum's opponent Henry Goodwin cited Rhode Island's lack of a written constitution, and attacked as insufficient Varnum's reliance on British constitutional precepts. The report of *Bayard v. Singleton*, a case in which a North Carolina court invalidated a state law which barred former holders of property confiscated during the Revolution from suing present holders whose titles were derived from the acts of confiscation, mentions "long arguments from counsel on each side, on constitutional points," which apparently included judicial review. Perhaps the substance of their argument on that question can be inferred at least partially from correspondence of James Iredell, one of the counsel, who later became a justice of the U.S. Supreme Court. In Iredell's view, as subsequently in Hamilton's and Marshall's, the supremacy of the constitution necessarily endows courts with power to pass on the constitutionality of legislation. The position opposed to Iredell's in *Bayard v. Singleton* was articulated by North Carolina judge Richard Spaight, who corresponded with Iredell while Spaight was a delegate to the U.S. Constitutional Convention in Philadelphia. Spaight maintained that the power of judicial review would make judges "more despotic than the Roman Decemvirate, and equally insufferable," and that the only constitutional remedy for an unconstitutional law was to defeat legislators who enacted it when they ran for reelection. In 1803 the Pennsylvania Supreme Court heard judicial review argued in *Emerick v. Harris,* the case involving a constitutional challenge to a legislated increase in the monetary limits of the small claims jurisdiction of justices of the peace, which was still pending for decision when *The Cost Award Cases* and *Rutherford v. M'Faddon* were decided in Ohio in 1806 and 1807, respectively. Counsel on both sides in *Emerick* were leaders of the Philadelphia bar. As was sometimes the practice in early American case law reporting, arguments for the losing side—here essentially similar to those which Spaight had made to Iredell—were summarized before the court's opinion was set forth.[11]

The formalism which characterized submissions on both sides as counsel argued judicial review in these state court cases—"the constitution is supreme, and therefore the courts must enforce it against the legislature," versus "the legislature is at least equal in status with the courts, and therefore it is responsible for the constitutionality of its own acts"—did not appeal to the Litchfield students who argued judicial review in their moot court. For them the question was "who could better be trusted" to observe the limits of constitutionally delegated powers, legislative or judicial. "Encroachment" was the buzzword in postrevolutionary America which epitomized widely held concern that a governmental body or officeholder would exceed such powers and trespass on another's rightful function. Thus it was Hamilton's contention in *The Federalist, No. 78* that, compared with other branches, "the judiciary, from the nature of its functions, will always be the least dangerous to the political rights of the Constitution," and Swift's contrary assertion in *The System of the Laws* that it was "as probable that the judiciary will declare laws unconstitutional which are not, as it is that the legislature will exceed their constitutional authority," that would frame the issue over judicial review as the students debated it. Their submissions reflect familiarity with both works.[12]

It was still daylight that July evening in 1797 as law students who were members of the Litchfield moot court society left the private homes where they boarded, joining up by two's and three's for the walk along South Street to Reeve's lecture building where moot court sessions were held. Rearranging the desks to simulate a courtroom and judicial bench would have left little room for spectators, but if the society's members could invite guests they might well have included some who were students at Sarah Pierce's Female Academy, established in Litchfield in 1792 as one of the nation's first institutions to provide women's education beyond grammar school. For the argument over judicial review Cyrus Swan presided as chief justice; his associates were Elijah Hubbard, another of Tod's Yale classmates, and the previously mentioned John Starke Edwards, a Princeton graduate who would later emigrate to Ohio. Edwards was a grandson of Jonathan Edwards, the renowned Calvinist theologian who ended his ministry as Princeton's president, and a son of Pierpont Edwards, a prominent New York lawyer. Tod's co-counsel Thomas Scott Williams additionally acted as the court clerk, and compiled the record.[13]

Stephen Twining might well have supposed that in appearing for the affirmative in the debate over judicial review he had drawn the more difficult assignment, for the aggressiveness of his choices in framing his contentions is typical of a combative underdog. Of Hamilton's theoretical arguments Twining made only a perfunctory reaffirmation. His principal effort was to expand on Hamilton's "least dangerous" characterization of the judiciary, comparing legislators unfavorably to judges both as to competence to pass on constitutional questions and as to trustworthiness in observing proper limits of their respective constitutional mandates. Twining did not pull his punches. Taking direct issue with Zephaniah Swift's contention that judges and legislators were equally likely to err in matters of constitutional interpretation, he replied, "in point of *judgment*, the judiciary are *superior* to the legislature. Greater abilities are required for the discharge of their office than to perform the duties of a legislator." Twining also cited the judges' professionalism. "By their exercises and their habits," he said, "they are better fitted to judge with coolness and deliberation what laws interfere with the constitution, than the legislature, in which laws are sometimes passed rather from the heat of party than the strength of reason."[14]

Driving home the implication of Hamilton's characterization of the judiciary as "least dangerous," Twining attacked the legislature as the *most dangerous* branch. "Do we not find," he said, "that legislatures are always endeavoring to extend their power, and is it safe to entrust a body of men with *power to extend their power* [by making them sole determiners of the constitutionality of their acts]?" Judges were the safer choice: "their ambition would not aspire" to misusing their judicial powers to usurp legislative functions. Turning around an anticipated opposing argument that Connecticut's practice of having its judges appointed by the legislature for annual terms made the judiciary a subordinate branch, Twining portrayed the practice as a constitutional safeguard, making it "impossible for [judges] to encroach upon the Legislative, upon which they depend for their very existence." Summarizing, Twining returned to his theme, a paramount concern of contemporary American political thought. "It is *more safe* to entrust this power in the hands of the judiciary," he said. The power of judicial review "is a power which in their hands cannot be abused."[15]

The clerk's report sets forth Tod's and Williams's arguments as a single submission, but it seems likely that both addressed the court. They began by citing nonjudicial constitutional checks on the legislative branch which safeguard against adoption of unconstitutional measures: the division of legislative power between two houses each with a negative on the other's enactments, and ultimately the supervening power of the electorate. Connecticut's governor did not then have a veto, as Ohio's would not under its 1802 constitution. As Twining had anticipated, Tod and Williams urged that the legislators' power to select the judges made the judiciary a constitutionally subordinate branch. "If the legislature are so corrupt as to need the checks gentlemen wish to impose [by judicial review], will they not appoint men to fill the seats of justice, who will be subservient to their pleasure, who will declare only those laws void which the legislature are willing should be annulled?" Tod and Williams also cited the absence in the constitution of any express grant of the power of judicial review.[16]

But it was to the final question addressed in Twining's argument—whether the legislature or the judiciary was the safer choice for placement of responsibility for passing on the constitutionality of laws—that Tod and Williams gave most attention. A "rage" to expand power, they insisted, is common to all who possess governmental authority. If courts were to exercise the power of judicial review "they will show to the world that [they] are not less free from a desire to increase the power which they now enjoy than any other department of the government." A likely means of gratifying that desire, they argued, would be for judges to ignore the distinction between constitutional questions and policy issues: the power of judicial review would become a license to "intervene, and prevent the carrying into execution any law which they may think likely to be injurious to the public." The result, Tod and Williams claimed, would be a judicial usurpation of legislative authority, "put[ting] all the power of the legislature into [the judges'] hands, and our legislatures will become mere ciphers in the government." The evil of that result would be compounded, as Zephaniah Swift had observed, by the great number of courts which might exercise the claimed power of judicial review. Tod and Williams warned that "not only the highest tribunals, but the lowest courts of judicature throughout the U.S.A." might strike down any law, merely "because their minds are not sufficiently enlarged to discover the design of the legislature in passing it."[17]

Thus, as debated by the moot court's advocates, the constitutional legitimacy of judicial review came down to a question of trustworthiness.

Like college literary society debates, moot court arguments had no stated time limit, and we wonder whether the students whose turn it was to provide candles or other means of illuminating the courtroom after dark had that reason to remember this case as unusually lengthy. Perhaps there was a recess, or at least a few moments of quiet after the advocates had finally exhausted themselves. We do not know whether the judges conferred before announcing their decisions. Each gave his own opinion, Hubbard and Edwards, the two associate justices, speaking first.

Hubbard would recognize the power of judicial review. He was not impressed by any of Tod's and Williams's objections; he saw no contradiction between the judges' exercising the power and the fact that they were put in office by legislators whose acts they might strike down. Nor, said Hubbard, was there any danger that judges might exceed the proper limits of judicial review to invalidate legislation for reasons of policy as opposed to constitutional infringements. Acknowledging that the electorate could eventually bring about repeal of an unconstitutional law by voting out the legislators who had adopted it, Hubbard deplored the slowness of that process and the injury the law might work meanwhile. But he found most forceful Twining's claim that judges were better qualified to determine constitutional questions. "Brought up to the study of the law [and] being men of greatest eminence," Hubbard said, judges were "generally superior to the same number of men in the legislature" and "better fitted for the exercise of this power than the legislative body."[18]

Edwards would not recognize judicial review. For him the issue was simple: nothing in the constitution expressly confers such a power, and the omission must be taken as deliberate. "We can hardly suppose," he said, "that if it had been designed to invest [judges] with a power so great and important, it would not have been mentioned in the constitution."[19]

That left the casting vote to Cyrus Swan, the moot court's chief justice. Born in Stonington, a Connecticut seaport town, Swan was among the approximately half of Reeve's students who had not attended any college. A skeptical Yankee whose subsequent career was mostly devoted to small-town law practice, Swan heard little on this occasion that impressed him. He began by dismissing arguments on both sides. Tod's and Williams's professed concern over the multiplicity of tribunals that might exercise the power of judicial review was entitled to "no weight," since lower courts were subordinate to a supreme court to which their decisions could be appealed. On the other hand Swan incisively rejected the formalistic argument Twining had briefly asserted, asserting the supremacy of the constitution as the basis of judicial power to set aside conflicting laws. "The question," Swan observed, "was whether the judges had a right to determine that there *was* such a [conflict], and whether they might act in direct opposition to a positive act of the supreme legislature."

But Swan was completely unmoved by the submissions urged by Twining and supported by Associate Justice Hubbard, that judges were better qualified than legislators to judge the constitutionality of laws, and that they were less susceptible to ambition which could lead to illegitimate use of that power. While a legislature might abuse its authority to judge the constitutionality of its acts, Swan said, "this is a power which the judges may likewise misuse." For him those possibilities were precisely offsetting. "It would be of little service," he declared, "to take power from one body of men [the legislators] and place it in the hands of another set of men [the judges] *if*"—as Swan maintained—*"they were equally likely to abuse it."*[20]

With that dour prediction judicial review lost in the Litchfield Law School Moot Court.

CHAPTER FIVE

Judicial Review Challenged: ". . . lest we again be Marshall'd"

The journalistic voice of Pennsylvania's radical Republicans was the Aurora, *a* widely read Philadelphia newspaper of which William Duane became editor in 1798. Duane was a colorful polemicist, and the derisive name he coined for Pennsylvania Governor Thomas McKean and other Republican moderates entered the nation's political vocabulary. Duane called them "quids," after *tertium quid:* "a third something"—neither Federalists nor, in Duane's view, true Republicans. In Ohio as in Pennsylvania "quid" was an opprobrious designation, the radicals' label for one who identified himself as a Republican and supported the presidential candidacies of Jefferson and Madison, but resisted demands for greater implementation of popular democratic rule. Quids called themselves "independent Republicans." In jurisprudential matters they supported the common law, were skeptical of proposals for procedural reform, valued judges' and lawyers' professionalism, defended the judiciary against threats to its independence, and accepted judicial review. They voted with Federalists, who shared these views, whenever issues respecting the character of the judicial system were predominant in political controversy.[1]

Newspapers were an important forum for public debate of those issues. Virtually anyone with a printing press could establish one, and partisan identification was part of the formula for success both in developing circulation and gaining lucrative government printing contracts. A practical requirement for filling up pages with material that could be obtained without cost resulted in extensive reprinting of items from other newspapers. Many such items were devoted to foreign news. Professor Utter once remarked of the press in frontier Ohio that it was "easier for the subscriber to follow the career of Bonaparte than of

Jefferson." Domestic political content was not always one-sided; alert to their readers' appetite for controversy many newspapers gave substantial access to advocates on opposite sides of public questions regardless of the paper's editorial stance. Exchanges of published letters often extended over several weekly issues. In respect to their capacity for interactive communication early nineteenth-century newspapers have aptly been compared to the Internet. Much of the dialog for which they acted as common carriers was at a level of sophistication not attainable in modern journalism, where most electronic media reporting of discourse by principals is limited to sound bites, and print-media pieces are also greatly restricted in length.[2]

Curiosity excited by correspondents' use of assumed names added to public interest in what they had to say, and some editors were steadfast in refusing to disclose their true identities. In November 1807, in the issue which carried Chief Judge Huntington's opinion in *Rutherford v. M'Faddon*, the *Liberty Hall and Cincinnati Mercury* reported in an unrelated story that its editor had been assaulted, knocked down, beaten with a "large bludgeon . . . and otherwise severely bruised and wounded . . . in a most barbarous and brutal manner" for refusing his assailant's demand to name the authors of letters the paper had recently published under the pseudonyms "PLAIN TRUTH" and "MORE TRUTH." The assailant on this occasion was Jacob Burnet, one of the city's most highly respected lawyers. His uncharacteristic loss of temper cost him a hundred dollars, the jury's damage award for assault and battery.[3]

It is sobering to ponder what might have become of the first claims of Ohio courts to the power of judicial review, had Ohio judges lacked the means of explaining those claims to the citizenry which Ohio newspapers then provided. It was not unusual during the first decade of statehood for judges to give oral explanations of legal rulings, speaking from the bench. But those explanations reached only those present. The practice of reducing them to written form when they dealt with novel or important questions was, for Ohio, some years away. A requirement for noting reasons for legal rulings in writings filed with county clerks of court was imposed on the Ohio Supreme Court by a statute enacted in 1813. Written opinions of Ohio courts during the first decade of statehood are rarities; indeed we have found none which antedate the writings of Judge Pease and his Jefferson County associates in *The Cost Award Cases,* which appeared in the Chillicothe *Scioto Gazette* in December 1806.[4]

Apart from being written for a lay readership and published in newspapers the opinions in these cases and *Rutherford v. M'Faddon* are distinctive for two other reasons. One relates to the interactive nature of newspapers of the time, as a communication medium. No one nowadays who disagrees with a court's legal decision (except a dissenting judge) can express that disagreement in the same medium in which the court publishes the decision. The Ohio State Reports does not print letters from concerned citizens. But the opinions by which Ohio courts first expounded their claims to the power of judicial review were written for a medium in which citizens could, and were expected to respond. That expectation was especially strong in respect to the opinions in *Rutherford v. M'Faddon*, published while the legislature was out of session and opponents of judicial review were temporarily without access to that forum. Judges Huntington and Tod well understood that they were writing to open a dialogue with correspondents who disagreed with them, and would be eager to engage them in debate.

Another distinctive feature of the *Rutherford* opinions, one shared with those of Judge Pease in *The Cost Award Cases,* is that their authors were well aware of the likelihood that their conclusions would be challenged in impeachment prosecutions. That prospect made uniquely valuable the opportunity newspaper publication gave the judges for explaining their rulings directly to the public. Pease had narrowly escaped prosecution in the last legislature. But Huntington and Tod could hardly count on being let off by the radical Republicans in the next General Assembly.

The Huntington and Tod opinions in *Rutherford v. M'Faddon* ran first in the Steubenville *Western Herald,* the paper which previously broke the news of the decision.[5] Huntington's appeared in the *Herald*'s weekly edition of October 2, 1807. Beginning with a point that might have opened his defense at an impeachment trial, he acknowledged the skepticism and hostility with which he expected the court's claim to the power of judicial review would be met. Citizens who had given the matter only "hasty and superficial examination" would conclude, he supposed, that "the exercise of this power would operate to repeal the laws; that it would be an assumption of legislative authority, and that it would be judging over the head of the legislature." Huntington's response to this charge repeated arguments others had used, including a sophistry Chief Justice Marshall employed in *Marbury*—that since laws which violate the Constitution are void, they are *not laws* at all, and accordingly, whenever a court declines to give effect to an unconstitutional enactment it cannot be said to have repealed a *law.* Huntington also cited the oath judges took upon assuming office, promising to support the federal and state constitutions. But all these contentions begged the question of placement of responsibility for determining the constitutionality of legislative acts. If only the legislature has that responsibility under the constitution, then all its enactments *are* law, and judges would not violate their oath by enforcing any enactment whatever they or any other citizen might privately think about its constitutionality. Legislators likewise take an oath to support the constitution.

Huntington next addressed an opposing argument that could arise only under state constitutions where judges were chosen by members of the legislature, as in Ohio. This argument, which Huntington identified as "the chief source of the erroneous opinions entertained on [judicial review]," was that judges are constitutionally subordinate to the body which gives them their offices. But, answered Huntington, the fallacy was to "suppose that the judiciary received their *authority*, as well as their *appointments* from the legislature," an error which "arises from not considering the judiciary as a coordinate branch of government deriving its authority from the constitution." That response again begged the question whether the judiciary's constitutionally granted authority includes the power to pass on the constitutionality of the legislature's acts.

In the last part of his argument on judicial review Huntington gave examples of situations in which constitutional objections to legislation might arise. He admitted that extreme cases such as Marshall cited in *Marbury*—laws introducing slavery, imposing religious tests, infringing freedom of the press, abolishing jury trial—were unlikely to be encountered. More plausible, he suggested, were cases in which a law's conflict with the constitution arose inadvertently, as one of those "mistakes from haste or inattention" which occasionally afflict the legislative process.

Like Hamilton and Marshall, Huntington compared judicial cognizance of conflicts between a statute and the constitution with the familiar work of courts in resolving conflicts between two statutes. But the comparison was inapt, for a finding of conflict between statutes presents only a *first* question; the next is to decide which of the two statutes should apply in the case at hand. The court will then look for evidence of the legislature's intent, or finding none it will invoke some general principle of presumptive intent—supposing that the legislature meant its more recent enactment to govern, or the one which applies more specifically. But on the other hand, where a statute is found in conflict with the constitution there is no *second* question as to which should apply; the statute is struck down regardless of what the legislature might have intended.

Huntington's invocation of the "two conflicting statutes" comparison immediately after his suggestion that conflicts between a statute and the constitution might often arise inadvertently, is significant, for he wanted to portray the power of judicial review as a means of *implementing* the legislature's intention. Huntington wrote, "I firmly believe that it was not the intent of the legislature to infringe the constitution by extending the jurisdiction of justices of the peace, and that if they [the legislature] should be convinced that any part of the law in question is unconstitutional, they will correct the error." But there was no basis in fact for this belief. Huntington could not have supposed that members of the Ohio General Assembly would be "convinced" that they had mistakenly violated the state constitution by adopting the Fifty Dollar Act. Nor could he have perceived any likelihood of their "correcting" such a mistake by repealing the act and limiting the justices' monetary jurisdiction to twenty dollars. The Ohio House had deliberated the act's constitutionality in its 1806–07 session. There was no doubt as to what its members had concluded, or that they had intended to reach that conclusion.

Indeed this was precisely the situation that Zephaniah Swift had identified as the hard case for advocates of judicial review. In his *Marbury* opinion Chief Justice Marshall cited examples of obvious and gross constitutional violations (Congress's imposing a tax on exports, passing a bill of attainder, adopting an *ex post facto* law, or allowing convictions for treason without the proofs the Constitution required), and Huntington expanded on this litany of dreaded possibilities ("slavery may be introduced; a religious test may be established; the press may be fettered or restrained; the trial by jury may be abolished; *ex post facto* laws may be made; standing armies may be raised; and the whole train of evils against which our constitution meant to provide, may be let in upon us"). But "a little reflection," Swift had said, "will make it evident that no question [of a statute's unconstitutionality] will ever arise" in such "very clear cases: where the point is really doubtful a question may arise." "Really doubtful" cases are the hard ones for the doctrine of judicial review. Swift continued, "there may be some instances where good men may very honestly differ respecting the construction of the constitution, because from the imperfection of language the expressions may be ambiguous. It is therefore only with respect to such questionable points, that we are to consider who ought to be vested with the power of ultimate decision, and not in those extreme cases which may be easily stated, but probably will never happen." By suggesting that the court was dealing with an instance of "haste or inattention" rather than a case where the "good men" of the state's legislature had "very honestly differed" with the state's courts on the Fifty Dollar Act's constitutionality, Huntington avoided the fundamental issue his claim to the power of judicial review addressed. He was not the first judge to have ruled on an important question of law by mischaracterizing the case which presented it.[6]

Near the end of his opinion Huntington made passing reference to decisions elsewhere which supported his ruling: "the judgment of the supreme court of the U.S. and of every court of the individual states which has had the question [of judicial review] before them." But, he said, he had considered the case before him "as depending on the construction of our own constitution and laws," and he "would not have hesitated to give a different opinion had I been convinced the decisions [he had referred to] were erroneous." That was as close as either Huntington or Tod came to relying on *Marbury v. Madison.* Indeed, throughout the ensuing controversy over the Ohio judiciary's claim to the power of judicial review, no instance has been found of any proponent of the claim ever having supported it by citing *Marbury* expressly, or Chief Justice Marshall by name.

Tod's argument for judicial review also hypothesized inadvertent constitutional violations, citing "the haste with which laws are passed," which precludes "that deliberate attention to constitutional objections, which the nicety and importance of the subject makes requisite." He grounded his argument on Article III of the 1802 Ohio Constitution, which vested "the judicial power of the state" in its courts, and according to Tod, "expressly cloaths [*sic*] the judiciary with the power of deciding on all 'matters of law and equity.'" He contended that "all" meant that the grant of judicial power was comprehensive, and thus included constitutional questions. But the constitution did not say "all." Article III, section 1 provided that "The judicial power of this state, both as to matters of law and equity, shall be vested . . . [in the courts]." Tod added "all," leaving the word outside the quotation marks as he copied from the constitution's text. He was not the first judge to mischaracterize a legal source cited as authority for a ruling on an important question of law.

But Tod's opinion is impressive for its suggestion of applications for the doctrine of judicial review that are more typical of twentieth-century American constitutional jurisprudence. Many of the cases in which the power had heretofore been exercised by American courts involved legislation which assigned or divided up governmental functions: the allocation of small-claims jurisdiction, as did the Fifty Dollar Act; the hearing of *mandamus* proceedings, as did the pro-

vision of the Judiciary Act of 1789 struck down in *Marbury;* the administration
of war veterans' pension claims, as did the statute struck down in the federal
pension act cases. Comparatively few were early instances where the power of judicial review was exercised to invalidate legislation found to violate individual
civil rights other than the right of jury trial. Even the claimed denial of the jury
right was often simply a vehicle for attacking legislation to defeat its attainment
of some other object. In *Trevett v. Weeden,* the 1786 Rhode Island case where the
court struck down a law requiring acceptance of the state's depreciated paper
currency at face value, the judges found a constitutional violation not in the
law's uncompensated taking of property or its interference with contractual relations, but in its subjecting accused violators to trial without a jury. The courts'
concern in these cases was not with a denial of constitutional rights as it affected a disfavored particular class of individuals. As Professor Nelson has observed, American courts before 1820 "did not see judicial review as a mechanism
for protecting minority rights against majoritarian infringement." Before then,
there were practically no cases in which the power of judicial review had been
exercised to invalidate laws objected to as infringing personal freedoms of
speech, religion, or the press, or rights of contract or property ownership.[7]

But Tod's opinion looked ahead to such cases. A citizen's "natural and unalienable rights," he noted, were defined in Article VIII of the Ohio Constitution as "enjoying and defending life and liberty, acquiring, possessing and protecting property, and pursuing and obtaining happiness and safety." But does the
constitution "in itself guarantee the enjoyment of those unalienable rights, or
does it simply point to them as rights to be secured by legislative provision?" For
Tod the answer was "too obvious to be mistaken": constitutional rights are held
directly by individual citizens, and courts are *their* instrument for vindicating
those rights against legislative infringement. Tod was the first Ohio judge to find
that vindication in the Ohio Constitution's "open courts" provision, that "all
courts shall be open and every person for an injury done him, in his lands,
goods, person or reputation, shall have remedy by the due course of law, and
right and justice administered without denial or delay."[8] Tod's opinion also dis-
plays his rhetorical flair, with sentences that seem to have been written for quotation. "Among the various duties which are imposed on any court," he wrote,
"that of guarding and protecting the constitution is of importance paramount
to all others." And again, "I hold myself as strongly bound to test all legislative
acts by the constitution, as I do to administer justice without partiality."

As to the Fifty Dollar Act, Huntington and Tod both made the argument Judge Pease had earlier articulated, that the right of trial by jury was adopted into the Ohio Constitution in all respects as it stood at the time of the constitution's framing. Neither acknowledged that the twenty-dollar limit on single magistrates' small-claims jurisdiction in force at that time had been the latest of a series of increases of such limits, which prior to statehood had been subject to legislative adjustment from time to time. Nor was Huntington willing to concede to the Ohio General Assembly any assumption of reasonableness or good sense as to any future adjustments. "I do not conceive it to be any answer . . . that the legislature, being the immediate representatives of the people, will never so far forget their duty as to destroy this important right," he wrote. "If they can take it away in cases under fifty dollars, they can take it away in cases of five thousand dollars." Responding to the contention that defendants in cases subject to the Fifty Dollar Act could obtain a jury trial on appeal, with a new trial in the court of common pleas, Tod's opinion similarly invoked extreme hypothetical possibilities of legislators' perversity and oppression. The requirement for an appellant's giving bond as in other appeals was one which "may be carried to any extent," he said, "until that boasted right [of jury trial] shall be wholly abrogated." The same argument, we might note, could apply to the right of appeal itself.

Tod concluded his opinion with a point which struck politically sensitive nerves. The Ohio House and Senate had interpreted the Ohio Constitution's disqualification of any "judge of any court of law or equity" to serve concurrently in the General Assembly, as not applying to justices of the peace who, as we have noted, sometimes amounted to near-majorities in those bodies. But as Tod pointed out, expanding the justices' powers effectively altered the demarcation between the constitutionally incompatible offices of judge and legislator. If such powers were enlarged "to an indefinite extent," Tod warned, justices of the peace would be made functionally equivalent to common pleas or supreme court judges. His concluding observation, that the question whether they were "judge[s] of a court of law or equity" within the meaning of the constitution's prohibition of concurrent legislative and judicial service was "not on this occasion, necessary to be adjudicated," would have seemed quite ominous to the many justices of the peace who served in the Ohio General Assembly. A supreme court judge in Tod's position might have thought better about raising that question unnecessarily, as he confronted the likelihood of an impeachment trial.[9]

Responses to the *Rutherford* opinions came quickly. On October 17, 1807, two weeks after it ran the Huntington opinion, the Steubenville *Western Herald* carried the first of a two-part rebuttal, *"Observations on the Opinion of the Court, Addressed to the Citizens of the State of Ohio. By a Farmer."* This "farmer" was articulate and well read. Leaving no doubt as to where he stood politically, he denounced the decision as one that would take back all the gains of statehood, "annihilate the legislative department, sap the foundation of our state government, and thus, at this early hour, while yet in the bud, just emerged from the filth and corruption of a Territorial government, ere *Aurora* shall have beamed forth his enlivening rays from the Eastern Horizon, blast all our fond hopes as a free, Democratical and independent state." Farmer's arguments against judicial review were sophisticated. He condemned it as a usurpation of legislative authority, citing a provision of the Ohio Constitution's bill of rights that reserved to the legislature the power of suspending laws, and denouncing as empty rhetoric Huntington's rejoinder that since an unconstitutional enactment was "no law," a court would not be suspending or setting aside a "law" by declaring it void. Farmer also criticized Huntington for failing to cite legal authorities. Regrettably the *Herald*'s next weekly edition, one which contained the second part of Farmer's letter in which he argued for the constitutionality of the Fifty Dollar Act, is lost.[10]

Some weeks later the judges' supporters weighed in, with letters from "Agricola" and "Mechanic." Noting that Farmer had "forsaken his plow" to assume the role of political commentator, Agricola advised Farmer's readers not to be dazzled by *Aurora*'s "enlivening rays from the Eastern Horizon," but to "wait for the coolness and calmness of the evening." Mechanic, claiming to be "intrigued by Farmer's letters" but finding them "so elegant and sublime as to perhaps be incomprehensible to the unlettered," undertook to provide "the following little Dictionary as an expositor to the Farmer's address:

Constitution. A subordinate and explanatory appendix to the laws of the state.

Court. A place for the administration of injustice where the constitution and people are tried and condemned by order of the legislature.

Judge. A perjured sycophant.

Legislature. An omnipotent assembly, invested with power to quash the constitution and repeal the moral laws.

Law. Whatever the General Assembly direct their Clerk to write and their printer to publish. . . .

Unconstitutional. Contrary to the opinion of the legislature.

Readers for whom these letters were written understood allusions to *Aurora* as the organ of Pennsylvania's radical Republican views, and to "perjured sycophant" as a judge who enforced legislative enactments which violated the constitution despite his oath to support it.[11]

The *Herald's* succeeding weekly issues are lost; the hiatus in coverage extends until the issue of December 12, 1807. By then the exchanges have become personal, Farmer calling Agricola "a petty, insignificant, aristocratical lawyer." "If I be petty and insignificant," Agricola rejoined, "it is for want of genius, and the means of information." But, he continued he could do little to remedy the first failing, since "all the genius in this side of the great mountains" was possessed by a "single individual"—apparently he meant Farmer. As for means of information, Agricola continued, "I have sent to the state of New York for books to the amount of *one hundred and fifty dollars.*" Those were probably law books; indeed we have little difficulty in surmising that Farmer, Agricola, and Mechanic were all lawyers. We would be left to speculate about their true identities but for a letter written to Tod by M'Faddon's counsel, Obadiah Jennings, and found among Tod's papers:

You have probably heard of the conversion of H. Lane. Until the decision of the Sup. Court he declared himself a strenuous advocate for the principles embraced by the decision. Shortly afterward he became as warm for the other side, and published in the W. Herald two numbers . . . [illeg] with the signature of the Farmer, in opposition to the opinion published by Judge Huntington. You have probably seen the *trash* alluded to. Lane . . . probably calculates on being employed in presenting the [your—i.e., Tod's] impeachment if it is preferred. I forgot to mention that Lane appears to have given up the Farmer in consequence of an attack made upon him by Walker of N. Lisbon under the title of Agricola.[12]

With the publication of the last Farmer-Agricola exchanges in December 1807, the *Western Herald's* editor directed readers' attention to the coming Ohio General Assembly session, "in which the right of courts to decide on the constitutionality of legislative acts will probably be inquired into." Noting that the supreme court's invalidation of the Fifty Dollar Act had caused "some inconvenience to our citizens," the editor defined succinctly the issue facing the General Assembly's members. "It therefore remains to the legislature," he wrote, "to determine whether the decision of the courts on that subject, or their own act, is to be obeyed." Elections that fall were dominated by a contest for governor, confused by Thomas Worthington's unexpected withdrawal of his candidacy. Worthington had been widely expected to succeed his brother in law, Edward Tiffin, in the governor's chair. The election's apparent winner, Return Jonathan Meigs Jr., was disqualified when the General Assembly found that he failed to meet a residency requirement. But Meigs's opponent, Nathaniel Massie, de-clined to accept the office as the voters' second choice. Thomas Kirker, Speaker of the Ohio Senate who had succeeded to the governorship when Tiffin resigned to become Worthington's replacement in the U.S. Senate, then stayed on as act-ing governor. Worthington meanwhile offered himself as a legislative candidate and was elected to the Ohio House. Another new House member was Benjamin Hough, the justice of the peace whose $32.50 judgment had been struck down in *Rutherford v. M'Faddon.*[13]

The Ohio House began its 1807–08 session with a message from Acting Governor Kirker which reported "difficulties in the collection of all debts" for amounts between twenty and fifty dollars, resulting from the decisions overturn-ing the Fifty Dollar Act. Kirker spoke of the "necessity of acting on this subject at an early period," but made no recommendation for action. A special commit-tee of the Ohio House was appointed to consider the matter, "with leave to re-port by bill or otherwise."[14]

The committee's original three members were Worthington, Hough, and William W. Irwin, a Fairfield County lawyer (not the William Irwin, formerly an Associate Judge in that county, impeached by the 1805–06 legislature for delin-quencies in attending court). In floor votes during the previous session Irwin had supported Judge Pease's common pleas court decision both as to the power of judicial review and as to the Fifty Dollar Act's unconstitutionality. He had also voted in favor of the resolution, which lost on a tie, declaring that the legis-lature had no right to interfere with a court's judgment as to the constitutionali-ty of a law unless the judges had acted with "corrupt motives." Worthington, on the other hand, was seeking to solidify the position as leader of Ohio's Republi-cans which he had gained with his campaign for statehood. In attempting now to unite the party behind opposition to judicial review and rejection of the judi-ciary's claims to be a constitutionally independent branch, he returned to an is-sue he had confronted for the federal judiciary while serving in the U.S. Senate. There was certainly no question where Squire Hough stood. Obadiah Jennings, M'Faddon's counsel, had told Tod in the same letter in which he identified "Farmer" and "Agricola," that if Tod's prosecution by impeachment were "to depend upon the opinion of such men as Benj. Hough & Co. there can be little doubt of the event. Hough has been heard frequently to say insultingly that the judges would be brought before '*them*' for usurpation of power."[15]

After augmenting the committee's membership by additional appointments of Alexander Campbell and William Corry, representatives from Adams and Butler counties respectively, the House received its report on December 25, 1807. (Christmas was not celebrated as a public holiday in early nineteenth-century Ohio.) Worthington was spokesman. He stated that the first question to be considered under the committee's charge to inquire into the decisions invalidating the Fifty Dollar Act was "how far the judges of this state, under the provisions of the [Ohio] constitution, have the power to declare acts of the legislature unconstitutional, or null and void." Worthington noted that on that question all House members already had before them the same information the committee did. Were they to find that the judges have such power, Worthington said, then "the committee are of opinion that any further enquiry on that subject on their part will be unnecessary." Worthington then proposed the following resolution:

Resolved, that the judges of this state are not authorized by the constitution to set aside any act of the legislature, by declaring the law unconstitutional or null and void.

Worthington's choice to present this question first, without any recommendation as to impeachment charges or other action to be taken against the judges, proved to be a sound tactic for marshaling support. The resolution was extensively debated. Votes turning aside proposed amendments were close, and revealed that the committee itself was divided. William Corry and William Irwin, the dissenting members, supported efforts to emasculate the resolution by amending it to deny the judges power to set aside any *constitutional* act, or by substituting a caution that they should be "answerable to the legislature" for any abuse of their power to invalidate legislation on constitutional grounds.[16]

House members were well aware of public interest in the issue. Reporting the Worthington committee's appointment, the Steubenville *Western Herald* claimed that a "large majority of the General Assembly are of opinion that *their* acts ought to be obeyed and not trampled on by the judges of any court," and predicted that "the representatives of the people will show themselves worthy of the confidence of their constituents on this occasion." A letter from a Chillicothe correspondent published two weeks later in the *Liberty Hall and Cincinnati Mercury* reported an atmosphere of "bustle and contradiction" surrounding the legislative session, "legislators, governors, judges, lawyers and farmers all together pell-mell." He went on to state the issues with remarkable clarity:

"The constitution of the state is violated," say the judges, "and your fifty dollar act is void."

Legislators retort and enquire of the judges, who authorized them to arraign the constitutionality of the laws sanctioned by the legislature: "Hath not the potter power over the clay?"

Lawyers support the judges as a co-ordinate, not a subordinate branch of government, and . . .

Farmers contend that all the justices and constables in the state are ruined if the fifty dollar act be not supported at all hazards.

The first arguing from principle, the latter from consequences.[17]

After a debate lasting three days, described by the Chillicothe *Scioto Gazette* as "a very animated and argumentative discussion," the Ohio House adopted the Worthington committee resolution without amendment, by a final vote of eighteen to twelve. The tally confirmed an assessment House member John Sloane made in a letter to Benjamin Tappan, both highly partisan Worthington allies, reporting that body's political composition as including "ten decided feds and two or three quids" who were judges' supporters. Judicial review, as Sloane described it to Tappan, was an issue "more warmly contested than any that has ever come before this legislature."[18]

The House debate on the Worthington Committee resolution was not recorded; most of what we know of it comes from two floor speeches subsequently published in Ohio newspapers. Both were arguments against judicial review, and in favor of the resolution. Sloane's was the more elaborate; the other was by Worthington Committee member Alexander Campbell. From references they both made to "the member from Fairfield," we surmise that William Irwin of that county, one of the Worthington Committee dissenters, took part in the debate as a supporter of judicial review.[19]

After adopting the resolution the House appointed a committee to draw impeachment charges against judges Huntington, Tod, and Pease for "assuming the power" of declaring the Fifty Dollar Act unconstitutional. But from that point the prosecution effort lost momentum. The resolution condemning judicial review was never taken up by the Senate, and, as the session ended, the House voted to postpone further consideration of impeachment charges to the following year's session. Sloane explained the postponement by saying that the House "members were mostly new [and] it was some time before they could properly understand each other."[20]

The General Assembly dealt with other matters besides a gubernatorial election contest, the Fifty Dollar Act and judicial review during this session. We cannot resist mentioning the "Act to encourage the killing of squirrels." These animals had eaten more than their fair share of the 1807 corn crop, and the legislators' response provided lessons in environmental regulation and tax policy, if not in animal rights. The regulatory scheme was ingenious. The act required township trustees to make each taxpayer responsible for dispatching a certain number of the creatures, the number to be fixed by setting a numerical target for squirrel population reduction in the township and allocating that target among individual taxpayers in proportion to their property assessments, but not to exceed one hundred squirrels for any taxpayer. Compliance was to be demonstrated by turning in squirrel scalps to the township clerk. For any delinquency a fine of three cents per scalp was to be paid. On the other hand, for each scalp delivered in excess of the required number, clerks were to pay a bounty of two cents out of the fine moneys collected. "A Citizen of J.C. [Jefferson County]" whose letter was published in the June 8, 1808 Steubenville *Western Herald* indignantly denounced the law's tax benefits for the rich:

> The poor man, who owns no taxable property but one cow, of ten dollars value, for which he has not to pay more than ten cents County Tax, must produce ten scalps or pay thirty cents, while the wealthy Rich Man who owns six horses, eight cows, and three thousand dollars worth of other taxable property, shall not produce more than one hundred scalps or pay three dollars, although his County Tax would not be less than sixteen or seventeen dollars, to which if his squirrel tax was apportioned, it would amount to about fifty dollars. Is this Equity? Is it Republican? Is it consistent with correct principle, in a Republican government?

The legislature failed, moreover, to insure that squirrel tax collection receipts would be sufficient to cover claims for bounty payments. An April hunt conducted by enthusiastic citizens of Hamilton County's Anderson Township, reported in the *Liberty Hall and Cincinnati Mercury* as yielding a scalp count of two thousand, eight hundred and one, must have bankrupted that township's fund. The law, which could hardly have gained for its legislative sponsors a single vote from a township clerk, was quietly repealed in the legislature's next session.[21]

A more lasting product of the 1807–08 General Assembly was legislation which took the first step in a direction which would eventually lead to the Ohio Supreme Court's becoming, as it is today, an exclusively appellate tribunal with responsibility as a court of last resort for the body of state law established by judicial decisions. The 1802 constitution provided that after the year 1808 the General Assembly might add another judge to the supreme court, making a total of four, and that the state might then be divided into two supreme court circuits within each of which any two of the judges could hold court sessions. The constitution also provided for increasing the number of common pleas circuits and their respective presiding judges after 1808. There was no constitutional limit on that increase, and so as the state became populated and new counties were established the legislature continually added to the number of common pleas circuits. It began at this 1807–08 session by adding one such circuit, making for the time being a total of four. By the same act the legislature added a fourth judge to the supreme court and divided the state into two supreme court circuits. Supreme court judges' individual assignments to circuits was left for them to agree upon among themselves. With the constitution's requirement for holding an annual session in each county, the travel required of a supreme court judge would become an increasingly burdensome incident of that office.[22]

The conduct of circuit sessions by less than a majority of the court's total membership raised an additional possibility of conflicting rulings, now as between the circuits as well as between the members of any two-judge panel whenever they disagreed. Addressing these possibilities, the same act provided for special court sessions to resolve such conflicts as well as "any new and difficult question" upon which it was considered especially desirable to secure a ruling by the entire court. Attended by all members of the court, these were known in Ohio, as elsewhere, as *"en banc"* sessions. There were to be four such sessions a year, one in each of the four common pleas circuits. The act thus established the essentials of a modern two-tiered appellate system, with review at the intermediate level given to parties as a matter of right, and review by the system's highest court provided only where the judges find either that there is a conflict in the rulings of intermediate-level tribunals or that the case presents a question which is novel and of great public interest. Under the 1808 act the Ohio Supreme Court functioned on both levels, with its two-judge circuit panels serving as an intermediate appellate tribunal. But its circuit sessions also included considerable trial work. The court had original jurisdiction over civil cases involving title to land or where the amount in question exceeded one thousand dollars, and over criminal matters more serious than justices of the peace could adjudicate. In those matters its jurisdiction was exercised concurrently with common pleas courts. Over divorce and capital crimes the supreme court's original jurisdiction was exclusive, except in capital cases where the defendant might elect trial in the court of common pleas. And as we have noted, civil cases originally tried in the common pleas could be retried in the supreme court. Only in *en banc* sessions, limited to consideration of questions of law, did the early Ohio Supreme Court function exclusively as an appellate tribunal.[23]

On February 13, 1808 as the legislative session was winding down, members of the House and Senate met to fill judicial vacancies. Only single ballots were necessary to elect William Wilson presiding judge of the newly established fourth common pleas circuit, and Return Jonathan Meigs Jr., the disqualified winner of the recent gubernatorial election, to the newly established fourth seat on the Ohio Supreme Court. To fill the vacancy created by supreme court Judge Daniel Symmes's resignation the legislators chose William Sprigg on a second ballot. A native Marylander who had been one of the Ohio Supreme Court's first judges, Sprigg had returned to Chillicothe after serving meanwhile in a succession of territorial federal appointments in Michigan and Louisiana. He was noted for his legal learning. For the coming year, 1808, the Ohio Supreme Court would accordingly consist of Chief Judge Samuel Huntington and judges George Tod, William Sprigg and Return Jonathan Meigs Jr. The junior judges were separated in the circuit pairings, Sprigg sitting with Huntington, Meigs with Tod.[24]

With the judiciary as the principal issue, public interest in the 1808 gubernatorial and legislative elections began to build early. In July, from Canton in eastern Ohio, Sloane reported the outlook. "The feds are in great hopes of success and say that after next election Ohio will be federal," he wrote. "But my letters from the westward give me encouragement that all is not lost. We will be obliged to support Worthington for governor. There is no other choice. If we divide, Huntington is elected and Federalism will triumph." Radical Republicans were beginning to call their own party's independents "Feds" as well as "quids," and disparaged them as supporters of Federalist principles.[25]

Public interest in the issue the election presented with respect to the Ohio Supreme Court's claim to the power of judicial review and its invalidation of the Fifty Dollar Act had intensified. A Fourth of July toast drunk in Cincinnati that summer as members of the city's Republican and Mechanic societies gathered to celebrate the holiday leaves no doubt either as to their position on that issue, or—and this is especially impressive—their members' understanding of it:

—The judiciary—but not to remain so independent as to place it without control or responsibility, *lest we again be Marshall'd!*

One gun, three cheers! [26]

CHAPTER SIX

Charles Hammond and "The Rights of the Judiciary"

Newspaper publication of John Sloane's and Alexander Campbell's speeches against judicial review, made in the Ohio House as it deliberated the Worthington Committee's resolution, began in February as soon as the 1807–08 legislative session ended. A correspondent writing anonymously more than a year later denied that Sloane ever gave his speech on the House floor, but "only wrote the best arguments he could advance in favor of his opinion and had them printed." However that may be, the publications rekindled public debate, which then became more focused and sophisticated. Campbell's speech ran in the Steubenville *Western Herald*, which printed it in two installments shortly before the close of the session. Sloane's is here cited from its text as it was appended to Charles Hammond's *The Rights of the Judiciary*, a brilliant responding work of considerably greater historical interest, set forth in its entirety in appendix B. Hammond there spelled Sloane's name without the *e*.[1]

"I have waited," Campbell began, "to hear the arguments of the gentlemen on the other side of the question." But despite "all the libraries in this town [Chillicothe] having been ransacked" in search of precedents, Campbell dismissed as irrelevant the authorities—"opinions of foreign courts, or even those of the United States"—cited by supporters of judicial review. The question before the House, he insisted, was governed only by the Ohio Constitution. Sloane began his speech with the same point. Not surprisingly, neither could find anything in the Ohio Constitution to indicate, as Campbell put it, "that the judges have any right, either expressed or implied, to set aside any act of the legislature."[2]

Campbell recounted the disagreement with the judiciary over the Fifty Dollar Act's constitutionality as it developed in the previous legislature when a

House committee disputed the ruling of Judge Pease's common pleas court, and redeveloped when the Ohio Supreme Court disregarded that committee's judgment, and by its decision in *Rutherford* held the act unconstitutional. Referring to the oath to support the constitution which legislators as well as judges swore as they took office, Campbell asked, "Can the legislature be *equal* to the judiciary, if the latter can set aside the acts of the former *after they have passed* [upon it] *under all the solemnities of an oath, &c declaring it* [the Fifty Dollar Act] *to be within the pale of the constitution?*" Sloane went further, attacking the premise of equality of the branches. "The idea that our [Ohio] constitution has delegated to different branches of government a coordinate or equal authority is incorrect," he declared, citing, as to the executive branch, the severely limited authority the 1802 constitution granted to the governor, who could make only interim appointments and lacked the power of veto.[3]

Campbell and Sloane were effective in refuting the claim of some of judicial review's supporters that the oath the Ohio Constitution required judges to take, "to support the constitution of the United States and of this state," implied that courts were empowered to pass on the constitutionality of laws. Both pointed out that the constitution required the same oath from all persons holding state office. Would a militia commander, Campbell asked, be justified in defying any law which he privately believes to be unconstitutional? And if the oath justifies every officeholder's acting on his own view of a measure's constitutionality, how could that be reconciled with systems of hierarchal authority within the judiciary or other branches of government? Suppose, said Sloane, that all the common pleas courts were to agree in pronouncing a law unconstitutional, but the supreme court held the opposite opinion. How then could common pleas judges discharge their obligation of "oath and conscience" if they deferred to the supreme court's ruling? The problem with the "judges' oath" argument for judicial review, as Campbell and Sloane thus demonstrated, was that it proved too much.[4]

Campbell was not impressed by assurances of judicial review's supporters that the power would did not amount to a hunting license for judges to go through the statute book and kill off whatever laws they found constitutionally objectionable. The power could be exercised, supporters had insisted, only when a statute subject to a constitutional question came before the courts to be applied or enforced in the regular course of judicial proceedings, and then only if one of the parties raised the question under applicable rules of pleading and procedure. Campbell was a practicing physician. Perhaps the ethical mandate of his profession obliging doctors to treat patients who come under their care is reflected in Campbell's questioning of a judge's not treating the affliction of unconstitutionality in *any* law which should come to his notice, had he the power to do so. Why, Campbell wondered, should "the sagacity of some attorney" in perceiving and challenging a law as unconstitutional, be necessary for the *court* to act?[5]

Confronted with arguments based on extreme examples of unconstitutional legislation, Campbell and Sloane cited political remedies: legislators who voted for egregiously unconstitutional laws would be defeated at the next election; their successors would repeal the offending statutes. But Sloane, a lawyer, went further. In a concession unprecedented among judicial review's opponents, he suggested that while the legislature was out of session both the governor and the courts could act against a law perceived to be unconstitutional, by granting temporary relief to keep the law from operating until the legislature could reconsider it. Thus the governor might pardon convicted violators of a constitutionally challenged criminal statute. In civil cases where a law claimed to be unconstitutional affected contract or private property rights, courts could postpone those consequences by granting continuances or ordering new trials. This was an intriguing suggestion, for it would allow the governor or the courts in the performance of their official duties to question a law's constitutionality and inhibit its operation until the legislature had an opportunity to reconsider it in the light of such questions. But the legislature would still have the last word.[6]

Members of the House minority who supported judicial review cited works of Thomas Jefferson and James Madison, authorities that, unlike the U.S. or foreign courts whose opinions Campbell had rejected, could not simply be dismissed. In his *Notes on the State of Virginia* criticizing his state's 1776 constitution for its concentration of power in the legislature, Jefferson had urged the adoption of a state constitution "in which the powers of government should be so divided and balanced among the several bodies of magistracy, as that no one could transcend their legal limits, without being effectually checked and restrained by the others." "An *elective despotism*," said Jefferson, "is not the government we fought for." His *Notes* were published in 1787 and written a few years before. He clearly favored a constitutional balance with governmental powers distributed among three coordinate branches that were "equal" in the sense that each exercised its powers independently as it functioned within the constitutional limits of its responsibility. Madison described the legislature in *The Federalist, No. 48,* as "an assembly which is inspired by a supposed influence over people, with an intrepid confidence in its own strength," and identified it as the branch most likely to need checking. "It is against the enterprising ambition of this department," he wrote, "that the people ought to indulge all their jealousy, and exhaust all their precautions."[7]

Sloane could not ignore these "elective despotism" and "enterprising ambition" quotations. No national political figures were more revered by early Ohioans who identified themselves as Republicans, than Jefferson and Madison. Their warnings against abuses of legislative power commanded attention wherever a state constitution like the one in Virginia which Jefferson had criticized, and the one later adopted in Ohio, made the legislature the dominant branch. Sloane's response was to contend that the nation's experience with the constitutional theory of three equal and independent branches had been so adverse in respect to the judiciary, that were Jefferson and Madison "to write now after the Union has fully discovered the effect that this independence is likely to produce, they would have ample reason to recant their opinions." Jefferson later flirted with that suggestion, as we have seen.[8]

The threat to individual liberties presented by malignant growth of a popularly elected legislature's power was vividly portrayed by an advocate of consummate skill, who carried on the debate in a more public forum after the session ended. In this next round Sloane would meet a formidable adversary:

You [Sloane] deny that the different departments of government are intended as checks upon each other. . . . The [Ohio Constitutional] Convention, you say, "carefully guarded the Legislature from every kind of clog, or control from the other branches"; and yet we find not a word like this in the constitution. If we resort to the opinions of statesmen on this subject, you turn a deaf ear. We say, that the different departments of government are intended as checks upon each other. We read the opinion of Mr. Jefferson, that the "powers of government should be so divided and balanced among the several bodies of magistracy, that no one could transcend their legal limits without being effectually checked and restrained by the others". . . .

Power, not right, is the foundation of your system. On power, regardless of right, all despotism is founded. "The will of a majority of the citizens shall conduct the operations of the government." The act of the Legislature is the will of the majority. Hence all the powers of government, legislative, executive and judiciary, result to the Legislative Body. The concentrating these in the same hands is precisely the definition of despotic government. It will be no alleviation that these powers will be exercised by a plurality of hands, and not by a single one: one hundred and seventy-three despots would surely be as oppressive as one. Let those who doubt it turn their eyes upon the Republic of Venice. As little will it avail us that they were chosen by ourselves. "An elective despotism was not the government we fought for." Such is the opinion of Mr. Jefferson. It is an opinion founded on experience, observation, and reflection, and cannot be shaken by the assertions of a minor politician.

WARREN[9]

"Warren" was Charles Hammond, the prevailing counsel in *Rutherford v. M'Faddon*, whose response to Sloane's speech was given in seven letters published during the summer of 1808, at first serially in Ohio newspapers, and shortly after in collected form, in a pamphlet entitled *The Rights of the Judiciary, in a Series of Letters Addressed to John Sloan, Esq., Late a Member of the House of Representatives.* The work is an impressive demonstration of Hammond's talent as a polemicist as well as his skill in the courtroom. His later career would extend both to journalism and to an admired, though losing argument in the U.S. Supreme Court. In 1823 Hammond became the first official "reporter" (editor for publication) of opinions of the Ohio Supreme Court, which then began to be regularly published.[10]

Heretofore virtually unnoticed by legal historians and constitutional scholars, Hammond's *Rights of the Judiciary* is remarkable for the originality as well as the eloquence of his arguments for judicial review. Responding first to the objection that the power of courts to pass on the constitutionality of legislation is not mentioned in the 1802 Ohio Constitution, Hammond noted that its grants of governmental powers were made in general terms—the "legislative authority of this state" to the General Assembly, the "judicial power of this state" to the courts—without specifying the purposes for which such "legislative authority" or "judicial power" might be exercised. Having shown that neither the legislature's authority to enact laws nor the judiciary's power to decide cases depends "upon an express enumeration [in the constitution] of the several grants of legislative and judicial powers," Hammond proceeded in his second letter to drive home the next point of his argument. He is no longer addressing Sloane. He writes as though, in a courtroom, he had turned away from the bench and opposing counsel to speak directly to the jury—here a jury of citizen readers:

The constitution is not made and written for either Legislature or Judges. It is made by the people, for themselves, and is expressive of their sovereign will. It contains, if I may be allowed the expression, the articles of association between the people. Every individual is a party to it. Every individual is bound by it, and every individual has a right to claim its protection. To the Legislature, under certain restrictions, the people give the power of "prescribing a rule of civil conduct:" to the Judiciary they give the power of deciding all controversies which arise under the social regulations. Both the Legislature and the Judiciary are the immediate representatives of the people. By their Legislature the people enact laws; by their Judges they pronounce judgment.[11]

Hammond's next point was remarkably forward-looking. If, as Professor Nelson has noted, "Judges of 1820 . . . did not see judicial review as a mechanism for protecting minority rights against majoritarian infringement," here is an Ohio lawyer who did, in 1808. Constitutions, Hammond said, are written

to secure the rights of the few against the many. Every limitation, every prohibition of the exercise of power, contained in a constitution, is a declaration by the people, that they cannot trust each other upon that subject. A constitution is not, as seems to be supposed, needed to secure power to a majority of the community. This power a majority must always possess, in the very nature of things, until they surrender it by compact, or constitution. A constitution is intended to impose restraints upon a majority, and to place the minority upon an equal footing. It is intended to compel the majority, in the exercise of power, to pursue a certain course, and observe certain principles; and it is written, that the few may at all times appeal to its provisions for protection.

Only the courts, he declared, could provide such protection.[12]

In his next letter, continuing to write as though he were addressing his readers as a jury of citizens, Hammond gives examples of two cases to demonstrate that constitutional jurisprudence is part of the everyday business of courts, and that lawyers cite the constitution as they do today, as a guide to interpreting and administering laws as well, though less frequently, as a basis for challenging them. Hammond's two examples are so realistic as to seem that he took them from actual trial experience. In fact he did.

The setting of each case was familiar to early Ohioans: a conflict between a landowner and a public official engaged in taking the owner's property for road building. Such takings were frequent, for much of the land in southern Ohio was originally platted and sold without providing for public rights of way. In December 1805 in the Jefferson County Court of Common Pleas Hammond's client Robert Carothers, a county road commissioner, was held liable for twenty five dollars damages for cutting down trees on the plaintiff John Taggart's land. Carothers's defense of official immunity—that he had cut down the trees in the performance of his duties—was disallowed by Judge Pease when it appeared that Carothers had not taken the oath of office required by the state constitution.[13]

Respectfully

Charles Hammond (1779–1840). Admitted to the bar of the Northwest Territory, 1801, and of Ohio, 1803; editor, Ohio Federalist, *St. Clairsville, 1812–1818;* Cincinnati Gazette, *1825–1840; Reporter, vols. 1–9,* Ohio Reports.

(*Courtesy Ohio Historical Society*)

Hammond tried the other case in December 1807 in the Court of Common Pleas of Muskingum County, another county on Judge Pease's circuit. Hammond's clients this time were Isaac Zane and several of Zane's friends, whose violent opposition "with clubs, swords and guns" to the construction of a road across Zane's land resulted in their being indicted for riot. The court record shows only that having waived a jury they were tried by Judge Pease and his associate judges, and the result of the trial. Hammond's third letter to Sloane in *The Rights of the Judiciary,* wherein he cites the case by name, tells the rest of the story. Pursuant to an Ohio statute which provided for appropriating property for public roads Zane had received an order on the county treasurer for payment of the compensation assessed for the taking of his property. Zane did not question the adequacy of the amount assessed. The order, however, had not been paid before the road builders entered on Zane's land to begin construction. Local governments then lacked credit facilities for borrowing against anticipated tax revenue, and it must not have been unusual for county treasuries to be temporarily out of funds. But the 1802 Ohio Constitution's bill of rights declared that "possessing and protecting property" was one of the "natural, inherent and inalienable rights" of man, and it made private property "inviolate, but always subservient to the public welfare, *provided a compensation in money be made* to the owner." After stating this case, Hammond continued in his third letter, addressing himself first to Sloane:

Now, Sir, I ask you whether the Court could refuse to hear [these citations]? Could the Judge say to [Isaac Zane], "It is nothing to us whether you have received a 'compensation in money' or not. We do not look at the constitution. The Legislature are the sole judges of its meaning and application." Would it be proper for the Court to hold this language?

Hammond then suggests the ruling the court might properly make. Now he addresses his readers, people who well knew that the paper money of time was not legal tender:

If the people themselves cannot rightly substitute paper orders for money, the Legislature, who are no more than agents of the people, certainly cannot do it. But it is not perceived that the Legislature have attempted to do this. The law directs that the [County] Commissioners shall give the party an order on the Treasurer. It does not declare that such order shall be accepted as payment. It is no more than pointing out the course by which the party shall get his compensation. . . . By giving this construction to the act of the Legislature, we prevent any collision between it and the constitution. The consequence is, that until the money was paid, the road ought not to have been opened.

Did Hammond actually make this argument in the Muskingum County court? Or was it one of those summations that lawyers make in their always-brilliant second thoughts, after the case is over? We only know for sure that he gained the verdict: the record shows that Judge Pease and his associates found Zane and his codefendants not guilty. Hammond's recounting of this case made another point—a corollary of the doctrine of judicial review—that whenever possible courts will construe a law in a manner which makes it constitutional.[14]

But the possibility of a saving construction did not exist for other Ohio laws Hammond offered as examples of constitutional violations. His fourth letter cited statutes which purported to authorize Ohio courts to order persons accused of certain noncapital crimes to be held in pretrial confinement despite their constitutional entitlement to bail. That example was put only in black-and-white legal terms, without any factual portrayal. In his fifth letter, on the other hand, Hammond colored an example of another statute he condemned as unconstitutional, with assumed facts that were arresting and to some readers, disturbing.[15]

Despite Northwest Ordinance's providing that "there shall be neither slavery nor involuntary servitude" in the territory out of which Ohio was established, blacks who emigrated to the state were not free in any practical sense. Among the repressions imposed by what became known as Ohio's "Black Laws," enacted shortly after statehood, was a requirement that Negroes who came into the state register with the clerk of the court of common pleas in their county of residence, and provide a five-hundred-dollar bond, with freeholders as sureties, to assure their good behavior and secure against their becoming a public charge. Upon any failure to comply with this registration requirement, a practical impossibility for most emigrating blacks to meet, the overseers of the poor were required to "remove immediately such black or mulatto person, in the same manner as is required in the case of paupers." Another statute made paupers who lacked a "legal settlement within the state" subject to removal "to the state or county where they have a legal settlement." But the Ohio Constitution provided that "no person shall be liable to be transported out of this state, for any offense committed within the state." Hammond argued that a Negro emigrant's failure to register was such an offense, and that his forced removal would constitute "transportation out of this state" in violation of this constitutional provision.[16]

Hammond might have left it at that, making his argument in abstractions, citing the Black Laws' registration requirement and the constitutional prohibition of transportation out of the state as conflicting. But he proceeded to put a hypothetical case which all his readers could—though most would have preferred not to—see portrayed in their own minds' eyes. A Negro emigrating to Ohio fails to give bond, but resists being forcibly deported. Suppose, said Hammond, that overseers of the poor "should tie him neck and heels, fasten him upon a litter, or a horse" to carry him off. But then suppose, Hammond continued, that the Negro brings an action against the overseers for false imprisonment. "Would this not be a *civil case in law?*" And what would be the matter in controversy? "The overseer would rely on the legislative act; the Negro would rely on the constitution." But Hammond did not stop there; he made the hypothetical case more disturbing. Resisting deportation, the Negro unintentionally kills the overseer and is indicted for manslaughter. As then defined by Ohio law, manslaughter was the "*unlawful* killing of another . . . unintentionally in the commission of some *unlawful* act." But, said Hammond, the Ohio Constitution declares that the "defending life and liberty" is a "natural, inherent and inalienable right." The Negro accordingly "rests his defense on the ground that his resistance was lawful; that the act of the Legislature authorizing the overseer to remove him was unconstitutional and void, and therefore could give him no authority." Then suppose, Hammond continued, that the court and jury conscientiously believe this defense to be meritorious. "Must they decide according to their own opinions, or must they decide according to the opinions of the Legislature?" [17]

No American lawyer before Hammond had ever—even hypothetically—invoked the power of judicial review against laws which enforced racial repression. In this feature Hammond's argument in his fifth letter to Sloane is a milestone in American constitutional jurisprudence.

In his sixth and seventh letters Hammond sought to rehabilitate the judges' contention that judicial review was mandated by their oath of office, and he protested the adoption of the Worthington Committee resolution denying the power of judicial review, as a prejudgment of an issue the House was likely to encounter as it took up impeachment charges against judges who had claimed and exercised the power. But it is for his summing up of that claim in the conclusion of his fifth letter that Hammond deserves especially to be remembered. A model of forensic skill, with the phrasing of an experienced speaker, the summation is written as Hammond would have delivered it in court. His successors at the Ohio bar might do well to read it aloud:

To show that individuals have a right to call upon the courts to decide all controversies between them, and all the questions upon which those controversies arise, I have examined the constitution and our statutes, and stated a variety of cases which have arisen or may arise under them. I have shown the manner in which those questions may be brought before the court, and the necessity of their being determined. I have explained the nature and extent of judicial power under a limited constitution, as it was understood by the first framers of the American constitution, and as it had been practiced upon and previous to the framing of our own constitution. From a full view of the "whole ground" I infer, that the power of deciding legislative acts unconstitutional, is vested in the judiciary by the general grant of judicial power; that it results to the courts incidentally, being necessary to enable them to try all civil and criminal causes; that it is a power necessary to the preservation of a limited government; and that our constitution, by declaring that "all courts shall be open, and every person, for an injury done to him in his lands, goods, person, or reputation, shall have remedy by due course of law, and right and justice administered without denial or delay," has emphatically enjoined upon our courts, to decide promptly, and without hesitation, all questions which may be brought before them, whether they arise under the law or the constitution.[18]

CHAPTER SEVEN

The Judges Impeached: The Opposing Contentions

"The independence and infallibility of the judiciary is now the last recourse and stronghold of Tory federalism,'" said the *Scioto Gazette*, taking a quotation from the Boston *Chronicle* as its theme for assessing the situation in Ohio in March 1808, shortly after the 1807–08 legislative session closed. "It has now become a serious question," the *Gazette* continued, whether and how long Ohioans "are to submit to the disposition of an *independent* judiciary in the hands of Federalists, combined with the shameful uncertainty of the law."[1]

The uncertainty was over the continued applicability of English common law, a question which heightened misgivings over the Ohio judiciary's claimed independence. State statutes enacted after the Revolution had provided for adopting the common law where it was not superseded by state or federal legislation, with an additional exception for situations where the court might deem English law unsuited to American conditions. But in his message to the 1805–06 legislature Governor Edward Tiffin pointed out that access to English legal reference sources was difficult for Ohioans, and he intimated that they might not find the common law to their liking even if they could know what it provided. The legislators reacted by repealing the adopting statute without substituting any other body of law. Ohio courts responded as Chief Judge Huntington had predicted at the time of the repeal, holding that they still had "liberty so far to apply the principles of [the common law] to give a remedy when the statute law applies none, and when the reason of it subserves the great end of Justice." Thus the common law continued to define legal rights and remedies relating to real and personal property, debt collection and other contractual matters, injuries to person or reputation, domestic relations, conveyancing, and succession to property on death. Moreover, despite the complexity of writs with Latin titles and arcane forms of action, the common law continued to govern court procedure. Finally, not least significant, was the acceptance in Ohio and elsewhere of the common law's recognition of precedent as the rule of decision in subsequent cases, along with its capacity for continual revision and refinement by decisions on new legal questions. If submitting to the "disposition" of an independent judiciary was a "serious question" for Ohioans, as the *Scioto Gazette* declared in its March 1808 editorial, the answer would ultimately come from citizens' experience with common law jurisprudence.[2]

The 1808 judicial season added another dimension to that experience. The advent of *en banc* sessions of the Ohio Supreme Court gave focus to its responsibility as an appellate tribunal of last resort, serving to unify and guide judicial law-making by inferior courts including the supreme court itself, functioning as an intermediate tribunal in two-judge circuit sessions. As previously noted in chapter 5 the 1808 circuit pairings were Chief Judge Huntington with Judge William Sprigg, and Judge Tod with Judge Return J. Meigs Jr., both Sprigg and Meigs being newly elected.

In a circuit session in October of that year, at West Union, the seat of Adams County, Huntington and Sprigg presided over the trial of William Beckett, indicted for murder, a capital crime over which the supreme court had original jurisdiction. The killing had occurred on a boat tied to a tree on the Adams County bank of the Ohio River. Beckett was represented by two capable lawyers, Henry Brush and William Creighton Jr. The evidence of his guilt was circumstantial, and the prosecution called numerous witnesses. With still more time taken by counsel in arguing legal points, a situation arose which no Ohio court had thus far encountered in a jury case: the trial would last more than a day. The question was what to do with the jurors overnight. Must they be kept together for the duration of the proceeding, or might they be allowed to separate and return to their homes? Chief Judge Huntington would have permitted separation after admonishing the jurors not to discuss the case with anyone. Judge Sprigg had misgivings about that expedient, and was persuaded to consent to it only provisionally. The trial lasted four days. The jurors went home the first two nights; on the third they stayed up deliberating; on the fourth they reached a verdict, finding the defendant guilty. But Judge Sprigg was still not convinced that allowing the jurors to separate was permissible, and he declined to enter judgment on the verdict, a judgment of execution from which Beckett would have had no right to appeal.[3]

The case might have been certified for determination of the jury-separation question by the entire court pursuant to the newly enacted statute providing for *en banc* sessions, the next of which was due to convene in Chillicothe a month later, in November. Whether this procedure was actually followed cannot be confirmed, the record of the trial having been destroyed years later, in an Adams County courthouse fire. It does appear, however, that Beckett and his counsel agreed that judgment might be entered provisionally, and that Beckett would be executed December 10, two months later, unless the county clerk of court were sooner notified that the supreme court at its *en banc* session had ordered a new trial.

The brief record of that session, kept in Ross County of which Chillicothe is the seat, makes no mention of any argument or appearance by Beckett's counsel. Indeed, whether counsel were expected normally to have any role in *en banc* proceedings is uncertain. There was no mention of their participation in the 1808 act which first provided for such proceedings. Rules for *en banc* sessions adopted pursuant to a similar statute enacted fifteen years later made only limited provision for participation by attorneys, who were allowed to submit written briefs but not to present oral argument unless the court specially requested it. A more fundamental question is whether, as originally conceived, *en banc* sessions were adversarial proceedings. In English practice such sessions were conducted more as colloquies among the judges and counsel than as arguments in a debate format with opposing counsel speaking in turns and occasionally being interrupted by questions from the bench. In Beckett's case the judges prepared for the issue they would confront at the *en banc* session. Chief Judge Huntington wrote to Jacob Burnet, a prominent member of the Cincinnati bar, stating that while he understood British law to require jurors to be kept together during a trial he did not know what consequence that law imposed, were they to be separated. He asked for Burnet's opinion on that question, and also whether Burnet had known of any instance in which a jury trial had lasted more than a day. We do not have Burnet's response. Sprigg wrote to the court's other two members, judges Tod and Meigs, briefly stating the case and citing English authorities, "all of which you will find here [in Chillicothe, where Sprigg resided]."[4]

On November 18, 1808 the four judges met in Chillicothe and denied defense motions for new trial and arrest of judgment. The record simply states that "no opinion can be certified in favor of the Petitioner on either of the said motions." Beckett's execution was carried out the following month on the day set by the provisional judgment. His hanging attracted an enormous crowd of onlookers, and it being the time of the Great Revival Movement they were addressed by clergymen including Lorenzo Dow, a famous camp meeting orator. Moved by Dow's exhortations Beckett himself spoke for three quarters of an hour, exonerating the individual upon whom his counsel had sought to redirect suspicion at trial, and confessing his own guilt, attributed his crime to "intemperance, gambling and base company."[5]

Since issues of the *Scioto Gazette* from the end of September to mid-December 1808 are missing, we cannot say whether the *en banc* proceedings in the Beckett case were reported at all in that Chillicothe paper. But from the absence of secondary evidence such as reprinting in another paper or later mention in correspondents' letters, we may conclude that the judges did not write and publish opinions explaining the Beckett decision. Their having done so would have provided a public demonstration of the court's role as an appellate tribunal, and its work in shaping English common law to fit the needs and circumstances of frontier Ohio. But by that time at least two of the court's members were preoccupied with the results and portents of the October 1808 elections, held a month before they rejected Beckett's appeal.

Public interest in controverted issues relating to the independence and powers of the state's judiciary had grown continuously since the 1807–08 legislative session, when the Ohio House adopted the Worthington Committee resolution against judicial review but deferred action to initiate impeachment proceedings against the three judges who had claimed the power. By March 1808, Ohio newspapers were reporting inconsistent lower court rulings around the state. Judge Francis Dunlavy, presiding judge of the common pleas circuit which included Chillicothe, defied the supreme court's decision in *Rutherford v. M'Faddon* and upheld judgments of justices of the peace for amounts greater than twenty dollars, citing the Fifty Dollar Act apparently without addressing objections to its constitutionality. On the other hand, from courts on Judge Pease's common pleas circuit decisions limiting the justices' jurisdiction to twenty dollars were reported. "Are the inhabitants of [counties in these circuits] governed by different laws?" the *Scioto Gazette* asked. "Can it be the law in Chillicothe, which is no law in Steubenville?"[6]

By that summer Thomas Worthington had announced his intention to run for governor in the October election. His principal opponent, who had declined Worthington's intimation of support for a U.S. Senate seat if he chose not to run against him, was Samuel Huntington. Worthington's objective was to re-unite the state's Republicans behind a platform of rejection of judicial review and support of greater control by the legislature over the judiciary. Sloane had written to him the previous April with an optimistic assessment of his prospects in eastern Ohio, observing that "the question [presented by the election] I am pretty confident will be tried by the principles of federalism and republicanism, except in the county of Trumbull," Huntington's home county, a locus of inde-pendent Republican strength. There, said Sloane, "are some who have wished to be called democrats [Republicans] although they are generally found acting and associating with the Federalists."[7]

"Acting and associating" of independent Republicans with Federalists be-came an important political phenomenon starting with that election, as former political adversaries found common ground as upholders of the independence of the judicial branch. In April Sloane thought that they would not "make a majority of [Trumbull] county, as [Huntington] is not popular even there." But by August, when acting governor and speaker of the Senate Thomas Kirker en-tered the gubernatorial contest as a third candidate, Sloane's confidence had be-gun to erode. Kirker was a radical Republican. Although Sloane professed to "flatter myself there is no danger" of Kirker's taking votes from Worthington, his anxiety increased when Huntington supporters demonstrated organizational strength at a political meeting in September in the Trumbull County town of Warren. Benjamin Tappan, who witnessed the meeting, reported to Worthing-ton that it had been organized "by Mr. Pease and his friends, to procure Mr. Huntington's nomination for our governor." Tappan gave the attendance as a hundred or so, a good turnout; Sloane, who was not there, estimated sixty. They concurred in reporting a two-to-one majority for Huntington's candidacy, with Kirker receiving some of the other votes cast.[8]

The Steubenville *Western Herald* and the Chillicothe *Scioto Gazette* weighed in on the judiciary issue during that same month of September. Both papers were Worthington supporters. The *Herald*'s coverage included publication of letters from correspondents who opposed his antijudiciary platform, the editor declar-ing that "however contrary to our own opinions are the arguments of those in favor of the judges having the right of setting aside acts of the legislature, we consider it a duty to give them publicity, if for no other reason than that the honest and independent freemen of Ohio may detect their evident absurdities." The *Herald* accordingly published "Agrippina's" reply to "Caius Graechus's" open letter to Calvin Pease, wherein Graechus had referred to Pease as the judge "who commenced the usurpation of legislative power . . . even before the judges Huntington and Tod seemed to have been aware of their great strength." But, Agrippina responded, "I do not see why Judge Pease is charged with commencing this contest. The lawyers in the neighborhood of Steubenville brought the question before the court, and it was certainly the duty of Judge Pease to determine upon it." Agrippina made this point to argue that the power of judicial review would not encourage any evil ambition on the part of a judge, since the power "can never be exercised, [unless] some of the citizens [who are parties in the case] call for it to be done." Finally, as Agrippina correctly noted, Caius Graechus was mistaken in attributing the authorship of *The Rights of the Judiciary* to Pease.[9]

Correspondence the *Scioto Gazette* published was one-sided. "Attention! Republicans of Ohio" cried "Plain Farmer" in a letter appearing in the September 6 issue. "No candidate should be elected to the legislature who does not declare his sentiments" on the "long agitated question" as to whether "our next legislature [ought] to repeal [the Fifty Dollar Act] or to remove the judges who refuse to act in conformity with [it]." In the same issue "A Friend to the Rights of the People," identifying himself as a nonlawyer, denied that there was any need for an independent judiciary. In contrast to England under monarchial rule, he argued, sovereign power in Ohio was held by the people, and exercised through their elected legislators. Now, he warned, a "dangerous aristocracy is fast forming, which threatens, like Pharaoh's lean kine, to swallow up" citizens' rights and usurp the powers of their popularly elected representatives. Voters' "supineness" in recent elections would "forge the chain which shall bind you to the foot of the judicial altar." But in the coming election Ohioans could remove that threat by voting to "put down the rising aristocracy which is forming around the judges and the courts." "If," Friend said, "you wish to avoid binding your rights, your persons and your property at the feet of an aristocratical judiciary, give no man who holds those monstrous doctrines an undue influence, by placing him in the [governor's] chair, or in your Senate or House of Representatives." Two weeks later in the same newspaper "Horatius" condemned Huntington for his decision in *Rutherford*, denouncing his claim to the power of judicial review as "unwarranted" and "aristocratical," and his invalidating the Fifty Dollar Act as having "thrown the state into more confusion than it has ever been in since its first organization." "Good Heavens!" Horatius cried,

Are we reduced to this lamentable state of oppression by the arrogant conduct of the judges, who pretend to be the safe-guards of the people? And shall we continue . . . to put such men in office to trample down our liberties, and bind us fast in slavish chains? No, fellow citizens! Assert your liberty, maintain your rights, and vote for no man on the day of election, whom you know to possess such tyrannical principles of aristocracy.[10]

Huntington won the election for governor with a plurality of 45 percent. The vote that would have gone to Worthington in a two-man contest was split with Kirker. Worthington and his supporters were bitter over his defeat, Sloane writing that "it will be very gratifying to Federalism" and blaming "men who although they make a general profession of republicanism understand nothing of [its] application but are ready at all times to join the federalists in opposing those who have been continually engaged in protecting the rights of the people." But the views of the composite majority of Ohio electors who believed that a vote for either Worthington or Kirker would help protect those rights against an overly powerful judiciary, were vindicated by the results of elections for legislative seats. The next General Assembly would have increased anti-court majorities in both houses, eager to avenge Worthington's defeat.[11]

Having received several petitions from citizens complaining of the "power exercised by the judiciary" in declaring the Fifty Dollar Act unconstitutional, the House of Representatives moved immediately to reopen the impeachment inquiry which it had tabled at the close of the previous session. This time the committee given charge of the business would speak without dissenting voices. Its three members were Thomas Morris, newly elected from Clermont County; Joseph Sharp of Belmont; and Samuel Monett of Ross. It took only eleven days for them to prepare, and for the House to vote articles of impeachment against judges Pease and Tod.[12]

Huntington had also been named in the resolution appointing the committee. But the House members apparently recognized that his leaving the court to become governor placed him beyond the reach of an impeachment prosecution, and no further action was taken against him. Nor, on his part, did Huntington do anything to assist Tod or Pease, to defend the court on which he had served, or to justify its decision in which he had joined. He was undoubtedly sensitive to his political weakness, having failed to gain statewide majorities either for the office or, evidently, for the issue on which he had run. He had been defeated decisively in his home county of Trumbull, Sloane's observation about his personal unpopularity there having proved quite accurate. All during his two-year term as governor, Huntington distanced himself from the controversy over judicial review and judicial independence, seeking to make himself agreeable to the judiciary's opponents in the legislature. His inaugural address contained only an oblique reference to that controversy, citing a "leading principle of republican governments, that the will of the people manifested through the constitutional organ [the General Assembly] should be the guide and rule of our actions."[13]

Judge Meigs's brief tenure on the Ohio Supreme Court was also ended by taking a new office; the legislature elected him to the U.S. Senate shortly after Huntington took the oath as governor. This left William Sprigg as the only incumbent judge whose tenure on the Ohio Supreme Court had thus far been unchallenged. But Sprigg lacked political skills or influence. His memorial to the House with unsolicited suggestions for composing the legislature's differences with the courts, apparently by amending the Fifty Dollar Act, was ignored.[14]

The articles of impeachment the House voted separately against Pease and Tod were adopted by majorities on the order of three to one. Of the three articles voted against Pease, the first two concerned cases over which he had presided in Trumbull County in June 1808, in which he had held the Fifty Dollar Act unconstitutional. In the first case Pease had set aside a justice's judgment for more than twenty dollars; in the second he had awarded costs to a plaintiff in a case brought in the common pleas on a claim for which the act would have denied costs. In both cases the articles of impeachment charged Pease with having acted "wickedly, wilfully and corruptly." The third article was badly drafted. It began by charging that "at diverse other times" Pease had determined "that the courts had full power to set aside, suspend and declare null and void any act or acts of the legislature." But it went on to allege redundantly that "at the times and places last aforesaid"—apparently in the two Trumbull County cases—he had "proceeded to set aside, suspend, and declare null and void" the Fifty Dollar Act. This third article charged Pease with having acted "unjustly, illegally and contrary to the constitution and laws of this state."[15]

Tod was charged in a single article for his decision in *Rutherford v. M'Faddon.* His indictment is here copied in appendix C. The conduct constituting the alleged offense was that Tod "did in his judicial capacity adjudicate and determine that [the act] was unconstitutional, null and void," and "for that cause only" had reversed Justice of the Peace Hough's judgment for a sum greater than twenty dollars. In so doing Tod was charged with being "unmindful of the solemn duties of his office," and with having acted "wickedly, wilfully, and maliciously" with intent to nullify the Fifty Dollar Act, "thereby to bring the acts and doings of the General Assembly into contempt and disgrace, and to induce the good citizens . . . to disregard them, and thereby to introduce anarchy and confusion into the government of the State of Ohio," all to the "evil example of all good citizens of the State of Ohio . . . contrary to its constitution and laws, disgraceful to his own character as a judge, and degrading to the honor and dignity of the State of Ohio."[16]

The House took final votes on the articles against Pease and Tod on December 23 and 24, respectively. On the twenty-fourth it appointed five members to act as managers to conduct the prosecutions upon trial of the charges by the Senate. The managers were all three members of the committee which had initially drafted the charges, Thomas Morris, Joseph Sharp, and Samuel Monett, along with James Pritchard and Othniel Looker. Morris was designated chairman, and thereafter served as lead prosecutor. Then thirty-two years of age, he was a lawyer with little trial experience.[17]

The building in which the legislature met while Chillicothe was the temporary state capital was a two-story structure with single rooms on each floor. Constructed in 1801, it had been used as the site of the convention which adopted the 1802 Ohio Constitution. An oversized replica of the building may be seen today in Chillicothe, where it houses the editorial offices of the *Chillicothe Gazette,* formerly the *Scioto Gazette.* In the original structure the House occupied the ground-floor room, through which members of the Senate had to walk in order to reach a stairway leading to their second-floor chamber. Proceedings in each chamber were audible and must sometimes have been distracting to members of the other house gathered above or below. But at least as recorded in their respective official journals, communications between the houses were always conducted decorously and with carefully observed formality. That was especially true of the Pease and Tod impeachment proceedings, for which the record of the prosecution and trial of Justice Samuel Chase furnished the forms of procedure used by both houses of the Ohio legislature in the Tod and Pease impeachments.[18]

Service of process on the respondents was the first order of business after the charges against both judges were formally presented to the Senate. Directions as to return dates of the summonses—the date when each respondent

judge was to appear to answer the charges—reveal both the Senate's decision to try Tod first, and something of his whereabouts. Monday, January 2 was the return date of his summons; service was to be made at least three days beforehand. The Senate's sergeant at arms subsequently certified that he had served Tod personally at his "residence" on December 29, the day after the summons was issued. This "residence" could not have been Tod's home in Youngstown. Its distance from Chillicothe at the time was considerably longer than the 220-mile route now provided by modern highways, and could not have been traveled in a day's journey. Since Tod appeared in the Senate on January 2, the return date of which summons had given such short notice, his "residence" for the time being must have been someplace nearby, likely a Chillicothe tavern. It probably also served as headquarters of the effort organized for his impeachment defense.[19]

After the senators had been sworn to try his case Tod sought and obtained a week's extension, until the following Monday, January 9, to submit his written answer to the impeachment charge. He then rose and, as recorded in the Senate Journal, "informed the court [the Senate, now sitting as the High Court of Impeachment] that the most respectable gentlemen of the bar had tendered their services, in order to assist him in conducting his defense." Tod then moved the admission of Jacob Burnet, Arthur St. Clair Jr., William Creighton Jr., Henry Brush, and Lewis Cass to serve as his counsel. They were indeed among the Ohio bar's "most respectable," and respected. Burnet, senior in standing, was a pioneer and leader of the Cincinnati bar. St. Clair, son of territorial governor Arthur St. Clair, was also a Cincinnati lawyer and, like Burnet, a Federalist. Creighton and Brush were from Chillicothe; having broken with Worthington over the judiciary issue, they were beginning to identify themselves as independent Republicans. Both were experienced and capable trial lawyers. Creighton was a graduate of Pennsylvania's Dickinson College and had until recently served as Ohio's first secretary of state. Lewis Cass, then twenty six, was in his sixth year of a successful law practice which included service as Muskingum County prosecutor. Behind his "rough eloquence and noisy bluster" were nascent abilities. As a member of the Ohio House in the 1806–07 legislature he had supported the committee findings acknowledging the power of judicial review but disagreeing with its exercise by the Pease court in holding the Fifty Dollar Act unconstitutional. Cass's conduct of the House's investigation of Aaron Burr's conspiratorial activities at Blennerhassett Island on the Ohio River had been rewarded with an appointment as U.S. marshall for Ohio, a position compatible with Cass's law practice. As Tod hinted when be acknowledged their offer to serve as a "great honor to themselves and society," it is virtually certain that none of his five defenders was compensated. There was no provision for paying them with public funds, nor could Tod himself have done so out of the meager judicial salary which was his only substantial source of income.[20]

The House's response when Tod introduced his counsel indicates that its leaders viewed the proceedings before the Senate as more a political contest than a trial, with prosecution of the impeachment charges calling for skills of legislative, not legal advocacy. They were confident of having the votes to convict the judges by the required two-thirds Senate majority. The same October 1808 election which had increased the House's anti-court majority from a proportion of three to two when the Worthington Committee resolution was adopted in the 1807–08 session, to three to one when the House in this next session voted articles of impeachment, was believed also to have strengthened anti-court forces in the Senate. An unusual number of the members of that body were newly elected, Senate membership having increased that year from sixteen to twenty-four with the establishment of new counties.

On Wednesday, January 4, the House augmented its prosecution team by appointing Alexander Campbell and Robert Lucas to assist the managers. Campbell, who had spoken against judicial review in the previous House session, had just been elected Speaker of the House. Lucas, new to the legislature, had been a boisterous participant in the political affairs of Scioto County and an enthusiastic member of the militia. Both these additional appointments appear to have been intended to consolidate political support for the prosecutions. The House managers might well have regretted the loss of the forensic ability of John Sloane, the most articulate opponent of judicial review in the last legislative session, who did not serve in this next legislature. Morris was convinced that his prosecution team needed capable reinforcements, but he failed to persuade his House colleagues. On Friday, January 6 they voted down his motion to permit the managers to employ counsel.[21]

By then it was clear that Tod's defenders not only had the advantage in ability, but that they had already been at work. What was in effect the first defense brief in the case was made public even before the charges were voted. On Monday, December 12, 1808, the week after the legislature convened, the *Scioto Gazette*—to its great credit, for its editorial position was against the judges—published the first of four letters by "Examiner" which ran in successive weekly issues through

Monday, January 2, 1809, the day Tod appeared before the Senate in compliance with the summons. Despite his deference to "men more competent to the task than I am," Examiner was clearly someone of consequence, an authority on Ohio law. His language was courteous and dignified, his style expository, not aggressive like Hammond's. "I believe," he wrote in his first letter's beginning paragraph, "that the power exercised by the judges of deciding on the constitutionality of law, is essential to the preservation of our rights and liberties. I think it is as capable of demonstration as any abstract proposition can be. Without it," Examiner warned, "everything lies in the mercy of the legislature. The constitution becomes an instrument in their hands, liable to be wielded to the most destructive purposes." On the other hand, he continued, "I am far from wishing to see the judges throw down the gauntlet to the legislature. . . . [for] an opinion deliberately formed and expressed by [legislators] is entitled to great weight." But when constitutional questions raised by their enactments "cannot, without a dereliction of principle, be avoided, [courts] should meet them with regret and decide them with firmness." Once made and until reversed, Examiner noted, such decisions establish "the law of the land." But they are nonetheless "liable to be investigated, and are proper subjects for discussion."[22]

Proceeding to discuss the Ohio Supreme Court's decision in *Rutherford* overturning the Fifty Dollar Act, Examiner again led with his conclusion. "As an individual," he said, "I believe that decision to be erroneous. I think the court were right in the exercise of the power, but wrong in its application. Right in deciding upon the constitutionality of laws, but wrong in deciding this law to be unconstitutional." The first ruling, he said, "involves everything dear to us: the duration of our laws and the permanence of our government," while the court's holding the Fifty Dollar Act unconstitutional was "comparatively of little consequence." He proceeded, however, to demonstrate the error of that holding in the remainder of his first, and all of his next three letters.[23]

Although the *Gazette* issues containing the second and fourth letters are lost, it is possible to discern from the third letter the main points of Examiner's defense of the act's constitutionality. Conceding that the right of jury trial which the Ohio Constitution made "inviolate" was the right as it existed at the time of the constitution's adoption, he showed that under territorial law the mode of trial depended on the court which heard the case, not the amount in controversy. Since trials before justices of the peace had never been conducted with juries, he argued, the territorial legislature was empowered to increase the justices' monetary jurisdiction, and it had done so, he noted, notwithstanding the Northwest Ordinance's guarantee that the inhabitants of said territory "shall always be entitled to the benefits of . . . trial by jury." The state legislature, Examiner maintained, had the same power. "It therefore follows," he concluded, "that the [constitution's guarantee of jury trial] leaves to the state legislature the power of increasing the jurisdiction of justices of the peace to any amount, and of requiring them to try those causes of which they have cognizance without the intervention of a jury."[24]

Examiner's grasp of territorial statutes establishes his likely identification as Jacob Burnet, who drafted many of those statutes while serving on the territory's Legislative Council. Perhaps Burnet was in Chillicothe when he wrote the Examiner letters, the third of which mentions not having the territorial statutes before him. It is thus plausible that during the period of two or three weeks before Tod's January 2 summons return date, Burnet met in Chillicothe with Tod and the other lawyers who would appear in the Senate as Tod's counsel, to develop the strategy and coordinate the work of his impeachment defense.

The strategy was clearly evident before the trial began. No attempt would be made to justify Tod's holding the Fifty Dollar Act unconstitutional. In his answer to the impeachment charge, submitted to the Senate on Monday, January 9, he simply asserted that the ruling was "sound, correct and tenable," but that "time will not permit" Tod's stating "the principles and reasons" for it. Burnet's "Examiner" letters affirming the act's constitutionality made declining to put the ruling in issue a provident concession. More importantly, the letters justified a hope the defense intended to encourage, that the Fifty Dollar Act could remain in effect and no longer be subject to judicial attack. Prospects for that hope appeared favorable. Pease's term on the common pleas bench had only a year to run, and two of the four supreme court seats (the two recently vacated by Huntington and Meigs) were available for the legislators to fill at the end of the present session. Judge Sprigg, who would continue on the supreme court, had indicated in the memorial the House had rejected his willingness to accept a compromise; presumably one that would have allowed the act to remain in force. Perhaps it was to get Sprigg's proposal before the Senate Tod that requested permission for Sprigg to appear for him as an additional counsel. But the Senate denied that request and would not allow Sprigg to participate.[25]

On Friday, January 6, Stephen Wood, senator from Hamilton County, wrote to his friend Ethan Allan Brown, an eager candidate for a supreme court judgeship, reporting rumors of defections among Tod's counsel. "Cass refuses to appear," Wood said, and Burnet and St. Clair "plead press of business." The rumor of Cass's defection was false. Burnet and St. Clair did retire, Burnet making his last appearance before the Senate the following Monday at a session mostly taken up by Tod's reading of his answer to the impeachment charge. St. Clair likewise took no further part in the case. But it may be doubted that Burnet and St. Clair were defectors. Both were well known as Federalists, and they and Tod's other defenders might have thought that those appearing for Tod in trial proceedings in the Senate should be lawyers with Republican, albeit independent Republican credentials. Added to the weight of that political consideration was the incomparable advantage of representation at trial by capable and experienced trial lawyers. Creighton, Brush, and Cass all possessed that qualification. Tod would be as fortunate in the allocation of responsibility for his defense as he was in his choice of defenders.[26]

Tod's answer to the impeachment charge had the faults of excessive length and awkwardness characteristic of "committee" authorship. It began with what lawyers today call a "statement of the case," recounting the background of *Rutherford v. M'Faddon* and Tod's own part in the decision. He admitted essential facts pleaded by the Article of Impeachment—that he had acted with Chief Judge Huntington to reverse the judgment awarded to Rutherford by a justice of the peace, asserting as a ground of that action that the statute which empowered justices to hear claims in the amount of the judgment was unconstitutional. Tod's answer also asserted something not alleged in the impeachment article, that it was the appellant, Rutherford, who had raised the issue of the act's claimed unconstitutionality on which the court had ruled. Along with arguments in favor of judicial review previously articulated by Hamilton and Marshall, Tod put the exercise of power as he had in his own judicial opinion, in the context of litigation between individual parties:

It will not, I trust, be denied that the citizens of this state have certain rights under the constitution. A controversy concerning those rights may arise, out of which will grow a constitutional question; which question presents itself to the court for a hearing and determination. The courts cannot turn their backs on such questions.[27]

In the third part of his answer Tod spoke personally. He said that if he had erred either in claiming the power of judicial review or in exercising that power to hold the Fifty Dollar Act unconstitutional, he had done so in good faith, as a judge ruling on questions duly brought before him for determination in a judi-

George Tod (1773–1841)
Ohio Senate, 1804–1806
Judge, Ohio Supreme Court, 1806–1810
Ohio Senate, 1810–1812
Major and lieutenant colonel, U.S. Army, 1812–1815
Presiding Judge, Third Common Pleas Circuit, 1816–1830

cial proceeding; and that he had not acted for any such base motives or evil purposes as had been alleged in the Article of Impeachment. His mind, he said
"has ever soared against the unhallowed temptations of corruption"; his "conscience, in accents sweetly encouraging, whispers to him her approbation." Tod
claimed that his belief in the propriety of courts passing on the constitutionality of legislation had been "wrought in his mind at an early hour of his political
life." Maintaining that he "was not bound to answer" to the Senate for the correctness of his judicial decisions, Tod asserted that a contrary view would con-
vert that body "from a court of impeachment, into a court of errors and appeals," making every error in judgment on the part of an Ohio judge a
punishable offense. Moreover, he warned, if the impeachment charge against
him were sustained, every judge's tenure would thereafter depend on the arbitrary will of legislators "ungoverned by any established principles."[28]

We may wonder whether, as he wrote these words, Tod remembered the time,
ten years before *Rutherford v. M'Faddon* was decided, when he and his classmate
Thomas Scott Williams argued against judicial review in their law school moot
court. Of course Tod might have explained away that argument, either as foreign
to his personal beliefs at the time or as preceding the "early hour of his political
life" when he said he came to an opposite conclusion. But for not having to offer
any such explanation he must or should have been thankful. There is no indication that anyone in Ohio ever learned of the Litchfield moot court case.

Responding to Tod's protestations of his personal innocence and purity of
motive, the House managers backed away from the impeachment article's allegations of willful, wicked and malicious conduct, asserting in their replication
that "it is not believed necessary to inquire" into such matters. To the contrary,
they said, the only "legitimate and proper" issue was whether Tod had violated
the constitution and laws of the state "in the exercise of power not delegated to
him." It was that last element—the usurpation of a power which did not belong
to the courts—which in the managers' submission made the case different from
one involving "mere error of opinion in a judge, on a subject legally and constitutionally before him." They pointed out that unlike the U.S. Constitution
which specified the jurisdiction of the federal courts, the Ohio Constitution
had left it to the General Assembly to establish the jurisdiction of each of the
courts of the state, a distinction from which they argued that the Ohio judiciary
derived its powers solely through intermediate legislative grant, not directly

from any conveyance of the "judicial power of the state" by the Ohio Constitution. "It is not perceived," the managers said

> that the authority claimed and exercised by the respondent [Tod] in declaring void an act of the legislature, is incident to any power granted to the judicial courts or necessary to its execution—consequently such power cannot pass by implication, and its exercise is an usurpation of authority not to be submitted to by the people of a free and independent state.[29]

But the managers were compelled to address Jefferson's expressed belief that judicial power to pass on the constitutionality of laws was a necessary "check" on the legislature. Not mentioning Jefferson by name, they acknowledged that belief as "the only argument meriting consideration." The Ohio legislature, they asserted, is sufficiently checked in other ways. Laws require passage by two houses; every law is "published, promulgated, and submitted to the inspection of the people"; and if the members of the General Assembly were "so corrupt as to . . . attempt to break down the barriers of the constitution" the people would have an effective remedy "by means of the annual elections." Moreover, should the legislature attempt to subvert the constitution by a law taking away the right of suffrage itself, the people would simply ignore such a law, hold elections in the usual manner, and so *"by their conduct . . . declare void such legislative act."* This suggestion of a remedy for unconstitutional legislation by popular nullification contrasts with Sloane's proposal in the previous session's Ohio House debate, that the courts or the governor could respond to any law which they believed to have violated the constitution, with temporizing actions (e.g, pardons of convicted offenders, or judicial orders for continuance or new trial) until the legislature could reconsider the measure in the light of constitutional objections. The managers' replication made no mention of that suggestion.[30]

Tod's answer was lengthy, and he must have taken a long time to read it to the senators. But if they had difficulty keeping all of his points in mind, they would certainly have remembered what they heard at the end. Tod's final summation had nothing of the mawkishness of his earlier protestations of personal innocence. It was simple, dignified, and professional, and the eloquence of its concluding words describing the significance of the issue on which the senators would pronounce their verdict is profoundly moving:

> This respondent, with cheerfulness, submits his cause to this honorable court.—On its integrity, and the justice of his case, rest his hopes, *that the issue will give stability and value to our rights and liberties.*[31]

CHAPTER EIGHT

The Judges Tried:
Proceedings in the Ohio Senate

The rules the Senate adopted for the conduct of the Tod and Pease trials dispensed with opening statements and provided for presentation of evidence immediately following readings of the respondent's answer and the managers' replication. After the evidence was in argument would be heard, with the managers opening and closing. As each session was about to commence the House was formally notified, and its proceedings were adjourned to permit members to attend the trial. Although the 1802 Ohio Constitution provided for all sessions of each house to be public, "except in such cases as, in the opinion of the house, require secrecy," there are no express indications either that other spectators were present, or that any of the trial proceedings apart from the senators' deliberations on the verdict were closed. The official record, printed as an appendix to the Senate journal and maintained in the same manner, recounts only the formal course of proceedings in each trial. It identifies participants (e.g., "Mr. Creighton on behalf of the respondent opened his defense"), records Senate votes on objections and procedural matters, and sets forth in their entirety the Articles of Impeachment, the respondent judge's answer, and the managers' replication. But the journal record does not report what was said by senators, witnesses, or counsel. After completion of the arguments, as the rules went on to provide, the managers, the respondent and his counsel, and all attending House members were to retire, and in the ensuing closed session each senator was "at liberty to offer reasons for the vote he intends to give." The parties and House members were then to be invited back, to be present to hear each Senator openly cast his vote as the clerk called the roll.[1]

Tod's reading of his answer took up most of the first day of his trial. After a few days' adjournment to allow the managers to prepare it, their replication was read to the Senate on Saturday morning of the same week, January 14. That afternoon the managers put on their only witness, Benjamin Hough, the justice of the peace whose $32.50 judgment for Daniel M'Faddon was reversed by the Ohio Supreme Court decision for which Tod was on trial. Hough produced a copy of his docket, which included his return to the writ of *certiorari* which brought the case to the court of common pleas. Tod's counsel objected to the part of the return which indicated that Rutherford had confessed the judgment entered against him (that is, that he had admitted being indebted to M'Faddon for the amount claimed, and had waived trial), on the ground that no such confession of judgment had been alleged in the Article of Impeachment on which Tod was being tried. This detail was important. Evidence that Rutherford had confessed judgment would have permitted the managers to argue that he had no standing to complain of being denied a jury trial before the justice, and so counter a point Tod's counsel are likely to have emphasized, that the power of judicial review could be exercised only at the behest of a party to a case who could show prejudice from the application or enforcement of the law claimed to be unconstitutional. Rutherford might, of course, have first demanded a jury trial before Justice Hough and then confessed judgment after the demand was rejected. But there was no indication that he did so. On Tod's motion, after a lengthy argument in which all three of his counsel and two of the managers, Morris and Campbell, participated, the Senate voted unanimously to sustain the objection. Tod would improve on that success when, at the end of the trial, his counsel got the managers to agree to a stipulation which established an additional reason for excluding the evidence of Rutherford's confession of judgment, that the confession had not been "made a point in the pleadings before the supreme court." Strictly speaking that was true: M'Faddon's formal plea in the supreme court was merely a general denial of error: *"in nullum est erratum."* But the supreme court's own record set forth Hough's return to the writ of *certiorari*, and thus Rutherford's confession of judgment was before that court when it acted. The managers, however, had neglected to put the supreme court's record (as contrasted with Justice Hough's) into evidence. Tod had good luck as well as good lawyering.[2]

The evidence offered on his behalf was mostly documentary. Creighton gave notice that he would read from the 1806 House journal, and from "the journal of the Senate, when the bill extending the jurisdiction of justices of the peace was pending" before that body. Presumably both records were introduced when trial resumed Monday morning, January 16. The evidence from the House journal undoubtedly consisted of the two House committee reports in the 1806–07 session, both with respect to Judge Pease's decision in *The Cost Award Cases.* The Lewis Committee, it may be recalled, had declared that "notwithstanding they consider the [Fifty Dollar Act] to be constitutional, yet [they] are of opinion that courts have the right to judge the constitutionality of our statutes." The Committee of the Whole's report that the "House has no right to interfere with the court in giving an opinion as to the constitutionality of a law, unless they [the judges] have acted through corrupt motives" was the basis for the last of the defenses asserted in Tod's answer, that he was not guilty of any corrupt motive in pronouncing the Fifty Dollar Act unconstitutional. The Senate journal excerpt supported that defense by showing that other members of that body had joined with Tod as a colleague in opposing any increase of the justices' monetary jurisdiction above twenty dollars. John Bigger, one of the senators and the only witness in Tod's case, had served with Tod in the Senate when the Fifty Dollar Act was passed, and had voted in favor of its passage. He was probably called to establish that other senators in the minority voting against the act's adoption had likewise expressed the opinion that it was unconstitutional.[3]

Tod's counsel did not succeed in getting into evidence "a paper purporting to be a record of the Washington district court, of the Commonwealth of Kentucky." His answer had mentioned recognition of the power of judicial review by the Kentucky Supreme Court as well as by the U.S. Supreme Court; perhaps the Kentucky district court case concerned an exercise of the power. Objecting to this proffered evidence as having "no bearing on the question under consideration," the managers argued successfully that only the Ohio Constitution governed the claim of Ohio courts to the power of judicial review.[4]

Neither side offered any further evidence, and by midday Monday, January 16 the Senate was ready to hear from counsel. Regrettably, there is nothing approaching a complete account of their arguments. A source for what little is known of them is the highly partisan reporting of a Chillicothe newspaper, the *Supporter,* established during the summer of 1808 and avowedly Federalist in its political stance. From the few issues which survive from the remainder of that year it appears that the paper's coverage of the impeachment prosecutions was at first limited to brief reports of the progress of Tod's trial, along with publication of his "very long and argumentative" answer and the managers' comparably

The Old Statehouse, Chillicothe, where Tod was tried in the second floor Senate Chamber. Ohio's first capital building, it was the Northwest Territory's first stone structure when in was erected in 1800.

(Chillicothe Gazette, *May 21, 2000 Bicentennial Supplement*)

lengthy and argumentative replication. But after Tod's acquittal, defense of the state's judiciary became the *Supporter*'s principal editorial cause.

It is not in our power to give even a satisfactory sketch of this interesting trial—it would occupy too much of our paper. The subject was under discussion [i.e., tried in the Senate] from Monday until Friday. The proceedings were perfectly novel, as it was not pretended by the managers that Judge Tod was guilty of any criminal act.

The managers' argument-in-chief was made on that Monday, after all the evidence had been presented. Morris led, followed by Monett and Looker. The *Supporter*'s report went on to recount how Morris acknowledged the novelty of his case as he began his argument:

The chairman of the managers, in the opening of the prosecution, declared that he set out, Columbus-like, to navigate a new ocean, and trace out an unbeaten path.

Morris would come to rue this choice of Columbian imagery.[5]

Submissions of Tod's counsel took up the next two and a half trial days. On Tuesday and Wednesday, January 17 and 18, Brush and Creighton argued for the power of judicial review. The only account we have, a brief passage in a letter by William Woodbridge, indicates that they emphasized the right of individual Ohioans to claim the protection of the Ohio Constitution, including the right to be relieved against the application of unconstitutional laws whenever such laws should be confronted in court proceedings. Woodbridge was one of a small minority of House members who supported the judges. He described Tod's, then Pease's impeachment trials in two letters he wrote to Paul Fearing, a fellow Federalist who had represented the territory in Congress prior to statehood. In the first letter written January 20, 1809, the day Tod's trial concluded, Woodbridge awkwardly described Brush and Creighton's argument as having asserted "the right of the people, in order to enforce in favor of any one of them to demand of the court to extend to the applicant his constitutional privilege, 'tho in contravention of an act." The casting in Tod's answer, of judicial review in the setting of litigation between individual parties was thus reinforced in his counsel's final remarks.[6]

During the trial Tod wrote a note on a slip of paper and passed it across to Alexander Campbell, one of the House managers, who read it, smiled, and passed it back. According to the *Supporter* Tod then gave the paper to "one of his friends" and thereafter, somehow, it came to a senator who was the subject of the note, Thomas Elliott of Jefferson County. Elliott had formerly served in the

House, and had voted in the 1806–07 session in favor of the committee report which had affirmed the power of judicial review. "Can a man who had it as his opinion, a few months before my [*Rutherford*] decision that the courts had the power in question," Tod wrote, "*now* tell me that my conduct was criminal?" Elliott's reported reply is puzzling. "Did I ever give it as my opinion," he wrote back, "that a judge had a right to decide a judicial question . . . without knowing the nature of the case, and declare null and void acts of the Legislature and suffer himself to be misled, by lawyers at the bar?" Perhaps he was referring to Tod's and Huntington's overlooking the fact the impeachment Article had omitted to plead, that Rutherford had confessed judgment before the justice of the peace. Publishing the exchange, the *Supporter's* editor added a journalist's last word: "Is it more criminal for a judge to be misled by lawyers, than for a Senator to be *led* by fear of losing his election?"[7]

On the morning of Thursday, January 19, Cass rose to argue Tod's defense of good faith and innocence of improper motive, a defense which the managers had sought to dismiss as irrelevant. But they could hardly complain of Tod's asserting it, their Article of Impeachment having alleged that he had acted "wilfully, wickedly and maliciously." As is often the case with unprovable allegations, these now became an embarrassment. Woodbridge recounted in his first letter the haste with which the House had framed them, telling Fearing that the Article of Impeachment "had been sent up in a very crude state, for the [House] majority were determined to suffer no amendment from the minority and listened to no suggestions of impropriety in pushing the business without evidence."[8]

Cass's argument defending Tod against the charges of bad faith and corrupt motives was powerful. "Stranger," writing for publication in the *Supporter,* praised it as a performance "such as would have done honor to any man before any tribunal in the United States," its submissions were "correct, bold and energetic," and its conclusion "beyond description, beautiful and sublime." Woodbridge's praise was not as lyrical. Cass had performed "very ably," he told Fearing, going on to describe the strong impression the argument had made. "Cass could I think beyond a doubt be elected judge if he would. He had resolved to be a candidate, but has I believe altered his mind."[9]

After Cass finished, Looker, Campbell, and finally Morris spoke for the managers in rebuttal, and the Senate adjourned until the following morning of Friday, January 20, the last day of the trial. It began with a stipulation between the parties, Tod waiving any objection he might have had to technical defects in the impeachment article, the managers agreeing that the indication in Justice of the Peace Hough's record that Rutherford had confessed judgment should be disregarded as evidence, for the reason, as previously noted, that it "had not been made a point in pleadings before the supreme court." What the Senate journal describes as "a few remarks" were then made by Tod himself, followed Creighton, and finally Morris.[10]

There is no record of what Tod said on this occasion. If we imagine that he followed the practice of some trial lawyers to make closing remarks as though they were directed to a single juror, then Tod might have directed his to Senator David Abbot. Abbot had emigrated to the Western Reserve's Trumbull County at about the same time as Tod. His anti-court views were well known and sincerely held. He had put his objections to judicial review in a letter to Tod, undated but almost surely written before the impeachment trial ended, which challenged Tod to explain how the "evils" of judicial review could be avoided. "Government would be at an end," Abbot wrote, if the people "had no power left" except to elect legislators whose acts the courts could set aside. Admitting that without judicial review the legislature had no "check," and that legislators might be "so corrupt" as to pass unconstitutional laws, Abbot asked:

But if the people allow the judges to set aside the laws, does it not make the judiciary a complete aristocratic branch by setting the judges over the heads of the legislature? Nothing, I think, could have originated the idea, except it is the Scripture account of God and the devil—one to create, the other to destroy.

Tod kept this letter; it is now among his papers at the Western Reserve Historical Society. Perhaps he responded to it in his "few remarks" at the conclusion of his trial. It expressed fundamentally the charge he had to meet—that judicial review, a work of Abbot's devil, would be destructive of democratic rule.[11]

About this time a legal development occurred elsewhere which would have impacted a modern trial as breaking news. On December 24, 1808 the Pennsylvania Supreme Court finally announced its decision in *Emerick v. Harris,* the case which presented the same questions under Pennsylvania law as the Ohio courts had addressed with respect to the Fifty Dollar Act: are state courts competent to judge the constitutionality of state statutes; and if so, is a statutory increase in the monetary limit of the small claims jurisdiction of justices of the peace unconstitutional, as a denial of the right of jury trial? The case had been pending for decision for more than five years after the Pennsylvania court heard it argued in 1803, by counsel who were leaders of the Philadelphia bar. Impeachment prosecutions of three of the court's members intervened while the case was being held under advisement. The ruling endorsed judicial review, and held that the increase in the monetary limit was constitutional. But although it was published in 1809 in the first volume of Horace Binney's Pennsylvania reports, the decision is not known to have been cited in Ohio at any time while judicial review and the Fifty Dollar Act were in controversy in this state. The opinion by Justice Jasper Yeates, one of the three Pennsylvania judges tried by impeachment and narrowly acquitted, contains an especially poignant paragraph. Tod's lawyers, if later in life they ever read it, must have regretted being unable to quote it in their final argument to the Ohio Senate:

> Every one can readily see that the judges may be thrown into a delicate situation by the exercise of this constitutional right [of judicial review]. They are subjected to the lawmaking power by impeachment . . . and may therefore in one sense be supposed to owe their existence to the lawmaking power. I can only answer, the constitution of this state contemplates no willful perversion of the power of impeachment . . . and it is to be hoped, for the honour of human nature, that such instances will seldom occur. Whenever it does happen, the judge must derive consolation from the integrity of his own mind, and the honest feelings that he has discharged his duty with fidelity to the government. When he accepted his commission he knew the tenure of his office, and it is much better that individuals should suffer a private inconvenience, than the community sustain a public injury. Posterity sooner or later will do him complete justice.[12]

After the arguments in Tod's trial were concluded the twenty-four senators who comprised the Ohio Senate's entire membership retired into closed session to deliberate pursuant to the rule permitting each "to offer reasons for the vote he intends to give." One senator, Warren County's John Bigger, subsequently published the reasons he offered. Bigger stated that while he himself believed the Fifty Dollar Act to be constitutional, a minority of the legislators, "men as good and as honest as any in our country," had a contrary opinion when the act was debated in the legislature prior to passage, as Bigger had likely testified when he appeared as a witness for Tod. "The question," Bigger said, "must ultimately turn on this point: Shall the judge be displaced—shall he be hurled from office with all the ignominy which such a fate would incur—merely for giving an opinion which a minority of the legislature did once give, [and] without the imputation of a crime? If so, it is a hard case!" Bigger got that far before the Speaker cut him off for "arguing, not explaining." No account of other senators' explanations of their votes has survived.

When the closed session ended Tod, his counsel, the House managers and other House members were invited back in to the Senate chamber to be present when the verdict was taken. The clerk asked each senator: "Mr. _____, how say you, is the respondent, George Tod, guilty or not guilty, as charged in the article of impeachment?" Fifteen senators including Abbot and Elliott answered "guilty." Nine including Bigger answered "not guilty." The vote to convict having fallen one short of the constitutionally required two-thirds, Speaker Kirker, who had himself voted "guilty," was compelled to pronounce the Senate's judgment of acquittal.[13]

Many legislators believed that the devil had won.

When the House members returned downstairs to their chamber Morris moved that a committee be appointed "to enquire into the state of the commonwealth, and of the expediency of adjourning the session of the legislature without day"—in effect, that they all simply quit and go home. Writing to Fearing later that night Woodbridge predicted that Morris's motion would be withdrawn, as it was the next day. Woodbridge had learned that at "a sort of caucus" held after the end of the day's session "too many moderate men" were opposed to giving up. But the atmosphere remained heavy with despair and foreboding. Many believed that Tod and Pease would have to resign. Tod's friends "pretty generally" urged that course, Woodbridge reported, "and if he should, [Judge] Sprigg will undoubtedly resign also. Pease it is said will also resign." Woodbridge also heard "much talk" of the legislature's calling a constitutional convention, the only means by which the 1802 Ohio Constitution could be amended. Had it been possible to do that expeditiously the result would surely have been fatal to judicial review as a doctrine of Ohio constitutional law. But the amending process was slow: voters would have to approve the legislature's call for a convention; next October's elections was the earliest that could be done; the next legislature would then have to set a place and time for a convention to meet; another election would be needed to choose delegates; it would be almost two years before they could convene; another election would be required to ratify whatever constitutional change they produced. That timetable did not suit the judges' adversaries.[14]

Over the weekend Tod made it clear that he would not resign. Nor—as had also been rumored—would he repudiate his decision invalidating the Fifty Dollar Act. But lawyers who had stood by him were alarmed. They might have differed over how immediate was the possibility that irresponsible and destructive legislative actions which "moderate men" could no longer prevent would render the state's judicial system dysfunctional. But all agreed that the situation was highly volatile, and with Pease's impeachment trial due to begin in a few days, that it would likely remain so. These lawyers—Charles Hammond who had prevailed in *Rutherford v. M'Faddon;* Tod's defenders Cass, Creighton, and Brush; and William Woodbridge and his House colleague Jesup Couch—resolved to do something to cool the heat they could feel rising in Chillicothe as frustration over the Tod impeachment verdict gave way to anger. The initiative they decided upon was extraordinary.

In a remarkable letter here set forth as appendix D, dated Monday, January 23, three days after the Tod verdict and thereafter published in newspapers, six of Ohio's most distinguished lawyers urged all their professional colleagues to join them in disregarding the Ohio Supreme Court's ruling invalidating the Fifty Dollar Act. Acknowledging that the effort to impeach Tod for his part in that ruling had been supported by "a large majority of the legislature," and that it was "at least possible" that the court had erred in declaring the act unconstitutional, they doubted whether the "gentlemen of the bar should convulse the country by adhering to [that decision]." Accordingly, they recommended that Ohio lawyers cease to bring actions in common pleas for demands under fifty dollars "or any other sum which the Legislature may limit," and pledge themselves not to seek reversal of any judgment of a justice of the peace "upon the point of unconstitutionality." As to pending actions they recommended that questions as to the constitutionality of the justices' jurisdictional limit "be kept out of view," and that lawyers forgo taking any fees for common pleas court costs in cases within that limit. By and large, it appears that Ohio lawyers complied with these recommendations. While never expressly overruled by the Ohio Supreme Court, *Rutherford v. M'Faddon* does not appear ever to have been cited to challenge the constitutionality of any legislated increase in monetary limits of cases triable by justices of the peace.[15]

Pease's defense was slow to get organized. He did not appear on Tuesday, January 24, the day for which he had been summoned, when his trial officially began as the senators were sworn. On the next day the Senate postponed further proceedings until the following Monday, January 30, when Pease was present and introduced William Creighton and Henry Brush as his counsel. A letter Creighton wrote the same day to a friend reported that Pease "has just waited on me and asked me to defend him," and opining that "the result in his case is very doubtful." Creighton and Brush promptly moved to disqualify Senator Thomas Elliott for having "formed and delivered an opinion prejudicial to the cause of the said Calvin [Pease], and pledged to support the same by his vote." Elliott was the senator whom Tod had chided for switching his position on judicial review. The Speaker overruled the motion for disqualification on the ground that the objection had not been raised when Elliott was sworn, despite that having occurred without Pease or his counsel being present. The vote to overturn this ruling was watched closely, as an indication of how senators were leaning. Now only eight of the nine who had voted for Tod's acquittal voted in Pease's favor. The ninth, Columbiana County's Lewis Kinney, voted with the anti-court majority to sustain the Speaker's ruling and allow Elliott to sit.[16]

On Wednesday, February 1, Pease submitted his answer; the afternoon of the same day the managers submitted a brief replication. The taking of evidence began Saturday morning, February 4. At least four witnesses testified with respect to the second charge, which concerned Pease's allowance of costs in an action originally brought in the Trumbull County common pleas court. The prosecution maintained that the allowance was in violation of the Fifty Dollar Act's prohibition of such allowances in cases that might have been brought before a justice of the peace. But the case was complicated by multiple claims and set-offs, and questions as to whether Pease had actually approved the judgment entered by the court clerk, which granted the costs. The third charge, which asserted that "at divers other times" Pease had declared for judicial review and against the Fifty Dollar Act's constitutionality, was dismissed for vagueness. The first charge, on the other hand, alleged a specific instance in which Pease had set aside a judgment of a justice of the peace for a sum exceeding twenty dollars, on the ground that the Fifty Dollar Act's grant of monetary jurisdiction in excess of that amount was unconstitutional. Pease's answer to this charge did not deny the alleged facts.[17]

The pace of trial picked up after four witnesses called by the managers were examined. Pease's evidence consisted of an affidavit of Elisha Whittlesey, a lawyer and a friend; it is plausible to suppose that he affirmed Pease's innocence of any personal wrongdoing. Arguments, at most, took just half a day: the managers waived opening; Creighton and Brush gave their summations; Campbell and Morris replied. Then five of the managers including Campbell and Morris made what were noted as "a few" additional remarks or observations. Trial was then adjourned until the following Monday, February 6, when the senators would vote on the two remaining charges.[18]

If the clerk had gotten the verdicts mixed up in writing them down, noting for the first charge the votes actually cast on the second and vice versa, the Senate journal's record of the outcome would make sense. If corrected for that assumed mix-up it would show that the Senate voted unanimously to acquit Pease on the second charge with its troublesome evidence of multiple claims and set-offs, and uncertainty as to authorship of the judgment entry which awarded costs. On the first charge, alleging the setting aside of a justice's judgment for more than twenty dollars and thus cleanly presenting the issue the senators were concerned with, they voted fifteen to nine to convict. Eight of the nine had previously voted to acquit Tod. The senator who cast the remaining Pease acquittal vote, Thomas Irwin of Butler County (not the William Irwin of Fairfield who had supported judicial review in the 1806–07 House), had voted for Tod's conviction. Senator Lewis Kinney, one of the nine who had voted for Tod's acquittal, now voted for Pease's conviction. Why Kinney and Irwin each switched sides is unknown. The result in any event was the same as for Tod: Judge Pease was acquitted by a single vote, one short of the required two-thirds.[19]

Reporting this outcome a week later in his second letter to Fearing, Woodbridge wrote that "you can hardly form an adequate idea of the degree of fervor and irritability which has unfortunately pervaded the minds of Members of the Legislature," the House having "fostered in its bosom a fire whose heat I fear will be felt in the extreme parts of the state." If "our most valuable civil institutions" were to be saved from being "consumed in a general conflagration," Woodbridge thought, that could only result from "external pressures and our neighborhood to other States," not from "any spirit of moderation among us." Ever since Pease's acquittal, he continued, "our Assembly has been held together only by the fear and shame of going home without doing anything and involve the State immensely in debt [it owed twelve thousand dollars, according to the auditor], without preparing some bill by way of a general law to satisfy the people."[20]

In fact such a bill was then being deliberated, and would be adopted later in the session, making the Fifty Dollar Act a Seventy Dollar Act. No protest against its passage was entered on the journals of either house, as had been done in other cases in which an enactment's constitutionality was questioned. Nor, so far as is know, did any member of either house otherwise question the constitutionality of the increase, or object that in adopting a measure which deliberately compounded what the state's highest court had determined to be a violation of the Ohio Constitution, the General Assembly was itself acting to subvert constitutional rule. If the impeachment trials, the ensuing actions of the General Assembly and the bar, and the ultimate demise of *Rutherford v. M'Faddon* as to justices' jurisdiction had proven anything for certain, it was that judicial supremacy had been overwhelmingly rejected as a doctrine of Ohio constitutional law, whatever might be left of the courts' claim to the power of judicial review.[21]

It was on July 28, 1809, some months after the session had concluded, that Leonard Jewett wrote his letter to Thomas Jefferson, asking for Jefferson's opinion as to whether judges had the right to pass on the constitutionality of laws, and reporting the controversy and "unpleasant forebodings" over the issue in Ohio.[22] Since Jefferson did not answer the letter we cannot say whether it prompted him to reflect on how it might be possible to have judicial review without judicial supremacy—for courts to judge the constitutionality of laws and decline to enforce or apply those found unconstitutional, but not infringe what Jefferson held to be the equal rights of other branches of government to determine such questions. The formula he would propose a few years later in his letter to W. H. Torrance, that the "branch which is to act ultimately, and without appeal, on any law, is the rightful expositor of the validity of the law," did not solve the dilemma. Jefferson himself recognized that "contrary decisions may arise and . . . produce inconvenience . . . a necessary failing in all human proceedings."[23] What was lacking as an alternative to judicial supremacy was not a formula for allocating power to make constitutional judgments to one branch or another, but a process for consultation between the branches to insure the constitutionality of legislation as a matter of shared responsibility.

But events in Ohio did not move in that direction.

CHAPTER NINE

The Judges Deprived:
The "Sweeping Resolution"

On February 17, 1809, a few days before adjournment of their session, members of the Ohio House and Senate met to fill the two supreme court seats made vacant by the resignations of Chief Judge Huntington and Judge Return J. Meigs Jr., Huntington to become governor and Meigs a U.S. senator. In a message calling the legislators' attention to the vacancies Huntington made a surprising recommendation, that the measure they adopted the previous year to add the fourth judgeship be repealed. Advocating restoration of the court's original membership of three, Huntington acknowledged that the fourth judgeship had reduced the judges' travel burdens by permitting a division of the state into two supreme court circuits. But he cited "serious inconveniences" he thought would result in cases of disagreement between members of a two-judge circuit panel, or between the panels. When a panel's two members could not agree, he said, "either the opinion of one judge must be the opinion of the court, or the parties must be subjected . . . to the expense and delay of another trial, in which one or both the other judges must sit." But those inconveniences had always been a risk in cases heard by two judges, whether they were two out of three, or two out of four. Huntington also suggested that the amount saved from not paying the fourth judge's salary might be divided up among the remaining three judges as a pay raise, to compensate them for having each to attend circuit sessions in about two-thirds, as compared to half the counties. They would indeed have to "ride like post boys," as Daniel Symmes had once remarked in a letter he had written to Huntington in 1805 when they were judicial colleagues. Symmes was commenting on the impact on judges' working conditions of additional supreme court circuit sessions required by the continual increase in the number of Ohio counties.[1]

Huntington also criticized the establishment of a four-judge court as presenting the possibility of disagreements between its two-judge circuit panels. "The decisions in one district may be different from those in the other district, upon the same points," he wrote, "and thus two opposite rules of conduct may be established in different parts of the state—though governed by the same laws, under the same jurisdiction." This second criticism is very curious, for it ignores the provision for *en banc* sessions to resolve such disagreements contained in the same law which increased the court's membership. Huntington himself had participated in at least one such session in the Beckett case, recounted above in chapter 7. Perhaps he found impracticable the law's requirement for holding four *en banc* sessions a year, one in each common pleas circuit. But members of the General Assembly had no interest in any proposal for reducing the number of places on the state's highest court which they could award to political favorites compliant with their views of the judiciary's proper place and function. Huntington's recommendations were ignored. After a perfunctory reference to committee, and the Houses resolved to fill both of the two vacant seats, and thus retain a four-judge court.[2]

The candidates were voted on together, each legislator voting for two, until one candidate received the votes of a majority of the House and Senate members. That occurred on the second ballot with the election of Thomas Scott, the Senate's longtime clerk, a loyal servant of Worthington-faction Republican interests. Balloting continued with the legislators each casting a single vote, until, on the fifth ballot, a candidate who could claim to be uniquely deserving was chosen. He was House member Thomas Morris, leader of the prosecutions at the Tod and Pease impeachment trials.[3]

Two days later John Bigger, the senator who had published his explanation of the acquittal vote he cast at Tod's trial, wrote to Tod with news of the election of Tod's new supreme court colleagues. "We have at length filled up the measure of our iniquity, and brought to a grand climax the modern system of judge-killing," Bigger exclaimed. "Oh God of heaven, what have we done . . . that we should have two such Monkies placed on our Supreme Bench?" Yet, he reflected, the selection of Scott and Morris "may perhaps be one of the best things that could have happened to us, for although it may seem like a death blow to the respectability of the judiciary, yet, sir, it will display, emphatically display, the primary object of the principal actors in the game." The people of Ohio, Bigger thought, are "certainly too discerning not to apply to these circumstances a proper construction." He concluded by expressing a hope that those in the "eastern end of the state" who had supported the impeachment prosecutions "will have the honor of Judge Morris and Judge Scott to preside over their District," and that Tod and Judge Sprigg would hold court in the western circuit where Bigger resided.[4]

But the four judges, apparently by agreement, chose different pairings for that year's campaign: Scott with Sprigg in the west, and on the eastern circuit Tod with his erstwhile prosecutor Morris. These pairings sealed the judicial fate of *Rutherford v. M'Faddon,* insuring that no more justices' judgments for amounts exceeding twenty dollars would be overturned, either on circuit or *en banc.* Tod's refusal to eat at the same table with Morris doubtless made it awkward for lawyers accompanying them as they traveled the circuit. To Tod's and Morris's credit, however, there is no indication that unfriendly personal relations affected their performance as colleagues on the bench.[5]

Morris's characterization of the prosecution's case at Tod's trial as "Columbus-like" in its exploration of new grounds for impeachment was taken up by the *Supporter,* Chillicothe's avowedly Federalist newspaper, in coverage which made entertaining contributions of ridicule and allegory to the literature of political discourse in Ohio. Morris's "Columbus" characterization was "strictly true," the editor wrote, and "our sister states will no doubt be surprised that Ohio, the youngest state in the union, should embark on such a novel and adventurous expedition, and they will no doubt rejoice that a few skillful and patriotic senators have stood firm at the helm, and navigated her back to port, her crew all safe and her constitution sound." Three weeks later as Judge Pease's trial was just beginning, the *Supporter* announced that "Columbus's destination in his late voyage was the *Judiciary Islands.*" With "squally weather, a heavy sea rising ahead, and his upper works being much damaged, some doubts are entertained of his ability to reach a port in safety." But, the *Supporter* reassured its readers, if "Columbus" should "again be defeated [by Pease's acquittal], he intends to make a homeward bound voyage and will probably never again *refit.*"[6]

With publication of the *Supporter*'s March 2, 1809 edition "Columbus's" ship acquired a name. The *Anarchy Brig Impeachment,* "of fifty-two guns, having been several weeks at sea . . . was wrecked on a plain even coast, unknown to either officers or crew, but which has since been ascertained to be a well known part of the continent of America, called Constitution Harbor." Fifty-two was the total number of House and Senate members who voted for the impeachments. Signed "Nauticus," the voyage account continued with portraits of the expedition's principals.[7]

The "projector" was Worthington, who by a vote split with another candidate had lost the governorship to Huntington in the October 1808 election. During the 1808–09 legislative session Worthington was at Adena, his home near Chillicothe, where he kept in close contact with his supporters in state political affairs. He certainly approved of the impeachment prosecutions against Tod and Pease, and the Nauticus account suggests that his role went beyond encouraging, to directing it:

Having been disappointed in several projects which he had formed, for the purpose of seating himself in the governmental chair of his country, [Worthington] determined at length to attempt an entire revolution in naval tactics, by which means he contemplated being able suddenly to invade some new country and make prize of the liberty and wealth of its inhabitants.

Recalling events of the previous (1807–08) legislative session when the House adopted Worthington's resolution against judicial review but failed to vote impeachment charges, Nauticus reported that "a few of her [the anarchy brig's] timbers were set up, when the projector for a time suspended his operations." Thereafter, he continued, "about the middle of September, 1808, the workmen resumed their labor, and the projector, having in October met with a new disappointment [his gubernatorial election defeat] he resolved to complete her for sea early in December, which his indefatigable industry effected."

This is the most direct evidence for Worthington's very plausible role as the impeachment prosecutions' éminence grise. His influence was powerful, but he exercised it discreetly. So far as is known he never addressed the judiciary issue in any public forum apart from the Ohio House's 1807–08 session during the single term in which he served in that body.[8]

The "captain, who on account of the novelty of his expedition, assumed the name of Columbus," was Morris. Nauticus mistakenly made him a "native of the ancient dominion [Virginia]"; in fact he had moved there with his parents during infancy, emigrating across the Ohio River in 1795, when he was nineteen. We wonder how well Morris really answered to Nauticus's description: "forehead flat and gloomy . . . eyes small and heavy . . . cheek bones remarkably prominent . . . eyebrows very large and black . . . nose short and stubby . . . lips and chin give a mark to his phiz, that is by many esteemed a complete index of malignity and presumption." The "second mate" and fellow ship's "officers," whom we may take to be the other House members who served as managers for the impeachment prosecution, were saluted with portrayals only slightly less grotesque. As in the previous allegorical account, the ship which symbolized their undertaking was wrecked and lay derelict. But the outlook for the future had changed: this crew would not give up. "It is understood," Nauticus reported, "that they are preparing a new vessel, and are determined to make another venture, being fully persuaded that they will not again be arrested in their course by the impertinent interference of Constitution Harbor, or any other land marks whatever." Perceptive readers might have wondered about this prediction. What "new vessel" was being fitted out for "another venture" to defy the "impertinent interference of Constitution Harbor"?[9]

As we speculate on the extent of Worthington's role in the impeachment prosecutions we may also puzzle over the *Supporter's* suggestion that he might be a candidate for a supreme court seat. In its issue of February 16, 1809, the eve of the election to fill the two vacancies, the paper warned that Worthington might put himself forward:

Is it possible that Retiring Modesty has become a candidate for the important office of Judge of the Supreme Court, so destitute of legal knowledge, and all the necessary qualities to enable him to discharge the duties of that office. . . ? Oh disappointed ambition! . . . do you wish to make an innovation on declarations, pleas, demurrers, etc.? For shame, sir, continue in that retirement, and under that benign influence which you have so eagerly desired.

Members of the Ohio House and Senate gave Worthington nineteen, then fifteen votes, to gain fourth place on each of the first two ballots, the second of which elected Scott. These meager totals negate any hypothesis of serious interest on his part in gaining election to the court. Perhaps Worthington or his confederates recruited these votes to hold in reserve, to be given to a genuinely favored candidate on a later ballot. If so, that candidate was Morris. Worthington received one vote on the third ballot, none on the fourth, and none on the fifth, the ballot on which Morris was elected. Reporting that development in its next weekly edition under the ironic headline "Merit Rewarded," the *Supporter* asked, "But what signifies this? He [Morris] is a good democrat, and has bawled aloud for the 'rights of the people.'" The report concluded:

Come, tickle me, Tommy, do, do, do!
And in my turn, I'll tickle you.[10]

Two months later Morris was back in the news, with a scandal. On May 25, before that year's supreme court circuit sessions were to begin, the *Supporter* reported that he had been arrested in his home county of Clermont, for the crime of rape. The complainant having no supporting witnesses, Morris immediately responded by charging her with perjury. Her prosecution on that charge was initiated by Morris's brother, an associate judge of the county common pleas court, along with "lawyer Rodgers, who is the sheriff." To his report of Morris's arrest the *Supporter*'s editor could hardly have resisted adding: "Query. Is the above not an *impeachable* offense?"[11]

The following week the *Scioto Gazette*, a radical Republican organ, published the alleged rape victim's name but not Morris's—an omission which the *Supporter* promptly denounced. Nor was the performance of Clermont County's judicial system any more commendable. When Morris and the woman, Mary Ireland, each appeared before the county court of common pleas on June 20 the charge and countercharge were referred to the same grand jury. Only eleven of those called for that duty having appeared, the sheriff, Rodgers, chose four bystanders to fill out the panel, then resigned, announcing that he had been engaged as one of Morris's counsel. When the county prosecutor also quit Joshua Collet was appointed *pro tem*, despite Morris's lawyers' objection that Collet was not a resident of the county. The only Clermont County attorney who had not been retained for Morris's defense was reputed to be on intimate terms of friendship with him.[12]

Disregarding their secrecy obligations, two of the grand jurors not only leaked, but published accounts of their deliberations. "P. Light," the foreman, probably a Morris partisan, sent his story to the *Scioto Gazette*, but the July 31 edition in which it appeared is regrettably lost. "J. Huber," a fellow juror who had apparently read Light's account and thought it less than "full and impartial," composed one of his own for publication in an issue of the *Supporter*, attested to by Jonathan Hunt, another grand juror. That issue having survived, we have only Huber's version. He stated that after the jury heard Mary Ireland they discussed whether they should first decide whether to indict on the rape charge, noting that Morris and his supporters were the only other witnesses waiting to be called. Proceeding to a vote, they found that they were eight to seven for returning a rape indictment. But then some jurors argued that they should not consid-

er the vote as final until they had heard from Morris and his friends on the perjury charge. Having done that, they first agreed to consider each charge and its
supporting evidence separately. But, as Huber reported, they found that impossible, "the testimony being known and being so opposite." Despite one juror's
objecting that "consolidating" the cases, i.e., weighing all the testimony together, "would be traveling out of the ground of grand jurors, and taking upon us
the duty of a traverse [trial] jury," they did just that. In the end only two jurors
voted for the rape indictment against Morris. But that was twice the number
who voted to charge Ireland with perjury. One grand juror, disgusted, refused to
vote at all. Morris thereupon brought a civil action against Ireland for slander,
reported in the same issue of the *Supporter* in which Huber's account was published. "In what part of the state," the editor wondered, can "a jury of their
peers . . . be found, so that the parties can have a *constitutional* trial? The disposition of the civil case is unknown; it seems unlikely that it went forward."[13]

Shortly after this affair became public the supreme court circuit pairings
were announced. The awkwardness of Morris's sitting that year in his home
county might well have dictated his being paired with Tod as the lesser embarrassment. Tod's and Sprigg's seniority on the court would have enabled each to
choose to serve in the circuit where he lived—Tod in the eastern, Sprigg in the
western. Since Clermont County was in the western circuit, Morris's avoiding
that circuit would have required his sitting with Tod in the east. It should be
noted, however, that he did so sit, and performed the duties of his office. *The
Ohio Hundred Year Book*, a compilation of state officeholders published at the time
of the centennial of Ohio statehood and often cited as authoritative, mistakenly
lists Morris as "failing to qualify as a judge" following his election.[14]

On the western circuit a case known as *Reed v. Moore*, an action for thirty-five
dollars originally brought in the Montgomery County Court of Common
Pleas, gave Judge Scott an opportunity to uphold the Fifty Dollar Act's validity
while disclaiming any power to pass on its constitutionality. By statute Ohio
common pleas courts had jurisdiction "where the matter in dispute exceeds the
jurisdiction of a Justice of the Peace." Thus, if courts were obliged to enforce
the act the common pleas court in this case lacked jurisdiction. Judge Scott's
ruling to that effect was expounded in an opinion published in the *Scioto Gazette*,
pointedly declining to address the Fifty Dollar Act's constitutionality. "It is not
the business of the court to enact, repeal, set aside, annul or make void any law,"
he wrote, "but simply to declare what the law is, and apply it to the particular

case before them." Scott did not cite or refer to *Rutherford v. M'Faddon*. Putting a we-told-you-so spin on its publication of the Scott opinion, the *Gazette* observed that, had Huntington and Tod similarly ruled, "our state would never have been convulsed as it has [been], and is." Judge Sprigg, Scott's colleague on the bench who favored judicial review but might not have agreed with *Rutherford*'s holding the Fifty Dollar Act unconstitutional, apparently expressed no opinion. But Judge Pease continued to act on his determination of the act's invalidity as he presided over his common pleas circuit. A correspondent wrote to the *Gazette* in April to complain that since Pease's impeachment trial "he has attended court at Geauga [County], and again pronounced the law unconstitutional."[15]

Around September the *Gazette* began to print letters denouncing legislators who had voted against the impeachment prosecutions, and urging their defeat in the October election. "A Farmer" asked: "Shall we this year elect representatives . . . who will exert, as three of them did last year, the whole weight of their authority and influence, to re-assume those alarming and anti-republican doctrines which have, for several years, agitated the public peace . . . and made the servants greater than their masters—THE PEOPLE?" Another correspondent, "a plain unlettered man" who nevertheless seemed remarkably literate, wrote to say:

You must place none but democrats in office . . . not those who would clothe four men with supreme power . . .

Is there a farmer, or mechanic, that does not like the [Fifty Dollar Act]? Is there one who believes it necessary for the public good that all debts over twenty dollars would be collected by a lawyer? Is there one who would spend six days at [common pleas] court, waiting for trial of his cause, rather than be six hours at a magistrate's, and in his own township?

Other correspondents denounced independent Republicans for supporting the judges:

Let Ross County at the ensuing election convince the sticklers for judicial aristocracy that its voters are made of sterner stuff than to bestow their suffrage on . . . men who wish to "carry water on both shoulders"—upon men formed of such pliable materials as to sacrifice your rights to gratify individual infirmity and the voraciousness of Federalism.

The plain honest farmer . . . looks with amazement at the specimens of reiterated insult and outrage offered by the Judges of the supreme court to the sovereignty of his legislature and asks himself, if the judges are to rule in this way, there is no necessity to elect representatives to make laws.[16]

Other newspaper correspondents in 1809 raised fundamental questions respecting the state's legal system. The declaration Hammond and other leading lawyers published immediately following Tod's acquittal, promising not to challenge the constitutionality of any law establishing whatever monetary limit the legislature might enact respecting the small-claims jurisdiction of justices of the peace, was scorned in the same issue of the *Scioto Gazette* by a correspondent who condemned Hammond and his colleagues as "the *primum mobile* of all the mischief, vexation, tumult and wickedness which has [*sic*] convulsed the courts of this state for two years past." "What!" demanded "One of the People," writing two weeks later from faraway Fort Defiance, "is the execution of our laws, and of the laws themselves, and the interests and liberties of the citizens, to depend on the whims, views, and follies of a few mercenary lawyers" who had taken upon themselves to determine "whether these usurpations of the court shall be persevered in or not." The "great question," he continued, was "whether the judges should disregard the laws and statutes of the state . . . and the rights of a free representative government be changed for that of a judicial aristocracy." But, countered "Old Jowler" in the March 16, 1809 *Supporter*, "never was there a more absurd proposition, than that the legislature is the *creator*, the judiciary its *creature*. . . . The judiciary has its existence from the constitution. The legislature can claim no higher origin. They are both the representatives of the people: the legislature of their interests, the judiciary of their rights."[17]

Additional support for judicial review came from an unexpected source. At a public meeting held in the court house at Xenia "for the purpose of inquiring into the rights of the judiciary," citizens of Greene County adopted a resolution particularly condemning two assertions they had found in the Ohio House's replication, its formal response to Judge Tod's answer at his impeachment trial. They objected to the manner in which the replication framed the issue at the trial, as whether judges "have a right to set aside an act of the Legislature under the pretense of the same being unconstitutional." And they were alarmed by the House's asserting that "the Legislature should assist the understanding of the Judges, force their prejudices and inclinations, and subject their will to simple, fixed and certain rules." "These expressions," the Greene County citizens said, "tend to show that [the legislators] wish to subvert our government by destroying that most useful branch thereof, the Judiciary, turn themselves into a base aristocracy, and place themselves at the head."[18]

With the approach of the October election the *Supporter* published a series of five articles by "Seventy Six," a supporter of judicial review. Ably written, each article concisely made a different point. The first two argued that judicial review was a not a general license to set laws aside, and that making the legislature solely responsible for the constitutionality of its enactments would create in its members "an aristocracy with a vengeance," making the judges "a poor cringing set of menials looking up to their masters (the legislature) for every decision they give." "What kind of confidence," the fourth article asked, "can you place in judges, elected in the manner you know those were last winter—men blindly devoted to this abominable arrogance of power by the legislature?"[19]

The fifth article is especially interesting, for it assumes that its Ohio readers were familiar with the Sedition Act cases, including "the trial of Callender [Duane Callender, a Republican newspaper editor], at which [Justice] Chase presided." Noting that Callender's counsel pleaded that the Sedition Act was unconstitutional, Seventy Six asked, "If [judicial review] was a Republican doctrine in 1800, how comes it to be a Federal one in 1809?" Only one explanation, he claimed, could possibly account for some Ohio Republicans' reversal of position—their ambition for judicial office. Anyone acquainted with the last legislature's proceedings could "point out the candidates that were to fill the offices of judges Tod, Sprigg and Pease, even down to the associates [common pleas associate judges]." Seventy Six's comment on the "chagrin and regret" of those candidates over the election of Morris to the supreme court is especially interesting. More than being disappointed, Seventy Six claimed, those candidates and their supporters had been betrayed by Morris's selection: "So secret was the affair managed by the 'Choice Spirits' of the band, that honest and well meaning men of the party were kept behind the curtain until they saw, and saw too late, to retrieve the error they had fatally been led into." Seventy Six did not name the "Spirits" or their leader, almost certainly Worthington. Even the disclosures he had made, he declared, would expose him to "the persecution and malice of this overbearing and irritated party."[20]

By the fall of 1809 that "overbearing and irritated" party had resolved to act. The *Supporter* broke the story in its September 29 issue, reporting that "the leaders in these affairs, having been defeated in . . . sacrificing at the altar of party the judiciary of the state, are now brooding a scheme . . . to sweep off the *whole* of our judicial officers at one blow . . . and thus effect by a *legislative vote* what could not be done by *impeachment!*" The report would prove to be accurate.[21]

In the same message in which he had recommended return to a three-judge supreme court Governor Huntington presented the 1808–09 legislature with a question Secretary of State William Creighton Jr. had earlier raised with respect to his own official tenure. The 1802 Ohio Constitution provided for the secretary of state to be elected by members of the legislature for a three-year term. The question was whether a candidate elected to replace an officeholder who had not completed his term would serve for a newly commencing three-year term, or only for the remainder of the original officeholder's term. In the setting in which Huntington presented it in the spring of 1809, near the end of the second triennial of statehood, the question's immediate significance was in respect to whether the legislators then needed to conduct new elections for secretary of state and auditor (the latter office having similar tenure), both current occupants of those offices having served less than three years from the time each was first elected. Thus squarely confronted with this question, the Ohio House and Senate resolved not to conduct new elections for these offices, and hence established a clear precedent for interpreting constitutional terms to run separately for each officeholder from the time of election. There is no indication that the members of the 1808–09 legislature who had narrowly failed to impeach judges Tod and Pease then realized that essentially the same question would come up the following year, 1810, seven years after the first holders of most Ohio judgeships had been elected. For judges who had been elected as successors to those first holders, the same question would arise as had been presented with respect to the secretary of state and auditor. Were the successors to serve each for a new seven-year term, or only for the remainder of the original incumbent's term? The tenure clause of the 1802 Ohio Constitution's judiciary article provided that supreme and common pleas court judges "shall hold their offices for the term of seven years, if so long they behave well." The spring of 1810 would be the seventh anniversary of original elections to Ohio judicial offices: the original three supreme court judgeships, the first three common pleas circuit presidencies, and all associate judgeships in the state's first counties. In almost all of those offices, however, holders first elected were no longer serving. Pease was an exception: the original holder of his seat, he would not be affected by the question. But Tod and Sprigg were, both having succeeded judges whose terms had not expired.[22]

Whenever a judge or other state officer was elected by members of the legislature the speakers of the Houses would notify the governor, who would thereupon issue a commission for the office. During the first decade of statehood, however, the terms of judicial commissions were not consistent as to their provisions for tenure. Tod's commission, issued by Governor Edward Tiffin upon Tod's election by House and Senate members in January 1807, simply made him a judge of the Ohio Supreme Court "vice Wm. Sprigg Esquire resigned." Many other judicial commissions were issued in like form, without setting forth the term of office. But other commissions provided specifically for the length of tenure—always seven years from the date of election. The commission issued to Judge Sprigg when he was again elected to the court in February 1808, states that he was "commissioned Judge of the Supreme Court of Ohio in the room of Daniel Symmes Esquire resigned, to continue in office for and during the term of seven years from the 13th day of February, 1808 if he shall so long behave well." Apparently, however, no one ever tried to make anything of this difference in the form; all judges having been elected in the same manner. It is thus fair to conclude that, prior to the fall of 1809, the understanding as to the tenure of judges had been consistent with the position the previous legislature had taken in its 1808–09 session with respect to the secretary of state and auditor, that the term of office specified in the constitution ran anew for each officeholder from the time of his election. But the "scheme . . . now in agitation" reported in the *Supporter's* September 29, 1809 issue would abrogate that understanding. The scheme called for a joint resolution of the legislature, ordaining that the terms of officeholders elected to fill vacancies should extend only until the end of the term for which the original incumbent might have served.[23] Tod and Sprigg were the expected casualties of this measure, Tod the principal target. Pease would lose his seat when his seven-year term expired in the spring of 1810; he had no hope of reelection.

In his "Autobiography," written in 1840 after he had become prominent in national Democratic political life, Benjamin Tappan related that in December 1809, while he was employed by a client to attend the 1809–10 legislative session as a lobbyist, he and Morris were invited to attend a caucus of about thirty members, held at Irwin's Tavern in Chillicothe as the session was about to begin, and presided over by Worthington's brother-in-law Edward Tiffin, lately a member of the U.S. Senate. The caucus discussed the question of judicial tenure. When asked for his opinion Tappan argued that the constitution's providing that judges' salaries "shall not be diminished during their continuance in office," implied that successors would serve only for the remainder of original incumbents' terms. He reached that conclusion by assuming that the framers intended that reductions of judge's salaries which the legislature might impose should take effect for all judges at the same time. He recalled that he then drafted a joint resolution "declaring what I thought to be a true construction of the constitution and resolving to proceed on such a day to elect three judges of the supreme court." But no such resolution was adopted by the General Assembly. Its actions to reinterpret the constitution's tenure clause and to set a date for judicial elections were taken three weeks apart; they were not accomplished by a single piece of legislation. It must have been during those three weeks, moreover, that the radical Republican proponents of the reinterpretation came to a realization which caused them—as well as Tappan, if he had been advising them—great embarrassment.[24]

Since its membership was increased at the end of the 1807–08 legislative session the Ohio Supreme Court had had four judges. The tenure clause reinterpretation would have no immediate effect on the current occupant of court's fourth seat, for its original holder had been elected only two years before, in February 1808. It will be recalled that the legislators then had two supreme court seats to fill—a seat made vacant by the Judge Daniel Symmes's resignation, and the new fourth seat which had just been established—and that they held separate elections to choose Judge Sprigg as Symmes's successor and Return J. Meigs Jr. for the fourth seat. But the following year, when members of the 1808–09 legislature proceeded to fill the vacancies created by the resignations of Chief Judge Huntington and Judge Meigs, they voted for both positions on the same series of ballots, electing first Scott, then Morris as each received the requisite majority vote. Under this procedure neither elected candidate could be identified to the seat held by a particular predecessor, and accordingly, it could not be known which of Scott or Morris had succeeded Huntington in one of the three original seats, and which was Meigs's successor in the fourth seat. That difference was immaterial if, as the House and Senate members had understood at the time, they were electing judges each for a newly commencing seven-year term. They had acted on the same understanding just a few days before, when Governor Huntington raised the question whether the three-year terms of office specified in the constitution for secretary of state and auditor ran for each officeholder from the time of his election. Concluding that the terms did so run, the members of the 1808–09 General Assembly found it unnecessary to conduct new elections for those positions.[25]

Looking for a way out of this embarrassment, the 1809–10 legislative leaders called for production of the governors' commissioning records, hoping to find an indication of which of Scott or Morris had succeeded to the fourth seat. But that hope was forlorn: the record stated that they were "severally commissioned Judges . . . to continue in office for seven years commencing the 17th day of February." The only way to escape the embarrassment of not being able to say which incumbent occupied the fourth seat—for a term which even according to the anti-court Republicans' new-found interpretation of constitutional tenure had five more years to run—was to abolish that seat and reduce the court's membership back to the original three.[26]

The General Assembly's work had five components. The first was a joint resolution voted on January 16, 1810, ungrammatically declaring that "in filling vacancies by the legislature [the constitution] cannot of right be construed to extend beyond the end of the original term for which [electees'] predecessors could have constitutionally served, had no such vacancies taken place." The adoption of this measure without implementing legislation suggests that its supporters were eager for prompt passage. The absence of any provision to deal with the question over who held the fourth supreme court judgeship further suggests that they were not yet aware of that problem.[27]

They apparently had discovered it, however, by Monday, February 5. On that day the houses resolved to meet the following morning, to "elect . . . three judges of the supreme court of this state." The members purported to do that when they met the next day, February 6. But no legislation abolishing the fourth judgeship was adopted until February 16, when the legislature amended the Judiciary Act to fix the number of supreme court judges at three. Another such amendment repealed the law establishing two supreme court circuits and providing for *en banc hearings*, adopted in 1808 when the number of judges was increased to four. On February 19 the General Assembly implemented the January 16 interpretative resolution by amending the Commissioning Act to require that commissions thereafter issued should specify the term of office—the "residue" of the previous holder's term in the case of anyone elected to fill a vacancy.[28]

The key vote on January 16 to adopt what became known as the "Sweeping Resolution" was twenty-seven to eighteen in the House, fourteen to ten in the Senate. Three of the senators who had declared for conviction at Tod's impeachment trial were opponents of the Resolution, and subsequently entered their protest of its unconstitutionality on the Senate journal. On the other hand were three of the nine senators who had voted to acquit Tod; they now voted *for* the Resolution. The tenth vote against it was cast by Leonard Jewett, who had been promoted to the Senate after serving in the House the year before. Opponents of the Resolution in the lower chamber also entered protests on its journal.[29]

Credit for managing the effort to enact the Sweeping Resolution belonged to Edward Tiffin, who was elected Speaker of the House for that session. Duncan McArthur, one of the senators who had voted Tod guilty but opposed the Resolution and joined the protest against it, called it "Mr. Tiffin's Sweeping Resolution." McArthur claimed that Tiffin got the votes needed to pass it by promising in exchange to move the temporary state capital to Zanesville, where the next two legislative sessions would be held. Again, however, it was Worthington who provided critical support and encouragement for Tiffin's effort. All during the 1809–10 legislative session he entertained legislators by the dozen, two or three times a week, at Adena, his stately home. In nearby Chillicothe he frequently attended their caucuses, and sessions of each house of the General Assembly.[30]

On February 6, 1810 the legislators held an election to fill the three supreme court seats which the Sweeping Resolution would shortly make vacant, upon the expiration of the original incumbents' seven-year terms. Two of those three were the seats currently occupied by Tod and Sprigg. No one could say which of Scott or Morris held the third seat. The balloting opened with all three seats voted on together. Judge Scott and a newcomer to the bench, William W. Irwin of Fairfield County, were chosen on the first ballot, on which neither Tod nor Sprigg received a single vote. On the second and third ballots Hamilton County's Ethan Allen Brown, an eager judicial aspirant who had been in the running the year before, gained a plurality well short of a majority, with Morris and two other candidates including Tappan all nearly tied for second. On the fourth ballot the other candidates' votes went to Brown, and he was elected over Morris.

In the balloting for common pleas circuit presidencies Benjamin Ruggles was chosen as Pease's successor, in a vote in which Tod made a surprisingly strong showing. Francis Dunlavy, an original incumbent, was reelected to the presidency of the first, or western common pleas circuit. Levin Belt, a reputed Federalist whose tenure as a successor holder of the second circuit presidency was cut short by the Resolution, was replaced by John Thompson. Thompson and the legislators' three supreme court choices thus became "Resolution Judges," as those elected under such circumstances came to be called.[31]

Writing the next day to newly elected supreme court Judge Ethan Allen Brown, his friend John Hamm exclaimed: "The Democracy is yet triumphant, the insidiousness of Quiddism and the wickedness of federalism to the contrary notwithstanding. Last night was a *jubilee!!* Such a scene of festivity and rejoicing has rarely been witnessed here."[32]

Worthington was present at the joint session at which these judicial elections took place, and shared in the celebration of the outcome. His biographer has supposed that "he doubtless laughed up his sleeve at the discomfiture of his aristocratic opponents [the ousted judges' supporters]." But he would find in one of the election results no reason to gloat. The choice of Brown over Morris for the third of the supreme court seats demonstrated either that Worthington did not control the legislators' votes, or if he did, that he had used that power unwisely. In either case he made an enemy.[33]

Tappan recalled being with Morris in the latter's room in Irwin's Tavern when he received word of the election results. "Morris behaved like a perfect madman," Tappan wrote. "He walked about the room striking his fists together, and, with great vehemence, declared that he would not submit to it, he would hold on to his commission as a judge of the supreme court which had several years to run yet to make up the seven years." According to Tappan Morris then declared "that before he would submit to being turned out of office in this way, he would carry the question up to the Supreme Court of the United States." Morris was convinced that he had been betrayed.[34]

With the enactment of the Sweeping Resolution and the elections of Resolution Judges the constitutional issue respecting the state judiciary's powers and position was transformed, and political divisions primarily defined by that issue became more contentious. A letter the *Supporter* ran in its December 30, 1809 issue notwithstanding the author's disagreement with the paper's own editorial position, epitomizes this change. After expounding on his construction of the 1802 Ohio Constitution's tenure clause, providing that judges "shall hold their offices for the term of seven years," "A Lawyer" addressed the significance of the dispute over the clause's meaning. If judges elected to fill vacancies were thereby each to commence a new seven-year term, different from other judges' terms, then, as A Lawyer contended, it would be virtually impossible for people to keep in mind the times when each judge's term would end. Accordingly, he continued, electing legislators who would in turn pass on whether such judges should continue in office, would be ineffective as a means of exerting popular influence in matters judicial selection and retention. "A door is immediately opened for placing the tenure of judicial office in the power of incumbents," who, without effective opposition, could either procure their own reelections or get "their coadjutors smuggled into office." It was, therefore, "most rational" as A Lawyer argued, to construe the tenure clause as the Sweeping Resolution did, to create an "entire, integral term, at the end of which all the offices become vacant, and the power of appointment returns again to the people."

Made more portentous by its practical consequence that initial terms of judges who were elected to fill vacancies would always be somewhat less than seven years, this "return to the people" epitomized the anti-court Republicans' ideal of a subordinate judiciary, whose members, though not chosen directly by the electorate, are bound to give effect to its wishes, articulated by and through elected legislators. The judiciary's constitutional independence had now become the paramount issue for Ohioans, supplanting the disputes over judicial review and the Fifty Dollar Act's constitutionality.[35]

On opposite sides of that issue were formed the political factions into which the state's Republicans continued to be divided at least for the next two years. The nomenclature of that division is somewhat assorted. Historian Andrew Cayton calls supporters of an independent judiciary "moderate Republicans"; they often referred to themselves as "independent Republicans"; their opponents called them "quids," "lordly aristocrats," or "the high court party." Together with Federalists, with whom they agreed on the judiciary issue, Ohio's independent Republicans became a formidable political force. Apart from the judges themselves their leaders included Nathaniel Massie, Duncan McArthur, and William Creighton Jr. The Chillicothe *Independent Republican*, which began publication in 1809, gave them an articulate editorial voice.[36]

The anti-court faction led by Worthington and Tiffin, which historians have sometimes designated as "regular" or "radical" Republicans, were now beginning to refer to themselves as "democratic Republicans" or "Democrats," and to their constituents as "the Democracy." As Professor Ratcliffe has recently pointed out, they paid greater attention to party organization than did independent Republicans, viewing it as an instrument for realizing democratic ideals, and its organizational strength as an "inherent virtue." But those ideals were to be compromised and the virtue tarnished by the radicals' infatuation with a bizarre fraternal organization with political objectives, the Society of St. Tammany.[37]

CHAPTER TEN

The Judges Defiant: Tod and Sprigg

Judge William Sprigg learned while he was away in Maryland of the legisla-
ture's acting to oust him. He immediately wrote to Judge Thomas Scott who, as
Sprigg said, was "now a judge by a two-fold title," having been reelected to a
new term after his previous term on the court had purportedly been cut short
by the Sweeping Resolution. Characteristically lengthy and verbose, Sprigg's letter essentially asked Scott to declare his position. If he should agree that the
Resolution and the judicial elections pursuant to it were invalid, then Sprigg
wanted to know whether Scott would join him and Tod in holding circuit sessions as the Ohio Supreme Court's only legitimate members.[1]

Morris was excluded from this proposal. "I am not giving any opinion on
the claim of that gentleman," Sprigg wrote, not mentioning Morris by name.
Sprigg probably thought that another encounter with the frustration of being
unable to say whether Morris or Scott was the former "fourth judge" would be
distracting, and unhelpful to his cause. Congress's action in abolishing newly
created federal circuit judgeships during the first year of Thomas Jefferson's
presidency would have been taken in Ohio as an authoritative precedent for the
legislature's eliminating the fourth state supreme court judgeship, and depriving
its incumbent—whether Morris or Scott. Sprigg wished to associate himself
with the first of Scott's "two-fold" titles, and did not want to cast it in the shad-
ow of that uncertainty. Sprigg ended his letter with a threat. He also wanted
Scott to declare his position if it were hostile, so "that I may determine . . .
whether to undertake the further discharge of my official duties in Ohio with
the sanction and cooperation of the chief judge only, in opposition to your
opinion, and that of the new judges *de facto*." (Tod's seniority had made him
chief judge of the pre-Resolution supreme court.) Sprigg's threat was thus one

of schism: that he and Tod would go on circuit that year as a rival Ohio Supreme Court.

Although Sprigg told Scott that "until I hear from you [I] shall not consider it necessary to make any communication to Judge Tod," Sprigg wrote to Tod the following day, stating the questions he had put to Scott, and asking, in the event Scott should prove uncooperative, "shall you and I ride the circuit without him?" On the same day, February 28, 1810, Sprigg wrote to Governor Huntington to inquire whether Huntington proposed to issue commissions to Irwin and Brown, "whom the [General] Assembly appointed or intended to appoint to supersede Judges Tod and myself?" But those commissions had already been issued. Huntington had done nothing to assist Tod or Pease in their impeachment trials, and he had carefully avoided mentioning any aspect of the controversy over judicial tenure in his messages to the legislature. He would keep a politically safe distance from that topic throughout his two-year term as governor.[2]

Back in Ohio on March 10 Sprigg wrote to Tod from Steubenville, saying that he was awaiting Scott's reply, and wanted to see Tod. Meeting two weeks later in Youngstown and still not having heard from Scott, they drafted a public announcement, the text of which has not survived, but which as later described in secondary sources condemned the Sweeping Resolution as unconstitutional, denounced as illegitimate the judges installed pursuant to it, and warned that their purported judgments would be invalid. On April 2, again from Steubenville, Sprigg wrote to inform Tod that a printer in New Lisbon with whom he had left their draft announcement had been instructed to wait to publish it until he heard from Tod, who "on further reflection" might decide against publication. "For my part," Sprigg continued, "I do not know what is best to be done and wish you to use your own discretion on the subject." Holding back from acting was characteristic of Sprigg. Tod published their announcement in the New Lisbon *Ohio Patriot* on April 7.[3]

Unaware that Tod had taken that step and now advising against it, Sprigg wrote from Chillicothe on the twelfth, reporting his recent conversations with Scott and William Irwin, another of the Resolution Judges. Scott was still temporizing, Sprigg said, and wanted "a fortnight to give a definitive answer." To Irwin, Sprigg proposed that they submit the controversy to arbitration: all claimants to supreme court judgeships would submit their titles to "any court or to the judges of any court in vacation," agreeing that those whose claims to office were not upheld would resign their commissions, and that the others would act as the court. Irwin and Scott had given Sprigg the impression that while they personally doubted the Sweeping Resolution's constitutionality they were inclined to hold themselves bound by the legislature's action in adopting it. "Thus," Sprigg wrote, "a new [supreme] court may be organized which the very judges who compose it do not believe to be a constitutional court but only hold their offices from deference to the opinion of the [General] Assembly."[4]

Scott's "definitive answer," given in an April 22 letter to Sprigg, confirmed the position he had forecast in conversation. He acknowledged that he personally disagreed with the Resolution, and said he would not have voted for it had he been a member of the legislature. But each department of government, Scott wrote, was responsible to the people for the constitutionality of its official acts, and it was improper "for one department . . . because they think another department has erred, in a certain point, to hurl defiance at, and usurp the authority properly belonging to that other department." Scott then addressed Sprigg's threat to go on circuit with Tod to hold a schismatic court. He could not say what he might have done had if he, like they, had "not been the choice of the late General Assembly." But he could not imagine responding by attempting to hold a rival court, setting up a claim to office "in such a manner that must, in the nature of things, convulse the state to its very center." "I am persuaded," Scott concluded, "that if the people of Ohio are convinced that the former judges are entitled to seats on the bench, they have virtue and will declare it." In the meantime he would hold the court with Irwin and Brown.[5]

Incensed over Scott's "hurling defiance" charge, Sprigg wrote a lengthy reply on May 1. "Has the judiciary undertaken to vacate some of the seats of the members of the legislature?" he asked. "In what way have the judges hurled defiance at those who have hurled them from their offices, except by declaring the constitution still exists?" Both correspondents then went public with their exchange. Scott provided a copy of Sprigg's letter to the *Scioto Gazette*, which excoriated Sprigg's "very outrageous and unjustifiable attempt to inflame jealousy and create discord between the legislative and judicial authority of our state" as it announced that it would publish Scott's "candid, dignified, mild, patriotic and very correct" response in its next issue. Someone, likely Sprigg, gave all three letters—his of February 20, Scott's of April 22, and Sprigg's May 1 reply—to the Dayton *Ohio Centinel*, which began publishing them on May 10.

Others weighed in. In its May 9 issue the *Scioto Gazette* carried the first of two letters from "Logan," which reported Sprigg's having sounded out officials of Scioto County as to whether he and Tod might be allowed to hold a supreme court session there. The second "Logan" letter exposed Sprigg's attempt to enlist "a malevolent factious spirit in Gallia [County]," but decried the notion that any of its inhabitants would join with the "two poor ignorant creatures in Scioto County" and "other disappointed, turbulent souls" to assist Sprigg and Tod in "producing a scene of anarchy and confusion throughout the state." Recalling the biblical Sampson, who died in the house he pulled down upon himself, "Justice" wrote in the May 30 *Scioto Gazette* that Sprigg and Tod "seem disposed to hold their offices, or bury them beneath the rubbish of the constitution." Some of Justice's other criticisms identify him as a lawyer. Although the cases they refer to are obscure, their themes are universal, ones which courtroom practitioners of later generations will have no trouble recognizing as emanating from a disappointed advocate. Thus Sprigg was denounced for refusing to grant "Mr. Bollman" a writ of *habeas corpus,* for having "truckled to the upstart insolence of Wilkinson," and for an occasion when "he lamely permitted a military despot to lord it over the law and the court." In a second letter published a week later Justice came to a weightier point. Suppose, he asked, that the legislature had instead adopted a resolution interpreting the constitution's seven-year tenure provision as Sprigg and Tod advocated, and so approved their continuing in office. But what of citizens who might disagree with that interpretation? Would they not be entitled to claim that Sprigg and Tod were illegitimate, and being kept in their seats by an unconstitutional act of the legislature? "Is it perfectly clear," Justice asked, "that an erroneous decision of the legislature is utterly void? Is not such a doctrine fraught with alarming and dangerous consequences?"[6]

On June 12 Sprigg wrote to Tod from Wheeling, advising that he had approached the Sheriff of Chillicothe's Ross County about their holding a rival court there, but had received no indication of how they would be received. "Whether we should be able to hold a court in Ross County or in any others is more than I know," Sprigg said, notwithstanding his own activities over the past two months as a promoter of such proceedings. He was just as tentative about whether he and Tod should appear in Chillicothe on July 9, when the first session of that year's supreme court circuit was scheduled to convene.[7]

Morris was the only ousted judge who attended that session. Tod chose to stay away, and Sprigg, who wished to disassociate himself with Morris's claim, would not act alone. In a long July 26 letter to Tod which the Chillicothe *Inde-*

pendent Republican published two months later, very likely at Sprigg's instance, Sprigg recounted for the record all the things he had proposed but never did, "having concluded to pursue such a course as we both have deemed advisable . . . and to do nothing without your preference and concurrence." "Had we [appeared and] taken our seats and postponed a decision of this case," he wrote, "the business and progress of the court might still have proceeded in a legal manner, you being the chief judge and a quorum existing, whether the title of Mr. Morris be destroyed or in force." By "postponing a decision" Sprigg presumably meant that any judge claiming a right to sit might have done so without prejudice. But the alternative Sprigg favored was that he and Tod should have gone on circuit by themselves. "We might . . . have brought the question more fully before the people by riding the circuit and holding a supreme court where we could," he wrote. "Had we done this in a barn (as has been the case) and left the court house to the new judges, I have no doubt that ours would have been the legal and constitutional court, and their proceedings *coram non judice* [*"before one who is not a judge"*]." Acknowledging the need for local officials' cooperation, Sprigg said he had "little doubt" that he and Tod would be "cheerfully recognized" in "a number of the counties (if not a majority of them)."[8]

Was Sprigg right? Would their schismatic supreme court been permitted to operate? Would lawyers have brought cases to it? It is not fanaticizing to ask such questions, for some such thing actually happened in a neighboring state a few years later. In 1823, when the Kentucky Supreme Court invalidated a popular debtor relief law as unconstitutional, the legislature, lacking the supermajority of members' votes needed to oust the judges, created another supreme court on which judges of a different persuasion were installed. The result will be summarized briefly. Refusing to acknowledge the legitimacy of the "New Court" the "Old Court" judges continued to function. Both supreme courts operated simultaneously for about two years, as attorneys took cases to whichever court they thought would be the more favorable forum. A statewide election at which the Old and New courts' rival claims to recognition was the dominant issue produced a legislature with an Old Court house and a New Court senate, along with a New Court governor. Then, the New Court having gotten possession of the Old Court's records, the governor almost had to call out the state militia when the Old Court sent its minions to get the records back. Finally in 1826 an act was passed declaring the measure which abolished the Old Court unconstitutional, and the schism ended after the New Court governor appointed a New

Court partisan to the Old Court bench as chief justice. That is what happened in Kentucky. There is no reason to think that something quite comparable would not have taken place in Ohio in 1810, had Tod yielded to Sprigg's importuning.[9]

When Morris appeared before the Resolution Judges at the July 9 Ross County circuit session he exhibited his commission "for and during the term of seven years from the 13th day of February, 1808," and claimed his right to sit on the court, declaring himself ready to do so. But the judges ruled themselves incompetent to determine that claim, and referred Morris to the legislature. They "quieted" him, as a correspondent reported to the *Ohio Centinel*, by giving Morris a certificate attesting to his appearance and willingness to sit. The correspondent's surmise that Morris intended to use the certificate in petitioning the General Assembly was only partly correct. Morris would use the certificate in confronting that body, but not as a petitioner. Morris's scheme was to get his Clermont County neighbors to elect him to the House, where there would be a contrived objection to his being seated. The 1802 Ohio Constitution barred judges from serving in the legislature. Responding to the objection, Morris would present his judicial commission along with the certificate confirming his attendance at the beginning of that summer's supreme court circuit and his willingness to perform the duties of judicial office, all to enable the House to perform its constitutional duty of judging the qualifications of its members. By demanding that judgment Morris intended at least to embarrass his betrayers.[10]

Tod also decided to pursue his cause as a legislator. Having served in the Ohio Senate in the 1804–05 and 1805–06 legislative sessions, he stood again for election to that chamber. He did not seek to embarrass it with an objection like the one with which Morris planned to confront the House. Unlike Morris's, Tod's judicial commission did not expressly set forth his term of office. Nor would he have wished to be associated publicly with Morris in a tactical ploy unlikely to secure their reinstatement. Tod would act circumspectly for the time being.[11]

The July 26 letter published in the September 27 *Independent Republican* proved to be the last Tod would receive from Sprigg, who thereafter withdrew from the controversy and from public and professional life in Ohio. He had put his house in Chillicothe up for sale the year before, and now he departed the state for good.[12]

Public interest in the October 1810 election began to build in midsummer, with the controversy over the judiciary continuing to predominate as an issue, along with speculation over who the candidates for governor would be. Writing for publication in the July 4, 1810 *Scioto Gazette,* "A Farmer," who could not find for himself the meaning the Sweeping Resolution declared the constitution to have in respect to judicial tenure, advised its proponents to "go back, and take a fair start, and if possible shew that the Resolution is constitutional, and if so, I will acknowledge my error." A week later, observing that "the next election will be very important to the people of Ohio," a correspondent signing himself "A Back-Woodsman" wrote the *Gazette* to warn that:

The federal[ist] lawyers and judges, who endeavored to set aside the Fifty Dollar law, have united throughout the state to send artful, ambitious, intriguing men to the legislature for the sole purpose of introducing anarchy and promoting lawsuits among the people. The story goes, that the judges and lawyers are conspiring to destroy the Resolution passed last winter, and give the courts the right to set aside laws, and what is worse than all the rest, to reduce the jurisdiction of the magistrates to twenty dollars. Now, if these things be true, it is a most infamous plot.

Militia musters that summer were another forum for public discourse on the judiciary's position. In August the *Scioto Gazette* reported that members of Captain Daniel Hare's company deplored "the violent measures that the judge-party, lawyers and Federalists, are making use of to undermine our constitution" by "giving the judges power to set aside, make null and void our best laws," and "holding up to the people two sets of supreme judges."[13]

Of public correspondence excoriating the Sweeping Resolution surviving issues of the Dayton *Ohio Centinel* provide notable examples. "A Lover of Good Government" wrote in September to denounce what he called the "mammoth resolution" as part of a plot to gain "sovereign power" for its proponents, warning that "if we give up one of our constitutional rights this year, another next year, and so on, in a short time we will have a lordly legislature." The same letter condemned as an "extraordinary low stratagem" the claim that the Resolution's opponents were plotting to repeal the Seventy Dollar Act. Several candidates for the legislature who opposed the Resolution were compelled to publish denials of that charge. For its refusal to publish such denials by William Creighton and Henry Brush, two of Tod's impeachment counsel who had decided to run for the Ohio House, the *Scioto Gazette* was anathematized by its journalistic adversary, the *Independent Republican:*

Ye enemies and revilers of worth and talents, what tale will ye next invent, to help thy poor sinking cause? Repent of the evil which thou has already caused, and ye will be pardoned by the people, whose "bowels yearn with compassion for you."[14]

By the end of August it was known that Meigs and Worthington would be the rival candidates for governor in the October 1810 election. But campaigning openly for political office was considered unseemly. A potential candidate's friends would encourage speculation about his prospects and promote calls for him to run; a subsequent, dignified statement of willingness to serve if elected was the accepted way of announcing a candidacy. On the other hand, adverse public reaction to speculation about becoming a candidate often discouraged interest in running. Rumors in late June that Judge Pease might run for the governorship as an independent Republican brought a sharp reaction from "A Watchman," who wrote the *Scioto Gazette* to ask rhetorically, "Who and what is Mr. Calvin Pease? Is [he] the late president of the third [common pleas] circuit, who set aside the fifty dollar law? . . . . If the late Judge Pease is the man, it appears to me [that] he will hardly be elected." This was a well-grounded assessment, and if Pease ever had any interest in running he did not pursue it. On the other hand Meigs's apparent detachment from the controversy involving the judiciary was unquestionably an advantage: he had not been on the Ohio Supreme Court when *Rutherford v. M'Faddon* was decided, and he was in the U.S. Senate when the Sweeping Resolution was adopted.[15]

In February 1810 the Grand Sachem of the Society of St. Tammany in Philadelphia granted a "dispensation" to establish a "Wigwam" at Chillicothe, with the right to "extend the chain of amity" by chartering Tammany organizations throughout the state. Ohio Wigwam No. 1 was founded in Chillicothe in March 1810, a month after the Resolution Judges were elected. Supreme Court Chief Judge Thomas Scott was the first Grand Sachem; Worthington and Tiffin soon joined as members. Under their leadership the Ohio Tammany societies functioned as an elite radical Republican political organ, whose object was "to make nominations and control elections." Support for the Sweeping Resolution became a principal objective. Tammany ritual was a patriotic overlay of Indian imagery. Under its Grand Sachem each Wigwam had thirteen Sachems (the number of the original states) who together formed its council. "Wiskini" carried the keys; "Sagamores" had charge of inducting new members, who were carefully screened for their political views. Although Wigwam meetings were secret Tammany's existence was flamboyantly publicized with parades by members wearing buck's tails in their hats. "Long Talks"—speeches by the Grand Sachem on St. Tammany's birthday—were given in gatherings to which all citizens with "Republican principles" were invited. Tammany had its own peculiar calendar. January, for example, was the "month of Colds," and May the "month of Flowers." Columbus's landing and the Declaration of Independence were the bases for dual systems of numbering years.[16]

Out of "Wigwam No. 1" in Chillicothe Tammany colonies were eventually established in Zanesville, Cincinnati, Hamilton, Xenia, Lancaster, New Boston, and Warren, among other places. Tammany activity in the October 1810 election was centered in the Chillicothe organization, which actively supported Worthington for governor. The *Scioto Gazette* became a principal organ for Tammany propaganda, a major theme of which was to vilify Meigs as the candidate of the "ex-judge party." Political historian Donald Ratcliffe has found evidence of considerable "ticket-voting" in Chillicothe's Ross County, where candidates in that 1810 election were tagged with "Tammany" or "anti-Tammany" identifications. Stands on the Sweeping Resolution were also a determinant of "ticket" alignments elsewhere in the state, and became a divisive issue in local nominating conventions.[17]

Aided by a reinvigorated Federalist minority, independent Republicans did well in the election. Meigs won the governorship with substantial majorities in eastern Ohio which Worthington's strength in the southwest could not overcome. Radical Republican control of the legislature was weakened by voters' choices of some of the Sweeping Resolution's most committed opponents as new members. Besides Tod and Morris were two of Tod's impeachment counsel, William Creighton and Henry Brush, whose election from Worthington's home county of Ross shocked the Tammanyites. Worthington out-polled Meigs there by a margin of better than five-to-one, but his political coattails were embarrassingly short. When the 1810–11 General Assembly met it returned Worthington to the U.S. Senate, choosing him over retiring governor Samuel Huntington by a close vote. Letters thereafter written to Worthington by political lieutenants in Ohio would provide a rich source of information and commentary on further developments regarding judicial tenure and the Sweeping Resolution, a subject in which he continued to maintain great interest.[18]

The radical Republicans retained the leadership of the House where Edward Tiffin was installed again as speaker. But they succeeded only partially in blocking consideration of Morris's bid to be disqualified for legislative office based on his claim to be an Ohio Supreme Court judge. An effort to gain summary approval of the Committee on Privileges and Elections' initial report that all members had been duly elected was turned aside. Morris was permitted to present his judicial commission and the certificate of his attendance at the supreme court's first circuit session that year, and the question of his disqualification was specifically referred to the same committee. But it spent little time deliberating. Its report came back the same day, December 26, for floor debate by the entire House sitting as a committee-of-the-whole. The decisive vote was taken two days later, December 28, on an attempt to defeat a proposed resolution declaring that Morris had been duly elected and was qualified for his House seat. The vote on an amendment which would have ratified his judicial commission and thus disqualified him as a House member was sixteen in favor, twenty-seven against. But Morris was allowed to address the House in remarks later published in newspapers, only a portion of which have survived. The Marietta *Western Spectator*'s issue of January 4, 1811 has the first of what was evidently a publication in two parts. This part is interesting, for it indicates that Morris elected not to base his claim to membership on the court on a contention that the Sweeping Resolution was invalid. Instead he claimed that the question whether, in 1809, he or Scott had been elected to the supreme court's fourth seat had been resolved by Scott's subsequent election, in 1810, to one of its three original seats. That action, Morris argued, confirmed him in the fourth judgeship, which the General Assembly had not yet abolished when, having adopted the Sweeping Resolution, it next proceeded to elect three members to the supreme court. Morris's argument would have allowed him to regain his seat without the legislature's having to displace the three Resolution members or restore Tod and Sprigg. But the argument turned on a point Morris did not address, that the members of the 1809–10 General Assembly were competent to revise the action of their predecessors in the 1808–09 Assembly, by designating which of Scott or Morris those predecessors had elected to the fourth judgeship.[19]

The closeness of the General Assembly's vote to elect Worthington as a U.S. senator gave additional evidence that political forces loyal to him were disintegrating. Four days before the election Benjamin Hough, who had been elected state auditor since his judgment as a justice of the peace had been set aside in *Rutherford v. M'Faddon*, wrote to Worthington to report that a caucus of legislators called to agree on the candidate for the U.S. Senate seat had "ended in a farce." On the eve of the election Carlos Norton, clerk of the Senate, saw Worthington's prospects as "at best, doubtful" and feared that Huntington would to be elected. Norton's letter mentioned defections of Meigs, Morris, Brush, and Creighton, with each of whom Worthington formerly had political ties. When Worthington won, James Caldwell's congratulating letter mentioned four other "old friends," members of the House or Senate, who "took an active part against you in favor of his late Excellency [Huntington]."[20]

Norton also had a guarded outlook for the Sweeping Resolution in the General Assembly during that session. "It is more than likely," he told Worthington, "that there is a majority in favor of rescinding the Resolution, in the House of Representatives." But, he added, "in the Senate it is safe enough." The latter prediction was made good on January 15, 1811, when the Senate rejected, thirteen to ten, Tod's motion to appoint a committee to reconsider the Commissioning Act which implemented the Resolution, and "to compare the provisions of the same with the [Ohio] constitution." But when amended by adding a proviso that judges elected pursuant to the Resolution should in any event hold their offices for the remainder of their terms, the motion was defeated only by a single vote. Here and thereafter, attempts to amend the Commissioning Act were the vehicle for effective repeal of the Sweeping Resolution, which the act implemented. Tod's joining with other Resolution opponents to support the amended motion put him on record as offering to sacrifice his own prospects for restoration to his supreme court seat. An effort by opponents in the House was also narrowly defeated when on January 14, 1811, the day before the Senate's action, the lower chamber rejected by a single vote Brush's motion for leave to bring in a bill for the Commissioning Act's repeal. Coming out openly against the Resolution, Morris supported the repeal motion.[21]

Gloating over the defeats of repeal efforts, Senator David Purviance reported to Worthington that "those champions [Tod, Morris, Creighton, and Brush] who were expected to overturn and disannul former legislative acts and proceedings and set the world aright again have done little more than exhibit an additional proof of human frailty." "Whether our former proceedings have been right or wrong," he concluded, "it is well that those lordly aristocrats have received a check. The 'Sweeping Resolution' (as they are heard to say) remains as it was." Norton reported in the same ebullient mood. "Brush and Creighton have been foiled in everything" he wrote to Worthington, adding that "the whole blame was laid [by opponents of the Resolution] on the shoulders of the sons of old Saint Tammany." "By the way," Norton added, "the titular Saint of America has gained many followers this winter. It is a common saying here among the feds and quids that 'there is too much Tammany' in the Legislature."[22]

St. Tammany had indeed gained followers among radical Republican legislators, many of whom were initiated into the Zanesville Wigwam during the General Assembly's 1810–11 session. But other Ohioans were beginning to view Tammany as a sinister influence, mistrusting its secrecy, resenting its exclusivity, and sensing in those features a conspiracy to acquire and hold power. A correspondent's letter to the *Liberty Hall and Cincinnati Mercury* warned that "such secret societies are at war with the first principles of Republican government, because every measure ought to stand the test of public opinion . . . they are the cornerstones upon which aristocracy, monarchy, and tyranny are built." Readers of the Chillicothe *Independent Republican* were alarmed by its report, as the 1810–11 legislative session ended, that "no less than SEVENTEEN MEMBERS OF BOTH HOUSES joined this nefarious association in ONE NIGHT." Opponents of the Sweeping Resolution began to portray the Resolution itself as a Tammany measure, deliberately adopted to subvert republican institutions. A correspondent signing himself "The Writer" and published in the June 27, 1811 *Independent Republican,* expressed "real concern" over "the unconstitutional and anti-republican warfare, which has been so successfully waged against our judiciary," adding that "when justice is seized by the nose . . . the ruling authority has all the features and motions of a cabal." And in an open letter to his constituents decrying as "entirely out of the ordinary course" the Ohio House's refusal even to permit introduction of a bill for the Commissioning Act's repeal, Greene County representative James Morrow expressed his "fear [that] this extraordinary decision was in some measure governed by the influence of a midnight society, where a *grand sachem* alias GRAND SATAN presides—for with a few exceptions a *Tammany man* and a *Resolution man* mean the same thing."[23]

Weighing at least as heavily in the development of public opposition to the Sweeping Resolution were its unintended consequences for the most numerous of the Ohio judicial officers it affected—the associate judges of the county courts of common pleas. A majority of the associates in office in January 1810 when the Resolution was adopted were, like Tod and Sprigg, successors of original holders of their seats, and their terms of office were similarly cut short by the Resolution. But unlike supreme court judgeships and common pleas circuit presidencies, associate judges' positions were rarely the subject of contested elections. Legislators customarily deferred to the choices of colleagues who represented the counties, respectively, where the associates were to serve. But such deference was not always accorded. Senator John Bigger, who voted for Tod's impeachment acquittal and wrote at the end of the 1808–09 session to inform him of the elections of Scott and Morris (the two "Monkies") to the supreme court, complained in the same letter that nominees favored by the legislative delegations of Fairfield and Gallia counties had been passed over—a development which might have had something to do with the acquittal votes Tod received from senators representing those counties.

The following year, when members of the 1809–10 legislature came to fill the sixty-nine associate judgeships whose incumbents' terms had been cut short by the Resolution, most were simply reelected for new seven-year terms. There is no indication of the legislators giving such reelections any particular thought, or of their making any comprehensive effort to secure incumbents' consents to re-election. Commissions specifying their new terms were then promptly issued by Governor Huntington. To qualify under their new commissions the incumbents were required to take another oath of office.[24]

Receipt of a commission for a term which began before the term of one's previous judicial commission had run must have surprised some common pleas associates. Most made no objection, they took another oath of office and resumed performing the duties of their judgeships. If a few—perhaps a few more than normal—resigned during the next several months, we cannot say how many such resignations were motivated by opposition to the Sweeping Resolution. But two of Greene County's associate judges left no doubt as to their position on the Resolution. The manner, moreover, by which they chose to affirm that position could not have been more disruptive.[25]

They insisted on continuing to serve under their old commissions.

CHAPTER ELEVEN

Greene County's Subversives: Snowden and Huston

Named for Revolutionary War General Nathaniel Greene and established in thickly forested country east of present-day Dayton in May 1803, Greene County, Ohio quickly acquired a robust judicial heritage. The county had no town when the inaugural session of its common pleas court was convened in August of that year to organize county government. The site of this auspicious proceeding was a rude and isolated wilderness habitation consisting of a one-room cabin, a small pole building used as a smokehouse, and a nearby block house constructed as a refuge from Indian attack. Presiding Judge Francis Dunlavy, prosecuting attorney Arthur St. Clair Jr., and others arriving from distant places to attend the session were all put up in the cabin. They slept in the loft with the regular occupants, Peter Borders and his family. The court was convened in the cabin, the grand jury met in the smokehouse. The block house was available to serve as a jail. Besides county residents who would have official duties as sheriff, clerk, and grand jurors, the inaugural session attracted a sizeable number of spectators, some from neighboring counties. In frontier Ohio as elsewhere on the American frontier, court sessions were public entertainment.[1]

Judge Dunlavy's charge to the grand jury would have been the first item of business. Such charges were works of patriotic oratory, intended to impress and inspire spectators as well as instructing the grand jurors in their duties. The inaugural session must have called forth a memorable performance, with Prosecutor St. Clair's panoply of cocked hat and sword lending additional dignity to the proceedings. With no building large enough to accommodate the grand jurors and all the spectators attracted to the event, Judge Dunlavy would have had to deliver his charge outdoors. The "instructions" portion might well have been perfunctory, since no crimes had been reported, and it did not appear that the grand jurors would have anyone to indict.

That prospect soon changed. Borders, the landlord, had been granted a tavern license, of which he took full commercial advantage. As spectators began to show the stimulating effects of the corn whiskey Borders was dispensing, the decorous setting in which the court had convened was rapidly transformed by rowdiness and brawling. Seldom, however, were wounds to the dignity of justice more swiftly salved. After summoning seventeen witnesses to testify, the grand jurors issued nine bills of indictment for "affrays, assaults and batteries," *all committed while they were in session.* Arrested and confined in the block house and brought before the court for arraignment and trial the same day, all defendants pleaded guilty, and were fined and released.[2]

Recounted by local historians as a comic affair, the episode's symbolic significance as a rite of passage to the rule of law was recognized by at least one participant. Owen Davis, known to his neighbors both as a brave Indian fighter and a "kind-hearted, obliging man" met up with a sojourner from nearby Warren County with whom he had had unsatisfactory business dealings. After adjusting their differences in the manner both were used to, Davis immediately took himself before the court, confessed that he had "whupped that damned hog thief," slammed his leather purse down on the cabin table which served as the judicial bench, and demanded, "What's the damage—what's to pay?" He was fined eight dollars.[3]

County organization proceedings at this first court session included appointment of a surveyor to locate the future county seat and lay out plans for its streets and lots, all soon to materialize as the town of Xenia. The common pleas court began holding sessions there in 1804, in a log house on the public square which also was used as a tavern. While some Ohioans were disgusted by what one described as the "noise, confusion and drunkenness" of the tavern settings in which many counties' first judicial proceedings were held, others regarded those settings tolerantly, realizing that they were temporary. Some judges were remembered for their use of humor to keep order while holding court in taverns. A favorite story features Benjamin Tappan, the claimed draftsman of the Sweeping Resolution, who was elected in 1816 as presiding judge of a common pleas circuit that included New Philadelphia, Ohio. While holding court there in a tavern, and chastising two lawyers for squabbling, he was interrupted by an

The Borders Cabin. Greene County's First Courthouse.
(*Henry Howe, Historical Collections of Ohio*)

onlooker at the back of the room—a backwoods character—who, as the story
went, "had been practicing at another bar."

"Give it to 'em, old gimlet-eye!" cried the woodsman.
"Who said that?" demanded the Judge. He spoke in a dry, nasal tone.
"It's this here old hoss," came the reply, as the inebriate stepped forward.

Turning to his attending law enforcement officer, Tappan pronounced a sentence for contempt which convulsed the spectators. "Sheriff," he commanded,
"take that old hoss and put him in the stable and see that he is not stolen before
morning." Tavern stables were used as holding cells for prisoners.[4]

Decorum improved with the advent of purpose-built court houses. It is remarkable how quickly, and how well some of the first were constructed. Xenia
was still "a little stumpy, struggling village" as Samuel Wright saw it when he ar-

rived there in 1811. But the courthouse had been completed two years before; it was forty feet square and made of brick; it had a cupola; and it cost the county's taxpayers over thirty-three hundred dollars, at a time when almost all of them were still living in log houses.[5]

Records of early Greene County court proceedings are another indication of the pride taken in the court of common pleas. Books of minutes and judgment entries were devotedly maintained, and the draftsmanship of legal instruments reflected careful attention to form. Nothing was dumbed-down. "Legal habit," deplored by Thomas Jefferson and a few other freethinking intellectuals, was characteristic of pioneers almost everywhere in America, from the Old Northwest to the Overland Trail. Frontier Ohioans had little interest in the sort of procedural reforms that would come later, in midcentury, when common law pleading, writs with Latin names, and other legal archaisms were abolished. Legal formality might have been mysterious, but it was comforting.[6]

In February 1809 James Snowden was elected an associate judge of the Greene County Court of Common Pleas. Born in New Jersey, he emigrated to Ohio in the 1790s and settled in what became Sugar Creek Township, about six miles west of Xenia. Snowden was an eccentric, remembered for his habit of rising on court days long before dawn to walk through the forest from his home to the county seat. John A. Taylor, an early chronicler whose work survives only in a fragment quoted by a later writer, wrote that "James, the son of Jupiter, got him up early in the mornings, put a few unleavened cakes in his scrip [a small wallet or bag, typically carried by a pilgrim], grasped his staff, and setting his face toward the sunrising took up his march for the great city of X-Zeninia." Taylor's readers would have recognized the classical allusion: Jupiter, the Greek Zeus, was the god of the sky, and of the outdoors.[7]

Snowden was also remembered for his intense preoccupations. He did not like to ride. Once when a friend had insisted on lending him a horse for the journey to town, he dismounted after traveling a short distance and continued on foot, leading the animal. So deeply was he engrossed in what acquaintances supposed were profound thoughts of legal matters that he failed to notice when the horse slipped its bridle and went off to graze. Continuing on, oblivious, Snowden arrived in town and was surprised when someone asked why he was holding an empty bridle.[8]

The other Greene County associate judges when Snowden came to the bench in 1809 were David Huston and James Barrett. Presiding Judge Francis Dunlavy had held the circuit presidency since it was established with the formation of state government in 1803. Barrett was likewise an original holder of his seat. Huston had been elected in 1806. An emigrant to the Northwest Territory from Pennsylvania, he settled in Greene County in 1803 and immediately became active in community affairs. He was a substantial landowner. At the court's inaugural session at the Borders cabin he volunteered to be one of the sureties for the surveyor hired to locate and lay out the county seat; a year later he and James Snowden became members of the county's first board of commissioners. Huston had an abiding interest in the administration of justice.[9]

As successor appointees to their respective judicial seats, Huston and Snowden each held commissions expressly providing for "a term of seven years from [their respective dates of election]"—until 1813 in Huston's case, 1816 in Snowden's. Both terms were purportedly cut short by the Sweeping Resolution at the same time that the full seven-year terms of Presiding Judge Dunlavy and Associate Judge Barrett, the original holders of their respective seats, were due to expire. Members of the 1809–10 legislature reelected Judge Dunlavy to a second term as circuit president and chose Samuel Kyle to succeed Associate Judge Barrett. Why Barrett was not reelected is unknown. Huston and Snowden were each reelected for new seven-year terms, pursuant to the Resolution.

A judge-elect took his oath of office after receiving his judicial commission, and was thereby qualified to sit. No law regulated this procedure. There was no requirement for a judge-elect's informing the governor of his accepting or declining the office, no time limit for his taking the oath, no provision for voiding the election if he failed to take the oath. Nor was the oath-taking required to be entered on the court record, although court clerks sometimes did that. In this case neither Huston nor Snowden took the oath upon receiving their new commissions, or made any response to Governor Huntington concerning their intentions. When Judge Dunlavy arrived in Xenia in May 1810 to preside over the first of the common pleas sessions to be held after terms of office for judges elected under the Sweeping Resolution had begun, Huston and Snowden simply took their seats on the bench. As reported in the Dayton *Ohio Centinel* each then declared that his new commission was invalid, that he refused to be sworn under it, and that he would continue to serve under his old commission for the time it had to run.[10]

A politician got in the first word. Jacob Smith, who represented Greene County as a member of the Ohio Senate and had voted to adopt the Resolu-

tion, was one of the citizens summoned to serve on the grand jury. Now he refused to be sworn, contending that Huston and Snowden's presence on the
bench made the court an illegal tribunal. The judges overruled Smith's objection, observing, as reported in the Dayton *Ohio Centinel,* that "if they were
usurpers, they were amenable to the laws." But the unity of the Greene County
bench in rendering this ruling was soon fractured as its members divided sharply
over Huston's and Snowden's insistence on continuing to sit. Unable to alter
their determination, and finding that the third associate, newly appointed Judge
Samuel Kyle, was disposed to acquiesce in Huston's and Snowden's participation, Presiding Judge Dunlavy refused to take any further part in the proceedings and departed. All this took place on the first day of the session.[11]

Being a majority of the common pleas bench the three associates were empowered to conduct proceedings in their president's absence, and they decided
to continue with the business of the session. That first day they completed a
jury trial in a civil action of trespass, *Jonathan Browder v. Martin Mendenhall,* entering judgment for the plaintiff on a verdict for $14.50. In another civil case tried
the following day the jury awarded an amount which suggests a compromise
verdict, thirty-three dollars, thirty-three and one-third cents. These two cases
appear to have been routine. Then on May 24, the third day of the session, the
judges reached the first of two related criminal cases. Arising on common facts,
the charges were sensational, and public interest in the case, aversion to delay in
bringing the accused to trial, and Huston's and Snowden's desire to demonstrate
that they were serious about performing the duties of the offices they claimed,
all might have influenced the associates' decision to continue with the session
despite Judge Dunlavy's departure. The criminal defendants, an unmarried
woman and her lover, were accused of having placed their unwanted baby girl
outside on the ground to die of exposure immediately after birth. The grand
jury which met the first day of the session returned separate indictments for
murder, alleging in the words of customary common law criminal pleading that
the defendants had acted "not having the fear of God before their eyes but being moved and seduced by the instigation of the Devil." Since the charge was
capital, each defendant had a right to demand to be tried in the supreme court,
which was due to hold its next circuit session in the county the following December. Trial in either case would be to a Greene County jury. Both defendants
opted for the court of common pleas. They had the same defense counsel,
Joshua Collet, the lawyer who the year before had served as special prosecutor

in the Clermont County rape case involving supreme court Judge Thomas Morris.[12]

The woman, Jane Richards, was tried first and acquitted. The next day, Friday, May 25, her lover William Cottrell was tried to a different jury on an indictment with virtually the same allegations, and convicted. The following morning Attorney Collet promptly moved for new trial. The minute entry which records the granting of the motion states only that "it appeared to the court that the Law is for the defendant." We are thus left to wonder whether the new trial was grounded on a legal ruling that the acts alleged in the indictment did not amount to murder; or that the verdicts, if rendered on the same evidence, were inconsistent; or if rendered on different evidence that the disparity of result was unjust. A speculative explanation for the last-mentioned possibility is that after Jane Richards had been acquitted and was no longer at risk for self-incrimination, she either volunteered or (more likely) was compelled to testify against Cottrell, supplying evidence for his conviction that was not available to the prosecution in her case. In any event there is no record of Cottrell's ever being retried on the charge, although he evidently remained a resident of the county. Two years later he was prosecuted for an unrelated assault.[13]

As senior associate judge, David Huston signed the clerk's minutes of the court's proceedings at this remarkable May 1810 term. They were to be the last that the court's associates would conduct without their president. Before the next term of court in September the newest associate, Judge Samuel Kyle, declined to continue to sit with judges Huston and Snowden. Lacking a quorum of judges willing to serve with one another, the court failed to hold either of its next two terms scheduled by law for the fourth Tuesdays of September 1810 and January 1811.[14]

The Ohio Supreme Court visited Greene County to conduct its regularly scheduled annual circuit session in December 1810. At that session the $14.50 judgment in *Browder v. Mendenhall,* one of the jury cases tried by the common pleas associates the previous May, came up on appeal. Vacating the judgment below, the court sent the case back to the court of common pleas "to be there tried when that court shall be organized agreeably to law." The brief entry signed by Chief Judge Scott records, as a basis for the disposition, a finding that two unnamed associates of the court of common pleas had "proceeded to act as Judges without taking the oath prescribed by law upon their last appointment." There was no mention of any challenge to the Sweeping Resolution. Here again, as when Morris appeared before them a few months earlier to claim his seat, the judges declined to rule upon the Sweeping Resolution's constitutionality and referred the question to the General Assembly.[15]

The reference was made through Governor Meigs, at whose suggestion supreme court Judge William W. Irwin wrote to report the judicial impasse in Greene County, observing that while "it is certainly very important to the administration of justice that the obstruction should be removed," his court was powerless either "to compel those gentlemen [Huston and Snowden] to accept their commissions under the[ir] last appointments," or, while they refused to do so, to "recognize their acts as judicial officers." In mid-January 1811 Meigs forwarded this letter to the Ohio House and Senate, with a message urgently calling attention to the consequences of a common pleas court's not being held in Greene County since the previous May. "Causes remain undecided, prisoners untried, and crimes unpunished," the governor warned, as a result of an impasse which "ought no longer to exist," and demands "speedy attention." His duty as governor, Meigs insisted, was only "to inform you of the evil . . . to provide for its remedy is solely within the sphere of legislative obligation and authority."[16]

But the legislators did not provide a remedy. Proposals in the House for calling a constitutional convention, for authorizing a special court session in Greene County, and for declaring Huston's and Snowden's offices vacant, all failed of adoption. The Senate did not even deliberate the matter. On the other hand, legislators opposed to the Resolution who had been unable to muster sufficient votes for its repeal did manage to secure adoption of a measure which many of them, Morris especially, must have relished as a payback. The Ohio Supreme Court's circuit was henceforth to run from the last week of March to the first week of December—almost nine months instead of the previous six, which had begun in July. The effect was to spread out the calendar, allowing more time for the sessions in each county which ended whenever it was time to move on to the next county on the circuit. Thus, without raising their one thousand dollar annual salaries, the supreme court judges' workload in terms of days on the bench was increased almost by half. Just as drastic was the curtailment of the time they had for individual pursuits in farming, business, or private law practice. The judges were suitably appreciative. Here is part of what Irwin wrote to Brown on February 4, 1811:

We are indebted for this additional duty to a sage committee of lawyers . . . [in the House]. Finding it impossible to subvert the present order of things, the regulation of the terms of the court furnished them a fair opportunity of gratifying those vindictive passions that never gain admittance in a noble or generous mind. Mr. Morris on this occasion took a very active part . . . I must ask your pardon for introducing the name of a creature so unworthy.[17]

Gains by independent Republicans in the October 1810 election included victories in close contests for Greene's County's House and Senate seats. Incumbents including Senator Smith who had voted for the Resolution were replaced by opponents of the Resolution, James Morrow in the House and John Sterett in the Senate. Reporting the outcome of repeal efforts in an informative letter to his constituents published in the Dayton *Ohio Centinel* after the 1810–11 session ended, Morrow concluded by expressing his hope that the Resolution "would not much longer disgrace our rising Republic." It was in that letter that Morrow had said that "a *Tammany man* and a *Resolution man* mean the same thing," and without naming him had referred to Speaker of the House Edward Tiffin, Grand Sachem of Tammany's Chillicothe Wigwam, as the "Grand Satan."[18]

In March, a month later, David Huston resolved to break the impasse which prevented Greene County's court of common pleas from functioning, by resigning his seat on the bench. His successor was John McLean, whose recess appointment by Governor Meigs was made March 22, 1811, the same day Meigs received Huston's one-sentence letter of resignation. Under whichever of his commissions Huston might have held his seat, his unqualified resignation left no question as to the existence of a vacancy, and McLean's interim appointment was thus indisputably valid. That it was made coincidently with Huston's resignation suggests that the succession was prearranged among Huston, McLean, and the governor.[19]

Judge Snowden did not resign. To the contrary, on March 21, 1811 he published in the *Ohio Centinel* a provocative letter "To the Resolution Judges of the Supreme Court of the State of Ohio" who, he said, had been put on the bench "by the usurped power of a perfidious legislature." Denouncing their action to vacate the judgment in *Browder v. Mendenhall* at the December circuit session, Snowden began with a remarkably lawyerlike argument, pointing out that the supreme court's finding that he and Huston had "proceeded to act as Judges without taking the oath prescribed by law upon their last appointment" was not supported by the record—either the record of the case, or the record of the court itself, there being no requirement for recording any judge's qualifying oath-taking. Had Snowden seen the letter from Judge Irwin which Governor

Meigs had forwarded to the legislature, he would have noted as deliberate the ambiguity of Irwin's carefully phrased statement that "I was advised *in a manner satisfactory to my mind*" of Snowden's and Huston's refusal to act under their new commissions.[20]

Coming to the question of the Sweeping Resolution's constitutionality, Snowden said that while he "would be far from speaking so plain" in any case where the constitution's meaning was uncertain in its application to a legislative act, that was not the situation here. As a contrasting example he cited a question he might have pondered as "James the son of Jupiter" during long walks through the forest, to and from court: Did the sun's heat came from the sun itself, or from its rays "coming in contact with our atmosphere?" On the other hand, Snowden said, he found nothing at all doubtful about the meaning of "shall hold their offices for the term of seven years" in the Ohio Constitution.

Snowden went on to discuss the constitution. A republic's legislature, he wrote, has only "a certain limited and delegated power, conferred by the people." The evidence of that power is the constitution, a "power of attorney, put into the hands of all state officers by the people." Whenever legislators enact laws which violate the constitution, "they do not act by a delegated power, consequently they must act by a tyrannical usurped power, such as our General Assembly assumed when they resolved your lordships upon a high seat of honor." Concluding by demanding that the supreme court judges address the question of the Sweeping Resolution's constitutionality, Snowden challenged, "If you differ with me in opinion, you are required to come out and defend [the Resolution] on rational and constitutional grounds." Reprinting this remarkable letter two weeks after its original publication in the *Ohio Centinel*, the Chillicothe *Independent Republican* asked its readers, "In what light do thinking men of understanding and honesty consider the persons who are now exercising the functions of a supreme court, in the state of Ohio? Judge ye!"[21]

Meanwhile a charter for establishing Tammany "Wigwam No. 4" in Xenia had been granted in January 1811. The principal organizer was ex-Senator Jacob Smith, who had objected to Huston's and Snowden's presence on the bench when called as a grand juror the previous May. In Greene County and elsewhere in Ohio, Tammany activity was coming to be met with spirited opposition. Writing to the Chillicothe wigwam on March 23, 1811 Smith reported that "great threats are thrown against us by the enemies of Columbia [the Tammany Society] and they go so far as to say they will tar & feather all of us at the next meeting." But the Xenia Wigwam's members were denied whatever protection the county court house would have provided as a site for their meetings. The Greene County sheriff, James Collier, refused to allow use of the building for activities not open to the public.[22]

The May 1811 session of the Greene County Court of Common Pleas was convened by Presiding Judge Dunlavy and two associates, judges Samuel Kyle and John McLean, the latter sitting for the first time as Huston's successor. The occasion was another rare instance (the Ohio Supreme Court's proceedings in *Rutherford v. M'Faddon* may have been the first) when an Ohio court's proceedings were covered as news by a professional journalist. In Xenia to attend the opening of the court was the editor of the *Ohio Centinel*, the Dayton weekly newspaper of Federalist and independent Republican politics. It had reported on the court's last session of twelve months before, and had since published Representative Morrow's constituent report and Judge Snowden's challenge to the "Resolution Judges." The *Ohio Centinel* editor's presence at the May 1811 term of the Greene County court of common pleas was unusual, for frontier newspapers did not regularly cover events with their own personnel. But the convening of a court which had been unable to function for a year as a result of a political and constitutional crisis in which the people of the county as well as the court's judges were deeply divided, was certainly a newsworthy event.[23]

The minutes indicate that the court met on Monday, May 28, 1811, the first day of the term, Judge Dunlavy presiding and associates Kyle and "McClure" (evidently McLean) joining him on the bench. If any business was conducted that day it must have been routine, for nothing but the court's convening is mentioned in the record. But the following day's proceedings were extraordinary. According to the *Ohio Centinel* editor's story James Snowden suddenly appeared in the courtroom and attempted to take his seat on the bench. A "warm altercation immediately took place," as Judge Dunlavy demanded that Snowden withdraw. Did Dunlavy speak for the court?[24]

Presiding judges typically ruled with their associates' silent acquiescence. On this occasion, however, Judge Kyle was moved to declare himself. Having sided with Huston and Snowden the year before Kyle now supported Dunlavy. As Snowden later recalled, Kyle said that while he personally believed that Snowden was qualified to serve under his old commission, "the legislature had said otherwise." Newly appointed Judge McLean was silent. Kyle's vote was critical. Of the three judges who had an unquestioned right to sit, Kyle's support of Dunlavy meant that at least a majority were against recognizing Snowden. Snowden, however, persisted in refusing to withdraw.[25]

Now Judge Dunlavy took a firmer hand, ordering the sheriff, James Collier to remove Snowden from the courtroom. Sheriff Collier refused to obey the order. Dunlavy ordered the sheriff committed for contempt, and directed the coroner to take the sheriff into custody. The coroner complied, and took the unresisting sheriff away. As soon as the coroner returned from that mission Dunlavy ordered him to arrest and confine Snowden, who gave every indication of resisting. The coroner said he would need assistance to carry out this order. Judge Dunlavy directed him to obtain it from bystanders. The coroner called upon four spectators for help. Two flatly refused. Judge Dunlavy summarily held them in contempt, fining each three dollars. A third pleaded infirmity on account of his age, and was excused. The fourth spectator finally obeyed the coroner's command. They seized Judge Snowden, and with what the *Ohio Centinel*'s editor described as "much violent exertion" Snowden was "dragged from the bench and taken to a place of confinement." His report does not say for how long Dunlavy ordered the confinement to run; most likely it was for the remainder of the term, expected to last the rest of the week. With that, Judge Dunlavy must have thought that his court could finally get on with the business of the term.[26]

But Associate Judge John McLean, who had said nothing and seen enough, now rose to pronounce what would be a last word. Disgusted by the conduct he had witnessed, he announced his immediately effective resignation. McLean's departure would leave the court without a quorum, and again unable to function. Presiding Judge Dunlavy could persuade him to remain only long enough to hear the minutes of the day's session read and join in a vote to adjourn. The minutes make no mention of the Snowden episode or McLean's resignation. If the concluding sentence, "Court adjourned until tomorrow morning nine o'clock," reflected Judge Dunlavy's hope that McLean would reconsider, that hope would be forlorn. The court did not reconvene during the week of its scheduled May term, and until McLean's seat was filled it would continue to lack a quorum and could not function at all. The supreme court's ruling in *Browder v. Mendenhall* the previous December had disqualified Snowden; Dunlavy and Kyle would have refused to sit with him in any event. After twelve months without a common pleas court Greene County faced a crisis over the failure of this vital organ, a crisis deepened by uncertainty over how and how soon it would be resolved.[27]

Who was John McLean? In his recently published, immensely valuable account of Ohio politics of the period Professor Donald J. Ratcliffe identifies him as the John McLean who in later life was Mr. Justice McLean of the U.S. Supreme Court, now especially remembered for his dissenting opinion in the *Dred Scott* case. This "future Justice" McLean was twenty-two years old when he moved to Lebanon in Warren County, a county adjacent to Greene, in 1807. He was admitted to the bar that year, having begun the study of law in Cincinnati. For a time he published a newspaper in Lebanon, the *Western Star.* Election to Congress in 1812 launched his career in a succession of high public offices, culminating with thirty-two years of service on the U.S. Supreme Court. From 1810 when he sold the newspaper until his election to Congress two years later the future Justice McLean engaged in the practice of law in Lebanon. There is no indication, however, that he ever resided in Greene County, a constitutional requirement for service as associate judge of its Court of Common Pleas. Another fact hard to reconcile with future Justice McLean's participating in any action hostile to Judge Dunlavy is that they recently had been political allies. Eight months earlier they had together walked out of a Warren County political gathering about to endorse Meigs for governor, leading an exodus of a minority of the attendees to hold a rump meeting to vote a Worthington endorsement. *That* McLean would not have embarrassed Dunlavy by resigning in protest from a court over which Dunlavy presided.[28]

County histories provide a likelier candidate. In the course of research for his *History of Greene County*, published in 1901, George Robinson found a "little book" listing inhabitants of the county's Sugar Creek township in 1803, among them a "John McLean." That McLean was the eccentric R. S. Dills wrote about in a county history he published twenty years earlier, with a character description that fits with the May 1811 conduct of the junior associate on the Greene County common pleas bench, as well as supplying a positive identification:

[A] confirmed bachelor ... much given to complaint against the school laws, which compelled him to school other people's children. He denominated the members of the legislature who passed these laws, "a sett of dung-hill gods" from whom he prayed for "deliverance." He succeeded James Snowden as associate judge, in 1810. He lived to be eighty-three years of age, and was buried as he lived, in a lone grave on his land north of Bellbrook.[29]

What followed the aborted May 1811 term is even more extraordinary. With the legislature out of session until the following December, another recess appointment to the Huston/McLean seat was the only means of reviving the court in time for its next term in September 1811. The situation was critical. No common pleas court proceedings had been conducted in the county for over a year. Prisoners were being held in jail awaiting trial, some for that long or longer. But the recess appointment was controversial. The setting for the controversy was a contest for the seat between John Wilson, favored by the Independent Republicans, and Jacob Haines, the candidate of the Tammany Society.

Such a contest was unheard-of. There might have been occasions when rival candidates for recess appointments to associate judgeships were promoted by their respective political patrons, but those campaigns were waged out of the public eye, and had few participants. In this case, however, the campaigning had not only public exposure but enormous public participation. Governor Meigs received no less than ten petitions from citizens of Greene County urging Wilson's or Haines's appointment, all sent around the end of May 1811 within a few weeks after the aborted court session. Wilson's backers submitted five petitions with a total of 150 signatures. The five Haines petitions altogether bore 270 signatures. The combined total, 420 signatures, is only seven short of the total vote which Worthington and Meigs received in Greene County as candidates for governor in the previous October's election. Great efforts on the part of petition circulators must have been required to obtain such numbers of signatures.[30]

Those efforts coincided with high points of Tammany and anti-Tammany activity in the county. In June 1811 opponents of the society convened a public meeting at the courthouse to hear Tammany denounced. John Sterett, who had moved the resolution supporting judicial review after Tod's impeachment trial two years before, was elected chairman. In the ensuing discussion of the Tammany Society's objects and organizational peculiarities selections from its published constitution were read, with particular emphasis on provisions which declared Tammany to be a secret organization, imposed a political test for membership, subjected membership applicants subject to blackballing, and gave the Grand Sachem control over the topical agenda of meetings. Citing these provisions, a resolution denouncing the society was voted unanimously and directed to be sent off for publication in Ohio newspapers. Referring obliquely to Tammany support of the Sweeping Resolution, it concluded by proclaiming that "to be an aristocrat in principle, and an open violator of the constitution in practice, disturber of the peace, and a promoter of divisions amongst the citizens—to be a secret underminer of our republican system of government, by means of midnight cabals—is the same thing as to be a member of the Tammany Society, or Columbian Order."[31]

About the same time David Griffin, secretary of Tammany's Xenia Chapter, wrote describing its situation to "our Elder Brothers in Wigwam No. 1 in Chillicothe." Griffin reported that although his chapter had encountered "strong and formidable" opposition, "we have weathered the Blast and are increasing rapidly." Griffin then turned to the court of common pleas. "Respecting our disturbed court," he continued, "the Federal Party here are numerous and are continually endeavoring to incite Confusions and Disturbances among the People. Crying out haughtily against the proceedings of the Legislature, the Judges of the court are so obstinate and impertinent here that it required force to remove Judge Snowden from his seat which he claimed with all the assurance imaginable." Now, Griffin continued, "we hope that with the concurrence of [Tammany organizations in] other counties we will be able to establish a court that will be contented with their constitutional powers without deserting their Posts." "It is said," he admitted, "that the governor is on their side and has promised to commission any Person that our last Senator [Sterett] and Representative [Morrow] will recommend." "How that may be," Griffin said, "we do not know." Yet he was optimistic, and proud to report that "we have addressed the Publick in favor of our Principles and Society."[32]

On August 15, 1811 Governor Meigs rejected Haines, the Tammany candidate, and gave John Wilson the interim appointment to the associate judgeship, good until the end of the next legislative session. Wilson would serve at least for the common pleas court's September 1811 and January 1812 terms. He would not serve longer, for Tammany regained control of the Greene County legislative delegation in elections that October, when the voters sent Jacob Smith back to the Senate and elected another Tammanyite, John McKnight, to represent the county in the House. At the end of the legislative session, in accordance with what must have been Smith's and McKnight's recommendation, the members of the General Assembly elected Jacob Haines to the Huston/McLean/Wilson seat on the Greene County Court of Common Pleas.[33]

Haines would be commissioned for a full seven-year term, not the five years he would have had under the Sweeping Resolution as a successor incumbent. But no one took any special note of that. For by the time the legislators had come to elect judges near the end of the General Assembly's 1811–12 session, the Resolution had already been repealed.[34]

CHAPTER TWELVE

The Resolution Repealed

When William Creigton wrote to Tod from Chillicothe in June 1811 they had not seen each other since their parting in Zanesville in February when the legislative session ended. Creighton had heard nothing meanwhile by way of political news from northeastern Ohio, which still lacked a newspaper. He was pleased to inform Tod that "the middle and western part of the state is in an uproar in opposition to the Tammany Society," whose establishment, he added, "has produced more warmth and division than anything that has occurred since the organization of the state government."[1]

Tammany's exclusiveness and secretiveness were becoming substantial political liabilities. On the thirteenth of May (Tammany's "month of Flowers"), when the Chillicothe Wigwam celebrated the society's anniversary, members gathered that morning in the Ross County courthouse for a closed meeting at which they "kindled their council fire, smoked the calumet of peace, and arranged their internal affairs." Those proceedings completed, nonmembers—provided they were Republicans—were let in to hear Grand Sachem Edward Tiffin deliver a "Long Talk." This Tammany event was countered two days later by a courthouse meeting called by Creighton and Nathaniel Massie, another influential citizen, to denounce the society as "a well concerted scheme and deep laid conspiracy to revolutionize and overturn our republican government, and establish in its stead an aristocracy or monarchy." Those who attended voted to publish a resolution declaring themselves "unanimously agreed that the secret aim and concealed design of the Tammany Society" was the acquisition of absolute power by "this secret, midnight, cabalitical convention." A few weeks later the *Independent Republican* published a letter from Samuel Monnett, who had formerly represented Ross County in the Ohio House, reporting that he had been rejected for Tammany membership when his independent political views had become known. Monnett now condemned the society for its "anti-Republican nature."[2]

If Tammany's exclusiveness and secrecy engendered hostility and suspicion, its members' parading about in Indian dress brought ridicule. A correspondent calling himself "Little Turtle" and pretending to be an agent of the Xenia Wigwam writing to "Whiniskee, at the Great Wigwam [No. 1, in Chillicothe], published this letter in the same June 13, 1811 issue of the *Independent Republican* that carried Monnett's letter:

> I see that you want a large quantity of buck's tails, clean breech clouts, and a number of other Indian artifacts, especially a Buffalo hide with the horns, for the use of the G. Sachem. As I have on hand more than I have present use for, I wish to exchange a number of the articles you require, for such commodities as will doubtless suit us both. . . .
>
> But to come to the point—we will give you seventeen breech-clouts (but not warranted clean) for one white man—13 bucktails for one other, so on in proportion . . . As for the Buffalo hide, I have none, but suppose an ass or a mule-skin with the ears would answer the same purpose.[3]

By midyear 1811 the Tammanyites were giving way on the Sweeping Resolution, no longer attempting to justify it on the merits but still opposing its repeal. Reporting to Worthington in January 1811 that repeal efforts had failed by a narrow margin, David Purviance, a Worthington supporter who served in the Senate in the 1810–11 session, wrote that "whether our former proceedings [in adopting the Resolution] have been right or wrong, it is well that these lordly aristocrats have received a check." But by then both the unsoundness of the Resolution in theory and its unworkability in practice were becoming ever more widely obvious.[4]

Continual establishment of new Ohio counties and the need for additional common pleas circuits made unattainable the advantage Benjamin Tappan had claimed for construing the Ohio Constitution's judicial tenure clause to give the terms of all judges the same expiration date. Tappan, it will be recalled, argued that if the constitution were construed to make judicial terms run simultaneously, any legislated reduction in judicial salaries could take effect for all judges at once. A weightier consideration was suggested by "A Lawyer," writing to the Chillicothe *Supporter*, who argued that public oversight of legislators' actions in respect to judicial selection would be improved if all judicial seats came up to be filled at the same time. But common pleas judgeships in counties established after 1803 had original terms beginning with the formation of the county, and each of those terms had a unique seven-year span. No one could claim constitutional authority for making them run concurrently with those of judgeships in original counties. The same would be true for presiding judgeships in the additional common plea circuits which the legislature would soon have to establish.[5]

The Resolution was also proving unwieldy in its application to existing judgeships. On the one hand were judicial seats which had become vacant only a short time before the seven-year term of the seat's original holder would expire. If the vacancy occurred while the legislature was in session the Resolution required one election to be conducted to fill the seat for that short time, and another election for the next seven-year term soon to begin. This requirement led to the absurdity of the 1810–11 legislature's filling a vacancy in one of Muskingum County's associate judgeships by electing a successor, Samuel Sullivan, for the term of *seventeen days.* Opponents of the Resolution lost no time in inviting citizens to compare "seventeen days" with the constitution's "seven years." The opportunity to use this anomaly as a rhetorical launching pad was irresistible. Writing as "Ploughman," Charles Hammond exclaimed that Sullivan's election portended no less than a complete overthrow of republican government. If the men could construe the constitution "to mean that a judge should be elected for *seventeen days,*" he asked, "might [they] not with the same propriety construe that part of the constitution which relates to the election of governor, senators and representatives to mean that they were elected for life?"[6]

An oversight respecting Muskingum County's two other associate judgeships also embarrassed the resolutionists. Incumbents Jesse Fulton and David Finlay held seats for which the terms of office, as cut short by the Sweeping Resolution, had been due to expire at the same time as Sullivan's, in February 1811 (seven years from Muskingum County's founding). But by an oversight the legislators neglected to reelect Fulton and Findlay for new terms, as had been done in the previous session for Huston, Snowden, and dozens of other associate judges whose tenures the Resolution had terminated in the spring of 1810. To keep the oversight from putting the Muskingum court out of business for most of the year, Governor Meigs had to grant Fulton and Findlay interim appointments. Hammond would also confront the resolutionists with this embarrassment.[7]

Writing in 1811 in the *Supporter* as "Calpurnius," and in the *Independent Republican* as "Ploughman," Hammond was in the early stages of another professional career, one for which he would be saluted as "the first great journalist of the

Old Northwest" in an article-length biography which the late Professor Francis Weisenburger published more than a century after Hammond's death. In 1813 when he started the first of his own newspaper publishing ventures, the St. Clairsville *Ohio Federalist*, Hammond announced the aggressive editorial stance of which "Calpurnius" and "Ploughman" were exponents:

It is common for the author of a prospectus to give assurances that all "low scurrility" and all personalities shall be excluded from his columns. I make no promise of that kind. . . .

Instead of excluding all personalities from the Ohio Federalist, it is my determined purpose to drag into public view, and expose in all its deformity the true character of every false and hollow-hearted demagogue that attempts to delude the public. The vocabulary of sophisticated jargon does not contain a more impudent falsehood than the proposition that a knave in private life may be safely trusted in public life.[8]

In the first two of ten "Calpurnius" letters published in the *Supporter* from March through December 1811, Hammond exposed the hypocrisy of the Ohio Supreme Court's Resolution Judges who, continuing to sit, refused officially to address the issue of the Resolution's constitutionality while privately expressing their personal opinions either that the Resolution violated the constitution, or that its constitutionality was questionable. These first two letters were addressed to one of the judges, William Irwin. Chief Judge Scott was not targeted in this salvo, since he possessed what Sprigg had called a "two-fold title" to his seat, one by election in 1810 under the Sweeping Resolution, another by election in 1809 for a term which would still have time to run were the Resolution held invalid.[9]

Hammond's first letter attacked Irwin for declining to defend the Sweeping Resolution, on which his claimed right to a seat on the court as one elected to a vacancy created by the Resolution, was based. As Hammond had done three years before when he confronted John Sloane in *The Rights of the Judiciary*, he put a hypothetical case. Describing the situation of Muskingum County associates Fulton and Findlay whom the legislators had recently failed to reelect to new terms pursuant to the Resolution, Hammond asked Irwin to suppose that they had continued to sit under their pre-Resolution commissions. (Hammond's letter was written before Governor Meigs gave them interim appointments.) Suppose further, Hammond said, that Fulton and Findlay were indicted for usurpation of office, and brought to trial before Irwin in the Ohio Supreme Court. The issue of their guilt is solely one of law: is the Resolution constitutional?

Again as he had done with Sloane in *The Rights of the Judiciary,* Hammond speaks to his readers as though they were a jury hearing the case. Here is part of his summation:

On this day there prevails in this state two practical legislative constructions of the same section of the constitution. One, as I have shown, the isolated decision of a single legislature, grasping at immense patronage. Upon this rests your title to office. The other supported by a long practice, and the concurring opinion of every respectable lawyer and politician in the state. Upon this rests the title of judges Fulton and Findlay. I appeal, sir, to your magnanimity. Which has the most respectable support?[10]

In his second "Calpurnius" letter, also addressed to Irwin, Hammond challenged Judge Brown's title. In an argument that demonstrates his formidable powers of legal analysis Hammond assumed that the Sweeping Resolution was valid, and that judges Scott and Irwin were both legitimately elected under it. But Judge Brown's purported election, which came on a ballot subsequent to the one by which Scott and Irwin were chosen, was void in Hammond's submission. His argument may be summarized as follows:

1. There never was any distinct seat for a "fourth judge" on the Ohio Supreme Court. The constitution provided for the legislature's adding an "additional judge"; when that was done in 1808 the so-called "fourth judge" immediately became "an integral part of the court," holding his office by the same tenure as other judges.

2. Assuming that the legislature had power to reduce the number of supreme court judgeships back to three, it could do so only by omitting to fill a vacancy on the bench when it occurred. No sitting judge's tenure could be affected by such reduction.

3. Since in 1803 the Ohio Supreme Court began with three judges whose successors' terms the Resolution cut short in 1810, the Resolution could produce only three vacancies for legislators to fill in 1810.

4. But by 1810 the court had four judges, and one of them had a term not cut short by the Resolution.

5. Thus, if the legislators wished to reduce the court's membership to three, they could do so only by filling two of the three vacancies the Resolution had created. Those two vacancies were filled when Scott and Irwin were elected. Brown's purported election, occurring on a subsequent ballot, was therefore void.

Concluding, Hammond placed himself rhetorically in the position of Irwin's counsel, making what he maintained was the best argument available for vindicating Irwin's right to his seat. "I should commence by asking leave to discard Ethan A. Brown from the bench," Hammond began. And "I would *assume* the sweeping principle [the Resolution's validity]." Then, he continued, he would argue that Scott and Irwin were elected as successors to Tod and Sprigg, whose terms had been cut short by the Resolution; that Scott thereby constructively abandoned the seat he had gained by the previous year's (1809) election, and hence his claim to have been the "fourth judge" chosen in that election; and that Morris, now the undoubted "fourth judge," was entitled to sit for seven years from the date of his election in 1809. "Miserable" as these arguments are, Hammond concluded, "they are the best which can be devised. I defy you to support your title by any more plausible arguments." Though Hammond did not mention it, this argument was essentially the one Morris had made to the legislature when he had tried to regain his seat a few months before.[11]

Hammond wrote this second "Calpurnius" letter in late March 1811, a month and a half before Tiffin delivered his "Long Talk" as Grand Sachem of Tammany's Chillicothe chapter. Subsequently published by the *Scioto Gazette,* Tiffin's speech is noteworthy for the absence of any mention of the Sweeping Resolution. In declining to defend it Tiffin joined the judges of the Ohio Supreme Court and the two committees of the Ohio House which had rejected Morris's protest of his ouster as a judge by affirming his eligibility to serve as a legislator in the session over which Tiffin had just presided as speaker. Indeed, during all of the year 1811 no supporter of the Resolution who held any position in state government attempted to defend it as a proper interpretation of the Ohio Constitution.[12]

Other issues were beginning to occupy Ohioans' attention. Population gains recorded by the 1810 census would shortly result in increasing from one to six the number of Ohio seats in the U.S. House of Representatives, and the legislature would decide whether they would be elected at large or by districts. Widespread dissatisfaction with Zanesville as a temporary capital prompted efforts to settle a location for a permanent seat of state government. The capital would return to Chillicothe after the 1811–12 legislative session, but only temporarily. Revulsion over Tammany activity contributed to the disappointment of Chillicothe's hopes to have it remain there. The split among Republicans became wider for some. The bitterness of Duncan McArthur's personal differences with the Worthington faction surfaced with a letter to the Chillicothe *Scioto Gazette* in October 1811, in which McArthur declared that recent efforts to promote him for the governorship "together with my opposition to Mr. Tiffin's office-hunting, unconstitutional Sweeping Resolution" had caused allies of Worthington and Tiffin to circulate "the base slander and malicious falsehood that I had changed my politics." On the other hand many Ohioans were moving away from organized factional alliances into looser affiliations, and toward more independent individual political behavior.[13]

A unifying concern was the threat of war on the state's northwest frontier. Tecumseh, the Shawnee chief, was organizing the tribes and recruiting British support for his armed struggle to preserve Indian lands. Inhabitants of isolated settlements in northwest Ohio surrounded by Indian territory were becoming fearful. In July 1811 Indiana Territorial Governor William Henry Harrison's meeting at Vincennes with Indians led by Tecumseh failed to produce agreement, and on November 7 tribesmen led by Tecumseh's brother Tenskwatawa ("The Prophet") were defeated at Tippecanoe by a force under Harrison, which itself suffered heavy casualties. Britain's interference with American maritime trade and shipping during its conflict with Napoleonic France was a source of growing international tension. "War Hawks," among them southern and western congressmen, were promoting a North American military campaign against the Indians and British Canada. Worthington, who opposed war, wrote Meigs on November 30 to acknowledge that the Battle of Tippecanoe "will be the means of exciting the greatest alarm on the frontiers of Ohio." President Madison was being urged to arm the Ohio militia with weapons from federal arsenals.[14]

The October 1811 election for legislative seats did not at first seem to change the numerical strength of supporters or opponents of the Sweeping Resolution in the General Assembly. Creighton and Brush each chose not to run in Ross County, Creighton citing his preoccupation with a busy law practice and his growing family's need for the income it produced. On the other hand Samuel Monnett, who had publicized his rejection as an applicant for Tammany membership, won election to the House from that county. Thomas Morris continued in the House, George Tod in the Senate. The Greene County delegation reversed its position, now becoming pro-Resolution as Jacob Smith returned to the Senate and John McKnight was elected to the House. Samuel Huntington returned to office, this time in the legislative branch to represent Geauga County in the House. Jessup Couch, a young Chillicothe lawyer, wrote to Worthington after the election predicting that Huntington would be a candidate for Speaker of the House for that session, but stating that he was unable to forecast Huntington's position on the Sweeping Resolution. Couch thought Huntington might support it, after "first see[ing] on which side the majority inclines."[15]

As to the Resolution's fate, predictions of Worthington's other correspondents were almost evenly split. Writing on December 2, 1811, a day before the legislature convened, John Hamm, Grand Sachem of the Zanesville Wigwam, reported a concern that some legislators' promises to oppose repeal were "only designed to lull us into a fatal security," and that it appeared that the friends of the "new order of things [the Resolution]" were "sliding into the minority." On the other hand, writing two weeks later, James Caldwell predicted that Huntington's attempt to "introduce confusion" by bringing up the "old resolution" would fail.[16]

That attempt took place on December 11, soon after Huntington lost his bid to be elected Speaker. Jeremiah McLene, the incumbent Ohio secretary of state, had been elected in January 1810. The constitutional term for the office was three years. Since the triennial anniversary of the expiration of the original holder's term would come in 1812, at the end of the present legislative session, the Sweeping Resolution would have required another election to be held at that time. Slyly, to test sentiment for repeal, Huntington moved that the election be so held. His motion lost by one vote. But the House was not ready to commit, for it tabled Morris's attempt to secure a resolution declaring that McLene had a right to stay in office until January 1813. In the balloting on these motions some members previously counted as Resolution supporters began to waver. Abraham Edwards, a freshman from Montgomery County, "voted with the Feds" as Isaac Van Horne, another Worthington lieutenant, reported, adding that "hopes are entertained [that] he will eventually go right." More portentous was House member William Ludlow's motion on December 12, the day after Huntington's and Morris's trial balloons were punctured, that "hereafter" anyone elected to a judgeship should hold office for seven years, or as secretary of state, for three years.[17]

On December 16 the House took definitive action. Section 2 of the Commissioning Act had implemented the Sweeping Resolution by providing that persons elected to fill a vacancy in any judicial or executive-branch office should be commissioned only for the "residue of the term of service" of his predecessor. A bill had been introduced early in the session to exempt militia officers and justices of the peace from this requirement. Morris moved to amend the bill by deleting the Commissioning Act's second section in its entirety. The effect would be to repeal the Sweeping Resolution, at least prospectively. The amendment was adopted by a vote of twenty-eight to eighteen, the majority including

Huntington, Edwards, Ludlow, Morris, and all five members from Ross County. With final adoption on third reading the following day the bill was sent to the Senate. It was there that those predicting the repeal effort's defeat thought it would occur.[18]

Mixed forecasts indicated that the Senate's vote would be close. Writing to Nathaniel Massie to report the House's twenty-eight to eighteen vote, Duncan McArthur said he had "little expectation that it [the bill] would pass in the Senate." But McArthur's colleague Robert McConnell, writing to Worthington the same day, and Isaac Van Horne, writing two days later, both regretfully predicted Senate approval of the measure. Benjamin Hough, who by then had become state auditor, still hoped that the repeal effort would be forestalled. His December 21st letter to Worthington predicted defeat.[19]

The Senate took up the bill on Saturday, January 4, 1812, debating it all day with what Van Horne described as "considerable warmth." When a motion to reject the bill lost by a tie vote, twelve to twelve, it was put over to the following week. Among the senators who sided with opponents of the Resolution in this vote were two surprises, David Purviance and Thomas Irwin. Purviance, it will be recalled, had written to Worthington to gloat over the defeat of the "lordly aristocrats" in their effort to repeal the Resolution in the previous year's session. Irwin had likewise voted then against repeal. In a letter to Worthington reporting that day's Senate proceedings Van Horne expressed concern that continued conflict over the Sweeping Resolution was harming radical Republicans' prospects for gaining at least some of the state's six new congressional seats. It was feared that the coalition independent Republicans and Federalists had formed in opposition to the Sweeping Resolution might endure and sweep all the seats, especially if the legislature should opt to have candidates run at large rather than by district. It would decide the question in this session. Another sign of trouble was the sidetracking of a resolution to fill judicial vacancies in Adams County, a matter ordinarily handled routinely. Opponents of the Resolution now comprised a majority of the total membership of both Houses, and they could block any further elections of judges.[20]

As he sat in the Senate Tod had a habit of recording votes on his own tally sheets. He listed senators' names along the left-hand margin, and checked off their ayes or nays in vertical columns, ruled off from left to right across the page. At the foot of each set of columns he noted the measure voted on. Tod saved the tally sheet on which he recorded votes when the bill to repeal the law

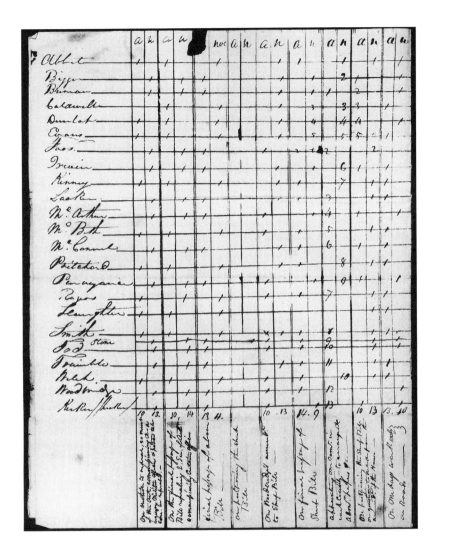

Tod's tally sheet of Ohio Senate roll call votes on the amendment to the Commissioning Act which effectively repealed the Sweeping Resolution. A record Tod made habitually as he sat in the senate, this portion shows key votes on January 7 and 8, 1812: 10–13 defeating a proposed amendment to make the repeal apply only to militia officers and justices of the peace, 10–14 defeating a motion to postpone, and 13–11 for final passage of the bill.

(Courtesy Western Reserve Historical Society, Cleveland, Ohio) implementing the Sweeping Resolution was before the Senate. He also saved his handwritten notes of the floor debate, but with entries not dated and some only partially legible, they are difficult to decipher.

When the bill came up in committee of the whole on Tuesday, January 7, it was amended to add a "grandfathering" proviso, against being construed "to invalidate or disannul any appointments made by a former legislature, nor in any wise affect commissions heretofore granted." The amendment ended any hope of Tod's being restored to his judgeship. It was adopted fifteen to nine, the majority consisting of Tod himself and eleven other senators previously identified as opponents of the Resolution, plus three who had formerly supported it, one of them the speaker, Thomas Kirker. Whether any of the three had changed his position fundamentally was unclear.[21]

The test came the following day, Wednesday, January 8, on a motion to postpone further consideration of the bill until the following session. This motion was defeated ten to fourteen, ten in favor of postponement now including two of the three senators who, the day before, had joined the twelve opponents of the Resolution to back the grandfathering amendment. Of the three only Speaker Kirker voted against postponement. Another senator who had previously sided with Resolution supporters, Levi Rogers of Clermont County, joined with Kirker to oppose postponement. Accordingly, to pass the bill, opponents of the Resolution needed either Kirker or Rogers. They got Kirker. Votes on third reading and for passage came swiftly, with majorities of thirteen to eleven. A day later the House concurred with the Senate's grandfathering amendment, completing the enacting process. Although deleting section 2 of the Commissioning Act effectively repealed the Sweeping Resolution, the Resolution itself was never formally rescinded.[22]

It was customary for each House to appoint one of its members as a messenger each time a bill was to be carried to the other chamber. On this occasion House Speaker Mathias Corwin chose Thomas Morris to carry the repeal bill to the Senate, and again to inform the Senate that the House had concurred with the Senate's grandfathering amendment. While the significance of Morris's selection for this task could not have been lost on members of both houses, Tod was not given the corresponding honor of carrying the amended bill back to the House. Senate Speaker Kirker might have thought that his own vote for it was enough.[23]

Writing on January 8, the day the Senate adopted the repeal bill with its amendment, Carlos Norton opined that Huntington and Meigs were "at the bottom of all the stir which has been made this winter about the Sweeping Resolution." But Tod's notes of the Senate debate, to the extent they are decipherable, suggest that the members of that body deliberated candidly, made up their own minds, and voted conscientiously. At first Purviance argued that the Resolution's validity had been confirmed by the last legislature, and that even if its constitutionality were doubtful they should not reconsider the question. In later remarks he wavered, acknowledging the constitution's lack of clarity respecting uncompleted terms of office but urging that a constitutional convention should be called, to amend it. Kirker, on the other hand, was troubled by present experiences of confusion and disruption, particularly in respect to common pleas associate judgeships. He twice mentioned the situation in Greene County. In the end, both seemed resigned to repeal as practical necessity. Tod's notes of one of Purviance's speeches cite (with Tod's underscoring) "*The Complaints in different parts of the State*" and "Expediency." Lawyer Benjamin Silliman's January 12 letter reported Kirker's "voting in favor of the repeal in consequence of the supposed dilemma in which some counties of the state would have been placed, as the majority of the House of Representatives had declared their intention of not entering into any elections until the [Resolution] should be repealed." That refusal, as Silliman told Worthington, "would in effect have suspended the function of the judges of the courts in some of the counties."[24]

Senator Jacob Smith, Greene County's Tammanyite, was not reconciled to the outcome. His January 9 letter to Worthington reported that "Enimeys [*sic*] to the resolution" had promised new members of the House that repeal would "not inter fear with any of the acts passed under [it]," and that key Senate votes had been swayed by "Congress being in view":

Perviens [Purviance] first failed then . . . Kirker Speaker lost his head and looked back and concluded that the team he was geared to was too weak to reach the City of Washington [i.e., to elect representatives to Congress if they ran at large] and so he flew back and left the people's rights at the foot of federal hill in a confused situation.[25]

But a week later, at least for some of Worthington's people, the mood brightened. John Pollock, a House member, described the session as "pleasant" although he acknowledged that the Sweeping Resolution's repeal had created "some warmth" over what "of course has been a disagreeable question in the legislature."[26]

The remainder of the session was harmonious and productive. A law for election of congressmen by district was duly enacted. The location for a permanent state capital was settled, the site to be on the east bank of the Scioto opposite the village of Franklinton and thereafter to be "known and distinguished by the name of Columbus." A state medical society was incorporated, with licensing powers, and duties which included providing information on matters affecting public health; every physician known to be practicing in the state was named in the act as a member. The Houses resolved that canal navigation between the Hudson River and the Great Lakes "would have the most extensive and beneficial effects . . . and that its tendency would be to encourage agriculture, manufactures, [and] internal commerce, and to strengthen the bond of union between the states."[27]

At the end of the session there were no vacancies on the Ohio Supreme Court or in circuit presidencies to be filled, all incumbents having been confirmed in office by the grandfathering amendment. But the legislators elected many to associate judgeships, including Muskingum County's Jesse Fulton and David Findlay, whose interim appointments had kept their court in operation during 1811. In deference to what must have been the wishes of Greene County's newly elected legislative delegation, John Wilson, the interim appointee to the Greene County bench, was replaced by Tammany petition candidate Jacob Haines. Presiding Judge Dunlavy and associates Haines and Kyle would provide the quorum which would allow the Greene County common pleas court to function. Nothing was done about James Snowden's seat, even after a committee appointed that session to consider his expulsion rejected his protest.[28]

The real import of the Resolution's repeal was reflected in the form of commissions issued to the newly elected associates. All were "to continue in office seven years from [commissioning date] if so long they behave well." The independence of the judiciary conferred by the security of tenure was vindicated.[29]

George Tod needed a job. He had not developed much of a law practice, and his Brier Hill homestead yielded little more than subsistence for his family. In a letter his wife Sally wrote to him in December 1811 expressing hope for his safe arrival in Zanesville for the General Assembly session, she spoke uncomplainingly of their meager circumstances and her own social isolation. Raised in genteel surroundings in the New Haven home of her sister and brother-in-law, Sally had never been able to return to Connecticut. "I have had somewhat of a struggle with myself," she wrote, "and have given up the idea of ever visiting my friends. Every spare penny shall be sav'd up for our children." Their youngest of six was then eight months old. A seventh child, George Tod Jr., would be born in 1816.[30]

On January 29, 1812, from Zanesville, Tod turned to the last person in his world that he would have wished to ask for help. With war threatening Congress had acted to raise new regiments for the U.S. Army; one of them, the Nineteenth Infantry, would be recruited in Ohio. Commissions for its field grade officers—a lieutenant colonel to command, and a major—were in the gift of the state's legislative delegation. New congressmen not yet having been elected, Ohio's delegation was dominated by Tod's longtime adversary Thomas Worthington. Tod wanted command of the new regiment, and although Ohio militia experience was his only military training he was probably as qualified as other seekers of the position. Diffidently, only three weeks after the Ohio Senate had enacted the Resolution repeal bill, Tod wrote to Worthington as follows:

Dear Sir:

I am an applicant for a Colonel's command in the army of the United States. Your personal interposition in my behalf will ever be grateful to my feelings. I am sensible of the great responsibility attached to such a command, and should my application prove successful I hope that neither my friends nor my country will find their confidence misplaced.

I am with considerations of respect your ob't and humble servant.

George Tod

Senate Chamber, January 29, 1812[31]

Tod was disappointed. John Miller, publisher of the Steubenville *Western Herald* and a longtime Worthington political ally, was made a lieutenant colonel and given command of the regiment. Tod was offered only a major's commission, and appointment as Miller's second in command. Several of Tod's friends urged him to decline, and refuse to serve, as one said, "under a trifling editor of a trifling newspaper." One of them quoted Governor Meigs as recommending that Tod return his commission to the president, with a protest. Adding to Tod's humiliation was a rumor that the result of his application "was known in town [Zanesville] by the Tammanies before the rising of the Legislature."[32]

But Tod accepted his commission, and with it the responsibility for recruiting and training that fell to the regiment's second in command. Informed of Tod's decision, Worthington wrote to him explaining that only two positions above the rank of captain had been allocated to Ohio, and that among the applicants passed over were three who outranked Tod in the state militia. Then Worthington added:

Knowing as you do the state of party in Ohio, and that unfortunately it has kept from that social intercourse so essential to happiness, many among us, and perhaps you and me particularly, I have on this occasion endeavored to give you the best evidence of my personal best wishes.

In as much as our spheres of action in the future will be very different—you will be employed in the noise and bustle of a camp, whilst I may be engaged in civil business— and if we may never meet again on this [side of the] grave, I beg you to be assured that you ever had and will continue to carry with you my best wishes. I make you this tender—[illeg] readily on this occasion because I am persuaded you have been altogether misinformed as to my personal feelings toward you. I have only to add that under the circumstances we are placed [in] it was not in my power to get you a higher appointment.

Yours respectfully,

T. Worthington

P.S. War in my opinion is inevitable.[33]

CHAPTER THIRTEEN

A New Constitutional Equilibrium

A week after the Ohio Senate voted to repeal the Resolution, lawyer Wyllys Silliman wrote to Worthington from Zanesville saying that while he "feared the consequences," the "healing disposition manifested by the majority" gave him hope that "all will yet be well." But, Silliman continued, as "important as these subjects are to the people of this state, they are lost when contrasted with the great and important objects which engross the attention of the national government." Ohio and the nation were preparing for the War of 1812, and controversy over the state judiciary's constitutional position would be suspended at least for the duration. What were the issues in that controversy, as they stood in 1812, immediately after the Sweeping Resolution's repeal?[1]

Opportunities the previous six years' events had presented for implementing Jefferson's distinction between judicial review and judicial supremacy had not been pursued, at least in any formal way. Nothing had come of John Sloane's suggestion during the 1807–08 Ohio House debate over *Rutherford v. M'Faddon,* that if the courts or the governor found a statute to be unconstitutional they might grant some temporizing relief—a court ordering a continuance or new trial, or the governor remitting a criminal penalty—until the legislature could reexamine the law and make a final determination as to its constitutionality. Nor was there any other proposal for communication or cooperation between the state's judicial and legislative branches to resolve questions regarding the constitutionality of legislative enactments. If courts were to decide such questions in the course of ordinary legal proceedings, then Ohioans, like other Americans, had given no thought to according such decisions any less than conclusive effect on the acts and proceedings of other branches of government. As Professor Raoul Berger has found in a survey of broader scope, "proponents and critics of judicial review expected the courts to have the final say."[2]

The inconclusive verdicts in the impeachment trials had also left each side in the dispute over judicial review's legitimacy with an objection its partisans had failed to meet. Opponents of the power had no answer to Charles Hammond's compelling human-scale portrayals of the urgency of addressing constitutional objections to legislation as they arose in court, exemplified by the real and hypothetical cases he propounded in *The Rights of the Judiciary*. Did Sloane and Campbell, Morris and the House managers, really mean to say that if the state had attempted to cut a road through Isaac Zane's land without having paid him for the right of way, and Zane were prosecuted for resisting, he could not even be heard to cite the 1802 constitution's requirement for a "compensation in money" for the taking of property? Would his counsel be silenced if he sought to protest that a statute purporting to authorize appropriation without payment should not be given effect because it violated the constitution? Disregarding Sloane's suggestion that courts might give temporary relief until the legislature could reconsider a statute of doubtful constitutionality, the House managers had taken an uncompromising position in the impeachment prosecutions. They would tolerate no judicial cognizance whatsoever, of claims that a statute about to be applied or enforced against a party in a legal proceeding was unconstitutional.

For proponents of judicial review, on the other hand, the unanswered question was one which Tod and his law school classmate Thomas Scott Williams had put when they argued against the doctrine in the Litchfield Moot Court:

If [the judges] declare a law void, because unconstitutional, which is not so, how are the people ever to receive the benefit of that law?

Most Ohioans thought that the Fifty Dollar Act was beneficial and wanted it to remain in effect. Lawyers of standing who supported judicial review believed, with "Examiner," that the Ohio Supreme Court's judges "were right in deciding upon the constitutionality of laws, but wrong in deciding this law to be unconstitutional." Tod's defense counsel concluded that attempting to justify his ruling against the act would prejudice, perhaps fatally, the outcome of his impeachment trial. The only response which judicial review's proponents within the legal profession could make was to treat the ruling as aberrational and pledge to ignore it. The General Assembly, with the same response, made the Fifty Dollar Act a Seventy Dollar Act.[3]

Rutherford v. M'Faddon was cited in a published opinion of the Ohio Supreme Court in 1999 when it was commented on by Justice Alice Robie Resnick, writing for the four-to-three majority of a deeply divided court in *State ex rel. Ohio Academy of Trial Lawyers v. Sheward.* The case was brought to challenge a comprehensive statutory reform of Ohio tort law. The majority upheld the challenge, holding the entire enactment invalid as a legislative usurpation of judicial power in violation of the constitutional doctrine of separation of powers. Justice Resnick quoted extensively from portions of the Huntington and Tod opinions in *Rutherford,* and she mentioned the impeachment trials and the Sweeping Resolution. But she did not describe the law which was held unconstitutional in *Rutherford,* noting only that the General Assembly had reenacted it "in even stronger form" in defiance of that holding.[4]

It was the adoption of a new constitution in 1851 which, in Justice Resnick's historical view, caused "the power of constitutional adjudication [to be] secured exclusively in the judiciary." This development was inferred from the 1851 constitution's providing for election of judges by popular vote, as well as from its curtailing the General Assembly's powers to incur public debt, and prohibiting the former practice of granting corporate charters by special acts. Justice Resnick also cited comments by delegates to the convention which framed the new constitution, predicting that it would result in a more equal division of powers among the state government's three branches. From an opinion in a case decided by the "new" Ohio Supreme Court in 1852, a year after the new constitution took effect, Justice Resnick quoted from Judge Rufus Ranney's declaration that judicial review was the "right and duty" of Ohio courts. It was "thereafter," according to Resnick, that "the power of constitutional adjudication was secured exclusively to the judiciary."[5]

This dating of the acceptance of judicial review as a doctrine of Ohio Constitutional law is in error by at least a generation. Changes similar to those made in Ohio in 1851 were made about the same time in other states' constitutions. While they were advertised as fostering a more assertive, as well as an expanded role for courts as enforcers of the constitution—judges would no longer owe their positions to the legislative body whose acts they scrutinized, and newly ordained limits on incurring public debt would make more laws subject to judicial scrutiny—these mid–nineteenth century state constitutional initiatives did not establish judicial review as a new, or newly effective doctrine. In lectures Timothy Walker delivered in the 1830s at his law school in Cincinnati he proclaimed the judiciary as the "tribunal to settle the question of constitutionality in the last resort, whose decision should be final and conclusive," and eulogized judicial review as "one of the noblest features in our system." Alexis de Tocqueville, who met Walker and other prominent Ohio lawyers in 1831 when his American tour took him to Cincinnati, described judicial review in his celebrated account of that tour as a doctrine "recognized by all the authorities; and not a party, not so much as an individual, is found to contest it." As early as 1825, when the Ohio Supreme Court rejected a constitutional challenge to a state law retroactively limiting time to levy execution on judgments, Ohio Supreme Court Judge Peter Hitchcock wrote that there "undoubtedly are cases where it is proper, nay, where it is the duty of a court, to refuse to enforce a statute, on the ground that it is inconsistent with the supreme law of the land."[6]

The eight cases cited in the endnotes are all published *en banc* decisions of the Ohio Supreme Court during the quarter-century before 1851, the last year of the "old" court's operation under the 1802 constitution. In one of the cases the court held that the legislature lacked constitutional power to grant divorces.[7] The other seven all involve rulings on the constitutionality of an Ohio law— three upholding, three invalidating the statutes in question, and one reversing a decision which had previously ruled a law unconstitutional.[8] In none of these cases was the court's power to pass on the constitutionality of laws questioned by any member of the court, or disputed by counsel in reported arguments.

The cited cases' time span coincides with Judge Hitchcock's long career as a member of the "old" Ohio Supreme Court, over which he presided as chief judge during its final years of operation. First elected to the court in 1819, Hitchcock was personally familiar with the controversy during the first decade of statehood, which culminated with the Sweeping Resolution. As a one-term member of the Ohio House in the 1810–11 General Assembly he had sided with Resolution supporters in the tie vote which rejected a motion to bring in a bill for the its repeal. Forty years later, in one of his last opinions as a member of the "old" supreme court, written while he was serving concurrently as a delegate to the 1850–51 Constitutional Convention, Judge Hitchcock reflected on the history of judicial review, a doctrine which, he said, "does not, at the present day, seem to be seriously doubted," but concerning which "a great change has come over the public mind" in Ohio. The "opinion entertained by a majority of the public men of this State, at the time of, and soon after the adoption of our [1802] constitution" was, as Hitchcock recalled, "that the power to correct unconstitutional as well as injudicious legislation rested alone with the people." He went on to note the impeachment prosecutions and narrow acquittals of the two judges who had undertaken to exercise the power of judicial review. But, Hitchcock continued, "this power seems now very generally conceded to the *Courts, and I cannot well see how it could be otherwise.*"[9]

Distinguished lawyers and judges who as delegates to the convention took a leading role in drafting the new constitution's judiciary article likewise regarded the power of judicial review as generally conceded. Except for a brief and condescending response to an individual delegate's proposal to withhold the power from the courts, a proposal never seriously considered, the topics of judicial review and the manner and extent of its exercise under the new state constitution had only passing mention in floor debate, as something already taken for granted by members of the legal profession.[10]

What produced the "great change" which brought about unquestioned acceptance of judicial review? In Ohio it apparently occurred after the Sweeping Resolution's repeal in 1812, and before 1825 when Judge Hitchcock could describe the power as one "very generally conceded to the courts."

Indicators of that change are striking. By 1825 the two judges who had been subjected to impeachment trials for claiming the power of judicial review and were thereafter forced out of office, had long since been restored to the bench. In 1816 George Tod was elected presiding judge of a common pleas circuit; re-elected in 1823, he would serve another seven year term. Calvin Pease, in 1816, was elected to the Ohio Supreme Court; shortly before his reelection in 1823 he became its chief judge. Both rehabilitations were aided by recognition of distinguished services in the War of 1812. Pease, a volunteer scout, organized the relay of dispatch riders that provided communications for General William Henry Harrison in the defense of Ft. Meigs in May 1813, against a besieging force of British and Indians. Tod, a major in the Nineteenth Regiment, was in the fort during the siege and was cited in Harrison's action report for his part in a sortie to capture a British battery. Not less valued were Tod's services in recruiting and training the soldiers of his regiment, a unit newly raised in Ohio. By war's end he had been promoted to lieutenant colonel.[11]

The "era of good feeling" after the war brought surcease from political rivalry. In Ohio "no party" elections for governor were won by Thomas Worthington in 1814 and 1816, and by Ethan Allen Brown in 1818 and 1820. The Ohio Supreme Court's membership stabilized as the average length of judges' service increased—to nearly nine years for the six who were first elected during the second decade of statehood, as compared with less than four years for the eleven,

including the Resolution Judges, whose tenure began before 1813.[12] No politically contentious matter implicated the judiciary. An episode of arbitrariness in
entering judgment on a jury verdict despite indications that the jurors were not
unanimous got Tod in trouble, but an ensuing impeachment threat did not materialize. Tod was generally well liked as a common pleas presiding judge. A
next-generation lawyer who traveled his circuit, Henry B. Curtis, knew him as "a
most genial and hilarious gentleman of the old school," and recalled evenings
"spent in characteristic jovial style" in rude lodgings Tod shared with members
of the circuit bar.[13]

In 1816, the year Pease was elected to the Ohio Supreme Court, the General
Assembly again increased its membership to four, the number it would have
throughout its remaining existence under the 1802 constitution. In 1823, a year
after Pease became chief judge, the court resumed holding *en banc* sessions, a
practice suspended when its membership was cut back to three after the Sweeping Resolution's adoption in 1810. Henceforth these sessions would be held in
Columbus, the new state capital, after the end of each year's two-judge circuits.
The statute which directed resumption of the *en banc* sessions required the
judges to provide written opinions explaining decisions which turned on legal
questions.[14]

The same statute provided that such opinions should be published by an official reporter. Appointed by the court, he would receive a salary for his services,
and his publishing enterprise would be supported by the state's purchasing one
hundred copies of each volume of reports. Ohio thus became one of the first
states to provide for official, publicly subsidized case law reporting. The pur-
chase commitment which formed part of the subsidy was significant as an ac-
knowledgment of the authority the decisions thus promulgated would command. In summary, by 1823, not only had Ohio legislators restored to office the
judges their predecessors had put on trial; they had acted to facilitate public dis-
semination of rulings of the court whose independence in a constitutionally
separate branch of government had been challenged in those trials.

Prospered by the judges' choice of Charles Hammond as the first reporter,
regular publication of *en banc* opinions was a major step in the court's transformation into an appellate tribunal of last resort. The first half dozen volumes of
the Ohio Reports provide striking evidence of the rapidity with which the
judges gained competence in legally sophisticated opinion-writing. Chief Judge
Pease sent Hammond their rough drafts, calling them "unlicked cubs, which

Calvin Pease (1776–1839).
An engraving made long after his death, the image is consistent with descriptions of Pease's appearance
when he was Chief Judge of the Ohio Supreme Court, 1822–1830.

you are to lick into shape and publish according to law." Hammond gave them good lickings. "I doubt very much whether there is any authority for this," he wrote back to Pease about one of the drafts he received in February 1824, and "I have made the court say nothing on this point." The point Hammond questioned was a dictum, a proposition of law not necessary for reaching the decision. It was omitted from the opinion in the case, *McArthur v. Porter*, as published in the first volume of the Ohio Reports.[15]

Pease encouraged the practice, which began during his time as chief, of explaining some decisions with an "opinion of the court" joined in by all the judges who concurred in the decision and the reasons for it. Like Chief Justice Marshall who had originated "opinions of the court" in U.S. Supreme Court practice several years before, Pease sought consensus in judicial lawmaking. He was an acknowledged leader. A lawyer who appeared before him recalled his "uncommon strength of mind and perfect integrity," and his intuitive grasp of the "great principles of law and equity," despite Pease's claimed aversion to reading law books and case reports. Eccentricities enhanced his effectiveness. Allen G. Thurman, who as a youngster saw Pease on the bench thirty years before Thurman himself would become a member of the "new" supreme court established under the 1851 constitution, remembered him as being elegantly "dressed in a way that would make a dude faint." Thomas Ewing, another lawyer of high repute, considered Pease "the greatest" of all the judges before whom he had appeared.[16]

If lengthier tenure, published and more learned opinions, and full-time service gained Ohio judges greater respect from members of the legislature, that sentiment was reciprocated. It is striking to compare the post-1820s judicial review cases with the Fifty Dollar Act decisions, as to the deference accorded to the General Assembly's express or implied affirmations of the constitutionality of its acts. In 1806, it may be recalled, Pease had used a newspaper to notify a sitting legislature that he and his colleagues had invalidated the act in *The Cost Award Cases*. The considered response of the Ohio House's Lewis Committee, acknowledging the power of courts to pass on the constitutionality of the laws but asserting its belief in the act's constitutionality notwithstanding the Pease court's ruling, had been ignored by the Ohio Supreme Court in *Rutherford v. M'Faddon*. Chief Judge Huntington's portrayal of the act's passage as an inadvertent constitutional violation which the General Assembly should be pleased to correct once it were made aware of its blunder, was more than condescending; it was required by doctrine. The orthodox Federalist justification for judicial review, which had set up the judiciary, in the words of *The Federalist, No. 78*, as the "intermediate body between the people and the legislature," did not allow for judicial notice of legislators' opinions in matters of constitutional interpretation.

But by the 1820s courts in Ohio and other states had new-found respect for affirmative judgments of constitutionality implied by a legislature's enactment of a statute. In *McCormick v. Alexander*, the Ohio Supreme Court's 1825 decision from which Judge Hitchcock's proclaiming the "duty of a court, to refuse to enforce [an unconstitutional] statute" was earlier quoted, Hitchcock went on to say, "Yet this ought not to be done, unless the statute in question is a plain and palpable violation of the constitution. It should be both against the letter and spirit of that instrument. So long as there is a doubt, the decision of the court should be in favor of the statute."[17]

Pennsylvania Justice John Gibson, a member of that state's supreme court, criticized this "plain and palpable" requirement for judicial findings of unconstitutionality, in a case decided the same year Judge Hitchcock articulated the requirement in *McCormick v. Alexander*. Gibson argued, in effect, that judges are paid to decide close as well as easy questions, constitutional or otherwise. But Judge Hitchcock put the requirement on a different footing. It was not meant to save judges from having to labor over difficult questions, or to foster harmonious relations with the legislature; it was a *constitutional* limitation:

Whenever courts, in doubtful cases, undertake to declare laws unconstitutional, they may, with propriety, be accused of usurpation. They lose sight of the object for which they were constituted, and interfere with the *rights of the people, as represented in a different branch of the government.*[18]

In subsequent rulings on the constitutionality of Ohio statutes prior to the 1851 constitution's coming into effect the Ohio Supreme Court consistently affirmed this *judicial* obligation of respect for the legislature's popular mandate, as it sustained enactments against objections such as might have prevailed with the Huntington court in 1807.[19] Such deference was a nationwide phenomenon. As Professor Nelson has observed, courts had come to regard statutes "as [acts] of the people at large," giving them effect "at least as long as a finding of inconsistency with the constitution was not plain and unavoidable."[20]

A case decided in 1858, in which the "new" Ohio Supreme Court effectively overruled its predecessor's decision in *Rutherford v. M'Faddon*, affords an illuminating look backward. The legal issues raised by the facts are already familiar. By the time the 1851 constitution was adopted the monetary limit on the small-claims jurisdiction of Ohio justices of the peace had been increased to one hundred dollars. Three years later the General Assembly enacted still another increase, to three hundred dollars. The constitutionality of *that* increase was challenged in *Norton v. McLeary*, the case the "new" Ohio Supreme Court decided in 1858. The 1851 constitution included the same provision for an "inviolate" right of jury trial as the 1802 constitution had contained, and again it was argued that "inviolate" froze the limit (now the hundred dollar limit) as it stood when the constitution (now the 1851 constitution) was adopted. But this time the court decided differently, holding that the constitution "leaves [the jurisdictional limit] to legislative discretion," and noting, moreover, that the defendant could always obtain a jury trial on appeal to the court of common pleas:

It is true, that the act of 1854 may subject a defendant to a trial, before a justice of the peace, before he can obtain a trial by jury; still, the right of trial by jury remains unimpaired and perfect. The mode of obtaining it may be more inconvenient than heretofore. But on this subject a discretion is given to the legislature, which must be so far abused, as to be clearly violative of the substantial right, before this court can interfere to nullify legislative action. We think the act under consideration does not present such a case.[21]

Remarkably, neither the opinion of the court nor the argument of counsel who challenged the Three Hundred Dollar Law cited *Rutherford v. M'Faddon*. Instead the court relied on *Emerick v. Harris*, the Pennsylvania Supreme Court decision just rendered, but apparently unknown in Ohio, at the time of the Tod and Pease trials.[22] Fifty years later it was *Rutherford v. M'Faddon* that was unknown in Ohio. The difference was official publication: *Emerick* in Horace Binney's reports, a work later incorporated into a regular series of reported Pennsylvania Supreme Court cases, while *Rutherford*, published only in newspapers of the time, had never found its way into the literature of the law.[23]

Another look backward reveals a profound change in the public attitude toward the legal profession. Perceptions of "horrid extortion, tyranny and oppression, practised [sic] among that order of men," which after the Revolution had prompted radicals to call for eliminating lawyers, and abolishing trials in favor of arbitration or informally conducted jury proceedings in which parties would be self-represented, had been superseded by a view of the profession as a meritocracy. Lawyers, said Alexis de Tocqueville, "belong to the people by birth and interest, and to the aristocracy by habit and taste"; they "form the only enlightened class whom the people do not mistrust." That class included the judges.

Even James Madison, an opponent of judicial supremacy, had by 1834 taken to describing the "co-ordinate and independent right of the three departments to expound the Constitution" as an "abstract view." Citing "the public deference to and confidence in the judgment" of the courts, he declared that "the judicial bench, when happily filled, will . . . most engage the respect and reliance of the public as the surest expositor of the Constitution."[24]

Ohioans' respect for the state's judiciary was powerfully influenced by experience of the administration of justice in frontier settings. Laid out to enable inhabitants to journey over primitive roads to the county seat and back in a day's time, Ohio counties had a total of four court sessions a year—one supreme court, three common pleas—each lasting about a week. People who attended these sessions constituted the greatest percentage of the citizenry ever to witness court proceedings firsthand. Many came to be entertained as well as informed. But whatever their purpose in attending, spectators were impressed with the dignity and competence with which they saw judicial business conducted by "the court," a term they applied to a circuit's bar as well as its judges. Few Ohioans, on reflection, would have joined with Federalist Levin Belt in ridiculing the 1802 constitution's requirement that the members of the state's highest judicial tribunal should hold court in every county, and, as Belt wrote sarcastically, "for the sake of carrying Justice to the doors of the people . . . risk their lives from bad accommodations to live meanly sparing to make their wages equal to their traveling expense, and give their time and trouble to boot." Belt could not have been more wrong in asserting that "if Justice is not worth coming after [by suitors traveling to faraway courts] it is not worth the having."[25]

Among themselves, the circuit bench and bar developed not only "a professional fellowship" but, as historian Willard Hurst observed, "a close sense of what was done and not done. If there was little formal discipline, there was nonetheless pressure to conform to group standards—pressure that made itself felt in long discussion and exchanges of professional talk as horses stumbled or wagons bumped their way." "Pressure" was Hurst's professorial way of putting it. Plainly stated, no lawyer with a reputation for suborning witnesses, misrepresenting facts or law to the court, cheating clients or neglecting their causes could have continued for long in circuit practice.[26]

Thus it is not surprising that the holding of supreme court circuit sessions was recalled fondly by delegates at the 1850–1851 Constitutional Convention, although they well knew that the number of Ohio counties—by then all eighty

George Tod (1773–1841)
Nothing is known of the current existence or whereabouts of this striking sculptural portrait.
The photograph here reproduced was donated to the Western Reserve Historical Society in 1908.

(*Courtesy Western Reserve Historical Society, Cleveland, Ohio*) eight had been established—made it impossible for such sessions to continue. The same Rufus Ranney who as a member of the "new" Ohio Supreme Court would declare that exercising the power of judicial review was a "right and duty" of the judiciary, spoke movingly as a convention delegate of "the importance of holding a good [supreme] court in each county, as a means of carrying home to the mass of the people a knowledge of their legal rights, and inducing respect for the administration of the law." Circuit practice was a showcase of character, and what Ohioans and other Americans saw in that showcase was decisive in gaining acceptance for the power of judicial review. The Litchfield students were right: the power's legitimacy depended on the integrity of the new Republic's judges.[27]

That quality was tested everywhere in the nation, but in Ohio, a part of the test was unique. Here between 1806 and 1812 judicial review was challenged by political processes—directly in legislative deliberations and impeachment prosecutions, indirectly by the Sweeping Resolution. But it was not the formal outcomes of these processes, but the fortitude and faith of men who stood against them, that counted in the end. Hammond's eloquence, Tod's and Pease's uncompromising claims to the power of judicial review in their impeachment defenses, Tod's and Morris's decisions to become members of the General Assembly and work as legislators for the Resolution's repeal, Tod's sacrifice of his own prospects for reinstatement to the bench in order to gain the Senate votes needed for the repeal measure's passage, and Huston's and Snowden's inspired stubbornness as Resolution resisters, all gave substance to the aspiration Tod articulated as he concluded his answer to the impeachment charge, *"that the issue will give stability and value to our rights and liberties."*[28]

APPENDIX A

"The Cost Award Cases"

Chillicothe Scioto Gazette, December 25, 1806
(Jefferson Co. Court of Common Pleas, 1806)

A very intelligent correspondent has politely communicated the following for publication in the Scioto Gazette:

IMPORTANT LAW INTELLIGENCE

Previous to December term, 1806, several suits had been brought in the common pleas of Jefferson county, in debt and covenant, in which judgements [*sic*] were confessed for a less sum than fifty dollars, reserving the question of costs. At the December term, 1806, the question was argued at length, upon different days, by Jenings and King, in favor of giving costs, and Paul and Hammond, against it.

In favor of giving costs it was contended that the law extending the jurisdiction of the justices of the peace to sums above twenty dollars, was unconstitutional, and the section of the same which took away costs from suits made cognizable before justices, being predicated upon, and made part of the same system, was also unconstitutional.

Against giving costs, it was argued that admitting that part of the act extending justices' jurisdiction, to be unconstitutional, yet that inasmuch as at common law, no costs were allowed, the giving or withholding costs was a matter of discretion, to be determined by the legislature.

On the last day of the term, the judges delivered their opinions *seriatim*, in substance as follows:

PEASE, President

Upon the important question which we are called upon to determine there is, unfortunately, a division of opinion among us. So much of the act of the legislature as extends the jurisdiction of justices to sums exceeding twenty dollars, I consider unconstitutional. By the 8th article of the constitution of this state, it is declared that the right of trial by jury shall be inviolate. To understand this section of the constitution we must refer to the laws regulating trial by jury, at the formation of the constitution. The right of trial by jury, though generally well understood, is of itself a very indefinite expression. In different states it is subject to different regulations, and so general a declaration might create much difficulty, did not a sound principle of law point out to the court a rule by which it may be rendered perfectly certain and definite. In construing a statute, or a constitution, where the words are ambiguous, we must resort to the subject matter. When the constitution speaks of the right of trial by jury, we must understand it as speaking of the right of trial by jury as it existed under the laws in force at the time the constitution was formed. At that time, the right of trial by jury existed in this country, without any shackle or restraint whatever, in all matters of dispute where the value exceeded twenty dollars. A reason for fixing twenty dollars as the utmost point, beyond which the right of trial by jury shall in no way be restricted, is to be found in the constitution of the United States. By the ninth article of amendments, it is declared that "in suits at common law, where the value in controversy shall exceed twenty dollars, the right of trial by jury shall be preserved." Though it may be objected, that this provision extends only to laws of the United States, yet I conceive it cannot be fairly contended that it does not extend to all laws formed under the authority of the United States. Such were the territorial laws which existed when our own constitution was formed, by which the right of trial by jury was preserved free from any restrictions whatever, where the value in controversy exceeded twenty dollars. These laws, or the rights secured by them, our constitution declares shall be inviolate.—Now I consider the restricting and shackling a right, tantamount to taking it away. An attempt to subject a complete and perfect right, to regulations and restrictions, is, to my mind, a *violation* of that right. We must test all principles by the extreme cases which they may produce. If the legislature can prohibit a trial by jury, where the value in dispute is fifty dollars, they may extend the prohibition to a thousand: If they can prohibit a trial by jury until security is given to pay the debt, or damages received, there is no placing limits to the amount of security they may require: If they can give justices jurisdiction over all disputes where the value in controversy is under fifty dollars, they may erect any tribunal they please, for the trial of civil causes, to any amount they may think proper. The system which the legislature have attempted to establish, by the act in question, totally changes the course of judicial proceedings. A defendant must submit to the arbitrary determination of a justice of the peace, or to obtain a trial by jury, must give security to pay the amount received. Men who are not able to give security for the payment of fifty dollars may be subjected to much loss and inconvenience by this system. They may be hurried to trial before a justice of the peace who is prejudiced against them. They may be forced to trial when they could not be prepared with the testimony requisite for their defense. A decision may be rendered against them upon doubtful or insufficient testimony, which, though satisfactory to the mind of one man, would never satisfy the minds of a jury. In these cases they cannot have a trial by jury, without giving security to pay the amount which may be recovered. It is much more difficult to obtain absolute security, than special bail. We are often unwilling to become security for payment of a debt, when we have the fullest confidence in the integrity of the debtor. Besides, even if a man cannot procure bail, he can nevertheless have the benefit of a jury trial; he may plead when in custody, and in spite of power, oppression or poverty, submit his case to the decision of twelve of his impartial fellow citizens.

I consider the constitution as the barrier between the people and their rulers. I esteem all attempts to obstruct, impede or shackle the rights secured to the people by the constitution, as violations of its fundamental principles. I never can consent, that what cannot be done directly, may be effected by indirect or consequential means. The constitution provides, that every person of a certain description, shall enjoy the rights of an elector. Suppose the legislature passed an act, declaring that no person should be permitted to vote, until he gave bond, with security in a heavy penalty, not to violate the election laws, could it be contended that this would not be a violation of the elector's right? Are not the cases similar? It is said, that by the act under consideration, the right of trial by jury is not taken away. It is preserved by appeal. True. Neither is the right of the elector taken away: He may preserve it by giving the bond. But the proper question is, does the right remain inviolate? It is clear to my mind that it does not, in either the one case or the other. It is equally clear to me, that whenever the constitution secures a right, it secures a perfect and complete enjoyment of that right, which the legislature have no authority to abridge, obstruct, or controul [*sic*].

The right of the court to decide upon the constitutionality of the acts of the legislature, is a subject upon which I have no doubt. The judges are sworn to support the constitution, and to do justice according to the law. The constitution is the supreme law by which all other laws must be tested; it is the source from which all other laws emanate. In interpreting laws, the judges or courts must necessarily decide, as well upon their constitutionality, as upon their meaning and application. It is supposed by some, that the courts, when they take upon them to decide a law unconstitutional, assume the power of suspending laws;—a power reserved by the constitution, to the legislature. This proceeds from a mistaken view of the subject. When the courts decide an act of the legislature unconstitutional, they declare that it never was law. They decide such an act to be a mere legislative abortion, which never had any efficient existence; which never had either life or force.

Many reasons of policy have been urged, as deserving consideration; but I consider all such matters out of the question. I am aware that many evils will arise in the existing state of things, from this decision, but I feel myself bound down by the constitution, and consider any mischief of less consequence than a violation of it. I must therefore declare, that I am of opinion, that so much of the act defining the duties of justices of the peace, &c, as extends the jurisdiction of justices to controversies where the value in dispute exceeds twenty dollars, thereby shackling the trial by jury in all such cases, is in collision with, and contrary to, the constitution, consequently null and void.

With respect to costs, I have had more difficulty. I agree that part of a statute being unconstitutional does not destroy the validity of other parts: but where the whole forms a complete system, for the perfection of which one part depends upon another, I do not see how they can be separated. It seems to me they must stand or fall together. The section of the act which respects costs provides: "that if any person or persons shall commence or prosecute any suit for any debt or demand, by this act made cognizable before a justice of the peace," &c. I have just declared my opinion, that this suit is not by the act made cognizable before a justice; of consequence, whatever was the intention of the legislature, the case is not within the words of the section. Considering this technical reason, and considering, as I above stated, the difficulty of separating these two parts of the act, I am of opinion that the plaintiff must have judgment for his costs, as in other cases.

MARTIN, associate:

I coincide in opinion with the president. The reasons he has advanced, seem to me conclusive on the subject, and unanswerable.

CABELL, associate:

Upon a former occasion, I conceived the court could not inquire into the constitutionality of an act of the legislature. I was then under the mistaken impression, that it was suspending a law. I am now satisfied of the mistake, and concur in the opinion with my brother judges.

PATTON, associate:

I differ with the other judges on this subject, and though I feel the force of the reasons upon which this difference of opinion is founded, I am conscious of being incapable of expressing them in detail, either to the satisfaction of myself or others. This act is said to be unconstitutional because it takes away the trial by jury. It certainly does not take away the trial by jury: It only subjects it to certain restrictions. Now I conceive a right may be restricted, in many cases, and not violated. The legislature have required plaintiffs, in certain cases, to give security for costs, under penalty of having their suits dismissed, yet no person has considered this a violation of the rights of a plaintiff.—There is scarcely any legislative act which does not, in greater or less degree, restrict the rights of individuals; but those regulations which are intended to controul [*sic*] the course of individual conduct, for the general benefit of society, have never been held violations of individual right. I cannot consider the mere regulating a right secured by the constitution, as a violation of the constitution. I lean against giving this construction to the act and the constitution, on account of the mischiefs it will produce. Justices and constables will not know what to do. They will be liable to actions for what they have done, supposing themselves protected by law.—There will be no uniformity in proceedings. What will be law in this circuit, will not be so in the next, perhaps not the next county. I fear the mischiefs and confusion which such a decision will produce, and cannot join in opinion with the other judges.

N.B. [by the *Scioto Gazette*'s editor] The same question decided in the above case, came before the court of common pleas in Belmont County, the next week.—In an action of assault and battery, the plaintiff had a verdict for ten dollars damages.—The court unanimously gave judgment for costs. The decision was grounded upon the principle, that the right of trial by jury can neither be taken away, or restricted, in any case in which it existed at the formation of the constitution. At the time the constitution was adopted, if plaintiffs in assault and battery recovered more than five dollars damages, they were entitled to full costs.

Warren [Charles Hammond], *The Rights of the Judiciary* (n.p. 1808)

THE
RIGHTS OF THE JUDICIARY
IN
A SERIES OF LETTERS
ADDRESSED TO
JOHN SLOAN, ESQ.
LATE A MEMBER OF THE HOUSE OF
REPRESENTATIVES

2

An *elective despotism* was not the government we fought for; but one which should not only be founded on free principles, but in which the powers of government should be so divided and balanced among the several bodies of magistracy, as that no one could transcend their legal limits, without being effectually checked and restrained by the others.

Jefferson, Notes on Virginia, 122

In a representative republic, where the executive magistracy is carefully limited both in the extent and duration of its power; and where the legislative power is exercised by an assembly, which is inspired by a supposed influence over people with an intrepid confidence in its own strength; which is sufficiently numerous to feel all the passions which actuate a multitude; yet not so numerous as to be incapable of pursuing the objects of its passions, by means which reason prescribes; *it is against the enterprising ambition of this department, that the people ought to indulge all their jealousy, and exhaust all their precautions.*

Madison, Federalist, No. 48

(Note: original page numbers are in left margin)

3

LETTER I
TO JOHN SLOAN, ESQ.

Sir,

IN addressing these letters to you, and thus drawing the public attention upon you, it is not my object either to wound your feelings, degrade your understanding, or lessen you in the estimation of the people. I am about to examine a constitutional question, in the examination of which you have borne a conspicuous part. I mean to attempt a refutation of doctrines maintained by you, in a speech delivered on the floor of the House of Representatives. As you have caused that speech to be published in a newspaper, it seems to me that an investigation of its principles may be addressed to you with peculiar propriety.

In discussing this subject, I shall endeavour to be cool and dispassionate. I shall address myself to your understanding, your candour, and your liberality. It will be my aim, in a public and perspicuous manner, to urge such arguments, and state such facts, as appear to to me calculated to convince you and the public, that your opinions are erroneous, and lead to consequences highly mischievous. It appears to my understanding, that the resolution of the last House of Representatives, respecting the right of the Courts to pronounce a legislative act unconstitutional, is not only erroneous in principle, but that in adopting it the House transcended their constitutional prerogatives. Though this is my opinion, I am not disposed to cast any imputation upon the motives of the members who supported the resolution. The integrity of the heart ought not to be impeached for the errors of the head. An attempt to demonstrate that a man has committed an error, is no attack upon his veracity. I shall attempt to prove that the House of Representatives were wrong; but I acquit them of any improper intention. I am at war with their judgment; with their motives I have nothing to do.

The House of Representatives, by solemnly resolving that the Judges of the state are not authorized by the constitution to declare an act of the Legislature unconstitutional, and therefore null and void, have assumed the position, that the Judges are bound by the legislative act; that for its constitutionality the Legislature are solely responsible. From this position it results, as a necessary consequence, that our Courts cannot compare an act of the Legislature with the constitution, for the purpose of judging between them. The advocates of this doctrine rest their arguments upon two propositions: First, that the Courts cannot exercise this power, because it is not expressly given to them by the constitution. Secondly, that if its exercise is permitted, the Courts become superior to the Legislature. Both these grounds deserve examination.

4

Upon the first proposition, it is triumphantly asserted, by yourself and others, that no express authority, upon this subject, is given by the constitution to the Courts. It is certainly true that the constitution is silent on this subject: and as this silence is the principal argument with the advocates of the resolution, it merits immediate examination. To illustrate its force, it will be necessary to analize [sic] the provisions of the constitution. It is declared by the first article, that "The legislative power of this state shall be vested in a General Assembly, which shall consist of a Senate and a House of Representatives, both to be elected by the people." The constitution then fixes the ratio of representation, the period at which the members shall be chosen, defines their qualifications, and declares a term for which they shall be elected. It proceeds to make provision for the organization of the Assembly; defines the rights and privileges of the members; prescribes the mode of filling vacancies, and the manner in which business shall be transacted. It next imposes certain restrictions upon the Legislature, with respect to certain salaries; prohibits the members from being appointed to certain offices; and forbids moneys being drawn out of the treasury without appropriations by law. It then disposes of the power of impeaching, and trying impeachments; points out who shall be liable to impeachment; declares the time the Legislature shall meet; and renders certain officers ineligible as members of the General Assembly.—This is a brief compendium of the provisions of the first article. It does not detail the particular powers of the Legislature. It does not authorize them to enact laws on any particular subject, but vests in them, in general terms, the whole legislative power of the state.

In like manner, the constitution, in general terms, declares that "the judicial power of this state, both as to matters of law and equity, shall be vested in a Supreme Court, Courts of Common Pleas for each county, in Justices of the Peace, and in such other Courts as the Legislature may from time to time establish." It goes on to prescribe the number of Judges which shall compose the different Courts, their terms of office, the manner of appointment, how often Courts shall be holden, &c. and, in general terms, provides that the Courts shall have criminal jurisdiction, common law and chancery jurisdiction, *"in such cases as shall be directed by law."* The constitution, it thus appears, has not empowered the Courts to determine this or that case. It has neither empowered them to take cognizance of an indictment for murder, nor an action of debt; but it has vested in them the *whole judicial power of the state*, without any restriction whatever, except that it is to be exercised by [sic] the manner prescribed by law. Let us then test your first proposition, and the arguments in support of it, by their application in these two articles of the constitution.

You commence your speech with a complaint, that "the arguments of gentlemen opposed to the resolution, are intended to prove the policy of vesting the courts with the power of *setting aside* the acts of the Legislature, on the ground of unconstitutionality, without ever attempting to *prove, by the constitution itself, that this power is vested*

5 ⅔

in them by that instrument. In vain," you exclaim, "may gentlemen resort to authorities written long before the existence of our constitution, to prove what are the powers granted by it to the different departments of the government. *It is by the constitution, and by it alone, that this question must be decided."*

No argument can be sound, no rule of construction, or interpretation, correct, which does not apply equally to every part of the same instrument. The argument which proves that one department of government can exercise no power, but what is expressly granted by the constitution, proves also, that the other departments must stand in the same predicament, or the argument will be good for nothing. It proves too much, and destroys itself. According to the doctrine under consideration the Legislature can enact no law, unless *expressly authorized by the constitution; and* whether they are authorized, or not, must be determined *by the constitution, and by it alone.*" I call upon you then, Sir, to name that section of the constitution which authorizes the Legislature to enact any law whatever. *"That any such provision* is [contained] in the *constitution, I do positively deny."* Read it over again and again. You will find that many things are to be provided for, and directed by law: but by whom the law is to be made, the constitution is altogether silent. Here you may be disposed to answer, that as the power of making laws can only be exercised by the Legislature, it results to them [by necessary implication]. Mark the bearing of you own argument upon this point. "Legislation," says your quotation from Blackstone, "is the greatest act of superiority that can be exercised by one being over another." Legislation then being such an important power, I might exclaim in your own words, "I hope the independent freemen of this state *will never suffer a power so important* as this, to be exercised from no other authority than mere implication. How easy it is for an ambitious man or set of men, to put such construction on our constitution, connected with the nature of their office, as will tend to promote their designs. *Whenever we submit to the exercise of implied power,* that moment we lay the foundation for the destruction of our liberties."

I repeat, Sir, that the constitution does not expressly authorize the Legislature to enact laws. But you will perhaps repeat your questions: "What are we to understand by the legislative authority? Is it not the power of making laws?" I answer in your own language, "it is by the constitution, *and by it alone,* that this question must be decided, and if the power contended for is not there to be found, I ask where are we to look for it?" Can you, Sir, escape from the dilemma in which this argument places you? Either it is absurd to require the Judges to shew an express provision of the constitution, authorizing them to decide upon the constitutionality of legislative acts; or the Legislature must shew an express authority to enact laws. No such provision can be shewn by either. Each is therefore guilty of an high "assumption of power, for which they ought to be called to an account."

But, further to illustrate your argument on this point, were I to admit that the laws named in the constitution were to be made by the Le-

6 ⅖

gislature, a question would arise, as you say, "concerning what is law, and whether it does not necessarily imply obedience?" You solve this question by resorting to Blackstone; but, in spite of your argument, I object to this procedure. Blackstone wrote "long before the existence of our constitution. In vain you [gentlemen opposed to the resolution] resort to an authority written long before the existence of our constitution, to prove what is law under it. It is by the constitution, *and by it alone*, that this question must be decided." Thus, Sir, I might progress through the whole constitution. By objecting to the exercise of every power not specially granted, and by rejecting every explanation of the meaning of the constitution, where that explanation is not furnished by the constitution itself. I could easily render it a dead letter. If the Judges are bound to shew that section of the constitution which, in express terms, authorizes them to decide upon the constitutionality of a legislative act, they may be called upon to point out where it has expressly authorized them to try an action for slander. And by the same rule of interpretation, the Legislature might be required to name that section of the constitution which authorizes them to enact a law "regulating negro and mulatto persons." Does not this view of the subject, this exposition of the consequence of your first position, and the tendency of your arguments in support of it, sufficiently demonstrate its weakness and absurdity? I will pursue the subject a little further.

How will this position operate, when applied to the whole powers of the Judiciary? "In examining," you say, "the third article of the constitution, the only one that treats of the powers of the Judiciary, we find that no such power as the opponents of the resolution contend for, is vested in the Judges; but on the contrary we find that when speaking of the supreme court in the second section, it provides that they shall have original and appellate jurisdiction, both in common law and chancery, *in such cases* as shall be directed by law." Does this article of the constitution vest the Judges with power to expressly try actions of debt or assumpsit? Does it authorize them to determine the difference between murder and manslaughter, or to sustain an action of ejectment? You must answer that it does not. The constitution gives the Judges power to decide no particular case. They are to take jurisdiction *"in such cases* as shall be directed by law."* They are to exercise no power by implication: it must be *expressly* vested in them by the constitution, or by the law. Such is the substance of your doctrine. Let us examine its consequences. Our Courts are in the daily habit of adjudging one man to pay damages to another, for slandering his reputation, assaulting his person or abusing his property. They have frequently determined that one individual should surrender up the possession of lands to another, and have issued process by which a citizen has been forcibly turned out of house and home. Upon what authority have the Courts proceeded in this manner? The statute has indeed provided, that they shall have jurisdiction in all civil cases, both in law and equity. But what is a civil case in law or equity? The constitution does not tell us. The statute book will not explain it. Put the

7 ⅔

question to a Turk, or an Indian, he can give you no answer. Neither the constitution, nor the statutes, nor the light of nature, are competent to explain those terms. How are we to come at their meaning? I anticipate your answer. Every man, you will say, in this country, knows their meaning. A civil case is a controversy between two or more citizens, respecting their rights and privileges, brought before a Court of Justice, for adjudication. But, Sir, whence do you derive this information? You can find no such definition in either the constitution or the acts of the Legislature. You must revert to law books and dictionaries, "to authorities written long before the existence of our constitution."

But I concede, that a "civil case in law or equity," is a controversy between two citizens, brought before a Court for determination. Still, let me inquire where you will find any express authority for the Courts to decide any particular case? Has the constitution, or the law, any where directed than an action of debt shall be brought upon a bond, or an action of assumpsit upon a simple contract? Or will you resort to Blackstone for an authority in support of these actions? Further: you have ascertained from Blackstone that "Law is a rule of conduct, commanding what is right, and prohibiting what is wrong?" This "rule is to be prescribed by the supreme power," the Legislature; and this rule, you say, is obligatory. We remember that the Courts are not to exercise any authority by implication. Suppose now that I publish to the world, that you are a murderer, a robber, a thief, a corrupt, perjured scoundrel: suppose you bring an action against me for defamation: would it not be a general sentiment that I had done you injury, and that the Courts of Justice ought to assist you to vindicate your reputation, by punishing your slanderer? Suppose we appear before a Court; a Jury is sworn to try the cause, and the libel exhibited before them. Should I then rise up, and holding your speech in my hand, demand of the Court to name that section of the constitution, or the law, which authorized them to take cognizance of the cause: what answer would I receive? Should your counsel, or the Court, begin to harangue about the principles of justice, common law or common sense, I would reply, "Mr. Sloan despises their assistance in a Court of Law. I aver you have no authority. *This question must be decided by the constitution and the law, and by them alone.* I appeal to them. Where is it provided that the Legislature have *prohibited* one man from slandering another, or annexed any penalty upon him for so doing; where it is *prescribed* that one citizen shall recover damages from another who has slandered him. *That there is any such provision, I positively deny.* I claim the benefit of these doctrines. Mr. Sloan has heretofore maintained their correctness. Here is his speech. He cannot object to what I advance." Do you believe that this harangue would be aplauded [*sic*]? Would not all who heard me be astonished at my assurance? And would not the Court tell the Jury, that what I had advanced was absurd and extravagant; that it was essential to the welfare of society, that such atrocious conduct should be punished; that the Legislature

8 {

could not provide for every case, but that the general powers given to the Court to try all civil cases, authorized the Court to try the case before them? Yes, Sir, this is the language which the court would hold, and every man who heard them would acquiesce in its correctness.—The power, then, of the Legislature to enact laws, and of the Judiciary to decide causes, does not depend upon an express enumeration of the several grants of legislative and judicial powers: otherwise the most absurd consequences must follow. What then becomes of your first proposition? It vanishes before the scrutiny of impartial investigation.

WARREN

LETTER II.

TO JOHN SLOAN, ESQ.

Sir,

WE must have some correct notions of the nature and object of a written constitution, before we can be qualified to understand "what are the powers granted to the different departments of government." We know nothing of the state of nature, where the regulations of society are altogether unknown. From the first commencement of our revolution to the present day, the American people have been bound together by political and social regulations. They have no idea of any other than a government of laws. Their political principles, nay their conceptions of a constitution, have all been formed upon existing institutions. It is owing to this, that they seldom examine into the nature and origin of government, or inquire how this or that proposition has been established. It is therefore necessary to take a cursory view of this subject.

It cannot be denied, that the right of self-government is one of the most inestimable privileges of man. The power of self-government is essential to the proper enjoyment of his existence. When a number of individuals agree to enter into a state of society, they find it necessary to delegate a portion of this right, and this power, to a few of their number, to be exercised for the benefit of the whole. Man possesses in his very nature, the power to prescribe rules for his own conduct. This is a legislative power. He possesses also the power to judge his own conduct, and determine how far he has conformed to the rules prescribed. This is a judicial power. In the breast of every man these two powers must, from the nature of things, be of equal extent.

$9\frac{2}{3}$

On whatever subject a man prescribes for himself, in his own mind, a particular line of conduct on that subject, his judgment is always competent to decide how far he has adhered to, or departed from, the rule prescribed. His judgment condemns, or approves, in spite of his self-love. These powers cannot be exercised, in a state of society, by every individual for himself. Hence results the necessity of a social compact, or constitution. Men agree to entrust to others a certain portion of their natural legislative and judicial powers, to be exercised under certain restrictions. The time, place, manner, and limitations under which these powers shall be exercised, are agreed upon, and the mode of selecting those who are to be entrusted with their exercise is pointed out; their qualifications and obligations are declared; and when the compact is thus concluded, it is called a constitution.

The patriots who framed the American constitutions were deep read in the lessons of experience, as well as history. They were sensible of the master errors which pervaded those forms of government with which they were acquainted. History had recorded them in the misery and suffering of the people, or the weakness and annihilation of the government. A proper balance of power had not been preserved; and to remedy this defect, those eminent statesmen determined to try a new system. To one body of men they entrusted the making of laws; to another body they delegated the power of judging and applying the law; to a third they gave the power of executing the law. These they denominated the departments of government; and these were devised, as checks and balances, to operate each upon the other, while the people, through the medium of elections, held the whole under proper control.

The history of past times taught them, that the Legislature could not always be trusted. Blighted by passions, or corrupted by power, it had frequently enacted laws highly injurious and oppressive. The republics of Greece and Rome, of Florence, Venice and Genoa, were striking examples of this truth. The conduct of the British Parliament was immediately and particularly under their observation. A slight knowledge of the human heart was sufficient to convince them, that the surest remedy against this mischief was to remove all temptation to commit it. The powers of the Legislature are therefore confined to making law; its application is entrusted to another set of men. To secure an upright application of the law, it is necessary that the Judge should be independent and honest. His ambition is restrained by confining him to that department where he cannot exercise force, but judgment. He is removed beyond the reach of ordinary temptations to corruption, by an adequate compensation. He is placed above fear, by a stable and permanent tenure of office. The Legislature, then, cannot hope to effect any sinister purpose without the concurrence of the Judiciary; and the Judge is neither vulnerable through ambition, avarice, or fear. The Judiciary cannot make any successful attempt upon the liberty of the country: they have no force to effect any thing, and if they travel out of their proper sphere of action, the gross impropriety of such conduct would subject them to just animadversion.

10 §

It must be remembered that, in this plan of government, both the Legislature and the Judiciary are creatures of the constitution, exercising under it a delegated authority. The constitution is not made and written for either Legislature or Judges. It is made by the people, for themselves, and is expressive of their sovereign will. It contains, if I may be allowed the expression, the articles of association between the people. Every individual is a party to it. Every individual is bound by it, and every individual has a right to claim its protection. To the Legislature, under certain restrictions, the people give the power of "prescribing a rule of civil conduct:" to the Judiciary they give the power of deciding all controversies which arise under the social regulations. Both the Legislature and the Judiciary are the immediate representatives of the people. By their Legislature the people enact laws; by their Judges they pronounce judgment.

If there were no designing, no ambitious, no dishonest men, there would be no necessity for a constitution. So, if men could trust each other, the constitution, when agreed upon, need not be reduced to writing. Unfortunately, this is not the case. Society and all its regulations grow out of the wickedness of man: it is devised and intended to protect the weak against the strong. When men are agreeing upon a constitution, no one of them can foresee how soon his fellow-citizens may adopt notions, or form designs, hostile to his ideas of liberty. Each, therefore, is anxious to introduce restrictions and limitations calculated, he supposes, to secure the rights of the few against the many. Every limitation, every prohibition of the exercise of power, contained in a constitution, is a declaration by the people, that they cannot trust each other upon that subject. A constitution is not, as seems to be supposed, needed to secure power to a majority of the community. This power a majority must always possess, in the very nature of things, until they surrender it by compact, or constitution. A constitution is intended to impose restraints upon a majority, and to place the minority upon an equal footing. It is intended to compel the majority, in the exercise of power, to pursue a certain course, and observe certain principles; and it is written, that the few may at all times appeal to its provisions for protection.

Having ascertained the origin of constitutions, and of the powers delegated by them, as well as the particular object of the constitutions of the different states, I shall proceed to examine the constitution of Ohio, and to explain my views of the authority vested by it in the legislative and judicial departments.

In framing the constitution of Ohio, the Convention adopted such language, and used such terms, as were supposed to be well understood in the United States at the time they met. The plan of vesting the power of government in three branches, as above explained, was at that time in the *"full tide of successful experiment."* It had produced so many good effects as to be the boast and pride of the American people. The meaning of the terms, legislative, executive, and judiciary, as containing fundamental principles of government, were well understood.

II $\frac{2}{5}$

An exposition of their meaning was to be found in the laws and usages of all the different states, and in every treatise on government which had been written in the country. The Convention therefore considered them as technical terms of known and certain interpretation, and used them to define the nature and authority of the different departments they were about to organize. Thus, it is provided by the constitution, that the *"legislative authority of this state* shall be vested in a General Assembly," and that the "judicial power of this state shall be vested in a Supreme Court, &c." To ascertain the nature of legislative and judicial power, we have only to inquire what was the interpretation of those terms at the time the constitution was adopted.

You have said, and correctly, that the *legislative authority* is the power of making laws. With equal propriety you have said, in your quotation from Blackstone, that "Sovereignty and Legislature are indeed convertible terms; one cannot exist without the other." To vest in any body of men an unqualified *legislative authority* is the same thing as to make them sovereign and supreme. The Convention knew this, but they did not intend to vest the Legislature with sovereign authority, they imposed certain limitations and restrictions upon the Legislature. "The Legislature," says the 19th sec. of the 1st art., "*shall not allow* the following officers of government greater annual salaries, &c." Here is an express limitation. The 8th article is altogether composed of restrictions and prohibitions. It commences with a declaration of individual rights: "That the general, great, and essential principles of liberty and free government may be recognized, and forever unalterably established, we declare, that all men are born equally free, and have certain natural, inherent, and inalienable rights, among which are, the enjoying and defending of life and liberty ; acquiring, possessing and protecting property; and pursuing and obtaining happiness and safety, &c." Then follows a declaration, providing that certain rights and privileges should at all times be respected by the government. Among other things it is declared, that "no preference shall be given *by law* to any religious society, or mode of worship—*No law* shall ever restrain the right to speak, write, or print, upon any subject.—*No ex post facto law* shall be passed.—The Legislature shall never levy a poll tax.—*No law* shall be passed to prevent the poor from an equal participation in the schools, &c." These restrictions must evidently apply to the Legislature, not only because it is expressly *the making of laws* which is prohibited, but because they are limitations of the exercise of sovereign authority. "Sovereignty and Legislature are convertible terms." The legislative authority is the supreme power; consequently, every limitation upon the exercise of sovereign authority is a limitation of the powers of the Legislature.

It appears, then, that the Legislature of Ohio are a power possessed of delegated and limited authority only. They are not clothed with absolute sovereignty. When they are about to enact a law, they must make two inquiries: whether the power they are preparing to exercise, comes within the sphere of legislative authority? Whether the constitu-

12 §

tion has imposed any restriction upon its exercise? Upon the solution of these two questions the legislative power is suspended, and not upon an express provision of the constitution.

The constitution declares, that "the *judicial power* of this state, both as to matters of law and equity, shall be vested, &c." Upon the exercise of judicial power the constitution has imposed no restriction whatever. It has vested, in general and unqualified terms, in certain Judges, the whole judicial power of the state. We have seen that the general grant of legislative authority, was not its exercise limited by the constitution, would have given the Legislature supreme, sovereign, uncontroulable [*sic*] authority. Does the general grant of judicial power vest the same authority in the Judges? Certainly it does. No controversy can arise between the citizens, respecting their liberty, property, or reputation, to which the judicial power does not extend. There was [no neces]sity to limit the powers of the Judiciary. The power of judging can only extend to subjects under the constitution of laws. Such a power cannot be dangerous. It is destitute of all force. It can neither unsheath the sword, nor touch the purse-strings of the people. Besides, the power of judging, under a limited constitution, is susceptible of no restriction, but that of being bound by the constitution and the law. Let it once be declared that the Judges cannot decide any particular question, and upon that question the Legislature immediately becomes supreme. Limitations on that subject are rendered nugatory. The majority are under no controul; the minority have no security. The symmetry of the whole system is destroyed.

If at this day we ask a man of any information, no matter to what party he belongs, what is the judicial power of the state? He would answer, that it is the department of government to which the people have granted the authority of determining all controversies which may arise between individuals in society. If we should ask him for a more particular definition, he would tell us, that if a man is accused of murder, it is by the Judiciary that his guilt or innocence must be determined. If one individual complains that another has done him an injury, or withholds from him a right, *"the judicial power of the state"* must determine between them. So generally is the nature of judicial power understood, that there is scarce an individual so ignorant as not to be in some degree acquainted with it.

But the right and power to decide upon the constitutionality of legislative acts, is not so generally understood or admitted. It is indeed denied by many; and it is loudly demanded that the grounds upon which it is claimed by the Judiciary should be explained. This I shall endeavor to do; and I shall insist that this power is vested in the Judiciary, by the general grant of judicial powers contained in the constitution; by the statutes which give the Courts jurisdiction of "all civil cases in law or equity;" by the constitutional provision, that "all Courts shall be open, and *every person*, for an injury done him in his lands, goods, person, or reputation, shall have remedy by due course of law, and *right* and *justice* administered without *denial* or *delay*."

WARREN

13 ⅖

LETTER III.

TO JOHN SLOAN, ESQ.

Sir,

IT is not so much with respect to the nature, as the extent of judicial power, that we differ. As a general proposition, you will no doubt admit that the Courts must decide all controversies between citizens of the state, respecting their rights and privileges, where such question is brought judicially before them. It is for this very purpose that the judicial power is created and organized. Have the citizens of this state, individually, any rights under the constitution? Can any controversy arise respecting those rights? Will not each controversy present a constitutional question for determination? Has not every citizen of this state a right to call upon the Courts to decide a controversy, in which his liberty or property is implicated? If I can shew that those questions must *all* be answered in the affirmative, I think it will be clearly demonstrated, that the Courts must frequently decide upon the constitutionality of legislative acts.

Have the citizens of this state, individually, any rights under the constitution? By that instrument it is declared, "that private property ought, and shall ever be held inviolate, but always subservient to the public welfare, provided a *compensation in money* be made to the owner." How is this constitutional declaration to be understood? Does it not include a solemn promise to every individual, that the majority of his fellow-citizens will not appropriate to public use any of his property, but upon one condition? *"A compensation in money"* shall be made to him. Every individual, according to my notions of political morality, has a right to claim the performance of this solemn promise. The government *ought not* to violate it: and if your institutions be not defective, the government *cannot* violate it, with impunity. Controversies respecting the rights secured by this constitutional provision may arise in various shapes; and in deciding them, it is absolutely necessary for the Courts to examine the constitution, not only for the purpose of deciding the validity, but for the purpose of ascertaining the true interpretation, of a legislative act. In order to illustrate this position, I will state a case which may arise: not a case of extreme profligacy, where the Legislature are made to disregard all appearance of propriety, but a case which might occur under an existing statute.

By the law for opening and regulating roads and highways, it is provided, that if any person through whose lands a road runs, feels himself aggrieved thereby, he may apply to the Commissioners, who shall appoint five land-holders to assess the damages occasioned by such road:

14 ⅖

that upon their return of damages, the Commissioners shall issue an order on the County Treasurer for the amount, payable to the person who may sustain such damage. Now, Sir, suppose, as is frequently the case, that when the Commissioners issue the order, there is no money in the treasury, and the amount of the order is not paid. Suppose that before such order is paid, the Supervisor comes and attempts to open the road. This might happen in the month of September, and the road might run through the cornfield of the man who held the order. Suppose the holder of the order collects round him a number of his friends, and by force prevents the Supervisor from opening the road. Suppose the holder of the order, and those who assisted him to resist the Supervisor, should be indicted for a riot.[1] Must not this indictment be tried before a Court and Jury, and would it not be their province to decide upon the defence the prisoners should set up.

Upon the trial of this indictment the prosecutor would prove to the Court and Jury, that a public road had been reviewed and established, according to the statute. He would prove, that the damage of the principal defendant had been assessed by five land-holders, and that he had received an order on the Treasurer for the amount; that the Supervisor went in consequence to open the road thus established, and was forcibly driven by the defendants from the performance of his duty. The defendants would then be called upon to produce their defence. The principal defendant would state to the Court and Jury, that by our constitution, "the acquiring, possessing and protecting property" is declared to be an inherent and *inalienable* right of all men. He would declare that he had done no more than protect his property. He would read the 4th sec. of the 8th art.: "Private property ought, and shall ever be held inviolate, but always subservient to the public welfare, provided a *compensation in money* be made to the owner." He would offer to prove, that when the Supervisor came upon his premises, when for the "general welfare" the Supervisor attempted to open the road through his cornfield, he had not received a *"compensation in money"* for the damage he would sustain. Now, Sir, I ask of you whether the Court could refuse to hear him? Could the Judge say to him, "It is nothing to us whether you have received a *compensation in money* or not. We do not look at the constitution. The Legislature are the sole, the exclusive judges of its meaning and application." Would it be correct and proper for the Court to hold this language? If your doctrine is correct it certain would be their duty to proceed in this manner; and what would be the consequence? A member of the community, a party to the articles of compact or constitution, looks into that

15 $\frac{2}{5}$

instrument. He finds it declared that his "private property shall be held inviolate," unless a *"compensation in money"* be made to him. He finds it declared that he has a right to *possess* and *protect* his property. A public officer attempts to *violate* his property, (for surely it is a violation of property to open a road through a cornfield). He has received no compensation in money. He protects it, as the constitution has declared he has a "natural, inherent and inalienable" right to do; and what follows? Why, behold, he is liable to "be fined in a sum not exceeding 100 dollars, and find surety for his good behavior for twelve months, and stand committed until sentence be performed"!!![2]

I, Sir, for one, hold a different doctrine. When the defendants, in the case above stated, had declared the nature of their defence, the Court, I conceive, should permit them to adduce their proof. If it appeared in evidence, that at the time they obstructed and resisted the Supervisor, the principal defendant had not received *a compensation in money*, but only held an order on the Treasurer, the Court, I presume, ought to address the Jury in language something like this:—"You are called upon, Gentlemen, to determine whether the defendants in this case *'assembled together with the intention to do an unlawful act, with force and violence.'* From the evidence which has been adduced before you, it turns out that the question, whether they assembled to commit an unlawful act, involves some very important considerations.

"The provision of the constitution, that private property shall be held inviolate, unless a compensation in money is made to the owner, cannot be misunderstood; nor can we mistake the reasons why this provision was introduced. During our struggle for national independence, the exigencies of the times demanded not only the service of the citizen, but the seizing of his property, for the use of the public. Much private property was seized for public use, without the consent of the owners, and nothing given them in return therefor, but receipts and memorandums, by which they were made public creditors. These pledges of public faith were not redeemed, until they had fallen into the hands of a few speculators. The real *bona fide* creditor derived little advantage from them. This was a serious evil; and to guard against its happening in this state, the Convention wisely provided, that private property shall not be violated; that it should not be taken for public benefit unless a *compensation in money* was made to the owner. The people of Ohio are not at liberty to depart from this constitutional provision. They cannot rightfully seize private property upon the credit of the government. They cannot make compensation in orders upon the State of County Treasurer, or in certificates of credit. The *compensation* must be made emphatically in money, in the current circulating medium of the country. Until such compensation is made, the owner may lawfully defend his property.

16 ⅔

"In this case, it is said that the Legislature have declared that the party shall accept an order on the Treasurer. If the people themselves cannot rightfully substitute paper orders for money, the Legislature, who are no more than agents of the people, certainly cannot do it. But it is not perceived that the Legislature have attempted to do this. The law directs that the Commissioners shall give the party an order on the Treasurer. It does not declare that such order shall be accepted as payment. It is no more than pointing out the course by which the party shall get his compensation. The Treasurer keeps the money; the Commissioners direct to whom it shall be paid. The order on the Treasury is not payment. By giving this construction to the act of the Legislature, we prevent any collision between it and the constitution. The consequence is, that until the money was paid, the road ought not to have been opened. This provision is highly reasonable. The public ought not to open a road through any man's fields, without first enabling him to make himself secure against the injury which might result. In the present case this was not done; and the defendants, in using no more force than was necessary for the protection of individual property, were not guilty of an unlawful act. They have done nothing but that which the constitution declares they have a *natural, inherent and inalienable* right to do."

It seems, Sir, that this course of proceeding would be nothing but a proper exercise of *"judicial power."* An attempt is made to give a legislative act a construction incompatible with a constitutional provision. Controversy arises. An individual acts upon his own judgment, and such a act is deemed criminal. He is accused by the Grand Jury of a crime, and brought before the Court for trial. He rests his defence upon his construction of the constitution. The Court hear him, compare the legislative act with the constitution, and find that by giving to the act a certain construction, not incompatible with its language, it may stand. They declare such opinion, and the defendant is acquitted. I ask you, Sir, if for doing this, the Court can be justly charged with *"an assumption of power?"* I demand whether this inquiry is not properly within the sphere of *judicial powers:* whether in this case the Court could not compare the legislative act with the constitution, for the purpose of judging between them?

WARREN

17

LETTER IV.
TO JOHN SLOAN, ESQ.

Sir,

In my last letter I pointed out one case, in which a controversy, respecting a right secured by the constitution, might arise under our existing laws. I trust it must appear manifest that this controversy was properly brought before the Judiciary, and that it could not, consistent with our constitution, have been determined any where else. Lest it should be considered that such a case can seldom arise, I will proceed to demonstrate that similar disputes may arise under other statutes of the state.

By the 10th sec. of the eights art. of the constitution, it is declared "that *all persons* shall be bailable by sufficient sureties, unless for *capital offenses* where the proof is evident or the presumption great." This constitutional provision is intended to establish a fundamental principle, for the better security of personal liberty. It was introduced for the purpose of restraining the government from confining its citizens in prison for any offences but those of the highest nature. Though the terms [*sic*] *"capital offense"* are no where explained by the constitution, we are not ignorant of their true meaning. If, indeed, we were under the necessity of determining their meaning *"by the constitution, and by it alone,"* we would be in some difficulty: but if we may be allowed to resort, as you have done, to a *"very celebrated author,"* all difficulties will be removed. From Blackstone we may learn, that a *"capital offence"* is the commission of a crime which the law punishes with death. Every person then in Ohio, though accused of atrocious crimes, has a constitutional right to be bailed by sufficient sureties, unless the law inflicts upon him, if guilty, the punishment of death.

This provision of the constitution the judicial officers are especially bound to notice. If a person is brought before a Judge, accused of committing a crime, and the Judge believes their is probable evidence of his guilt, he ought to be secured for further trial. If the prisoner does not request a special Court of Common Pleas, but offers bail for his appearance to answer the charge at the next term, the Judge must decide whether he can be bailed or not. This is a judicial question.

Suppose a man should be charged with stealing $100 before a Judge, and suppose upon investigation it should appear that he was guilty. Yet he offers sufficient surety for his appearance. No statute of the state has provided in what cases persons should be admitted to bail, but stealing is not a "capital offence, and the accused claims the benefit of the constitutional provision. Must not the Judge look at the constitution?

18 $\frac{2}{5}$

And when he had read it, would he not be bound to admit the accused to bail? This first sec. of the "act defining the duties of Justices of the Peace, &c," provides that a Justice shall have power "to cause any person charged with a crime or a breach of the laws of this state, to be arrested, and brought before him or some other Justice of the Peace, and such person to commit, discharge, or let to bail, *as the nature of the case requires*" him to do. In no other way can his judgment be correctly informed.

The "act to prevent certain acts hostile to the peace and tranquility of the United States within this state," provides that persons guilty of the offences therein specified shall, "upon conviction before the Supreme Court, be fined in a sum not exceeding $4000 dollars, and imprisoned for a term not exceeding three years." This is not a *capital punishment*; of course the person who violated this law could not be guilty of a capital offence. Yet it is provided by the third sec., that persons arrested under the law shall be brought before a Judge of the Supreme Court, or a President of the Court of Common Pleas, "whose duty it shall be, if he find probable cause for such arrest, *at his discretion, to commit the person or persons so arrested to close custody*, or admit him or them to bail." Here the Legislature, in express terms, authorize the Judge, *at his discretion, to commit a person to close custody* for an offense not capital, in direct contradiction to the constitution, which declares that all persons shall be bailable, unless for capital offences.

If, while this act was in force, Aaron Burr had been arrested under it and brought before a Judge of the Supreme Court, and if the most satisfactory evidence of his guilt had been produced, could the Judge have committed him to close custody, if he offered sufficient surety, without a palpable breach of the constitution? Ought the Judge to shut his eyes upon the constitution? Although the act directs that he commit or bail, "at his discretion," shall he, in violation of the constitution, which contains "such express and unequivocal terms as admit no doubt upon the subject," commit a man to close custody, and call such conduct the exercise of a sound discretion?

Suppose one of our Judges had, under this act, committed a man who offered sufficient surety, to close custody, and an action for false imprisonment had been brought against him. The Judge would justify under the legislative act : the plaintiff would rely upon the constitution. The Court have jurisdiction to try an action for false imprisonment. The dispute between the parties is brought to this single point: can a Judge lawfully commit a man to close custody, in direct contradiction to the plain, unequivocal letter of the constitution? I say to you, Sir, whe-

19 $\begin{smallmatrix} 2 \\ \overline{} \\ 5 \end{smallmatrix}$

ther this is not a "matter of law," and whether *"the judicial power of this state,"* which extends both "to matters of law and equity," is not competent to decide and settle this "matter of law" in controversy between two citizens?

Upon examining the constitution, and comparing it with the acts of the Legislature, we find that disputes may arise between citizens, which cannot be decided without comparing the one with the other. It cannot, I think, be denied but that the cases I have stated might have occurred; that others of a similar nature may occur; and that they must be decided by the Judiciary. It is then manifest, that frequently the Courts cannot give a correct interpretation to a statute, without compare it with the constitution.

The right of the Courts to decide upon the constitutionality of legislative acts, is not claimed for the honour or advantage of the Judges. Such power only enlarges the sphere of judicial duties. It increases the labour and responsibility of the Judge, without holding out to him any correspondent personal advantage. No, Sir, this power in the Judiciary is claimed for the safety and advantage of the citizens. It is insisted that this power in the Judiciary is necessary, to secure every individual his constitutional privileges. The constitution is in the nature of an article of agreement. It is a compact between each individual and society at large, by which it is agreed that certain principles shall at all times be adhered to by the majority; that certain individual rights shall at all times be respected by the government. This article of compact the majority ought not to violate; and it is very seldom that they will deliberately do it. But it is impossible to draft a constitution in language so concise and explicit, that men cannot differ in opinion with respect to its meaning; and when such difference arises, there should be some tribunal to determine it. This will not be denied.

When the Legislature enact a law, it may fairly be considered the act of a majority of the people: yet a great difference of opinion may exist with respect to its constitutionality. But if the Legislature are the sole judges of this matter, the constitution would seem to be made for them alone. The Legislature then might prohibit any person with a red head, or freckled face, from emigrating into the state, unless such person gave security for his maintenance, under the penalty of being set in the pillory.[3] Whatever act the Legislature shall declare criminal, they are the judges of the matter, and their judgment must be submitted to. They give the constitution their own construction, and punish those who hold a different opinion. It is to prevent such a proceeding as this, that the constitution is made. The judicial power is organized, that there may be one tribunal to decide all differences and controversies between the citizens respectively, and between the society

20 ⅜

and individuals. It is intended to weaken and restrain the physical force of a majority, to give to one solitary individual as much strength as is possessed by the whole state; to test the merits of every contest, not by the power or numbers of the parties, but by the eternal principles of justice.

In one part of your speech you assert that "experience has proved beyond all contradiction, that a difference of opinion, as to the constitutionality of some of our laws, has prevailed from the highest judicial officers down to the private citizen." When a difference of opinion exits, who is to decide? How is the question to be settled? When men differ in opinion respecting the meaning of a legislative act; when men differ in opinion concerning the principles of right and wrong; when men differ in opinion respecting their rights and privileges, who is to determine between them? If controversies arise in consequence of such difference of opinion, will they apply to the Legislature? Is it a legislative power, to settle differences of opinion, or to determine controversies? No, Sir, they will apply to the Courts. Common sense teaches them, that these matters are subjects of judicial cognizance. If then the termination of controversies, in general cases, does not appertain to the Legislature, how does it happen that those controversies, which arise under the constitution, are to be decided by the Legislature? Where is it declared that the legislative interpretation of the constitution shall be binding upon every individual in society? I call upon you to shew that part of the constitution which contains this declaration.

It is emphatically the province of judgment to decide between conflicting opinions. The judicial power is established purposely to determine controversies between individuals; and controversies originate in differences of opinion. If, then "a difference of opinion, as to the constitutionality of some of our laws" does exist, and the rights of individuals depend on the difference of opinion, the Judiciary must decide the question. The constitution has made it the duty of the Courts to decide. "All Courts shall be open, and every person, for an injury done him, in his lands, goods, person or reputation, shall have remedy by the due course of law, and right and justice administered without *denial or delay.*" The Court must decide whether an injury has been sustained. In making the inquiry necessary to decide this, the Courts are not limited to the consideration of any particular question. The whole subject matter is presented before them. When they find that an injury has been sustained, they are neither to deny nor to delay justice. They are not to *"continue the case, or grant a new trial,"* as you have supposed, but they are forthwith to do right and justice between the parties. Upon a full view of this subject, then, it seems to me that the power to decide a legislative act repugnant to the constitution, and for that reason to declare it null and void, is one of the attributes of judicial power, and is of course expressly vested in the Courts by the general grant of judicial power. It is given in as express terms as any other power whatever. It stands upon the same foundation with the power to decide between trespass and trover, or between contract and tort.

21 ⅖

There is yet another ground, upon which the general grant of "Judicial power" may be considered as vesting the Courts with power to decide upon the constitutionality of legislative acts. Though in the beginning of your speech you have said, that "the powers granted to the different departments of government" must be decided *"by the constitution, and by it alone,"* yet toward the conclusion of your speech you have yourself departed from this rule. "In order," you say, "to judge of the powers *intended* to be given by the constitution to the different departments, it may not be amiss to take a slight view of our situation under the territorial government, and the reasons that led to the establishment of an independent state government." This, Sir is pursuing the correct course to ascertain the true meaning of the constitution, and I shall not hesitate to adopt it.

In order to ascertain what power the Convention meant to give to the Judiciary by the general grant of the *"judicial power of the state,"* it may not be amiss to inquire what was the general understanding of the terms [*sic*] *"judicial power"* at the time the constitution was adopted. It cannot escape the most careless observer, that the framers of our constitution have endeavored to express their meaning in the language of the constitution of the United States. The similarity of language in the articles organizing the Judiciary, it is particularly my purpose to notice:

> "The judicial power of the United States shall be vested in one Supreme Court, and in such inferior Courts as the Congress may from time to time ordain and establish."
>
> *Con. U.S.*

> "The judicial power of this state, both as to matters of law and equity, shall be vested in a Supreme Court and in Courts of Common Pleas, &c."
>
> *Con. Ohio*

So early as the year 1791, the terms judicial power, as used in the con. U.S. were construed to create a separate and co-ordinate department of government. It was then decided, that the right to decide upon the constitutionality of legislative acts, was one of the power of this department. The Judges of the United States refused to execute an act of Congress which had received the sanction of Washington himself. No objection was made to the exercise of this power. Congress repealed the objectionable act, and thus, I conceive, recognized and acknowledged the right of the Court. In 1795 Judge Patterson pronounced an act of the Pennsylvania Legislature unconstitutional. Upon this decision the right to a very valuable property depended: yet the proceeding of the judges was never questioned. A law of Congress, laying a tax on carriages, was considered unconstitutional by many. In the year 1796 the question was brought before the Supreme Court of the United States, and decided in favor of the law. You, Sir, cannot but remember the famous trial of Callender. At that trial, which took place in 1800, it was contended that not only the Court, but the Jury, had a right to decide an act of Congress unconstitutional, and disregard it. This doctrine was then maintained by *genuine republicans,* by the celebrated Mr. Wirt, Mr. Hay, and Mr. Nicholas. Mr. Nicholas

22 ⟨

said, as appears from the testimony of David Robertson on the trial of Judge Chase, "it seems to be admitted *on all hands* that when the Legislature exercise a power not given them by the constitution, *the Judiciary will disregard their acts.*"

It appears then, that at the time our constitution was adopted, the judicial power of the state was understood to possess and exercise the right to decide legislative acts unconstitutional. The Judiciary of the United States had exercised this power at different times, from the adoption of the constitution to the year 1800. It had never been questioned by any attempt "to call the judges to account." The Judiciary in several states had exercised the same power. Yet the Convention have imposed no restrictions upon the exercise of judicial power. They have created the judicial department in terms of the same import with those used in the constitution of the United States, from which we have a just right to infer, that they intended to give to the judiciary of Ohio the same powers which the same creating terms had been construed to give to the judiciary of the United States. They adopted the words, with the interpretation they had received. Such is the sound rule of construction. If the Convention had designed that their Judiciary should possess less power than the judicial power was generally understood to possess, they would have said so. But they have been silent. This silence, connected with the terms they have used, and the known interpretation of those terms at the time they were used, is alone sufficient to warrant the Court in exercising this, until lately, acknowledged attribute of judicial power.

WARREN

LETTER V.
TO JOHN SLOAN, ESQ.

Sir,

FROM the view which we have taken of the *"judicial power of the state"* it appears that it was created to decide *all controversies* which might arise under the laws of the state, between individuals, whether such controversy arose under the constitutional, statute, or common law. It appears to be the particular province of the Courts, to *expound, apply, and pronounce the judgment of the law;* and it appears that, in the discharge of their functions, the Courts are not limited to any particular case, or question. On whatever subject the Legislature can *prescribe rules of civil conduct,* on that subject the Judiciary alone

23 {

can pronounce the meaning and application of the rule, as well as its constitutional force.

In organizing the judiciary department, the constitution speaks of *"the judicial power of the state,"* as a power, pre-existent, known, and understood. This power it vests in certain Courts, the jurisdiction of which it declares shall be directed by law. The Legislature cannot enlarge or abridge the judicial power, but it can apportion it among the different descriptions of Courts. It can declare to what cases the jurisdiction of the respective Courts shall extend. This it is expressly authorized to do by the constitution. In doing this, I contend that the Legislature have *expressly* authorized the Courts to decide upon the constitutionality of legislative acts.

The act of February 1805, organizing the Judicial Courts, gives the Supreme Court "original jurisdiction of all *civil* cases, both in law and equity, where the title of land is in question, or where the sum or matter in dispute exceeds 1,000 dollars." It gives the Court of Common Pleas "original jurisdiction of *all* civil cases, both in law and equity, where the matter in dispute exceeds the jurisdiction of a Justice of the Peace." This act and the acts to amend it, give the different Courts power to try all criminal offences which can be committed in the state of Ohio.

The Legislature have not taken upon themselves to enumerate the cases of which the Courts shall have cognizance. They have given them power to try *"all civil cases."* It is not merely the duty of the Court to render judgment, or pronounce sentence. They are to hear evidence, examine principles, and lay down rules of decision by which controversies arising among individuals, from discordant opinion or conflicting interests, may be terminated. The power to try an action of trespass includes the power to decide every question which may possible arise upon the trial; and very often such a cause is decided upon a matter very different from what would appear to be the matter in dispute.

Thus John Taygart brought an action against Robert Carothers, for cutting timber upon his land. Carothers pleaded that he was appointed by the Legislature a Road Commissioner, and commissioned as such by the Governor; that he had located the road through Taygart's land, and in clearing out the road cut the timber. Taygart replied that Carothers did not take an oath of office before he located and cleared out the road: and whether a Road Commissioner was bound to take an oath of office, was the question upon which the parties demanded the judgment of the Court. Carothers relied upon the act of the Legislature. He produced the different laws under which he held his appointment, and acted, and he showed that they made no mention of a Road Commissioner taking an oath. Taygart opened the constitution, and read the 1st sec. of the 7th art. "Every person who shall be chosen or appointed to any office of trust or profit under this state, shall, before the entering upon the execution thereof, take an oath or affirmation to support the constitution of the United States and of this state, and also an oath of office." Here two individuals differed in opinion

24 ⅔

respecting the constitutional obligation to take an oath of office. This difference of opinion brought on a controversy, which terminated in a law-suit. This was a *civil case in law.* The dispute grew out of the constitution. Could, or could not the Courts decide this controversy? Have they, or have they not, jurisdiction of this case?

Again, the constitution, art. 8, sec. 17, declares that "no person shall be transported out the this state for any offence committed within the state." The first section of the "act to amend the act regulating black and mulatto persons" provides that no "negro or mulatto person shall be permitted to emigrate into and settle within this state unless such negro or mulatto person shall, within twenty days thereafter, enter into bond, &c. And if any negro or mulatto person shall migrate into the state, and not comply with the provision of this actg, it shall be the duty of the Overseers of the Poor of the township where such negro or mulatto person may be found, to *remove* immediately such negro or mulatto person in the same manner as is required in the case of paupers." In the case of paupers, the Overseers of the Poor are authorized to remove paupers not having a legal settlement within the state, "to the state or county where they have a legal settlement." In other words, the Overseers of the Poor may *transport* paupers out to the state, to the state from whence they came; and in like manner the Overseers may transport negro and mulatto persons out of the state in certain cases. I say *transport,* for it is trifling to be quibbling about words, To *transport,* according to Johnson, means *to convey by carriage from place to place.* To *remove,* means to put from its place, to take or put away.

This act of the Legislature, authorizing the Overseers of the Poor to remove negro and mulatto persons out of the state, unless they give security for their maintenance and good behavior, I consider unconstitutional. Wherefore is a negro or mulatto person to be removed out of the state? Is it not *"for an offence committed within the state?"* He has refused to comply with the regulations of an act of the Legislature. The act of the Legislature does not extend beyond the state. It cannot operate upon any person until he comes within the state. In the nature of things it cannot be violated, unless it is done within the state. But the act, by its very terms, supposed the offence to be committed within the state. The penalty of transportation is not incurred until twenty days after the person has been within the state. The constitution says expressly "NO PERSON *shall be liable to be transported out of this state for any offence committed within the state."* The Legislature say, NEGRO AND MULATTO PERSONS *shall be removed out of this state* for refusing to give bond within the state. Is not here a clear and manifest contradiction? Is not here ample room for difference of opinion at least? Now, Sir, if a negro, emigrating from Pennsylvania into this state, should remain here twenty days, and refuse to give bond, by this act the Overseers of the Poor are required to remove him back to Pennsylvania. Suppose the Overseers should attempt to do this, and the negro should refuse to proceed. Suppose the Overseers should tie him neck and heels, fasten him upon a litter, or an horse, and trudge along with him to Pennsylvania; would not the negro exhibit every appearance of a malefactor? Suppose such negro should bring an action for false imprisonment against the Overseers: would not this be a *civil case in law?* And what would be the matter in controversy? The Overseer would rely upon the legislative act: the negro would rely upon the constitution. The negro says he has been injured in both person and property. He claims that the Court shall be open to hear him, that he may have "remedy by due course of law, and right and justice administered without denial or delay." Could or could not the Court administer a remedy in this case?

But further: suppose an Overseer attempts to remove a negro who refuses to give bond, and the negro resists. He puts himself upon his defence, and declares he will not submit to be removed. The constitution declares, that the *"defending life and liberty"* is a *"natural, inherent and inalienable right."* In defending his liberty the negro unintentionally causes the death of the Overseer. He is indicted for manslaughter. Manslaughter is defined by our statute to be, *"the unlawful killing* another, without malice express or implied, either intentionally on a sudden quarrel, or unintentionally in the commission of some *unlawful* act." The negro is put upon trial. He rests his defence upon the ground that his resistance was lawful; that the act of the Legislature authorizing the Overseer to remove him, was unconstitutional and void, and therefore could give him no authority. The Court, by the act of the Legislature, have cognizance of the crime of manslaughter. The guilt or innocence of the defendant depends upon the constitution. Both the Court and Jury are conscientiously of opinion, that the act is unconstitutional: that the defendant ought to be acquitted. You admit that a difference of opinion may exist on this subject. Are the Court and Jury bound to declare the defendant guilty? They are sworn to justice according to the law and evidence. Must they decide according to their own opinions, or must they decide according to the opinions of the Legislature? Must they, although they believe one thing, declare upon oath directly the contrary? Either they must do this, or they must disregard the legislative act, and pronounce the defendant innocent. This is a dilemma from which they cannot escape. They are involved in it without their own fault. The question has been incidentally brought before them. The parties to the controversy insist upon having it determined: and it is for the express purpose of determining *all questions involved in the issue,* that the Court and Jury have been brought together.

If, then, we take a cool and dispassionate view of the constitution, I think we will agree that its principal object is, to secure to the citizens, individually, certain rights.

When we examine our statute book, and the proceedings of our Courts of Justice, we shall find that various controversies may, and do, arise respecting those rights; and the deter-

26 ⅔

mination of such controversies, all must agree, is the deciding a constitutional question. To shew that individuals have a right to call upon the Courts to decide *all* controversies between them, and all the question upon which those controversies arise, I have examined the constitution and our statutes, and stated a variety of cases which ave or may arise under them. I have shewn the manner in which those questions may be brought before the Court, and the necessity of their being determined. I have explained the nature and extent of judicial power under a limited constitution, as it was understood by the first framers of the American constitution, and as it had been practiced upon [and] previous to the framing of our own constitution. From a full view of the "whole ground" I infer, that the power of deciding legislative acts unconstitutional, is vested in the Judiciary by the general grant of judicial power; that it results to the Courts incidentally, being necessary to enable them to try all civil and criminal causes; that it is a power necessary to the preservation of a limited government; and that our constitution, by declaring that "all Courts shall be open, and *every person*, for an injury done to him in his lands, goods, person, or reputation, shall have remedy by due course of law, and right and justice administered without denial or delay," has emphatically enjoined upon our Courts, to decide promptly, and without hesitation, *all* questions which may be brought before them, whether they arise under the law or the constitution.

WARREN

LETTER VI.
TO JOHN SLOAN, ESQ.

Sir,

ONE principal argument against the right of the Courts to decide the constitutionality of legislative acts, is drawn from what is considered a consequence of this doctrine. It is said to render the Judiciary superior to the Legislature. No process of reasoning can conduct the mind of man to a correct conclusion, so long as it refuses its assent to correct principles. Those who deny this power to the Courts, found all their arguments upon a mistaken notion of constitutional principles. They are hurried away with the idea of legislative omnipotence, which it seems impossible to remove. This idea has so fastened itself in your mind, that you deny that our government is composed of coordinate departments. "The grant of co-ordinate authority is not," you say, "to be found in the constitution." In this I apprehend you are mistaken.

The term co-ordinate does not mean of equal power, but of equal rank. The departments of government are co-ordinate, because each derives its power from the same source, and each is independent of the others. Thus the Register of the Land-office, and the Receiver of public monies, are co-ordinate officers. Both are necessary to the transacting the same business, though the duty of each is different. So the Legislature and Judiciary are co-ordinate departments of the government of Ohio. They both derive their power from the constitution. As it respects each other, they are of equal rank. Their functions are different; but, within its own sphere, each is independent of the other.

The constitution is the fundamental and supreme law. From it the departments of government derive all their authority. No act can be of binding force, unless warranted by the authority under which it is performed. The agent cannot be superior to the principal. The officers of government cannot be superior to the people. If the Legislature pass an act contrary to the constitution, such act is void. What acts are prohibited by the constitution, is matter of opinion. Opinion is the judgment of the mind, formed upon mature and deliberate investigation. The people of this state do nothing in their collective capacity but choose their officers. They act through, and by means of, the departments of government. To their Judiciary the people have entrusted the interpretation of their laws. By their Judiciary they pronounce judgment. If these positions are correct, it follows as a clear consequence, that the Courts are the organs of the people to declare the meaning of the constitution. When the Courts pronounce a legislative act unconstitutional, they exercise no controul [*sic*] over the Legislature. The legislative act becomes inoperative in consequence of such decision, because, from the very nature of the government, a judicial opinion upon any subject of law, becomes binding upon the citizens. Such is the structure of the human mind, that no words can be used as to convey the same meaning to every man. Difference of opinion will exist. When the Legislature prescribe a rule of civil conduct, the Judiciary must apply the rule to each particular case. They must consequently decide its meaning and application. Common sense requires that such decisions be uniform; and when pronounced by the superior Court, they must be conclusive. In deciding a legislative act unconstitutional, the Courts pronounce not only their own opinion, but the opinion of the people. The Legislature judge of the constitution for themselves: the Courts judge for the people. The judgment of the Courts is of more force than the judgment of the Legislature, not because the Judiciary are superior to the Legislature, but because judgment is the peculiar province of the Courts. The idea, then, that this power renders the Judiciary superior to the Legislature, originates in a mistaken view of the principles of a limited government.

Your arguments in support of your doctrine, like the doctrine itself, appear to have originated in misapprehension. It seems that your opponents in the House, had drawn some arguments from the oath of the Judges, the force of which you was [*sic*] desirous to invalidate. To do this, you in the first place declare, that the oath of a Judge is no more than an oath of allegiance or fidelity to the government. If you had looked at the 1st sec. of the 7th art. of the constitution, you would have found that

28

every officer is required to "take an oath or affirmation to support the constitution of the United States and this state, *and also an oath of office.*" A Judge, then, is not only to take an oath of fidelity, but he is to take an *oath of office* besides. This oath of office the Legislature has prescribed in the following words: "I A B to solemnly swear, that I will administer justice *without respect to persons* and do equal justice to the poor and the rich, and that I will faithfully and impartially discharge and perform all the duties incumbent on me as a Judge, according to the best of my abilities and understanding."[4] Is this an oath of allegiance? Can a Judge conform to this oath; can he "administer justice *without respect to persons*," and at the same time so far *respect the Legislature,* as to execute their unconstitutional acts?

In the second place, you attempt to invalidate the argument by insisting, that if this oath authorizes the Judge to decide a legislative act unconstitutional every officer who takes the same oath, must consequently possess the same power. But what officer takes the same oath? Will you be good enough to inform me what officer, besides the Judge, takes an oath to *"administer justice without respect to persons to do equal right to the poor and rich?"* In the third place, you object that if the Judges can exercise this power in consequence of their oath of office, they may, with equal propriety, *set aside the laws*[5] of the United States upon which they may be called to act.—This, you say, "would appear too absurd on the face of it." Here, again, you are mistaken. This power has been exercised by a state Court. The District Court of Virginia pronounced an act of Congress unconstitutional, in the case of the Supervisor of the Revenue against Alexander Campbell, and rendered judgment against the United States. No complaint was ever made on this subject. Besides, by the 20th sec. of the act of Congress establishing the Judicial Courts, passed in 1789, and now in force, is provided, "that a final judgment or decree, in any suit in the *highest Court of Law or Equity of a state,* in which a decision in the suit could be had, *where is drawn in question the validity* of a treaty or STATUTE of, or an authority exercised under, the United States, and *its decision is against their validity,* &c, may be re-examined, and reversed or affirmed, in the Supreme Court of the United States."—There, Sir, is express provision for re-examining the judgment of a state Court, where such Court shall decide *against the validity of a statute of the United States.* By this act of Congress, which received the sanction of Washington, the right of the state Courts to decide upon the constitutionality of acts of Congress is expressly recognized. Yet you say the doctrine is too absurd to be supposed. When you *wrote your speech,*

29

were you ignorant of these things? Or did you mean to oppose your *opinion* to that of Washington and Congress?

You seem sensible, that the Judge who has sworn to *support the constitution,* and also to *administer justice without respect to persons,* is placed in an awkward placement when called upon to execute an unconstitutional act. From this embarrassment you attempt to extricate him, by involving him in new difficulties. You suppose a case, where a Court of Common Pleas pronounces a legislative act unconstitutional, and the Supreme Court reverse their decision and declare the act constitutional. In this case, you ask, "how is the situation of the Courts of Common Pleas, in relation to their oath and conscience, bettered by carrying the case before the Supreme Court; of if these obligations are done away in consequence of this?" I answer, that to be bound by the opinion of the Supreme Court, is very different from being bound by the opinion of the Legislature.

Judges and lawyers differ in opinion on a great variety of important questions, and on the forms of actions and indictments, declarations and pleas; on the competency of witnesses, and the relevancy of testimony. When any of these matters are brought before the Supreme Court and decided, the question is considered as settled. Whatever difference of opinion previously existed, by the decision of the Supreme Court the law is fixed. The case becomes a precedent, and all inferior Court are bound to acquiesce. It is by this means that the law will become uniform. It is for this purpose that writs of error and appeals are allowed. If the decisions of the Supreme Court were not binding upon inferior Courts, as well as individuals, there would be no end of litigation. Besides, this difference of opinion between the Supreme Court and the Court of Common Pleas is not confined to constitutional questions. The Court of Common Pleas decided, that equitable estates in land could not be executed and sold for debt. The Supreme Court reversed this decision, and it is now considered a part of the law of the land, to seize equitable estates in execution.

That the Legislature may pass an unconstitutional act is a truth so self-evident that you could not deny it. That such act ought not to be executed, is equally manifest. In order to make such act obligatory, and at the same time prevent its execution, you have resorted to a curious expedient. You suppose, that if the Legislature should pass such an act, it would be repealed at their next meeting. "If, in the mean time, and decisions should take place that might affect the life or liberty of an individual, *the Governor is vested with the power to grant a full pardon;* and if it affected property, *the Court would be authorized either to continue the cause, or grant a new trial."* When a man is regularly convicted of a crime against the law of the state, the Governor, it seems, may grant a pardon because the law is unconstitutional. But who is to decide this question? The law is in full force. It has been wantonly violated. The violator is found guilty by a jury. The Court have pronounced sentence. He expresses neither sorrow nor compunction, but justifies his crime; and yet the Governor may step in, and ar-

30

rest the judgment of the law, because in his opinion it is unconstitutional. This is remedying the mischief, with a vengeance.

The Courts of Law ought not to grant a new trial, unless the verdict of the Jury is against law or evidence. They ought not to continue a cause, unless some legal ground for a continuance is shewn to them. An action is brought, grounded upon an act of the Legislature. The cause is tried, and a verdict rendered according to the act. The defendant asks a new trial. For what cause? Is the verdict contrary to evidence? No. Is the verdict against law? It is agreeable to an act of the Legislature. Wherefore is a new trial to be granted? Why, the act of the Legislature is unconstitutional. It is not law. The Court are of this opinion, and for this cause may arrest the proceedings; and yet the Court cannot decide upon the constitutionality of legislative acts!!! Was there ever a more glaring absurdity?

Your whole argument is a tissue of disingenuous sophisms and evasions. In one paragraph you reject all authorities, and in the very next resort to Blackstone. At one moment you exclaim against what you call the exercise of implied power, and in the next breath, claim that the Legislature have a right to exercise power by implication. You apply one rule to the Legislature, and another to the Judiciary. You declare that *it is not to be presumed* that the Legislature will be led to "disregard the sacred obligation of an oath, and hazard the forfeiture of their honour and reputation, by wantonly violating the constitution;" and yet you found your whole argument upon the *presumption*, that the Judges will abuse their power. You answer the authority derived from some of the founders of our independence, by boldly asserting that those opinions were "founded on their rather than experience." No answer can be given to such reasoning as this. When men, to support a favourite theory, denounce the wages of the revolution, and the statesmen who devised our happy systems of government, as theorists who had maintained erroneous opinions, there is but little hope that they can be convinced of error. Had they not the most unbounded confidence in their own wisdom, they would not venture to condemn the opinions of such eminent men, much less to declare, that those opinions would at this day be recanted.

You deny that the different departments of government are intended as checks upon each other. The people, by means of elections, are the only check upon the Legislature. The Convention, you say, "carefully guarded the Legislature from every kind of clog, or controul [*sic*], from the other branches;" and yet we find not a word like this in the constitution. If we resort to the opinions of statesmen on this subject, you turn a deaf ear. We say, that the different departments of government are intended as checks upon each other. We read the opinion of Mr. Jefferson, that the "powers of government should be so divided and balanced among the several bodies of magistracy, that *no one* could transcend their legal limits without being *effectually checked and restrained by the others*." You answer us by asserting, that "the official conduct of the writer is a complete contradiction to the inference attempted to

31 2/5

be drawn from his work." A bold assertion on your part, and calculated to cast a bitter assessment on the consistency of the President.

We argue that the Judges, by abusing their power, cannot do much mischief; that they can have no object to effect by abusing it. We contend, that the Legislature, being the most powerful and most popular branch of the government, can do more mischief than any other department; and hence we infer that they ought to be watched with jealousy. We shew you, that such is the doctrine maintained by the founders of our institutions. You cut us short by dogmatically telling us, that "there is more safety where the power is divided among a number, that where it is concentrated in the hands of a few individuals." Or you assert, "that the spirit and genius of our constitution is, that the *will of a majority* of the citizens shall conduct the operations of the government." Power, not right, is the foundation of your system. On power, regardless of right, all despotism is founded. "*The will of a majority* of the citizens shall conduct the *operations* of the government. The act of the Legislature is the *will of the majority.* Hence all the powers of government, legislative, executive and judiciary, result to the Legislative Body. The concentrating these in the same hands is precisely the definition of despotic government. It will be no alleviation that these powers will be exercised by a plurality of hands, and not by a single one: one hundred and seventy-three despots would surely be as oppressive as one. Let those who doubt it turn their eyes upon the Republic of Venice. As little will it avail us that they were chosen by ourselves. An *elective despotism* was not the government we fought for." Such is the opinion of Mr. Jefferson. It is an opinion founded on experience, observation, and reflection, and cannot be shaken by the assertions of a minor politician.

WARREN

LETTER IV
[corrected to VIII on OHS copy]
TO JOHN SLOAN, ESQ.

Sir,

I HAVE explained my views of the constitution, and the grounds upon which the Courts are authorized to inquire into the constitutionality of legislative acts. I have also reviewed and controverted the principles and arguments advanced upon the other side of the question. Here I might have brought these letters to a close, but there is yet another question which ought to be examined. When the House of Representatives adopted the resolution declaring the power of the Judges, did they not transcend their constitutional powers? I insist that they did.

The constitution vests in the *General Assembly* the "legislative authority of the state." The *General Assembly* consists of the Senate and

32 ⅖

House of Representatives. No *legislative* authority can be exercised by either branch separately. Both must concur. The resolution in question was adopted by the House of Representatives alone. It was not sent to the Senate for concurrence. This proves, that in adopting the resolution the House did not consider themselves as exercising a "*legislative*" authority. Besides, to declare the meaning or application of an existing rule, is not, in the nature of things a *legislative authority*. It is the province of the Legislature to prescribe new rules, and devise new remedies. To determine an abstract question, unconnected with the passage of any law, does not appertain to the Legislature. This resolution is intended to determine an abstract proposition, unconnected with the passage of a law. In no point of view, then, can the House of Representatives justify the adoption of this resolution, under the constitutional grant of *legislative authority*.

Besides the general grant of legislative authority the two branches of the Legislature are, by the constitution, specially authorized to exercise other powers. Those other powers are enumerated. The authority to declare what are the constitutional rights of the Judiciary is not especially given in the enumeration of special powers. If it is, I call upon you to name the section where it may be found. This resolution, then, is neither warranted by the general grant of *legislative authority*, nor by any special grant in the constitution. Upon what authority, then, did the House of Representatives proceed? I might answer in your own language, "that this is a power which the House of Representatives ought not to possess; that by the constitution they do not possess; and that the exercise of it is an unwarrantable assumption of power."

There is but one case in which the constitution gives the House of Representatives, alone, power to act. This is the power of impeaching. If there is any principle upon which the adoption of this resolution can be defended, it is upon the ground that the power to declare the rights of the Judges is incident to, and necessarily *implied in*, the power of impeaching. Upon this ground, I presume, you will not attempt to defend it. After the clamour you have raised against the exercise of implied power; after declaring that "whenever we submit to the exercise of *implied power*, that moment we lay the foundation for the destruction of our liberties;" after insisting that "if we submit to the exercise of one power not delegated, on the *pretence* that it is *implied*, it will form an excuse for the assumption of another," you will surely not claim to exercise this very dangerous power *yourself.* This ground of defence, nevertheless, deserves to be considered.

The House of Representatives are the Grand Inquest of the state. This is no law which prescribes rules for their government in exercising the power of impeaching, but common sense and common justice require an adherence to certain principles. If a Grand Jury, at the commencement of their session, should proclaim their opinion, that this or that was an indictable offence, every body would be disgusted at such conduct. It would be deemed an invitation to commence a prosecution. It would be deemed a manifestation of an indecent and un-

33 ⅔

becoming zeal to prefer accusations. It would be considered as pre-judging a question, before they were called upon to act. In what other point of light can the resolution in question be considered? The House of Representatives, with the Grand Inquest of the State, of their own mere motion, declare that the Judges have no right to exercise a certain power. No complaint has been made to them. No Judge has been accused of exercising this power, upon whom the declaration can operate. It is an *ex parte*, an extra-judicial proceeding. It is prejudging an important question. It is condemning the Judiciary unheard. This resolution has no legal, nor constitutional operation, until it is followed up by an impeachment. The House of Representatives and the Judiciary are at issue upon a certain principle. The Senate alone can determine between them. Until such determination is had, the question remains unsettled. The resolution of the House is a mere incipient proceeding. It can only be consummated by voting an impeachment. If, at the time this resolution was adopted, the House did not contemplate an impeachment, the adoption of the resolution was a dangerous assumption of power. It was calculated to overawe the Judiciary, to irritate and prejudice the public mind. In the case of Fries, Judge Chase delivered an opinion upon a question of law, relating to the case of the prisoner, before the jury was sworn, and before the accused was heard by his counsel. This conduct the House of Representatives of the United States declared to be "as dangerous to our liberties, as it is novel to our laws and usages." This resolution is not less dangerous; it is equally novel; it is unprecedented in the annals of government. It is the first time that ever a House of Representatives grasped at such a transcendant [*sic*] authority.

Thus, while the House of Representatives were laboring to prove the danger of confiding too much to the Judiciary; while they were accusing the Judges of assumption of power, and demonstrating that this assumption of power led to "judicial supremacy and tyranny, to slavery of the most degraded kind," they were themselves trampling the constitution under their feet. They were assuming a power, neither granted to them by their general authority, nor by express provision of the constitution. While preaching against the exercise of *implied power*, they were themselves either acting without any authority, or upon an authority resulting solely from *implication*. "Such, therefore, is the consequence of submitting to the exercise of *implied power*; and such is the influence which *power and ambition* have over the minds of men."

Before I conclude, permit me to inquire when this doctrine, that the Courts cannot decide the constitutionality of legislative acts, was first advanced. It was in the winter of 1801–2, when Congress determined to repeal and destroy the new Federal Judiciary system. On the constitutionality of this measure, there was great diversity of opinion. It was carried in Congress by a small majority. Among eminent men

34 ⅖

of all parties, its constitutionality was doubted. The friends of the repeal apprehended that the Supreme Court of the United States held the same opinion with the minority. They feared that their object would be defeated by a decision of the Supreme Court. They therefore preached the doctrine, that the Courts of the United States could not question the constitutionality of acts of Congress: and from this period this doctrine has been maintained, in the different states, by adherents of the majority. Such is the origin of this pernicious doctrine, the sole object of which is to carry a doubtful question by dint of numbers. Hence it has become the favourite doctrine of a majority.

Here, Sir, let me remind you of the instability of popular opinion. The time may not be far distant, when you will find yourself in the minority; when your interpretation of the constitution may be voted down by a dead majority; when your only consolation against the abuse of power, shall be derived from the provisions of the constitution, and the integrity of the Courts. Look at the schisms among your political friends. Look at the increase of Federalists in New York, and the high tone assumed by some of the Federalists of Pennsylvania. Recollect that Massachusetts has returned to her ancient ground; that a great dissatisfaction at the measures of the administration, pervades New Hampshire and Vermont. Nay, look around you, and you will find discontent brooding over the whole country. Prospects of war, alien and sedition laws, and a direct tax, drove the Federalists from office. Prospect of war, non-importation and embargo laws, seem likely to have the same effect upon the present administration. I give no opinion upon the propriety of these things. I speak of notorious facts, which cannot escape the eye of the most careless observer.

At present you feel no distrust of the Legislature, but you are abundantly jealous of the Judiciary. You are then no advocate for the *perfectibility* of man, unless he happens to be a Legislator. If the next Congress or the next Legislature of Ohio, should by any possible chance contain a majority of Federalists, would you have the same confidence in their virtue? Be not too sanguine that you will always float with the current. You may be dashed upon shoals and breakers. Political opinions may change, and you and your friends may be proscribed by an overbearing majority. *"The doors of honour and confidence"* may again be closed upon you. While, therefore, you have power in your hands, use it in wise moderation. *Do unto others as they should do unto you.* So that if any chance should throw you into a minority, you may then find the constitution unimpaired, and may resort with confidence to its provisions for protection.

WARREN

END OF THE LETTERS

1. All this happened in the case of the State against Isaac Zane and others, indicted for a riot, and tried before the Court of Common Pleas of Muskingum county, December term, 1807.

2. The statutory punishment of riot. See act respecting crimes and punishments, sec. 28.

3. Why not, as well as to prohibit the emigration of negro and mulatto persons unless upon similar conditions? I see no great difference, in the nature of things, between a black and a speckled face; a red and a woolly head.

4. See act of February, 1808, organizing the Judicial Courts, art. 10.

5. Little minds place great reliance upon an imposing form of words. The advocates of the Legislature never speak of this power of the Courts but they take care to call it the power of setting aside the laws of the state. They know the Courts claim no such power. Why charge them with it, is not for me to say.

35 ⁊

APPENDIX MR. SLOAN'S SPEECH

The foregoing letters having commented at considerable length upon Mr. Sloan's speech, it was considered no more than fair, to publish it as an appendix. It might be inconvenient for many persons, who may read these letters, to refer to the speech. Its publication will enable them to judge of the merits of the controversy, by hearing both sides at once. Besides, many people in the world, when they find a favourite argument entirely refuted, or turned against themselves, are apt to deny that ever such argument was used by them or their friends, unless you have the proof ready at hand to convict them. The publication of the speech may answer some good purposes in this point of view. It is also desirable to preserve this speech, as containing a compendium of principles upon which the advocates of the resolution rely, and which they at this time maintain. The speech is copied from the Scioto Gazette. As no person took notes during the debate, except one gentleman, who took no notes of Mr. Sloan's speech, it is presumed Mr. Sloan furnished it himself for publication. So that it does not merely contain doctrines urged in the ardour of debate. Its principles must be considered the best that could be advanced upon deliberate reflection.

MR. CHAIRMAN,—Much has been said on this subject, but it appears to me that it has not been considered in a proper point of view. The arguments of gentlemen opposed to the resolution, are intended to prove the policy of vesting the courts with the power of setting aside acts of the legislature, on the ground of unconstitutionality, without ever attempting to prove, by the constitution itself, that this power is vested in them by that instrument. In vain may gentlemen resort to authorities written long before the existence of our constitution, to prove what are the powers granted by it to the different departments of the government. It is by the constitution, and by it alone, that this question must be decided; and if the power contended for is not there to be found, I ask where we are to look for it? And that any such provision as this is contained in our constitution, I do positively deny.

The first section of the first article of the constitution says, "That the legislative authority of this state shall be vested in a general assembly, which shall consist of a senate and house of representatives." I ask, Mr. Chairman, what we are to understand by legislative authority? Is it not the power of making laws? I presume this will not be denied, and here a question arises concerning what is law, and whether it does not necessarily imply obedience. Law, by a very celebrated author, is defined to be, "a rule of civil conduct, prescribed by the supreme power of a state, commanding what is right and prohibiting what is wrong." *Blackstone's commentaries, vol. 1, page 43.* In page 47 he says, "It is called a rule, to distinguish it from a *compact or agreement,* for a compact is a promise proceeding from us—law is a command directed to us. The language of compact is

I will or will not do this; that of a law is, *thou shalt or shalt not do it.* It is true there is an obligation which a compact carries with it, equal in point of conscience to that of a law; but then the original of the obligation is different. In compacts, we ourselves determine and promise what shall be done, before we are obliged to do it; in laws, we are obliged to act without ourselves determining or promising any thing at all.—Upon these accounts, law is defined to be a rule." Again, in page 46 he says, "But further, municipal law is a rule of civil conduct, prescribed *by the supreme power in a state:* for

36 §

legislation, as before observed, is the greatest act of superiority that can be exercised by one being over another. Wherefore, it is necessary to the very essence of a law, that it be made by a supreme power. Sovereignty and legislature are indeed convertible terms; one cannot subsist without the other." Law, therefore, being a rule of action, emanating from the supreme authority of the state, prescribing the duty not only of citizens individually, but also the duty of officers of the different departments of the government, where the constitution has not gone into detail: would it not be absurd, in the extreme, to say that any other authority than that which gave existence to a law, should be competent to set it aside, on any pretence whatever?

If the doctrine of gentlemen is to prevail, in vain has the constitution provided that the power and duties of the several officers of the state should be prescribed by law: for if the power is vested in the officer to annul and set aside the law which is to define his powers, and regulate his duties, then indeed will all government be at an end, and the intention of the constitution be defeated. It was impossible for the constitution to law down the whole duty of each and every officer; it therefore provided that those not mentioned therein, should be prescribed by law, but never could have intended that any of the officers were at liberty to disregard the law. No, sir; reason and common sense forbid such a construction of the constitution.

In examining the third article of the constitution, which is the only one that treats of the powers of the judiciary, we find that no such power as that which the opponents of this resolution contend for, is vested in the judges; but on the contrary, we find that when speaking of the supreme court in the second section, it provides that "they shall have original and appellate jurisdiction both in common law and chancery, in such cases as shall be directed by law"; and also in the third section of the same article, we find similar provisions with respect to the court of common pleas. But gentlemen, because they have figured to their imagination the necessity of the judges possessing this power, contend that it is necessarily implied, from the nature of their offices. But I hope, Mr. Chairman, that the independent freemen of this state, will never suffer a power so import ant as this, to be exercised from no other authority than mere implication. How easy is it for an ambitious man, or set of men, to put such a construction on our constitution, connected with the nature of their office, as will tend to promote their designs? Whenever we submit to the exercise of implied power, that moment we lay the foundation for the destruction of our liberties.

I contend that the constitution, in relation to such an important power as this, must be construed strictly according to the letter, as the convention, if they had intended to delegate it to the court, would have delegated it in such express and unequivocal terms as would have admitted of no doubt on the subject—and as they have not so done, we are bound to believe that they never intended it; and the 28th section of the 8th article of the constitution declares, "That to guard against the transgression of the high power which we have delegated, we de-

clare that all powers not hereby delegated, remain with the people," who, in my humble opinion, are the only judges in this case—they having a sufficient check on the legislature to prevent them violating the constitution and disregarding the public good, which carefully provided that n one of them should hold their appointments for a longer term than two years.

It is not to be presumed that the legislature, composed of men elected from the body of the people, and who are to return to them again at very short periods, and on whom the laws will operate equally the same as on their constituents, will be led to disregard the sacred obligation of an oath, and hazard their forfeiture of their honor and reputation, by wantonly violating the constitution. Nor have I ever seen any thing to convince me of the correctness of that doctrine which is such a favourite topic with some gentlemen, viz. that the legislature is composed of men too ignorant to understand the provisions of the constitution. The members of the legislature, from their being collected from various parts of the country, can have no interest different from the great body of the people; the case of the judges may, in some measure, be different. At all events I think there is more safety where power is divided among a number, than where it is concentrated in the hands of a few individuals, who are possessed of all the weaknesses of the many, and who, from the increase of temptation which the distribution of power among a few will naturally produce, are liable to fall into the same errors. But, suppose the worst that can possible happen, and that the legislature were to pass a law that infringed upon the constitution, few or none of those evils that gentlemen apprehend would take place, as it cannot be supposed that such a law would continue in force longer than the next meeting of the legislature, when it would be repealed—and if, in the mean time, any decisions should take place under it, that might affect the life or liberty of an individual, the governor is vested with the power to grant a full pardon; and if it affected property, the court would be authorized either to continue the cause, or grant a new trial.

Great stress has been laid by gentlemen on the other side of the question, on the judges taking an oath to support the constitution of this state, and of the United

States; but the subject has been so able discussed by the gentleman from Greene, that I shall offer but a few remarks in addition.

This oath which is taken, not only by the judges, but by all other officers of the state, I cannot consider in any other point of view, than what is generally understood by an oath of allegiance and fidelity to the government, by which they are bound to support the laws, and not privileged to violate them. In monarchies, where the people have no share in making the laws, this oath is frequently required of each individual subject; but in a government like ours, where every citizen is considered as a part of the state, and feels an equal interest in supporting it, this oath is only required of those who are promoted to public stations, and are charged with the concerns of the government, and is exacted of them as a security and pledge of their fidelity.

But to prove the absurdity of the position which gentlemen have taken, let us examine this subject a little farther. If, as they contend, the judges, in consequence

38 ⅔

of the oath which they have taken, are vested with power to set the laws of this state aside, surely every officer who takes the same oath, must consequently possess the same power—and what then, I ask, would be our situation? Could it be said that our government is a government of laws? No sir, *it would be nothing more than a government of opinion,* varying in the different districts of the state, according to the whim and caprice of the officers who were appointed to administer it. That which would be law in one judicial district, would be declared null and void in another, or even that which would prevail in one township, would be disregarded in the adjoining one; for experience has proved beyond contradiction, that a difference of opinion as to the constitutionality of some of our laws, has prevailed from the highest judicial officers down to the private citizen.

But farther—If the judges of this state, in consequence of the oath they are required to take, are authorized to set aside the laws of this state, they may, with equal propriety, set aside any of the laws of the United States on which they may be called to act; and are gentlemen prepared to say that they possess this power? I presume not; this would appear too absurd on the face of it—however it differs from the power contended for only in its extent. But say they, it is extremely hard to compel a judge to act under a law which he believes is contrary to the constitution which he has solemnly sworn to support. This, at first blush, appears plausible; but when we reflect, that the constitution gives him no power to disobey the law, and that deciding on its constitutionality is beyond his jurisdiction, the difficulty does not appear so great. And I would ask gentlemen if the position they assume themselves, is any better calculated to quiet the tender conscience of the judges. Suppose, for instance, that a law is passed, which one, or all of the courts of common pleas in this state shall think unconstitutional, and decide accordingly—the case is carried up before the supreme court, and the judgment is there reversed, by the court declaring the law to be constitutional: I ask how is the situation of the courts of common pleas, in relation to their oath and conscience, bettered by carrying the case before the supreme court—or if these obligations are done away, in consequence of this? No sir, their situation is precisely the same now that it would have been had they been compelled to obey the law in the first instance. Thus much for the anxiety about the tender conscience of the judge. But some are so extremely solicitous to have the constitution preserved, that in the heat of their zeal, they are willing to break it to accomplish their purpose.

The gentleman from Fairfield appears to apprehend, that this resolution is to be the entering wedge which is to make a breach in the constitution, through which an innumerable train of evils is to enter. But let that gentleman look well to it, that he is not himself supporting a principle which is calculated to produce all the evils he appears to dread. I am well aware of the importance of guarding the constitution from the slightest violation, and that one encroachment gives rise to another; and I am also convinced, that if we submit to the exercise of one power not delegated, on the pretence that it is implied, it will form an excuse for the assumption of another,—and the courts, if this principle is acceded to, will be seeking, by degrees, to increase their power, and laws which at this time would be suffered to pass unnoticed, would, as they felt their importance increase, be set aside. For proof of this, I will state a case which I am credibly informed does exist. By the act declaring the duties of justices of the peace and constables, in criminal and civil cases, it is provided that if any person commences a suit in court, for any debt or demand made cognizable before a justice of the peace, he shall not recover any costs, unless he file an affidavit in the clerk's office, before serving out the capias or summons, stating that he did truly believe that the debt due, or damage sustained, amounted to fifty dollars or more, exclusive of costs of suit; ut it is said that the courts, regardless of the provisions of this act, have in several instances allowed costs where the sum in demand was over twenty and under fifty dollars. What right, I would ask, have the courts to act in this way? Will it be contended, that the legislature have not a constitutional right to say what costs a plaintiff shall recover, or even that he shall recover no costs? I presume costs is not a matter of right, which any plaintiff is entitled to claim, either by virtue of the constitution or common law: It can only be recovered

by the provisions of a statute made in that behalf, and is not a matter of right, but is given as an equivalent for a right withheld. Such therefore, is the influence which power and ambition have over the minds and actions of men.

A considerable part of the arguments on the opposite side of the question, have been drawn from the difference between our constitution and that of England. I am willing to agree, that there is a very striking difference. In England they have no written constitution, and parliament possesses the whole power of the nation, and can change and model the government at pleasure; but their acts can only be tested by their operations on the public welfare, and this requires time and experience to prove, therefore the power of such a legislature is more to be dreaded than in a government like ours, where there is a written specific constitution, which every member is sworn to support, and which he cannot violate without being detected; besides, our representatives are immediately responsible, while the situation of England is such, that parliament is neither the representatives [*sic*] of the people, nor responsible for their conduct; they are the mere creatures of the crown, such as the legislature would be reduced to here, if you consent to give any other branch a complete negative over their acts.

It has been often asserted, that the three branches of our government are co-ordinate in authority; but I think the arguments on this subject tend to defeat themselves. If the constitution has defined the powers of the different branches of the government, and they are co ordinate in authority, how comes it that the judiciary have the power to annul the acts of the legislature? Can it be said that the department which possesses the power to nullify the acts of another, possesses no more than a co-ordinate or equal authority? No, sir, it cannot; but on the contrary, this goes at once to establish judicial supremacy and tyranny. The idea that our constitution has delegated to different branches of government a co ordinate or equal authority, is incorrect, and for proof of this, I will call your attention to the very limited powers granted by the constitution to the executive. If co-ordinate authority consists in one branch having the power to annul or set aside the acts of another, I would ask in what article of the constitution is there granted to the executive a power to set aside the acts of the legislature? No, sir, the grant of co-ordinate authority is not to be found in the constitution, and if it was, the doctrine contended for would go at once to destroy it. The opinions of a number of conspicuous characters in the union have been read to prove that this power is in the judges, or rather, that the judges ought to be completely independent. I am well aware that at the time they wrote judicial independence was a favourite [*sic*] doctrine with many, but it was one founded on theory, rather than experience, and I am of opinion, if some of them had to write now after the Union has fully discovered the effect that this independence is likely to produce, they would have ample reason to recant their opinions. There is one authority which has been produced on this occasion, that I think has no bearing on this subject; and if it has, it is in our favour [*sic*]—besides, the official conduct of the writer, is a complete contradiction to the inference that is attempted to be drawn from his work. I allude to Mr. Jefferson's Notes on Virginia: there is nothing in that work which goes to say, that this power ought to be exercised by the court; it only shews the danger of blending the powers of government, by concentrating the legislative, executive and judicial authority in one body; that is not what we contend for; no, sir, we only wish to see each branch of the government confined to the powers granted it by the constitution. But we are told that the judiciary is so very harmless, that there is no danger to be apprehended from its encroachments;

and that, if the judges act improperly, and declare a law unconstitutional that is not, you can apply the corrective by way of impeachment—but I would ask, if this power is once acknowledged to exist, how can they be impeached for it? What, impeach a judge for doing what he has a right to do? No, sir, the idea is absurd; but they say it is not for the exercise of the power that he ought to be impeached, but on account of the motives by which he is governed.

Who can pretend to judge of this; will it not be impossible to establish, as in most cases, the motives of men can only be judged by the nature of the act committed: if then you legalize the act by acknowledging the right of the part to perform it—

all inquiry about the motives with which it was committed will be unavailing, as they will always be able to shelter themselves behind technical forms, or by pleading an error of judgment. And I presume gentlemen will not contend, that a lack of understanding is a high crime or misdemeanor for which a judge can be impeached. But farther, should this favourite principle here contended for, be once established, it will tend to the destruction of the fundamental principles of our government.—No one will pretend to deny, that the spirit and genius of our constitution is, that the will of a majority of our citizens shall conduct the operations of the government; but will it not be otherwise should the judges possess this power? Let us suppose a case, that the legislature should pass a law which is, strictly speaking, constitutional, but two of the judges of the supreme court, from ignorance or some other motive, declare it otherwise. This I say is a supposable case, for experience has shewn that judges, on important points like this, do frequently differ. The judges are impeached, but the right being acknowledged and no corruption appearing, they are acquitted, notwithstanding every member of the legislature may be of opinion that the law is constitutional. I ask what is the situation of the state in a case of this kind? The constitution has granted rights, and for the more effectual enjoyment of these rights the legislature passes a law, but two ignorant or corrupt judges say it is no law, and set it aside—the people must submit. Is this liberty, is this independence? No, sir, it is slavery of the most degraded kind.

But, Mr. Chairman, in order to judge of the powers intended to be given by the constitution to the different departments, it may not be amiss to take a slight view of the situation under the territorial government, and the reason that led to the establishment of an independent state government? What was the principal grievance complained of under that government? Was it not that the will of the people was disregarded—the governor, by his *veto*, having a controul over all legislative acts? And have we made nothing by the change but a transfer of power from the executive to the judiciary? It is indeed, not barely a transfer of power, but a transfer and increase both at once, for the governor only had power of negativing the acts of the legislature before they went into operation, or were acted upon; but the judges are now to be vested with power to set a law aside, after it has been received and acted upon for years! Is it possible that the convention, sensible of the grievance which the people labored under on account of the powers exercised by the governor of the territory, could have intended that a power greater and more dangerous should be vested in the court? Or, if they had, would they not have delegated that power in such a manner as not to have admitted of a doubt? Yes, sir, if they had intended that the judges should have a negative on the acts of the legislature, they would have provided that before the laws should be permitted to go into operation; they should be submitted to the inspection of the judges of the supreme court, and not have trusted to time and chance to bring them up before them, after they had long been acted upon. In place of granting this power, we find that convention carefully guarding the legislature from every kind of clog and controul from other branches, and vesting them with the sole authority of enacting and suspending laws, in order that the public will might be the law.

There is only one observation that has fallen from the gentleman from Fairfield, that I think merits notice—that is, the Great Britain's denying this power to the judges was one of the causes which procured the revolution; and the declaration of independence has been cited as proof. It might not perhaps, be amiss for that gentleman to read the declaration again, and see if there is not a possibility of his being mistaken. Our complaints *were not,* that the judges were deprived of the right of setting aside the law, but *that they were the mere creatures of a despot,* and depended on him for the tenure of their offices.

Upon the whole, Mr. Chairman, I conclude that this is a power which the judges ought not to possess—that by the constitution they do not possess it; and that the exercise of it is an unwarrantable assumption of power, for which they ought to be called to an account. These are the principles by which I am governed in giving my vote upon this question, and notwithstanding that gentlemen have expressed their astonishment at the impudence of the supporters of this resolution, they are principles I have dared to express, unawed by any declaration whatever.

FINIS.

Article of Impeachment against George Tod

Ohio Senate, Seventh [misprinted "Sixth"] General Assembly, Journal (1809), 52–54:

Article Exhibited by the House of Representatives of the State of Ohio, in the Name of Themselves and all the People of the State of Ohio, against George Tod, one of the Judges of the Supreme Court, for the State Aforesaid, in Maintenance and Support of their Impeachment Against Him, for a High Crime and Misdemeanor.

ARTICLE I. [the sole article]

THAT whereas it is provided by the fifth section of an act of the general assembly of the state aforesaid, passed on the twelfth day of February, in the year of our Lord, one thousand, eight hundred and five, entitled "An act defining the duties of justices of the peace and constables, in criminal and civil cases," that the power of justices of the peace, in this state, shall, in civil cases, be co-extensive with the township in which they may respectively be elected and reside, and their jurisdiction in such cases, shall extend, under the restrictions and limitations therein after provided, to any sum not exceeding fifty dollars, &c. That unmindful of the solemn duties of his office, and contrary to the sacred obligation by which he stood bound to discharge them faithfully and impartially, the said George Tod, judge of the said supreme court, of the said state of Ohio, the said act of the said general assembly, not regarding, but wilfully, wickedly and maliciously, with intent to evade, nullify and make void the same, and thereby to bring the acts and doings of the said general assembly into contempt and disgrace, and to induce the good citizens thereof to disregard them, and thereby to introduce anarchy and confusion into the government of the state of Ohio aforesaid, at a supreme court, holden at Steubenville, in and for the county of Jefferson, in the month of August, in the year of our Lord, one thousand, eight hundred and seven, whereat the said George Tod sat as judge in a certain cause, then and there depending and undetermined, wherein [left blank] Rutherford was plaintiff and [left blank] M'Faddon defendant, did, in his judicial capacity, adjudicate and determine, that the said fifth section of the act of the general assembly aforesaid, was unconstitutional, null and void, and for that cause only, did reverse, set aside, annul and make void the proceedings had before the court of common pleas, for the county of Jefferson, aforesaid, and the justice of the peace in the said cause, to the manifest injury of him, the said [left blank] Rutherford, to the evil example of all the good citizens of the state of Ohio, aforesaid, contrary to its constitution and laws, disgraceful to his own character as a judge, and degrading to the honor and dignity of the state of Ohio.

And the house of representatives, by protestation, saving to themselves the liberty of exhibiting, at any time hereafter, any further articles, or other accusation of impeachment against the said George Tod; and of replying to his answers, which he shall make to the said articles, or any of them; and of offering proof to the aforesaid article, and to all and every other articles, impeachment or accusation, which shall be exhibited by them, as the case shall require, do demand that the said George Tod, may be put to answer to the said high crime and misdemeanor; and that such proceeding, examination, trial and judgment may be thereupon had and given, as may be agreeable to law and justice.

ALEXANDER CAMPBELL,
Speaker of the House of Representatives

ATTEST: TH: S. HINDE,
  Clerk of the House of Representatives
Saturday, December 24, 1808

Circular Letter of Members of the Ohio Bar,

Chillicothe *Scioto Gazette, February 13, 1809*

(Circular)

Chillicothe, January 23, 1809

We have observed with great solicitude the many mischiefs which the present unfortunate contest between the legislative and judicial departments of our government is calculated to introduce into the country. We all know that this contest originated from the decision of the supreme court, that the act extending the jurisdiction of justices of the peace above twenty dollars, is unconstitutional. We have attended to the progress of this contest from its commencement. We have witnessed the final issue in the impeachment and acquittal of Judge Tod. We have been present during the trial of that impeachment, and we have beheld it obtaining the support of a large majority of the legislature.

Upon a view of these things, we are compelled to pause, and look forward to the consequences; to enquire of ourselves where the matter in controversy is of so much importance, that the gentlemen of the Bar should convulse the country by adhering to it. Upon the most mature consideration, those of use who have considered the law unconstitutional, have determined that it becomes our duty to acquiesce, and we all believe that we ought to set an example of moderation; that no one should persevere in the maintenance of an opinion, the correctness of which is doubted by some among ourselves, is denied by many of our best informed men, and against which a large majority of our citizens have protested, in language too unequivocal to be mistaken.

We know that the gentlemen of the bar pretend not to infallibility, nor have they the arrogance to suppose, that they alone can affix to the constitution its legitimate construction. It is at least possible that with respect to the constitutionality of the act in question, an erroneous opinion may have obtained the sanction of the court. Under these impressions, and with an anxious wish to contribute to the removal of all embarrassments, we have looked around us for some remedy, and it has occurred to us that this remedy is within our own power. We conceive that if the gentlemen of the bar will cease to bring suits for any demand under fifty dollars, or under any other sum which the Legislature may limit, and will never demand the reversal of the judgment of a justice, upon the point of unconstitutionality, all difficulty must soon be removed. By this course of conduct it will be impossible to again agitate the question, except in suits now pending: in those we recommend, that the point be kept out of view, and as an inducement to compromise the question, we recommend that the plaintiff's attorney relinquish the docket fee.

Persuaded that this course of conduct is not, in any point of view, inconsistent or improper; persuaded also, that it will tend to introduce that harmony into the state, which at a crisis like the present is all important, we have taken the liberty to address this circular letter to the gentlemen of the bar, exhorting them to use every means in their power, to effect so desirable an object. And we trust that no member of the bar will be so lost to a sense of his own honor, and the interests of his country, as to persevere in a contrary line of conduct through pecuniary considerations, when individual harmony and public security will be the end and object of his sacrifices.

/s/ C. HAMMOND
LEW. CASS
JESUP N. COUCH
Wm. WOODBRIDGE
HENRY BRUSH
WM. CREIGHTON, junr.

Ohio General Assembly, Resolution on the Subject of Filling Vacancies in Office,

January 16, 1810, 8 Ohio L. 349 [the "Sweeping Resolution"]

WHEREAS it is provided by the eighth section of the third article of the constitution of this state, "That the judges of the supreme court, the presidents and associate judges of the court of common pleas, shall be appointed by a joint ballot of both houses of the general assembly, and shall hold their offices for the term of seven years, if so long they behave well:" And whereas the first general assembly of this state did appoint judges of the supreme court, presidents and associates of the common pleas, many of whose offices have, at different times, become vacant, and elections have been had to fill such vacancies; and whereas the original term of office is about to expire, and it becomes necessary for the general assembly to provide for that event:

Therefore,

Resolved, by the general assembly of the state of Ohio, That the constitution of this state having limited and defined the term of office which the judges of the supreme court, the presidents and associate judges of the court of common pleas, the secretary of state, the auditor and treasurer of state, and also the mode of filling vacancies which may occur in those offices, and that in filling such vacancies by the legislature, it cannot of right be construed to extend beyond the end of the original term for which their predecessors could have constitutionally served, had no such vacancies taken place.

EDWARD TIFFIN,
Speaker of the house of representatives

DUNCAN M'ARTHUR
Speaker of the senate

Attest, Th. S. Hinde, C.H.R.
Attest, Carlos A: Norton, C.S.
January 16, 1810

James Snowden,
"To the Resolution Judges
of the State of Ohio"

Dayton *Ohio Centinel*, March 21, 1811
(as reprinted in the Chillicothe *Independant Republican*, April 14, 1811)

To the Resolution Judges of the Supreme Court of the State of Ohio:

Gentlemen:

If you had passed through the county of Green, in your unauthorized route, without emitting reproachful insinuations derogatory to the character of the constitutional judges of the court of common pleas of said county, I would have treated you and your ministrations with silent contempt, for you have traveled through the state of Ohio bearing the title of judges of the supreme court of said state without any evidence of your claim to the important office, except that your were elected to it by the usurped power of a perfidious legislature, corrupting the minds of the people, and endeavoring to bring into contempt judges who were legally and constitutionally elected and commissioned, and solemnly sworn to support that constitution which you are daily violating. For these reasons I think it is time to inquire a little into your conduct, and compare it with the general rule of proceedings in courts of justice—and, first, with respect to evidence, various opinions have been entertained by the enlightened world as to the admission of evidence, but all, without exception, stress that in all controversies, either in law or equity, the best evidence the nature of the case will admit of ought always to be required, but your honors in your great wisdom, by your conduct, have declared that common fame shall be the only evidence required in this court of which you are the judges. Lest you should be alarmed at this assertion, we will present for your inspection and further consideration the case of Benjamin Browder against Martin Mendenhall as it stands in the record of the clerk's office in your honors' court of the county of Green:

Jonathan Browder)

      vs.) upon an appeal

Martin Mendenhall)

"In this case it was made to appear to the court that the trial and judgment was had in the month of May last, before the judges of the court of common pleas, two of whom proceeded to act as judges without taking the oath of office prescribed by law upon their last appointment, from which judgment the appeal was taken to this court. It is therefor ordered, that the appeal be dismissed and the cause sent back to the court of common pleas and there tried when that court shall be organized agreeably to law."

I would ask your honors, how was it made to appear in your court that two of the judges of the court of common pleas in Green county have not taken the oath of office prescribed by the last law upon their appointments? According to the best information I can gather, your evidence was common report; but I have been also instructed that your honors were informed by your clerk in court, that judge Huston and myself had not produced our commissions in open court, neither did we cause them to be entered on the records of the court, which was a convincing proof to your honors that we were not legal judges. If your honors had examined your evidence a little farther, you would have found that there was no such thing on the record respecting any of the judges that preceded us in Green county, therefore, according to your honors' judgment of things, there never has been a legal court of common pleas held in Green county, although notwithstanding all this, your honors sanctioned business that was done in common pleas by the same judges . . . [citing case]. But gentlemen, I must take the liberty of differing widely with you in opinion respecting this matter, Our commissions stand on record, and our qualifications to office are endorsed on the back of our commissions which we are ready to produce at any time when lawfully called upon for that purpose. These things, in my opinion, are much higher evidence of our claim to a seat in the court than (and supercedes [*sic*] every necessity of) such record as your honors require to be made. But it was expedient that your honors would proceed in that way, seeing record is all the evidence you have of being judges of the supreme court, and that record was effected by the unconstitutional conduct of a perfidious legislature, and an unquenchable and unwarrantable desire of gain prompted you to accept of your offices in an unconstitutional manner.—I would further enquire of your honors, what constitutes a judge of the court of common pleas? You say, in your remanding order above stated, "it was made to appear to the court (to wit, your honors' court) that trial was had before the judges of the court of common pleas," &c, and again you say, "when that court shall be organized agreeable to law." I confess that it appear to me that one part of your official conduct clashes with another. . . . Let us now enquire into the reason why this mysterious remanding order was exhibited, of which I have above required a solution. One of your honors says, "If we acknowledged them to be judges, we defeat our own titles," although your honors have acknowledged us to be judges of the court of common pleas in your above cited order. But, gentlemen, you need not use so much caution about your titles, for they defeat themselves, which I shall thereafter prove in such a manner as will convince every unbiased mind. Gentlemen you have traveled through the state of Ohio with the self-confidence and effrontery of Irish bullies, by your conduct bidding defiance to our constitution, and declaring that the judges of the court of common pleas of Green country granted a new trial to Cotterail [Cotrell] because they were fearful of committing a murder. Were your honors present at the trial, or did you hear the evidence? Certainly not. Then, gentlemen, I may justly infer that your honors intend to hang every person charged with a capital crime that is brought before your honors' court for trial, lest the propriety of your claim to a seat on the bench of the supreme court should be suspected. Are the judges of the court of common pleas of Green county fearful of committing murder? Most certainly they are, and so is every good man; and probably your honors would feel some comp———tion [?] in the crime. Whenever the right of an individual should come in contact with the will of the legislature, were the words of the constitution of doubtful interpretation, or did they carry with them an appearance of a double meaning, so as to render the subject in any degree a matter of opinion, I would be far from speaking so plain. If the convention that formed our constitution meant anything different from what they expressly said, they certainly would have made use of some other words such as would have shewn to the world their meaning. The constitution reads "the judges of the supreme court, the presidents and associate judges of the court of common pleas, shall be elected by . . . and shall hold their offices for the term of seven years," &c. Gentlemen, I will suppose that one man says, or asserts, that the sun, that bright luminary of heaven, is a body of fire, because he confers heat upon us; another says he is a luminous body, but not a body of fire, and such heat is produced in coming in contact with out atmosphere: Here it is self evident that the above stated controversy is a mere matter of opinion, and never can be properly decided. But if a man takes a silver dollar out of pocket and exposes it to public view, describing it to be a potato, the spectators will at once discover that he had declared a falsity because it carries its own invincible evidence with it: therefore it is a matter of certainty and not of opinion.

Now, gentlemen, . . . I shall proceed to enquire which of these two different species the meaning of the above cited clause of our constitution belongs to. . . .

The term legislative authority is a very indefinite expression, and when abstractly considered, may include an unlimited power, such as kings and emperors are vested with, who make laws according to their own will and pleasure and cause them to be put in execution; but when the term is made use in of [*sic*] a republican government it cannot possible mean or intend any thing farther than a certain limited and delegated power conferred by the people upon a certain body of men [constituted?] a general assembly. For what reason? Because the sole power of government is in the hands of the people. What is the evidence of that delegated and limited power? The constitution is the evidence. Do the general assembly swear that they will support the constitution? Certainly they do. Is the Mammoth resolution correspondent with the constitution? No, it is in direct opposition thereto. Are the general assembly guilty of perjury in passing the resolution? I leave that to the world to determine. The people confer upon, or transfer to, certain bodies of men, and certain individuals, limited and delegated powers, such as they believe will be most conducive or productive of their benefit and happiness: And the constitution is (if we may be allowed to use the expression) a power of attorney, put into the hands of all state officers by the people, wherein the duties of every department of government are plainly held forth and enjoined, with a reservation made, declaring that all powers not therein delegated remain with the people. Hence it is plain and self-evident that when the general assembly pass laws or resolutions variant from or diametrically opposite to the constitution, that they do not act by a delegated power, consequently they must act by a tyrannical usurped power, such as our general assembly assumed when they resolved your lordships upon a high seat of honor and power. What foundation have unconstitutional law and resolutions [to] support them? The question is easily answered. It is universally acknowledged by the ablest of judges, that in all republics such law and resolutions are of no authority, at all times null and void, and cannot possibly operate any farther than the bodily strength and crafty devices of their perfidious progenitors, aided by the ignorance and lookwarmness [*sic*] of the people, together with what assistance such men as you are will contribute, can enforce them. Hence, then, it is evident that if we (the people) tolerate every infraction of our constitution made by a designing and unfaithful legislature, we will foster tyranny in the very bosom of our country. Indeed, if we approbate such conduct we have no use for a constitution at all. Now, gentlemen, I have shewn to you upon what a flimsy foundation your claim stands, and if you differ with me in opinion, you are required to come out and defend it on rational and constitutional grounds; otherwise cease to pollute the sanctuary of our justice with your base insinuations.

JAMES SNOWDEN

P.S. Where I have spoken of the general assembly, I do not mean every individual member of that body, for I believe it had some men in that house whose hands were clean and whose hearts were pure: "who have not lifted up their souls to vanity nor sworn deceitfully."

Abbreviations

GCA   Greene County Records Center and Archives, Xenia

LC   Library of Congress

LHS   Litchfield Historical Society, Litchfield, Connecticut

MAR   Dawes Memorial Library, Marietta College

MCA   Muskingum County Archives

OHS   Ohio Historical Society, Columbus

OHS-Y   Ohio Historical Society, Youngstown Historical Center

RCA   Ross County Archives

WRHS   Western Reserve Historical Society, Cleveland

YALE-MA   Sterling Memorial Library, Manuscripts and Archives Division Yale University

Notes

Preface

1. C. V. Wedgwood, *Truth and Opinion* (New York: The Macmillan Co., 1960), 14 (italics added).

Introduction

1. Leonard Jewett to Thomas Jefferson, Athens, Ohio, July 28, 1809, *Thomas Jefferson Correspondence, Printed from Originals in the Collection of William K. Bixby*, ed. Worthington Chauncey Ford (Boston: Privately printed, 1916), 181.

2. *Marbury v. Madison*, 5 U.S. (1 Cranch) 137 (1803).

3. The first use of the term "judicial review" is believed to have been by Professor Edwin S. Corwin in his article, "The Rise and Establishment of Judicial Review," *Mich. L. Rev.* 9 (Dec. 1910): 102, 283.

4. Andrew R. L. Cayton, *The Frontier Republic: Ideology and Politics in the Ohio Country, 1780–1825* (Kent, Ohio: Kent State University Press, 1986); Donald J. Ratcliffe, *Party Spirit in a Frontier Republic: Democratic Politics in Ohio, 1793–1821* (Columbus: Ohio State University Press, 1998); William T. Utter, "Judicial Review in Early Ohio," *Mississippi Valley Historical Review* 14 (June 1927): 3–24; Richard E. Ellis, *The Jeffersonian Crisis: Courts and Politics in the Young Republic* (New York: Oxford University Press, 1971); William E. Nelson, "Changing Conceptions of Judicial Review: The Evolution of Constitutional Theory in the States, 1790–1860," *U. Pa. L. Rev.* 120 (May 1972): 1166–85; William E. Nelson, *Marbury v. Madison: The Origins and Legacy of Judicial Review* (Lawrence: University Press of Kansas, 2000), 84.

5. Marginal note by Jefferson on his Draft of First Annual Message to Congress, Dec. 8, 1801, Jefferson Papers, Manuscripts Division, Library of Congress, quoted in David N. Mayer, *The Constitutional Thought of Thomas Jefferson* (Charlottesville: University Press of Virginia, 1994), 269.

6. Thomas Jefferson, *Notes on the State of Virginia* (1787), ed. William Peden (Chapel Hill: University of North Carolina Press, 1954), 120; Jefferson to Madison, Mar. 15, 1789, *The Papers of Thomas Jefferson*, ed. Julian P. Boyd (Princeton: Princeton University Press, 1950–1982), 14:659.

7. Jefferson to John Dickinson, Dec. 19, 1801, *The Writings of Thomas Jefferson*, ed. Andrew A. Lipscomb and Albert Ellery Bergh (Washington, D.C.: Thomas Jefferson Memorial Association, 1905), 302.

8. Jefferson to Abigail Adams, Sept. 11, 1804, *The Adams-Jefferson Letters*, ed. Lester J. Cappon (Chapel Hill: University of North Carolina Press, 1959), 279–80.

9. Jefferson to W. H. Torrance, June 11, 1815, *The Writings of Thomas Jefferson*, ed. Paul Leicester Ford (New York: G. P. Putnam's Sons, 1892–99), 9:516. Jefferson reaffirmed but did not fur-

ther explain his theory of concurrent review in a September 6, 1819 letter to Virginia judge Spencer Roane, *id.*, 10:140. See generally Mayer, *Constitutional Thought of Thomas Jefferson*, 257–73; Wallace Mendelson, "Jefferson on Judicial Review: Consistency Through Change," *U. Chi. L. Rev.* 29 (winter 1962): 327–337.

10. Jefferson to Torrance, June 11, 1815, *Writings of Thomas Jefferson*, ed. Paul Leicester Ford, 9:516.

Chapter 1

1. William Winslow Crosskey, *Politics and the Constitution in the History of the United States* (Chicago: University of Chicago Press, 1953, 1980), 2:944–73; David E. Engdahl, "John Marshall's 'Jeffersonian' Concept of Judicial Review," *Duke L. J.* 42 (Nov. 1992): 279, 282 n.7, 283–84; J. M. Sosin, *The Aristocracy of the Long Robe: The Origins of Judicial Review in America* (New York: Greenwood Press, 1989), 251, 257; Larry D. Kramer, "The Supreme Court, 2000 Term, Foreword: We the Court," *Harvard L. Rev.* 115 (Nov. 2001): 4, 67.

2. Edwin Meese, III, "The Law of the Constitution," *Tulane L. Rev.* 61 (April 1987): 979–90. The "conniptions" Meese's suggestion evoked from commentators are recounted in Kramer, "The Supreme Court, 2000 Term," *Harvard L. Rev.* 115:4, 6–7.

3. Oliver Wendell Holmes Jr., "Law and the Court," Speech at a Dinner of the Harvard Law School Association of New York, Feb. 15, 1913, in Oliver Wendell Holmes Jr., *Collected Legal Papers* (New York: Harcourt, Brace and Howe, 1920), 291, 295–96. Holmes continued: "For one in my place sees how often a local policy prevails with those who are not trained to national views and how often action is taken that embodies what the Commerce Clause was meant to end."

4. "Brutus," Letter XI, *New York Law Journal*, Jan. 31, 1788, in *The Antifederalist Papers*, ed. Morton Borden (East Lansing: Michigan State University Press, 1965), 226, 228.

5. *The Federalist, No. 78* (Alexander Hamilton); *Marbury v. Madison*, 5 U.S. (1 Cranch) 137, 177 (1803).

6. In his introductory lecture to a course on the law which he taught as a young man in 1794 at what is now Columbia University, James Kent described the Constitution as "coming from the people themselves *in their original character* when defining the permanent conditions of the social alliance." Marshall, in *Marbury*, declared that "the people have an *original* right to establish" such conditions. Both may have sought a way around the obvious objection to Hamilton's construct of judges as direct representatives of the people, by giving the people an "original character" distinct from the political character in which they acted to choose legislative representatives. James Kent, "An Introductory Lecture to a Course of Lectures, Delivered November 17, 1794," reprinted as "Kent's Introductory Lecture," *Columbia Law Review* 3 (May 1903): 330, 336; *Marbury v. Madison*, 5 U.S. (1 Cranch) at 176.

7. *Marbury v. Madison*, 5 U.S. (1 Cranch) at 176, 177, 179; Sosin, *Aristocracy of the Long Robe*, 309.

8. Jack N. Rakove, "Constitutional Problematics, circa 1787," in *Constitutional Culture and Democratic Rule*, ed. John Ferejohn et al. (New York: Cambridge University Press, 2001), 43–44; Kramer, "The Supreme Court, 2000 Term," *Harvard L. Rev.* 115:4, 68. The first edition of *The Federalist* as a collection of essays was published in New York in 1788 by printers J. and A. McLean. The second edition was published by J. Tiebout in 1799.

9. Zephaniah Swift, *A System of the Laws of the State of Connecticut* (repr. New York: Arno Press, 1972), 1:35, 51–52.

10. *Reports of Cases Argued and Determined in the Supreme Court of the State of Vermont,* ed. Daniel Chipman (Middlebury, Vermont: D. Chipman & Son, 1824), 1:21; Kramer, "The Supreme Court, 2000 Term," *Harvard L. Rev.* 115:4, 49.

11. Act of July 14, 1798 1 Stat. 596, the Sedition Act, had a "sunset" provision making it expire on March 3, 1803 at the beginning of the next presidential term. As to the conduct of federal judges in Sedition Act cases, see James Morton Smith, *Freedom's Fetters: The Alien and Sedition Law and American Civil Liberties* (Ithaca: Cornell University Press, 1956), 221–46, 334–58. For their rejection of submissions that the act was unconstitutional, see Charles Warren, *The Supreme Court in United States History* (Boston: Little, Brown & Co., 1922), 1:159, 165; and Frank Maloy Anderson, "The Enforcement of the Alien and Sedition Laws," American Historical Association, *Annual Report for 1912* (1914), 113. The John Adams quotation is taken from a February 12, 1771 diary entry published in *The Works of John Adams,* ed. Charles Francis Adams (Boston: Little, Brown & Co., 1850), 2:254.

12. Engdahl, "John Marshall's 'Jeffersonian' Concept of Judicial Review," *Duke L. J.* 42: 279, 297–98. Madison's response to objections to Virginia's Resolution denouncing the Sedition Act is quoted from his "Report of 1800," reprinted in *Languages of Power: A Source Book of Early American Constitutional History,* ed. Jefferson Powell (Durham, N.C.: Carolina Academic Press, 1991), 139, 141.

13. Act of Feb. 13, 1801, 2 Stat. 89 (Judiciary Act of 1801, repealed by Act of Mar. 8, 1802, 2 Stat. 132); George Lee Haskins, *Foundations of Power: John Marshall, 1801–15,* Part I, *History of the Supreme Court of the United States* (New York: Macmillan Pub. Co, 1981), 2:169–77; Albert J. Beveridge, *The Life of John Marshall* (Boston: Houghton Mifflin Co., 1919), 3:122.

14. Thomas Jefferson to William Johnson, June 12, 1823, *The Writings of Thomas Jefferson,* ed. Paul Leicester Ford, 10:226. Section 13 of the 1789 Judiciary Act gave the Supreme Court "power . . . to issue . . . writs of mandamus, in cases warranted by the principles and usages of law, to any . . . persons holding office under the authority of the United States." Act of Sept. 24, 1789, sec. 13, 1 Stat. 73, 80.

15. Peter Charles Hoffer and N. E. H. Hull, *Impeachment in America, 1635–1805* (New Haven: Yale University Press, 1984), 193–236; Ellis, *The Jeffersonian Crisis,* 69–82, 157–70.

16. Hoffer and Hull, *Impeachment in America,* 188–98, 207–13.

17. Ibid., 254–55.

18. As reported by alarmed Federalists, Giles speech is recounted in "Extract of a Letter from Washington, December 20, 1804," Boston *Columbian Centinel,* Jan. 9, 1805, and in John Quincy Adams's, December 22, 1804 diary entry, published in *Memoirs of John Quincy Adams,* ed. Charles Francis Adams (Philadelphia: J. B. Lippincott & Co., 1874), 322.

19. Ibid.; Beveridge, *Life of Marshall,* 3:160–62, 176–79; *Dred Scott v. Sandford,* 60 U.S. (19 How.) 393 (1857).

20. United States Senate, *Journal of the Senate of the United States in Cases of Impeachments* (Washington, D.C.: 1805), 127–40; John Quincy Adams, *Memoirs,* 1:377.

Chapter 2

1. Stephen Gutgesell, *Guide to Ohio Newspapers 1793–1973* (Columbus: Ohio Historical Society, 1974). Regular reporting of Ohio Supreme Court decisions began with Charles Hammond's first volume of the Ohio Reports, published in 1823. Benjamin Tappan's *Cases Decided in the Court of Common Pleas of the Fifth Circuit of the State of Ohio* (Steubenville, Ohio: J. Wilson, 1831) is the first published volume of Ohio common pleas court opinions.

2. Act of Jan. 5, 1819, 17 Ohio L. 11, 13; Nelson W. Evans and Emmons Stivers, *A History of Adams County, Ohio* (West Union, Ohio: E. B. Stivers, 1900), 128.

3. George Turner to Governor Arthur St. Clair, Ft. Washington (Cincinnati), Oct. 25, 1790, and St. Clair to Turner, Fort Washington, June 18, 1791, both in St. Clair Manuscripts, OHS. Remarks of St. Clair on Proposals to Extend Powers of Single Magistrates, Cincinnati *Centinel of the North-Western Territory,* June 3, 1795.

4. Timothy Walker, "Letters from Ohio," No. II, *New England Magazine* 1 (Nov. 1831): 381, 382; 1802 Ohio Constitution, art. I, sec. 2.

A correspondent whose letter was published in the Chillicothe *Supporter,* Feb. 2, 1809, counted twenty-five of forty-eight Ohio House members as justices of the peace, and fourteen of twenty-four senators.

5. A Law for Establishing General Courts of Quarter Sessions, Aug. 23, 1788, in *Laws Passed in the Territory of the United States North-West of the River Ohio from the Commencement of Government to the 31st of December, 1791* (Philadelphia: Francis Child and John Swaine, 1792), 7 (setting $5 limit for single magistrates' courts); A Law for the Easy and Speedy Recovery of Small Debts, June 3, 1795, in *Laws of the Territory of the United States North-West of the Ohio* (Cincinnati: W. Maxwell, 1796), 32 (increasing limit to $12); Act of Dec. 19, 1800, in *Laws of the Territory of the United States, North-West of the River Ohio, Passed at the Second Session of the First General Assembly* (Chillicothe: Winship & Willis, 1801), 100 ($20 limit, in force at the time of statehood in 1803); Act of Feb. 18, 1804, 2 Ohio L. 146 (s/b 246) (limit increased to $35); Act of Feb. 12, 1805, 3 Ohio L. 14 (the "Fifty Dollar Act").

6. M. C. Reed, "History of the Ohio Judiciary," in Ohio State Bar Association, *Reports— Proceedings of the Annual Meeting* 9 (1888): 206, 259; Act of Feb. 16, 1820, 18 Ohio L. 100, 136 (attorneys excluded from appearing except to represent nonresidents or parties unable to attend on account of sickness, etc.). The exclusion was repealed by the Act of Feb. 24, 1814, 22 Ohio L. 337.

7. *Wallace v. Jaffree,* 472 U.S. 38, 49 (1985); *Minneapolis & St. Louis R. Co. v. Bombolis,* 241 U.S. 211 (1916). Art. VIII, sec. 8 of the 1802 Ohio Constitution provided that "The right of trial by jury shall be inviolate." Essentially the same provision is found in Art. I, sec. 5 of the present Ohio Constitution, originally adopted in 1851.

8. Act of Feb. 12, 1805, §16, 3 Ohio L. 14, 27; Mary Sarah Bilder, "Salamanders and Sons of God: The Culture of Appeal in Early New England," in *The Many Legalities of Early America,* ed. Christopher L. Tomlins and Bruce H. Mann (Chapel Hill: University of North Carolina Press, 2001), 47, 57. See also Bilder's "The Origin of the Appeal in America," *Hastings L. J.* 48 (July 1997): 913–68.

9. Art. III of the 1802 constitution established the Ohio Supreme Court and courts of common pleas and provided for their jurisdiction. Sec. 10 of that article provided that "the supreme court shall be held once a year in each county, and the courts of common pleas shall be holden in each county, at such times and places as shall be provided by law."

10. The 1802 Ohio Constitution provided in art. III, sec. 8 for appointment of judges by "joint ballot of both houses of the general assembly," and in art. II, sec. 8 for the governor's granting commissions to fill vacancies when the General Assembly was in recess. The terminology here employed in calling the process of legislators selecting judges an "election" was used by members of the houses themselves, in resolutions setting times to meet for that purpose. See, e.g., Ohio House of Representatives, Sixth General Assembly, *Journal* (1808), 151.

Ohio Supreme Court Judge Peter Hitchcock employed the same terminology in *State of Ohio v. McCollister*, 11 Ohio 46, 56 (1841).

11. Reed, "History of the Ohio Judiciary," 206, 230 ("a one and two ciphers"); Henry Howe, *Historical Collections of Ohio*, Ohio Centennial Edition (Columbus: State of Ohio, 1900), 1:972 (Tappan addressing a saddle-bag) ; A. G. W. [Alfred George Washington] Carter, *The Old Court House: Reminiscences and Anecdotes of the Court and Bar of Cincinnati* (Cincinnati: P. G. Thompson, 1880), 28–31 ("one mule and three jackasses").

12. Reed, "History of the Ohio Judiciary," 230.

13. 1802 Ohio Constitution, art. III, sec. 7.

14. The record of the case in the common pleas court is found in the Jefferson County Common Pleas Court Journal, 1803–1808, a single volume, at page 160. The record in the Ohio Supreme Court is found in the single volume of Jefferson County Supreme Court Records, 1803–1816, at page 47. Both volumes are now in the archives of the Ohio Historical Society's Youngstown Historical Center. As was customary these records contain only procedural history and judgment orders; they do not report parties' claims or contentions, the basis for rulings, or any judge's opinion.

15. The "M'Faddon" spelling first appeared in the *Liberty Hall and Cincinnati Mercury* in November 1807, as it published opinions of two members of the Ohio Supreme Court when the case was before that body. Those opinions were republished in 1952 in Ervin H. Pollack, *Ohio Unreported Judicial Decisions Prior to 1823* (Indianapolis: Allen Smith Co., 1952), 71–94, which in turn was the source for republication in Ohio Chief Justice Thomas J. Moyer's March 20, 2001 "State of the Judiciary" Report to the Ohio General Assembly, 91 Ohio St.3d cxxxii.

16. The account of the case in Carrington T. Marshall, *A History of the Courts and Lawyers of Ohio* (New York: American Historical Society, 1934), 3:722–27 has several discrepancies. *Rutherford v. M'Faddon* originated in Jefferson, not Trumbull County, and it was decided in the Jefferson County Common Pleas Court in December 1805, not in "1907" [*sic*]. More important than the decision's calendar date is that it was rendered *before* that court decided *The Cost Award Cases*, which are the subject of the judges' opinions published in the December 25, 1806 Chillicothe *Scioto Gazette*. Marshall's statement that the associate judges "overruled" Presiding Judge Calvin Pease in *Rutherford v. M'Faddon* is likewise incorrect. The record indicates that Pease did not participate in that decision.

17. Act of Feb. 12, 1805, 3 Ohio L. 14, 35.

18. Jonathan H. Cable, "Two Hundred Years of the Cable Family and the Legal Profession" (seminar paper, University of Toledo College of Law, 2001), 1–11; Austin Looper, *Two Centuries of Brothersvalley Church of the Brethren, 1762–1962* (n.p., privately printed, 1962), 145; Esther W. Powell, *Tombstone Inscriptions and Family Records of Jefferson County, Ohio* (Akron: n.p., 1968), xxxviii.

19. Anon., "Sketch of Hon. Calvin Pease," *Western Law Monthly* 5 (June 1863): 1, 12–13; William B. Neff, *Bench and Bar of Northern Ohio* (Cleveland: Historical Publishing Co., 1921), 57.

20. Judge Slaughter's defenses were set forth in his lengthy answer to the impeachment charges, Ohio Senate, Fifth General Assembly, *Journal* (1807), 98–102.

21. The charges against Judge Irwin are reported in Ohio Senate, Fourth General Assembly, *Journal of the Senate of the State of Ohio in Case of Impeachment of William Irvin* [*sic*] (1806), 10–11. Cases in other states in which judges were threatened with impeachment for having invalidated state laws include *Rutgers v. Waddington* (New York City Mayor's Court, 1784), recounted in

The Law Practice of Alexander Hamilton, ed. Julius Goebel Jr. (New York: Columbia University Press, 1964) 1:381–83; *Trevett v. Weeden* (Rhode Island Superior Ct. of Judicature 1786), in *The Bill of Rights, A Documentary History*, ed. Bernard Schwartz (New York: Chelsea House Publishers, 1971), 1:417–29; *"Ten Pound Act Cases"* (New Hampshire, c. 1786–87), recounted in Crosskey, *Politics and the Constitution in the History of the United States*, 2:968–71.

22. New Hampshire Act of Nov. 9, 1785, repealed by Act of June 28, 1787, *Laws of New Hampshire*, ed. Henry Harrison Metcalf (Concord, N.H.: Rumford Press, 1916), 5:101, 268; Portsmouth, New Hampshire *Spy*, June 30, 1787.

23. *Emerick v. Harris*, 1 Binn. 416 (Pa. S. Ct. 1808).

24. The Act of Feb. 22, 1805, 3 Ohio L. 36, 39, provided for issuance of writs of error or certiorari as a matter of course. No time limit was imposed.

25. Ohio House of Representatives, Fifth General Assembly, *Journal* (1807), 78–80.

26. Wyllys Silliman to Worthington, Zanesville, Jan. 20, 1807, and Edward Tiffin to Worthington, Chillicothe, Jan. 9, 1807, both in the Thomas Worthington Papers, OHS.

27. Jefferson County Supreme Court Records, 1803–1816, OHS Youngstown Historical Center, 47.

Chapter 3

1. 1802 Ohio Constitution, art. III, sec. 2. The title "Chief Justice" was introduced in 1912 by an amendment of art. IV, sec. 2 of the 1851 Ohio Constitution. In 1968 the same article and section were further amended to designate the court's other members as "Justices."

2. Act of Feb. 22, 1805, 3 Ohio L. 36, 36.

3. Levin Belt to Paul Fearing, Chillicothe, Dec. 3, 1802, Fearing Manuscripts, Dawes Memorial Library, MAR.

4. 1802 Ohio Constitution, art. I, secs. 2, 3, 5, 25.

5. 1802 Ohio Constitution, art. II, sec. 8; Calvin Pease to Edward Tiffin, Warren, Ohio, Mar. 7, 1806, Edward Tiffin Papers, OHS.

6. Ohio Senate, Fifth General Assembly, *Journal* (1807), 71.

7. John Tod, *Some Account of the History of the Tod Family and Connections* (n.p., privately printed, 1917), 45–55 (copy in WRHS Library); Jeffrey P. Browne, "Samuel Huntington: A Connecticut Aristocrat on the Northwest Frontier," *Ohio History* 89 (autumn 1980): 420, 421.

8. Act of Feb. 4, 1804, 3 Ohio L. 385, 387; Marshall, *A History of the Courts and Lawyers of Ohio*, 1:280.

9. Timothy Walker, "Letters from Ohio," No. I, *New England Magazine* 1 (July 1831): 30, 34.

10. Phi Beta Kappa Society, Alpha of Connecticut, *Minutes of Meetings, August 1787–June, 1801*, entry for Sept. 10, 1799, Sterling Memorial Library, Manuscripts and Archives Division, Yale University.

11. Howe, *Historical Collections of Ohio*, 2:660.

12. David Tod (George's father) to George Tod, New York, Jan. 4, 1801, George Tod Papers, WRHS; John Tod, *Some Account of the History of the Tod Family*, 175; George Tod, "Expenses of Building my House," memorandum dated Sept. 1802, George Tod Papers, WRHS; Zerah Hawley, *A Journal of a Tour Through Connecticut, Massachusetts, New York, the North Part of Pennsylvania, and Ohio* (New Haven: S. Converse, 1822), quoted in Harlan Hatcher, *The Western Reserve, The Story of New Connecticut in Ohio* (Indianapolis: Bobbs-Merrill Co., 1949), 84–85.

13. Jacob Burnet, "Letter from Judge Burnet to the Editor [Timothy Walker], on the Early

Bench and Bar of the West," *Western L. J.* 1 (Nov. 1843): 70, 76; Henry B. Curtis, "Early Judges, Courts and Members of the Bar," in *Bench and Bar of Ohio,* ed. George Irving Reed (Chicago: Century Publishing & Engraving Co., 1897), 62, 64.

14. Letter to Tod, Boston, June 27, 1804, Tod Papers, WRHS. The sender's name is illegible.

15. Cayton, *The Frontier Republic,* 68–83; Ratcliffe, *Party Spirit in a Frontier Republic,* 13–43.

16. Huntington to Moses Cleaveland, [from] Cleaveland [*sic*], Feb. 10, 1802, in Western Reserve Historical Society, *Tracts,* no. 95, pt. 2 (Cleveland: Western Reserve Historical Society, 1915), 73; Huntington to Tod, Chillicothe, Nov. 18, 1802, Tod Papers, WRHS.

17. Ohio Senate, Third General Assembly, *Journal* (1805), 76–77; Joseph Buell to Tod, Marietta, Feb. [date illeg], 1806, Tod Papers, WRHS; Edward Tiffin to Tod, Chillicothe, May 13, 1806, Manuscripts Relating to Early History of the Western Reserve, WRHS.

18. Daniel Symmes to Huntington, Cincinnati, June 21, 1807, Huntington Papers, OHS.

19. Jacob Burnet, "Judge Burnet's Second Letter," *Western L. J.* 1 (Dec. 1843): 97, 102–03 (1848); Francis P. Weisenburger, "A Life of Charles Hammond, the First Great Journalist of the Old Northwest," *Ohio Arch. and Hist. Soc. Publications* 43 (1934): 340.

20. Steubenville *Western Herald,* Aug. 22, 1807.

21. "Observations on the Opinions of the Court . . . by a Farmer," Steubenville *Western Herald,* Oct. 17, 1807; letters from "Agricola," and "Mechanic," ibid., Dec. 5, 1807; Chillicothe *Scioto Gazette,* Oct. 8, 1807.

Chapter 4

1. James Barr Ames, *Lectures on Legal History and Miscellaneous Legal Essays* (Cambridge: Harvard University Press, 1913), 354; Samuel H. Fisher, *The Litchfield Law School, 1774–1833* (New Haven: Yale University Press, 1933) and Marian C. McKenna, *Tapping Reeve and the Litchfield Law School* (New York: Oceana, 1986) are comprehensive histories of the school. Andrew M. Siegel, "'To Learn and Make Respectable Hereafter': The Litchfield Law School in Cultural Context," *New York Univ. L. Rev.* 73 (Dec. 1998): 1978–2028, addresses its social and cultural aspects.

2. Samuel H. Fisher, *Litchfield Law School 1774–1833: Biographical Catalogue of Students* (New Haven: Yale University Press, 1946); McKenna, *Tapping Reeve,* 174.

3. Fisher, *Biographical Catalog,* 3–4, 27, 47; Walter Theodore Hitchcock, *Timothy Walker, Antebellum Lawyer* (New York: Garland, 1990), 56–57; McKenna, *Tapping Reeve,* 197; Mary Tyler Mann, *Life of Horace Mann,* 2d ed. (Boston: Walker, Fuller & Co., 1865), 30–32, 383.

4. Don C. Skemer, "The *Institutio Legalis* and Legal Education in New Jersey: 1783–1817," *New Jersey History* 96 (autumn/winter 1978): 123–33; Armistead M. Dobie, "A Private Law School in Old Virginia," *Va. L. Rev.* 16 (June 1930): 815–18; Creed Taylor, *Journal of the Law School and of the Moot Court Attached to It, at Needham in Virginia* (Richmond: J. & G. Cochran, 1822).

5. J. H. Baker, *The Common Law Tradition* (London: Hambledon Press, 2000), 19–22; David Potter, *Debating in the Colonial Chartered Colleges: An Historical Survey, 1642 to 1900* (New York: Columbia University, 1944), 13–41; David Potter, "The Literary Society," in *History of Speech Education in America: Background Studies,* ed. Karl L. Wallace (New York: Appleton-Century-Crofts, 1954), 238–58; Edmund S. Morgan, *The Gentle Puritan, A Life of Ezra Stiles, 1727–1795* (New Haven: Yale University Press, 1962), 396–97; *The Literary Diary of Ezra Stiles,* ed. Franklin Dexter Bowditch (New York: C. Scribner's Sons, 1901), 15, 267, 289.

6. Potter, "The Literary Society," 241; Phi Beta Kappa Society, Alpha of Connecticut, *Minutes of Meetings, August, 1787–June, 1801,* YALE-MA.

7. Linonian Society, Yale College, *Minutes 1790–1797*, YALE-MA; Phi Beta Kappa Society, Alpha of Connecticut, *Minutes; Minutes of the Philolexian Society, Columbia College*, June 13, 1817, quoted in Potter, "The Literary Society," 250.

8. Donald F. Melhorn Jr., "A Moot Court Exercise: Debating Judicial Review Prior to *Marbury v. Madison*," *Constitutional Commentary* 12 (winter 1995): 327, 330–32.

9. Ibid., 332–33.

10. Julius Goebel Jr., *Antecedents and Beginnings to 1801*, in *History of the Supreme Court of the United States* (New York: Macmillan, 1971), 1:591; John Wickham, *The Substance of an Argument in the Case of the Carriage Duties, delivered before the Circuit Court of the United States, in Virginia, May Term, 1795* (Richmond: Augustine Davis, 1795), 15; Act of Mar. 23, 1792, 1 Stat. 243; *Hayburn's Case*, 2 U.S. (2 Dall.) 409, 410 n.2 (1792); *United States v. Hylton*, 3 U.S. (3 Dall.) 171 (1796).

Motion of Chandler (U.S. 1794) and *United States v. Yale Todd* (U.S. 1794), the Pension Act cases the Supreme Court decided without opinion, are recorded in Court minutes published in *The Documentary History of the Supreme Court of the United States*, ed. Maeve Marcus and James R. Perry (New York: Columbia University Press, 1985–), 1:222, 228, 375, 380, 494. In 1854 the Court itself published a note on the Yale Todd case in *United States v. Ferreira*, 54 U.S. (13 How.) 40, 53n (1854).

11. *Trevett v. Weeden* (Rhode Island Superior Ct. of Judicature, 1786), in *The Bill of Rights, A Documentary History*, ed. Bernard Schwartz (New York: Chelsea House Publishers, 1971); Samuel Greene Arnold, *History of the State of Rhode Island and Providence Plantation* (New York: D. Appleton, 1859–60), 2:525; *Bayard v. Singleton*, 1 Martin 48 (N.C. Superior Ct. 1787); *Emerick v. Harris*, 1 Binney 416, 417 (Penna. S. Ct. 1809).

12. *The Federalist, No. 78* (Alexander Hamilton); Swift, *A System of the Laws of the State of Connecticut* 1:51–52.

13. Siegel, "'To Learn and Make Respectable,'" 1995–2002; Fisher, *Biographical Catalog*, 65, 123.

14. *Continuation of Reports of Cases Argued and Determined in Moothall Society from August 5th 1797 to July 12, 1798*, 33–37, MS in the archives of the Litchfield Historical Society, Litchfield, Connecticut, reprinted in Melhorn, 347–49.

15. Ibid.

16. Ibid., 37–38 (349 in Melhorn reprint).

17. Ibid., 40–41 (350–51 in reprint); Swift, *System*, 52–53.

18. Ibid., 41–42 (351 in reprint).

19. Ibid., 42 (351 in reprint).

20. Ibid., 42–43 (351–52 in reprint).

Chapter 5

1. Ellis, *The Jeffersonian Crisis*, 159–60, 169; Ratcliffe, *Party Spirit in a Frontier Republic*, 124, 138. Members of other Republican factions were also called "Quids" by those who saw themselves in the mainstream. Virginians gave the name to "old Republicans" led by John Randolph, John Taylor and William Branch Giles, who in turn claimed to be "pure Republicans." James MacGregor Burns, *The Vineyard of Liberty* (New York: Alfred A. Knopf, 1982), 258.

2. William Thomas Utter, "Ohio Politics and Politicians, 1802–1815" (Ph.D. diss., University of Chicago, 1929), 55; Patrick M. Garry, *Scrambling for Protection: The New Media and the First Amendment* (Pittsburgh: University of Pittsburgh Press, 1994), 98.

3. Cincinnati *Liberty Hall and Cincinnati Mercury*, Nov. 3, Dec. 8, 1807. When the action came on for trial the following August in the Hamilton County Court of Common Pleas, Burnet conceded liability, and withdrew his not guilty plea in a parallel criminal prosecution. With only the amount of damages left to be contested in the civil case, the paper reported in its August 13, 1808 issue that "after a very lengthy examination and arguments, in which the independence of the court and the ingenuity of the bar were discovered, the Jury returned a verdict of 100 dollars damages." The court had not passed sentence in the criminal case when the August 13 issue went to press.

4. Act of Feb. 4, 1813, 11 Ohio L. 69, 74. Benjamin Tappan's, *Cases Decided in the Court of Common Pleas in the Fifth Circuit*, published in 1831, contains opinions in cases decided during the period 1816–1819 when Tappan was the circuit's presiding judge. In 1835 Ohio Supreme Court judge John C. Wright published a single volume of reports of decisions rendered on his supreme court circuit from 1831 to 1834. In a preface to that volume Judge Wright stated that for a time after he came to the bench his practice had been to discard his notes; but that "as he progressed, he took more copious notes, and transcribed them into a manuscript book in the form of reports, with a design of preserving some evidence of points decided." This book, on which the volume he later published was based, became Wright's "circuit companion." The Ohio Reports, the first series of officially published reports of Ohio Supreme Court opinions, was published beginning in 1823. Its coverage was limited to *en banc* decisions of the full court, together with a selected few of the circuit decisions rendered by two-judge panels like the one on which Judge Wright sat.

In Ervin H. Pollack's valuable compilation of Ohio judicial writings prior to 1823, the case next after *Rutherford v. M'Faddon* which contains an opinion on legal points is *State of Ohio v. Thomas D. Carneal*, decided by the Ohio Supreme Court in 1817. Pollack, *Ohio Unreported Judicial Opinions*, 133.

5. There is no official text of the opinions in *Rutherford v. M'Faddon;* they are known only as they appeared in newspapers of the time. The *Liberty Hall and Cincinnati Mercury*'s issues of Nov. 3 and 10, 1807 are the only surviving contemporary source for both the Huntington and Tod opinions. They ran earlier in other newspapers, Huntington's in the October 3, 1807 Steubenville *Western Herald* and the October 15, 1807 Chillicothe *Scioto Gazette*, Tod's in each paper's next weekly issue, but both of those issues are missing. The *Liberty Hall* text was reprinted in Pollack's *Ohio Unreported Judicial Decisions*, 71–94, and again as an appendix to Ohio Chief Justice Thomas J. Moyer's March 20, 2001 "State of the Judiciary" Report to the Ohio General Assembly, 91 Ohio St.3d cxxxii to cxlvii.

6. *Marbury v. Madison*, 5 U.S. (1 Cranch) at 179; Swift, *A System of the Laws*, 52.

7. *Trevett v. Weeden* (Rhode Island Superior Ct. of Judicature 1786), in *The Bill of Rights, A Documentary History*, ed. Bernard Schwartz (New York: Chelsea House Publishers, 1971), 1:417–29. Neither of the Pension Act cases decided by the U.S. Supreme Court, *United States v. Todd* (U.S. 1794) and *Motion of Chandler* (U.S. 1794) had a reported opinion. See Wilfred J. Ritz, "United States v. Yale Todd (U.S. 1794)," *Wash. & Lee L. Rev.* 15 (fall 1958): 220–31; Gordon E. Sherman, "The Case of John Chandler v. The Secretary of War," *Yale L. J.* 14 (June 1905): 431–51. A statement of the Yale Todd case was subsequently published by order of the Court in *United States v. Ferreira*, 54 U.S. (13 How.) 40, 52n (1851). For Professor Nelson's observation on early judicial review and minority rights, see his "Changing Conceptions of Judicial Review: The Evolution of Constitutional Theory in the States," *U. Pa. L. Rev.* 120 (May 1972):1166, 1177.

8. 1802 Ohio Constitution, art. VIII, sec. 7.

9. Ibid., art. I, sec. 26.

10. Steubenville *Western Herald*, Oct. 17, 1807.

11. Ibid., Dec. 5, 1807.

12. Obadiah Jennings to Tod, Steubenville, Dec. 26, 1807, Tod Papers, WRHS.

13. Steubenville *Western Herald*, Dec. 12, 1807; Cayton, *Frontier Republic*, 99–100.

14. Ohio House of Representatives, Sixth General Assembly, *Journal* (1808), 13.

15. Ibid., at 23; Jennings to Tod, Dec. 26, 1807, Tod Papers, WRHS.

16. Ohio House of Representatives, Sixth General Assembly, *Journal* (1808), 43, 61.

17. Steubenville *Western Herald*, Dec. 26, 1807; *Liberty Hall and Cincinnati Mercury*, Jan. 11, 1808.

18. Chillicothe *Scioto Gazette*, Jan. 4, 1808; Ohio House of Representatives, Sixth General Assembly, *Journal* (1808), 61; John Sloane to Benjamin Tappan, Chillicothe, Jan. 25, 1808, Benjamin Tappan Papers, LC.

19. Steubenville *Western Herald*, Feb. 12, 19, 1808 (Campbell); ibid., Mar. 4, 11, 1808 (Sloane). For a complete text of Sloane's speech, see the appendix to Hammond's *Rights of the Judiciary*, Appendix B.

20. Ohio House of Representatives, Sixth General Assembly, *Journal* (1808), 62; Sloane to Tappan, Chillicothe, Jan. 25, 1808, Benjamin Tappan Papers, LC.

21. Act of Dec. 24, 1807, 6 Ohio L. 132, repealed by Act of Jan. 24, 1809, 7 Ohio L. 108; Steubenville *Western Herald*, June 3, 1808; *Liberty Hall and Cincinnati Mercury*, Apr. 30, 1808.

22. 1802 Ohio Constitution, art. III, sec. 2; Act of Feb. 17, 1808, 6 Ohio L. 32, 35–36.

23. Ibid., 34–35; Act of Feb. 22, 1805, 3 Ohio L. 36,36.

24. Ohio Senate, Sixth General Assembly, *Journal* (1808), 157.

25. Act of Feb. 20, 1808, 6 Ohio L. 143; John Sloane to Benjamin Tappan, Canton, July 11, 1808, Benjamin Tappan Papers, Library of Congress.

26. Cincinnati *Liberty Hall and Cincinnati Mercury*, July 9, 1808.

Chapter 6

1. Chillicothe *Supporter*, Aug. 18, 1809; Steubenville *Western Herald*, Feb. 12, 19, 1808; Warren [Charles Hammond], *The Rights of the Judiciary, in a Series of Letters Addressed to John Sloan, Esq. Late a Member of the House of Representatives* (n.p., 1808), with appended text of Sloan[e]'s speech in the Ohio House of Representatives, to which the letters respond. The complete work is reprinted as appendix B. Citations below, to original page numbers, also retain Hammond's spelling of Sloane's name, without the *e*.

2. Steubenville *Western Herald*, Feb. 12, 1808; Sloan speech, *Rights of the Judiciary*, app. B, p. 35.

3. Steubenville *Western Herald*, Feb. 12, 1808; Sloan speech, *Rights of the Judiciary*, app. B, p. 39.

4. 1802 Ohio Constitution, art. VII, sec. 1; Steubenville *Western Herald*, Feb. 12, 1808; Sloan speech, *Rights of the Judiciary*, app. B, pp. 37–38.

5. Steubenville *Western Herald*, Feb. 19, 1808.

6. Sloan speech, *Rights of the Judiciary*, app. B, p. 37.

7. Thomas Jefferson, *Notes on the State of Virginia*, ed. William Peden (Chapel Hill: University of North Carolina Press, 1954), 120; see also Mendelson, "Jefferson on Judicial Review: Consistency Through Change."

8. Sloan speech, *Rights of the Judiciary*, app. B, p. 39.

9. Hammond, *Rights of the Judiciary*, Letter VI, app. B, pp. 30–31.

10. Francis P. Weisenberger, "A Life of Charles Hammond, the First Great Journalist of

the Old Northwest," *Ohio Archeological and Historical Society Publications* 43 (Oct. 1934): 337–427; *Osborn v. Bank of the United States*, 22 U.S. (9 Wheat.) 737, 744–93 (1824) (argument by Hammond, for appellants).

11. Hammond, *Rights of the Judiciary*, Letters I and II, app. B, pp. 5–6, 10.

12. Nelson, "Changing Conceptions of Judicial Review," 1177; Hammond, *Rights of the Judiciary*, Letter II, app. B, p. 10.

13. *Jefferson County Clerk of Common Pleas Record for 1806*, OHS-Y, 212. The entry reads: Judgments at December Term, 1806.

John Taggart v. Robert Carothers. Action for cutting down and destroying trees. Dec. term 1805 jury awarded $25 and costs. D's counsel (Hammond) moved for new trial "on the ground that the court misdirected the jury, instructing them that the justification set up under the Governor's Commission, commissioning the defendant as a road commissioner, could not avail him, he not having taken an oath of office." Consideration postponed to next term. Continued in August term, 1806. Now, Dec term, motion denied and judgment entered on jury award.

14. *State of Ohio v. Isaac Zane and Others* (Muskingum County, Ohio Court of Common Pleas, Dec. term, 1807), *Muskingum County Common Pleas Book*, MCA, 545; Hammond, *Rights of the Judiciary*, Letter III, app. B, pp. 13–16, B13–15; 1802 Ohio Constitution, art. VIII, sec. 4.

15. Act of Dec. 6, 1806, 5 Ohio L. 45; 1802 Ohio Constitution, art. VIII, sec. 12 (mis-cited by Hammond as sec. 10).

16. Ordinance of 1787, art. VI; Act of Jan. 5, 1804, 2 Ohio L. 63; Act of Jan. 25, 1807, 5 Ohio L. 53; Act of Feb. 22, 1805, 3 Ohio L. 272, 276; Hammond, *Rights of the Judiciary*, Letter V, app. B, p. 24.

17. Act of Jan. 15, 1805, 3 Ohio L. 1, 2; 1802 Ohio Constitution, art. VIII, sec. 1; Hammond, *Rights of the Judiciary*, Letter V, app. B, p. 25.

18. Hammond, *Rights of the Judiciary*, Letter V, app. B, p. 26.

Chapter 7

1. Chillicothe *Scioto Gazette*, Mar. 21, 1808.

2. Act of Feb. 14, 1805, 3 Ohio L. 248; Ohio House of Representatives, Fourth General Assembly, *Journal* (1806) 15–16; Act of Jan. 2, 1806, 4 Ohio L. 38; Huntington to Worthington, Chillicothe, Dec. 10, 1805, Thomas Worthington Papers, OHS. See generally, William T. Utter, "Ohio and the English Common Law," *Mississippi Valley Historical Rev.* 16 (Dec. 1929): 321–33.

3. The case is recounted in detail in Donald F. Melhorn Jr., "The First Trial in Ohio that Lasted More than a Day," *Ohio Lawyer* 9 (July/Aug. 1995): 16.

4. Huntington to Burnet, Chillicothe, Oct. 30, 1808, Samuel Huntington Papers, OHS; Sprigg to Meigs and Tod, Chillicothe, Oct. 31, 1808, Return J. Meigs Jr. Papers, OHS.

5. Judgment entry dated Nov. 19, 1808, Ross County Ohio *Supreme Court Journal, 1808–1815*, 43, RCA; Nelson W. Evans and Emmons Stivers, *A History of Adams County, Ohio* (West Union, Ohio: E. B. Stivers, 1900), 386–92.

6. Chillicothe *Scioto Gazette*, Mar. 18, 1808.

7. Worthington to Huntington, July 29, 1808, Western Reserve Historical Society, *Tracts*, no. 95, pt. 2 (Cleveland: Western Reserve Historical Society, 1915), 120; Sloane to Worthington, Columbiana County, Apr. 11, 1808, Thomas Worthington Papers, OHS.

8. Sloane to Worthington, Canton, Aug. 20 and Oct. 3, 1808, Benjamin Tappan to Wor-

thington, Ravenna, Sept. 15, 1808, all in Thomas Worthington Papers, Early Ohio Political Leaders Collection, OHS.

9. Steubenville *Western Herald*, July 22, Aug. 12, 1808.

10. Chillicothe *Scioto Gazette*, Sept. 6, 23, 1808.

11. Sloane to Worthington, Canton, Nov. 13, 1808, Thomas Worthington Papers, OHS.

12. Ohio House of Representatives, Seventh General Assembly, *Journal* (1808), 47, 79–80.

13. Ohio Senate, Seventh General Assembly, *Journal* (1808), 55, 57.

14. Ohio House of Representatives, Seventh General Assembly, *Journal* (1808), 136–37.

15. Ibid., 71–76.

16. Ibid., 79–80.

17. Ibid., 79–81.

18. *Chillicothe Gazette*, Bicentennial Supplement, May 1, 2000, 1, 24. The *Gazette* is the oldest continuously published newspaper west of the Alleghenies.

19. Ohio Senate, Seventh General Assembly, *Journal of the Senate of the State of Ohio in Cases of Impeachments* (1809), 54–55.

20. Ibid., 57; Willard Carl Klunder, *Lewis Cass and the Politics of Moderation* (Kent, Ohio: Kent State University Press,1996), 7–8.

21. Ohio House of Representatives, Seventh General Assembly, *Journal* (1809), 104, 113; John C. Parish, *Robert Lucas*, Iowa Biographical Series, ed. Benjamin F. Shambaugh (Iowa City: State Historical Society of Iowa, 1907), 18–24.

22. Chillicothe *Scioto Gazette*, Dec. 12, 1808.

23. Ibid.

24. Ibid., Dec. 26, 1808; *Northwest Ordinance*, §14, art. II.

25. Ohio Senate, Seventh General Assembly, *Journal of the Senate of the State of Ohio in Cases of Impeachments* (1809), 59, 93.

26. Stephen E. Wood to Ethan Allen Brown, Chillicothe, Jan. 6, 1809, Ethan Allen Brown Papers, OHS.

27. Answer of George Tod to the Article of Impeachment, Ohio Senate, Seventh General Assembly, *Journal of the Senate of the State of Ohio in Cases of Impeachments* (1809), 59, 60–61, 63–67, 68–69.

28. Managers' Replication, Ohio Senate, Seventh General Assembly, *Journal of the Senate of the State of Ohio in Cases of Impeachments* (1809), 70, 73–74.

29. Ibid., at 78, 85.

30. Sloan speech, *Rights of the Judiciary*, B37.

31. Answer of George Tod to the Article of Impeachment, Ohio Senate, Seventh General Assembly, *Journal of the Senate of the State of Ohio in Cases of Impeachments* (1809), 74.

Chapter 8

1. Ohio Senate, Seventh General Assembly, *Journal of the Senate of the State of Ohio in Cases of Impeachments* (1809), 9, 19; 1802 Ohio Constitution, art. I, sec. 15.

2. Ohio Senate, Seventh General Assembly, *Journal of the Senate of the State of Ohio in Cases of Impeachments* (1809), 94–95, 99–100.

3. Ibid., 95, 96; Ohio Senate, Third General Assembly, *Journal* (1805), 76–77; Ohio House of Representatives, Fifth General Assembly, *Journal* (1807), 78–80.

4. Ohio Senate, Seventh General Assembly, *Journal of the Senate of the State of Ohio in Cases of Impeachments* (1809), 70.

5. Ibid., 97; Chillicothe *Supporter,* Jan. 26, 1809.

6. Ohio Senate, Seventh General Assembly, *Journal of the Senate of the State of Ohio in Cases of Impeachments* (1809), 97–98; William Woodbridge to Paul Fearing, Chillicothe, Jan. 20, 1809, Hildreth Collection, MAR.

7. Chillicothe *Supporter,* Jan. 26, 1809.

8. Ohio Senate, Seventh General Assembly, *Journal of the Senate of the State of Ohio in Cases of Impeachments* (1809), 99; Woodbridge to Fearing, Chillicothe, Jan. 20, 1809, Hildreth Collection, MAR.

9. Chillicothe *Supporter,* Jan. 26, 1809; Woodbridge to Fearing, Chillicothe, Jan. 20, 1809, Hildreth Collection, MAR.

10. Ohio Senate, Seventh General Assembly, *Journal of the Senate of the State of Ohio in Cases of Impeachments* (1809), 99–100.

11. David Abbot to George Tod, undated [1808], George Tod Papers, WRHS.

12. *Emerick v. Harris,* 1 Binn. 416, 421 (Penna. Sup. Ct. 1808).

13. Chillicothe *Scioto Gazette,* Jan. 30, 1809; Ohio Senate, Seventh General Assembly, *Journal of the Senate of the State of Ohio in Cases of Impeachments* (1809), 100.

14. Ohio House of Representatives, Seventh General Assembly, *Journal* (1809), 164; Woodbridge to Fearing, Chillicothe, Feb. 12, 1809, Hildreth Collection, MAR.

15. Chillicothe *Scioto Gazette,* Feb. 13, 1809.

16. Ohio Senate, Seventh General Assembly, *Journal of the Senate of the State of Ohio in Cases of Impeachments* (1809), 21–24; William Creighton Jr. to Nathaniel Massie, Chillicothe, Jan. 30, 1809, in David M. Massie, *Nathaniel Massie, A Pioneer of Ohio: A Sketch of his Life and Selections from his Correspondence* (Cincinnati: R. Clarke & Co., 1896), 257.

17. Ohio Senate, Seventh General Assembly, *Journal of the Senate of the State of Ohio in Cases of Impeachments* (1809), 13–14, 24–33, 43–45.

18. Ibid., 45.

19. Ibid., 46–47.

20. Woodbridge to Fearing, Chillicothe, Feb. 12, 1809, Hildreth Collection, MAR.

21. Act of Jan. 24, 1809, 7 Ohio L. 43, 49.

22. Jewett to Jefferson, July 28, 1809, cited in the Introduction.

23. Jefferson to Torrance, June 11, 1815, cited in the Introduction.

Chapter 9

1. Message from Governor Samuel Huntington to the General Assembly, Jan. 30, 1809, Ohio House of Representatives, Seventh General Assembly, *Journal* (1809), 195–98; Daniel Symmes to Huntington, Chillicothe, Feb. 22, 1805, Samuel Huntington Papers, OHS.

2. Ohio House of Representatives, Seventh General Assembly, *Journal* (1809), 232.

3. Ibid., 285–86.

4. John Bigger to Tod, Chillicothe, Feb. 9, 1809, George Tod Papers, WRHS.

5. John Sloane to Worthington, Canton, Jan. 12, 1812, Thomas Worthington Papers, OHS.

6. Chillicothe *Supporter,* Jan. 26, Feb. 16, 1809.

7. Ibid., Mar. 2, 1809.

8. Ibid., Alfred Byron Sears, *Thomas Worthington, Father of Ohio Statehood* (Columbus: Ohio State University Press, 1958), 148.

9. Chillicothe *Supporter,* Mar. 2, 1809; *Dictionary of American Biography,* ed. Dumas Malone

(New York: Scribner's Sons, 1928–1936), 13:227–28 (entry for Thomas Morris).

10. Chillicothe *Supporter*, Feb. 16, 23, 1809; Ohio House of Representatives, Seventh General Assembly, *Journal* (1809), 285–86.

11. Chillicothe *Supporter*, May 25, 1809.

12. Chillicothe *Scioto Gazette*, June 5, 1809, reprinted in Chillicothe *Supporter*, June 8, 1809; "Extract of a letter from a gentleman in the lower part of the state, to a gentleman in this town, dated June 23, 1809," Chillicothe *Supporter*, July 6, 1809.

13. Chillicothe *Supporter*, Sept. 8, 1809.

14. Ibid., Aug. 4, 1809; Elliot Howard Gilkey, *The Ohio Hundred Year Book* (Columbus: F. J. Heer, 1901), 468.

15. *Reed v. Moore*, Chillicothe *Scioto Gazette*, Nov. 13, 1809 (Ohio Supreme Court, 1809); "Letter from a Gentleman in Warren, Trumbull County, dated Apr. 3, 1809," Chillicothe *Scioto Gazette*, Apr. 4, 1809.

16. Chillicothe *Scioto Gazette*, Sept. 25, Oct. 2, 1809.

17. Chillicothe *Scioto Gazette*, Feb. 13, 27, 1809; Chillicothe *Supporter*, Mar. 16, 1809.

18. Chillicothe *Independent Republican*, Nov. 20, 1809; Replication of the House Managers in the Trial of George Tod, Ohio Senate, Seventh General Assembly, *Journal of the Senate of the State of Ohio in Cases of Impeachments* (1809), 78.

19. Chillicothe *Supporter*, Aug. 11, 18, Sept. 1, 8, 1809.

20. Ibid., Sept. 22, 1809.

21. Ibid., Sept. 29, 1809.

22. Ohio House of Representatives, Seventh General Assembly, *Journal* (1809), 195; 1802 Ohio Constitution, art. II, sec. 16, art. III, sec. 8.

23. George Tod, Commission as Judge of the Ohio Supreme Court, Feb. 4, 1807, Rice Collection, OHS; William Sprigg to Judge Thomas Scott, Chillicothe, May 1, 1810 (quoting tenure provision of Sprigg's commission), Chillicothe *Independent Republican*, June 7, 1810. For the inconsistent practices in the framing of commissions for state offices with respect to statements of tenure, see *Ohio Governors General Record*, vols. 1 (1803–08) and 2 (1808–13), OHS.

24. Benjamin Tappan, "The Autobiography of Benjamin Tappan," ed. Donald J. Ratcliffe, *Ohio History* 85 (spring 1976): 109, 144; 1802 Ohio Constitution, art. III, sec. 8.

25. Ohio House of Representatives, Sixth General Assembly, *Journal* (1808), 161–62; Ohio House of Representatives, Seventh General Assembly, *Journal* (1809), 232, 285–86.

26. Ohio House of Representatives, Eighth General Assembly, *Journal* (1810), 181–82.

27. Resolution on the Subject of Filling Vacancies in Office, Jan. 16, 1810, 8 Ohio L. 349.

28. Ohio House of Representatives, Eighth General Assembly, *Journal* (1810), 305, 308; Ohio Senate, Eighth General Assembly, *Journal* (1810), 232–33; Act of Feb. 16, 1810, 8 Ohio L. 259, 314 (Judiciary Act) ; Act of Feb. 19, 1810, 8 Ohio L. 250 (Commissioning Act).

29. Ohio House of Representatives, Eighth General Assembly, *Journal* (1810), 429–30; Ohio Senate, Eighth General Assembly, *Journal* (1810), 235.

30. Sears, *Thomas Worthington*, 149–50; Chillicothe *Fredonian*, Sept. 19, 1811.

31. Ohio Senate, Eighth General Assembly, *Journal* (1810), 266–67.

32. Ibid., John Hamm to Ethan Allen Brown, Chillicothe, Jan. 6, 1809, Ethan Allen Brown Papers, OHS.

33. Sears, *Thomas Worthington*, 150.

34. Ratcliffe, "The Autobiography of Benjamin Tappan," 146.

35. Chillicothe *Supporter,* Dec. 30, 1809.
36. Cayton, *Frontier Republic,* 95.
37. Ratcliffe, *Party Spirit in a Frontier Republic,* 132.

Chapter 10

1. Sprigg to Judge Thomas Scott, Hagerstown, Maryland, Feb. 27, 1810, Dayton *Ohio Centinel,* May 10, 1810.

2. Sprigg to Tod, Hagerstown, Maryland, Feb. 28, 1810, Rice Collection, OHS; Sprigg to Huntington, Hagerstown, Maryland, Feb. 28, 1810, Rice Collection, OHS.

3. Sprigg to Tod, Steubenville, Mar. 10, Apr. 2, 1810, Rice Collection, OHS. A letter from "Civis" published in the Chillicothe *Scioto Gazette,* May 9, 1810, asks "with what propriety have Messrs. Tod and Sprigg, at Youngstown, on the 25th of March last, undertaken to declare the appointments made by the last session of the legislature, to be null and void? In a letter addressed to those gentlemen (those appointed) of that date, published in the Ohio Patriot, of the 7th of April, they are declared to be usurpers." "Justice," writing in the Chillicothe *Scioto Gazette,* June 6, 1810, quoted or paraphrased Tod's and Sprigg's assertion in that letter, that "a supreme court composed of the two new judges [Irwin and Brown] will be an absolute nullity to all intents and purposes."

4. Sprigg to Tod, Chillicothe, Apr. 12, 1810, Rice Collection, OHS.

5. Scott to Sprigg, Chillicothe, Apr. 22, 1810, Dayton *Ohio Centinel,* May 17, 1810.

6. Chillicothe *Scioto Gazette,* May 9, 16, 30, June 6, 1810.

7. Sprigg to Tod, Wheeling, June 12, 1810, Rice Collection, OHS.

8. Sprigg to Tod, Chillicothe, July 26, 1810, reprinted in the Sept. 20, 1810 Dayton *Ohio Centinel* from the Chillicothe *Independent Republican.*

9. Arndt M. Stickles, *The Critical Court Struggle in Kentucky, 1819–1829* (Bloomington: Graduate Council, Indiana University, 1929).

10. "Extract of a letter from a gentleman in Chillicothe, dated July 19," Dayton *Ohio Centinel,* Aug. 16, 1810; 1802 Ohio Constitution, art. I, secs. 8, 26; Ohio House of Representatives, Ninth General Assembly, *Journal* (1811), 91.

11. George Tod, Commission as a Judge of the Ohio Supreme Court, Feb. 4, 1807, Rice Collection, OHS.

12. Sprigg to Tod, July 26, 1810, reprinted in the Sept. 20, 1810 Dayton *Ohio Centinel* from the Chillicothe *Independent Republican.*

13. Chillicothe *Scioto Gazette,* July 4, 11, Aug. 22, 1810.

14. Dayton *Ohio Centinel,* Sept. 27, 1810; Chillicothe *Independent Republican,* Sept. 13, 1810.

15. Chillicothe *Scioto Gazette,* July 4, 1810.

16. William T. Utter, "Saint Tammany in Ohio: A Study in Frontier Politics," *Mississippi Valley Historical Review* 15 (Dec. 1928): 321–40.

17. Ratcliffe, *Party Spirit in a Frontier Republic,* 152–53.

18. Ohio Senate, Ninth General Assembly, *Journal* (1811), 66.

19. Ohio House of Representatives, Ninth General Assembly, *Journal* (1811), 14, 91–93, 96; Speech of the Hon. Thomas Morris, in Committee of the Whole, on the Subject of his Eligibility as a Member, Marietta *Western Spectator,* Jan. 4, 1811.

20. Hough to Worthington, Zanesville, Dec. 11, 1810; Carlos A. Norton to Worthington,

Zanesville, Dec. 14, 1810; James Caldwell to Worthington, Zanesville, Dec. 15, 1810, all in Worthington Papers, OHS.

21. Norton to Worthington, Dec. 14, 1810, Worthington Papers, OHS; Ohio Senate, Ninth General Assembly, *Journal* (1811), 112; Ohio House of Representatives, Ninth General Assembly, *Journal* (1811), 160.

22. David Purviance to Worthington, Zanesville, Jan. 29, 1811; Norton to Worthington, Zanesville, Feb. 1, 1811, both in Worthington Papers, OHS.

23. Chillicothe *Independent Republican*, Feb. 21, 1811 (letter published in *Liberty Hall and Cincinnati Gazette*, partially quoted without date; same issue has report of seventeen members joining, and report of James Morrow); ibid., June 27, 1811 ("The Writer").

24. Bigger to Tod, Chillicothe, Feb. 19, 1809, Tod Papers, WRHS, *Ohio Governors General Record 2* (1808–1813): 62–63, entries for Feb. 20 and 21, 1810, showing commissioning of sixty-nine associate judges for new seven-year terms.

25. *Ohio Governors General Record 2* (1808–1813): 63–101. Entries from Feb. 21, 1810 through the end of that year show interim appointments to fill vacancies created by resignations of sixteen associate judges.

Chapter 11

1. *Greene County, 1803–1908*, ed. Committee of Homecoming Association (Xenia: Aldine Pub. House, 1908), 37–39.

2. R. S. Dills, *History of Greene County* (Dayton: Odell & Meyer, 1881), 220; L. H. Everts & Co., *Combination Atlas Map of Greene County, Ohio* (Chicago: L. H. Everts & Co., 1874) 17.

3. Howe, *Historical Collections of Ohio*, 1:696.

4. *Greene County, 1803–1908*, 47; Chillicothe *Scioto Gazette*, Sept. 25, Oct. 2, 1809; Howe, *Historical Collections of Ohio*, 2:698.

5. George F. Robinson, *History of Greene County, Ohio* (Chicago: S. J. Clarke Pub. Co., 1902), 110; Dills, *History of Greene County*, 228.

6. John Phillip Reid, *Law for the Elephant: Property and Social Behavior on the Overland Trail* (San Marino, Calif.: Huntington Library, 1980), 19.

7. Robinson, *History of Greene County*, 52.

8. Ibid.

9. [Chapman Brothers], *Portrait and Biographical Album of Greene and Clark Counties, Ohio* (Chicago: Chapman Bros., 1890), 483.

10. Dayton *Ohio Centinel*, May 24, 1810.

11. Ibid.

12. *Greene County Clerk of Common Pleas Minutes, 1804–1813*, 80–88; *Greene County Court of Common Pleas Record, 1809–1815*, 120–21.

13. *Greene County Clerk of Common Pleas Minutes*, 89–91.

14. Chillicothe *Supporter*, June 12, 1811; *Greene County Clerk of Common Pleas Minutes*, 92, 93.

15. *Greene County Clerk of Courts Supreme Court Record*, Vol. A (1803–1822), 49.

16. Letter of Judge William W. Irwin to Governor Meigs, Zanesville, Jan. 5, 1811, forwarded with message from Governor Meigs, Ohio House of Representatives, Ninth General Assembly, *Journal* (1811), 161.

17. Ohio House of Representatives, Ninth General Assembly, *Journal* (1811), 169, 176–77, 204, 211–12; Act of Jan. 30, 1811, 9 Ohio L. 70; William W. Irwin to Ethan Allen Brown, Lancaster, Feb. 4, 1811, Ethan Allen Brown Papers, OHS.

18. Letter from Representative James Morrow to his Constituents, Feb. 4, 1811, Chillicothe *Independent Republican*, Mar. 7, 1811, reprinted from the Dayton *Ohio Centinel*.

19. David Huston to Governor Meigs, Greene County, Mar. 9, 1811, with marginal note: "Resignation of David Huston as Ass't Judge of Green County rec'd March 22, 1811. John McLean com'd to fill the vacancy same day," Return Jonathan Meigs Papers, OHS.

20. Letter of James Snowden "To the Resolution Judges," published in the Dayton *Ohio Centinel*, Mar. 21, 1811, reprinted in the Chillicothe *Independent Republican*, Apr. 4, 1811; letter of Judge William W. Irwin to Governor Meigs, Jan. 5, 1811, Ohio House of Representatives, Ninth General Assembly, *Journal* (1811), 161.

21. Letter of James Snowden "To the Resolution Judges," Chillicothe *Independent Republican*'s introduction, Chillicothe *Independent Republican*, Apr. 4, 1811. The complete work is reprinted as appendix F.

22. Handwritten note that "Council Fire No. 4" [Xenia] organizing petition granted Jan. 6, 1811; Jacob Smith to Thomas Scott, Grand Sachem, Chillicothe Wigwam, "23d of the month of Worms" [Mar. 11], 1811; both in Tammany Society—Chillicothe Wigwam Records, OHS.

23. Article in Dayton *Ohio Centinel*, reprinted undated in June 22, 1811 Chillicothe *Supporter* under the heading "More Confusion in the Judiciary."

24. Ibid.; *Greene County Clerk of Common Pleas Minutes*, 93.

25. Memorial of James Snowden, Ohio House of Representatives, Eleventh General *Journal* (1811), 80.

26. Dayton *Ohio Centinel*, June 22, 1811.

27. Ibid.; *Greene County Clerk of Common Pleas Minutes*, concluding entry for May 29, 1811: "Court adjourned until tomorrow morning nine o'clock. /s/ Francis Dunlavy."

28. Ratcliffe, *Party Spirit in a Frontier Republic*, 152; *Dred Scott v. Sandford*, 60 U.S. (19 How.) 393, 529 (1857); Francis P. Weisenburger, *The Life of John McLean: A Politician on the United States Supreme Court* (Columbus: Ohio State University Press, 1937), 4–9; Lebanon *Western Star*, Sept. 29, 1810.

29. Robinson, *History of Greene County*, 21; Dills, *History of Greene County*, 633.

30. Return Jonathan Meigs Jr. Papers, OHS. The petitions themselves are undated, but were likely all received around May 30, 1811, the file date under which the Meigs papers are chronologically filed. For the 1810 gubernatorial election returns, see Ohio Senate, Ninth General Assembly, *Journal* (1811), 25.

31. Chillicothe *Independent Republican*, June 13, 1811.

32. David Griffin to "Our Elder Brothers of No. 1 in Chillicothe, Green County, Xenia, Year of Discovery 319," Tammany Society—Chillicothe Wigwam Records, OHS.

33. *Ohio Governors General Record*, 2:139.

34. Ibid., 2:160.

Chapter 12

1. Creighton to Tod, Chillicothe, June 2, 1811, reprinted in Western Reserve Historical Society, *Tracts*, no. 95, pt. 2 (Cleveland: Western Reserve Historical Society, 1915), 157.

2. Chillicothe *Scioto Gazette*, May 8, 15, 22, 1811; Chillicothe *Independent Republican*, May 16, June 13, 1811; Chillicothe *Supporter*, May 18, 1811.

3. "Littlewigwam" to "Whiniskee, at the Great Wigwam," Xenia, "Month of Blossom 8" [May 8, 1811], Chillicothe *Independent Republican*, June 13, 1811.

4. Purviance to Worthington, Jan. 29, 1811, Worthington Papers, OHS.

5. Tappan, "The Autobiography of Benjamin Tappan," 144–45; "A Lawyer" in Chillicothe *Supporter*, Dec. 30, 1809.

6. Chillicothe *Independent Republican*, Aug. 22, 1811.

7. "Calpurnius" [Charles Hammond] to Judge William W. Irwin, Letter No. I, Feb. 25, 1811, in Chillicothe *Supporter*, Mar. 11, 1811; *Ohio Governors General Record* 2:159–160.

8. Weisenberger, "A Life of Charles Hammond," 346.

9. Chillicothe *Supporter*, Mar. 11, 23, 1811.

10. "Calpurnius" [Hammond] to Irwin, Letter No. I, Chillicothe *Supporter*, Mar. 11. 1811.

11. "Calpurnius" [Hammond] to Irwin, Letter No. II., Chillicothe *Supporter*, Mar. 23, 1811.

12. Chillicothe *Scioto Gazette*, May 22, 1811.

13. Cayton, *The Frontier Republic*, 108; Ratcliffe, *Party Spirit in a Frontier Republic*, 160; Chillicothe *Scioto Gazette*, Oct. 2, 1811.

14. Worthington to Meigs, Washington, Nov. 11, 1811, Return Jonathan Meigs Papers, OHS.

15. Creighton to Tod, Chillicothe, June 2, 1811, Western Reserve Historical Society, *Tracts*, no. 95, pt. 2 (Cleveland: Western Reserve Historical Society, 1915), 157; Couch to Worthington, Chillicothe, Nov. 18, 1811, Thomas Worthington Papers, OHS.

16. John Hamm to Worthington, Zanesville, Dec. 2, 1811, James Caldwell to Worthington, Dec. 14, 1811, both in Thomas Worthington Papers, OHS.

17. Ohio House of Representatives, Tenth General Assembly, *Journal* (1812), 47, 64, 69; Isaac Van Horne to Worthington, Zanesville, Dec. 12, 1812, Thomas Worthington Papers, OHS.

18. Ohio House of Representatives, Tenth General Assembly, *Journal* (1812), 84, 85.

19. McArthur to Nathaniel Massie, Zanesville, Dec. 18, 1811, in David Meade Massie, *Nathaniel Massie: A Pioneer of Ohio: A Sketch of His Life and Selections from His Correspondence* (Cincinnati: R. Clarke, 1896), 264; McConnell to Worthington, Zanesville, Dec. 17, 1811; Van Horne to Worthington, Zanesville, Dec. 19, 1811, Hough to Worthington, Dec. 21, 1811, last three letters in Thomas Worthington Papers, OHS.

20. Ohio Senate, Tenth General Assembly, *Journal* (1812), 120; Van Horne to Worthington, Zanesville, Jan. 4, 1812; Purviance to Worthington, Zanesville, Jan. 29, 1811, both letters in Thomas Worthington Papers, OHS.

21. Ohio Senate, Tenth General Assembly, *Journal* (1812), 130.

22. Ibid., 134; Ohio House of Representatives, Tenth General Assembly, *Journal* (1812), 165.

23. Ohio House of Representatives, Tenth General Assembly, *Journal* (1812), 85, 165.

24. Norton to Worthington, Zanesville, Jan. 8, 1812; Wyllys Silliman to Worthington, Jan. 12, 1812; both letters in Thomas Worthington Papers, OHS; George Tod, notes of Ohio Senate debate on repeal of Sweeping Resolution, George Tod Papers, WRHS.

25. Smith to Worthington, Zanesville, Jan. 9, 1812, Thomas Worthington Papers, OHS.

26. John Pollock to Worthington, Zanesville, Jan. 14, 1812, Thomas Worthington Papers, OHS.

27. Act of Feb. 14, 1812, 10 Ohio L. 89 (six congressional districts); Act of Feb. 14, 1812, 10 Ohio L. 92 (fixing permanent seat of state government); Resolution of Feb. 21, 1812, 10 Ohio L. 204 (naming it "Columbus"); Act of Feb. 8, 1812, 10 Ohio L. 58 (medical society); Resolution of Feb. 20, 1812, 10 Ohio L. 197 (canal from Hudson River to the Lakes).

28. Ibid., at 349.

29. *Ohio Governors General Record*, 2:159, 160.

30. Sally Tod to George Tod, Youngstown, Dec. 24, 1811, Tod Papers, WRHS.

31. Tod to Worthington, Zanesville, Jan. 29, 1812, Thomas Worthington Papers, OHS.

32. Ebenezer Granger to Tod, Zanesville, Feb. 27, 1812, Tod Papers, WRHS.

33. Worthington to Tod, Washington, Mar. 15, 1812, MSS separately held, in archives of WRHS.

Chapter 13

1. Silliman to Worthington, Zanesville, Jan. 12, 1812.

2. Sloan speech, *Rights of the Judiciary*, app. B, p. 37; Raoul Berger, *Congress v. the Supreme Court* (Cambridge: Harvard University Press, 1969), 188.

3. "Continuation of Reports of Cases Argued and Determined in Moothall Society from August 5th 1797 to July 12, 1798," 40, MS in the archives of the Litchfield Historical Society, Litchfield, Connecticut, reprinted in Donald F. Melhorn Jr., "A Moot Court Exercise: Debating Judicial Review Prior to *Marbury v. Madison*," *Constitutional Commentary* 12 (winter 1995): 327, 350; "Examiner" in Chillicothe *Scioto Gazette*, Dec. 12, 1808; Act of Jan. 24, 1809, 7 Ohio L. 43, 49.

Professor Larry Kramer would say that such acts of defiance of the *Rutherford* ruling by the bar and the legislature demonstrate what he calls "the practice of popular constitutionalism," something he admits is difficult to reconcile with judicial supremacy. But perhaps, as he suggests, this difficulty arises out of "much too simplistic a view." There is, Kramer insists, "a world of difference between [courts] having the *final* word and having the *only* word." Nothing in the doctrine of judicial supremacy, he insists, "requires divesting either the people or the political branches of legitimate interpretive authority." Kramer's hypothesis thus recalls Jefferson's invocation of "the prudence of the public functionaries" and "the authority of public opinion" to settle constitutional questions on which the branches of government disagree. Jefferson to Torrance, *Writings of Thomas Jefferson* 9:516. But unlike Jefferson, Kramer acknowledges the courts' word as final. Kramer, "The Supreme Court, 2000 Term," *Harvard L. Rev.* 115:4, 113.

4. *State ex rel. Ohio Academy of Trial Lawyers v. Sheward*, 86 Ohio St.3d 451, 463–67 (1999).

5. Ibid.; 1851 Ohio Constitution, art. VIII, secs. 4, 6, and 13, art. XIII, secs. 1 and 2.

6. Caleb Nelson, "A Re-Evaluation of Scholarly Explanations for the Rise of the Elective Judiciary in Antebellum America," *Am. Journal of Legal History* 37 (Apr. 1993): 190–224; Kermit L. Hall, "The Judiciary on Trial: State Constitutional Reform and the Rise of an Elected Judiciary," *Historian* 45 (May 1983): 337, 349–50; Timothy Walker, *Introduction to American Law* (Philadelphia: P. H. Nicklin & T. Johnson, 1837), 31, 72; Alexis de Tocqueville, *Democracy in America*, ed. Phillips Bradley (New York: A. A. Knopf, 1945), 1:100; *McCormick v. Alexander*, 2 Ohio 65, 75 (1825).

7. *Bingham v. Miller*, 17 Ohio 445 (1848).

8. *McCormick v. Alexander*, 2 Ohio 65 (1825) (rejecting constitutional objection to retroactive application of a law limiting time for levying execution on a judgment); *State v. Gazlay*, 5 Ohio 15 (1831) (upholding occupation tax on attorneys); *Lessee of Good v. Zercher*, 12 Ohio 364 (1843) (law purporting to validate defectively executed releases of dower rights, held unconstitutional); *Chesnut v. Shane's Lessee*, 16 Ohio 599 (1847) (overruling *Lessee of Good v. Zercher*); *Schooner* Aurora Borealis *v. Dobbie*, 17 Ohio 125 (1848) (act purporting to construe a previously enacted statute in its application to cases pending at the time the act adopted, unconstitutional as a usurpation of judicial power); *Bonsall v. Town of Lebanon*, 19 Ohio 418 (1850) (upholding consti-

tutionality of sidewalk assessment); *Griffith v. Commissioners of Crawford County*, 20 Ohio 609, app. (1851) (law for special hearing before supreme court held unconstitutional; in dicta judges disagree as to the constitutionality of law authorizing counties to subscribe for stock in railroads—the issue which the special hearing was intended to resolve).

9. *Griffith v. Commissioners of Crawford County*, 20 Ohio 609, app. 2–3 (1851) (Hitchcock, C. J. dissenting) (italics added). For a biographical sketch of Judge Hitchcock, see Marshall, *History of the Courts and Lawyers of Ohio*, 1:238.

10. Ohio Constitutional Convention (1850–1851), *Report of the Debates and Proceedings of the Convention for the Revision of the Constitution of the State of Ohio, 1850–51*, 2 vols. (Columbus: S. Medary, 1851), 1:279–81; 2:216, 696.

11. Pease to Tod. Lower Sandusky, Mar. 8, 1813, George Tod Papers, WRHS; "Extract of a Letter from Calvin Pease, Esq., dated Huron, May 3d, 1813," in Warren, Ohio *Trump of Fame*, May 5, 1813; Harrison to Secretary of War John Armstrong, Head Quarters, Lower Sandusky, Ohio, May 13, 1813, in *The Papers of William Henry Harrison*, ed. Douglas E. Clanin (Indianapolis: Indiana Historical Society, 1993–1999), microfilm reel 8, frame 247. For a comprehensive account of the battle see Larry L. Nelson, *Men of Patriotism, Courage, & Enterprise!: Fort Meigs in the War of 1812* (Canton, Ohio: Daring Books, 1985), 67–92. Tod's recruiting and training activities are chronicled in the Tod Papers, WRHS.

12. Ratcliffe, *Party Spirit in a Frontier Republic*, 208–18. In computing the average lengths of tenure of supreme court judges I have treated as separate the disconnected service segments of judges Meigs and Sprigg, who each resigned and thereafter returned to the court during the decade, and I have disregarded the later service of Judge Peter Hitchcock, who returned to the court after an intervening period of legislative service during the mid-thirties.

13. E. Cooke to Tod, Columbus, Jan. 15, 1823; Memorial to the Ohio House of Representatives, Dec. 1825 (mislabeled "Petition 1823"), Ephraim Brown Papers, WRHS; Order to Show Cause why Tod and Associate Judges should not be commanded to sign bill of exceptions, Ohio Supreme Court, Ashtabula County, Aug. 19, 1826; application for extension of time to file answer, Tod to the Ohio Supreme Court at Columbus, 1828; "Substance of an Affidavit prepared for me to make in the mandamus case," June 28, 1828; Writ of Mandamus commanding Tod to sign attached Bill of Exceptions, Ohio Supreme Court, Apr. 19, 1829; Jon Werner to Tod, Jefferson (Ashtabula County), Dec. 6, 1825, all in the George Tod Papers, WRHS; Henry B. Curtis, "Early Judges, Courts, and Members of the Bar," in *Bench and Bar of Ohio*, ed. George Irving Reed (Chicago: Century Pub. & Eng. Co., 1897), 1:65.

14. Act of January 20, 1823, 21 Ohio L. 9.

15. [Anon.], "Sketch of Hon Calvin Pease," *Western Law Monthly* 5 (June 1863): 5, 11, 14, 15; Hammond to Pease, Cincinnati, Feb. 16, 1824, Calvin Pease Papers, 1st series, WRHS; *McArthur v. Porter*, 1 Ohio 99 (1823).

16. Beveridge, *The Life of John Marshall*, 3:16; *The Bench and Bar of Northern Ohio*, William B. Neff, ed., 58. Chief Justice Marshall's first "opinion of the court" was in *Talbot v. Seeman*, 5 U.S. (1 Cranch) 1, 25 (1801).

17. *McCormick v. Alexander*, 2 Ohio 65, 75 (1825).

18. *Eakin v. Raub*, 12 Serg. & Rawle 330, 352 (Penna. Sup. Ct. 1825) (Gibson, J., dissenting); *McCormick v. Alexander*, 2 Ohio 65, 75 (1825) (italics added).

19. An example is *Chesnut v. Shane's Lessee*, 16 Ohio 599 (1847), where the court rehabilitated a statute adopted to remedy a defect in land titles which in *Lessee of Good v. Zercher*, 12 Ohio 364 (1843), it had previously held unconstitutional.

20. William E. Nelson, "Changing Conceptions of Judicial Review: the Evolution of Constitutional Theory in the States, 1790–1860," *U. Pa. L. Rev.* 120 (May 1972): 1166, 1176.

21. Act of May 1, 1854, 52 Ohio L. 100; 1851 Ohio Constitution, art. I, sec. 5; *Norton v. McLeary*, 8 Ohio St. 205, 209 (1858).

22. *Emerick v. Harris*, 1 Binn. 416 (Penna. Sup. Ct. 1808).

23. The Huntington and Tod opinions in *Rutherford v. M'Faddon* were reprinted in 1952 in Professor's Pollack's *Ohio Unreported Judicial Decisions*, and more recently as an appendix to Ohio Chief Justice Thomas J. Moyer's Mar. 20, 2001 "State of the Judiciary" Report to the General Assembly, published in the front of volume 91 of the Ohio State Reports (3d series), in pages numbered cxxxii to cxlvii. But while these reprintings have made the case somewhat better known than it was in Judge Ranney's time, they do not accomplish the result of regular publication in making decisions accessible to research systems on which judges and lawyers rely. *Rutherford v. M'Faddon* still has not been published in a way that would get it into either case digests, or the electronic data bases which now increasingly supplant printed materials as repositories of American case law. "91 Ohio St.3d cxxxii" doesn't call up anything on the computer.

Posthumous official publication of important judicial decisions is not unknown. In *United States v. Ferreira*, 54 U.S. (13 How.) 40, 53n (1854) Chief Justice Taney, by order of the Court, published a note on *U.S. v. Yale Todd*, a previously unreported case decided without opinion in 1794, before *Marbury v. Madison*, which Chief Justice Taney regarded as an early exercise by the Court of the power of judicial review.

24. "Instructions of the Town of New-Braintree [Massachusetts] to its Representative," *Worcester Magazine*, 1 (June 1786): 106; [Benjamin Austin], *Observations on the Pernicious Practice of the Law* (Boston, 1786); [Jesse Higgins], *Sermon Against the Philistines*, 2d ed. (Philadelphia, 1805); see generally, Maxwell Bloomfield, "Antilawyer Sentiment in the Early Republic," in *American Lawyers in a Changing Society, 1776–1876* (Cambridge: Harvard University Press, 1999), 32–59; Alexis de Tocqueville, *Democracy in America*, 1:279; James Madison, letter dated "1834," in *Letters and Other Writings of James Madison* (Philadelphia: J. B. Lippincott & Co. 1865), 4:349.

25. Levin Belt to Paul Fearing, Chillicothe, Dec. 3, 1802, Fearing Manuscripts, Dawes Memorial Library, MAR.

26. James Willard Hurst, *The Growth of American Law, The Law Makers* (Boston: Little, Brown and Co. 1950), 268.

27. Ohio Constitutional Convention (1850–1851), *Report of the Debates and Proceedings of the Convention for the Revision of the Constitution of the State of Ohio 1850–51*, 2 vols. (Columbus: S. Medary, 1851) 1:609.

28. Answer of George Tod to the Article of Impeachment, Ohio Senate, Seventh General Assembly, *Journal of the Senate of the State of Ohio in Cases of Impeachments* (1809), 59, 74.

Bibliography of Sources and Cited Works

Court Records

Greene County, Ohio Clerk of Common Pleas Minutes, 1804–1813. GCA.

Greene County, Ohio Court of Common Pleas Record, 1809–1815. GCA.

Greene County, Ohio Clerk of Courts Supreme Court Record, 1803–1822. GCA.

Jefferson County, Ohio Common Pleas Court Journal, 1803–1808. OHS-Y.

Jefferson County, Ohio Clerk of Common Pleas Record for 1806. OHS-Y.

Jefferson County, Ohio Supreme Court Records, 1803–1816. OHS-Y.

Muskingum County, Ohio Common Pleas Book. MCA.

Ross County, Ohio Supreme Court Journal, 1808–1815. RCA.

Manuscript Collections: Individuals

Brown, Ethan Allen. Papers, OHS.

Fearing, Paul. Manuscripts, MAR.

Huntington, Samuel. Papers, WRHS.

Jefferson, Thomas. Papers, LC.

Meigs, Return Jonathan, Jr. Papers, OHS.

St. Clair, Arthur. Papers, OHS.

Tappan, Benjamin. Papers, LC.

Tiffin, Edward. Papers, OHS.

Tod, George. Papers, WRHS.

Worthington, Thomas. Papers, OHS.

Other Manuscript and Record Collections

Continuation of Reports of Cases Argued and Determined in Moothall Society from August 5th 1797 to July 12, 1798. LHS.

Hildreth Collection. MAR.

Linonian Society, Yale College, Minutes 1790–1797. YALE-MA.

Ohio Governors General Record (1803–). OHS.

Phi Beta Kappa Society, Alpha of Connecticut. Minutes of Meetings, August, 1787–June, 1801. YALE-MA.

Rice Collection. OHS.

Tammany Society, Chillicothe Wigwam Records. OHS.

Western Reserve Historical Society. *Manuscripts Relating to Early History of the Western Reserve.* WRHS.
————. *Tracts.* Cleveland: Western Reserve Historical Society, c. 1870– .

Published Collections

Jefferson, Thomas. *The Papers of Thomas Jefferson.* Ed. Julian P. Boyd. 20 vols. Princeton: Princeton University Press, 1950–1982.
————. *Thomas Jefferson Correspondence, Printed from the Originals in the Collection of William K. Bixby.* Ed. Worthington Chauncey Ford. Boston: Privately printed, 1916.
————. *The Writings of Thomas Jefferson.* Ed. Andrew A. Lipscomb and Albert Ellery Bergh. Washington, D.C.: Thomas Jefferson Memorial Association, 1905.
————. *The Writings of Thomas Jefferson.* Ed. Paul Leicester Ford. New York: G. P. Putnam's Sons, 1892–1899.
Jefferson, Thomas, and John Adams. *The Adams-Jefferson Letters.* Ed. Lester J. Cappon. Chapel Hill: University of North Carolina Press, 1959.
Harrison, William Henry. *The Papers of William Henry Harrison.* Indianapolis: Indiana Historical Society, 1993–1999. Microfilm.
Hamilton, Alexander. *The Law Practice of Alexander Hamilton.* Ed. Julius Goebel Jr. 5 vols. New York: Columbia University Press, 1964–1981.
Madison, James. *Letters and Other Writings of James Madison.* 4 vols. Philadelphia: J. B. Lippincott & Co., 1865.

Newspapers

Boston, Massachusetts *Columbian Centinel.*
Chillicothe *Fredonian.*
Chillicothe *Independent Republican.*
Chillicothe *Scioto Gazette.*
Chillicothe *Supporter.*
Cincinnati *Centinel of the North-Western Territory.*
Cincinnati *Liberty Hall and Cincinnati Mercury.*
Dayton *Ohio Centinel.*
Lebanon *Western Star.*
Marietta *Western Spectator.*
New Lisbon *Ohio Patriot.*
Philadelphia *Aurora.*
Portsmouth, *New Hampshire Spy.*
St. Clairsville *Ohio Federalist.*
Steubenville *Western Herald.*
Warren *Trump of Fame.*

Constitutions, Statutes, Convention and Legislative Journals

Federal

United States Constitution.

Act of Sept. 24, 1789, 1 Stat. 73.

Act of July 14, 1798, 1 Stat. 596.

United States Senate. *Journal of the Senate of the United States in Cases of Impeachments.* Washington, D.C.: 1805.

Northwest Territory

Ordinance for the Government of the Territory of the United States Northwest of the River Ohio ("Northwest Ordinance"), 1787.

Act of Aug. 23, 1788. *Laws Passed in the Territory of the United States North-West of the River Ohio from the Commencement of Government to the 31st day of December, 1791.* Philadelphia: Francis Child & John Swaine, 1792.

Act of June 3, 1795. *Laws of the Territory of the United States North-West of the Ohio.* Cincinnati, W. Maxwell, 1796.

Act of Dec. 19, 1800. *Laws of the Territory of the United States, North-West of the River Ohio, Passed at the Second Session of the First General Assembly.* Chillicothe: Winship & Willis, 1801.

Ohio

Ohio Constitution (1802).

Ohio Constitution (1851).

Ohio Constitutional Convention (1850–1851). *Report of the Debates and Proceedings of the Convention for the Revision of the Constitution of the State of Ohio, 1850–51.* 2 vols. Columbus: S. Medary, 1851.

Act of Feb. 18, 1804, 2 Ohio L. [246].

Act of Feb. 12, 1805, 3 Ohio L. 14.

Act of Feb. 17, 1808, 6 Ohio L. 32.

Act of Jan. 24, 1809, 7 Ohio L. 43.

Resolution of Jan. 16, 1810, 8 Ohio L. 349.

Act of Feb. 16, 1810, 8 Ohio L. 259.

Act of Feb. 19, 1810, 8 Ohio L. 250.

Act of Jan. 10, 1812, 10 Ohio L. 23.

Act of Feb. 8, 1812, 10 Ohio L. 58.

Act of Feb. 14, 1812, 10 Ohio L. 89.

Act of Feb. 14, 1812, 10 Ohio L. 92.

Resolution of Feb. 20, 1812, 10 Ohio L. 197.

Resolution of Feb. 21, 1812, 10 Ohio L. 204.

Act of Feb. 16, 1820, 18 Ohio L. 100.

Act of Jan. 20, 1823, 21 Ohio L. 9.

Act of Feb. 24, 1824, 22 Ohio L. 337.

Ohio House of Representatives, Fourth–Tenth General Assemblies. *Journals* (1806–1812).

Ohio Senate, Fourth–Tenth General Assemblies. *Journals* (1806–1812).

Cases

Federal

Dred Scott v. Sandford, 60 U.S. (19 How.) 393 (1857).

Hayburn's Case, 2 U.S. (2 Dall.) 409 (1792).

Marbury v. Madison, 5 U.S. (1 Cranch) 137 (1803).

Motion of Chandler, (U.S. 1794).

Minneapolis & St. Louis R. Co., v. Bombolis, 241 U.S. 211 (1916).

Talbot v. Seeman, 5 U.S. (1 Cranch) 1, 25 (1801).

United States v. Ferreira, 54 U.S. (13 How.) 40 (1854).

United States v. Hylton, 3 U.S. (3 Dall.) 171 (1796).

United States v. Yale Todd (U.S. 1794).

Wallace v. Jaffree, 472 U.S. 38 (1985).

Ohio

Bingham v. Miller, 7 Ohio 445 (1848).

Bonsall v. Town of Lebanon, 19 Ohio 418 (1850).

Chesnut v. Shane's Lessee, 16 Ohio 599 (1847).

The Cost Award Cases, Chillicothe *Scioto Gazette*, Dec. 25, 1806 (Jefferson Co. Ct. of Common Pleas, c. 1806).

Griffith v. Commissioners of Crawford County, 20 Ohio 609, App. (1851).

Lessee of Good v. Zercher, 12 Ohio 364 (1843).

McArthur v. Porter, 1 Ohio 99 (1823).

McCormick v. Alexander, 2 Ohio 65 (1825).

Norton v. McLeary, 8 Ohio St. 205 (1858).

Reed v. Moore, Chillicothe *Scioto Gazette*, Nov. 13, 1809 (Ohio Supreme Court, Montgomery County, 1809).

Rutherford v. M'Faddon, Liberty Hall and Cincinnati Mercury, Nov. 3 and 10, 1807 (Ohio Supreme Court, Jefferson Co., 1807).

Schooner Aurora Borealis v. Dobbie, 17 Ohio 125 (1848).

State v. Gazlay, 5 Ohio 15 (1831).

State ex rel. Ohio Academy of Trial Lawyers v. Sheward, 86 Ohio St.3d 451 (1999).

State of Ohio v. David Beckett (Ohio Supreme Ct., Adams Co., 1808).

State of Ohio v. Isaac Zane, et al. (Muskingum Co. Ct. of Common Pleas, 1807).

Taggart v. Carothers (Jefferson Co. Ct. of Common Pleas, 1806).

Other States

Bayard v. Singleton, 1 Martin 48 (N.C. Superior Ct. 1787).

Eakin v. Raub, 12 Serg. & Rawle 330 (Penna. Sup. Ct. 1825).

Emerick v. Harris, 1 Binn. 416 (Pa. Sup. Ct., 1808).

Rutgers v. Waddington (New York Mayor's Court, 1784).

The Ten Pound Act Cases (New Hampshire, c. 1786–87).

Trevett v. Weeden (Rhode Island Superior Court of Judicature, 1786).

Books and Articles

Adams, John. *The Works of John Adams.* Ed. Charles Francis Adams. Boston: Little, Brown & Co., 1850.

Adams, John Quincy. *Memoirs of John Quincy Adams.* Ed. Charles Francis Adams. Philadelphia: J. B. Lippincott & Co., 1874.

Ames, James Barr. *Lectures on Legal History and Miscellaneous Legal Essays.* Cambridge: Harvard University Press, 1913.

Anderson, Frank Maloy. "The Enforcement of the Alien and Sedition Laws." In *American Historical Association Annual Report for 1912,* 113–26. Washington, D.C.: American Historical Association, 1914.

[Anon.] "Sketch of Hon. Calvin Pease." *Western Law Monthly* 5 (June 1863): 1–17.

Arnold, Samuel Greene. *History of the State of Rhode Island and Providence Plantation.* 2 vols. New York: D. Appleton, 1859–1860.

[Austin, Benjamin.] *Observations on the Pernicious Practice of the Law.* Boston: Adams and Nourse, 1786.

Baker, J. H. *The Legal Profession and the Common Law.* London: Hambledon Press, 1966.

Berger, Raoul. *Congress v. The Supreme Court.* Cambridge: Harvard University Press, 1969.

Beveridge, Albert J. *The Life of John Marshall.* 4 vols. Boston: Houghton Mifflin Co., 1919.

Bilder, Mary Sarah. "The Origin of Appeal in America." *Hastings Law Journal* 48 (July 1997): 913–68.

———. "Salamanders and Sons of God: The Culture of Appeal in Early New England." In *The Many Legalities of Early America,* ed. Christopher L. Tomlins and Bruce H. Mann. Chapel Hill: University of North Carolina Press, 2001.

Bloomfield, Maxwell. *American Lawyers in a Changing Society.* Cambridge: Harvard University Press, 1999.

Borden, Morton, ed. *The Antifederalist Papers.* East Lansing: Michigan State University Press, 1965.

Brown, Jeffrey P. "Samuel Huntington: A Connecticut Aristocrat on the Northwest Frontier." *Ohio History* 89 (autumn 1980): 420–38.

Burnet, Jacob. "Letter from Judge Burnet to the Editor [Timothy Walker], on the Early Bench and Bar of the West." *Western Law Journal* 1 (Nov. 1843): 70–76.

———. "Judge Burnet's Second Letter." *Western Law Journal* 1 (Dec. 1843): 97–104.

Burns, James MacGregor. *The Vineyard of Liberty.* New York: Alfred A. Knopf, 1982.

Carter, A. G. W. [Alfred George Washington]. *The Old Court House: Reminiscences and Anecdotes of the Court and Bar of Cincinnati.* Cincinnati: P. G. Thompson, 1880.

Cayton, Andrew R. L. *The Frontier Republic: Ideology and Politics in the Ohio Country, 1780–1825.* Kent, Ohio: Kent State University Press, 1986.

[Chapman Brothers.] *Portrait and Biographical Album of Greene and Clark Counties, Ohio.* Chicago: Chapman Bros., 1890.

Chipman, Daniel, ed. *Reports of Cases Argued and Determined in the Supreme Court of the State of Vermont.* Middlebury, Vt.: D. Chipman & Son, 1824.

Corwin, Edwin S. "The Rise and Establishment of Judicial Review." *Michigan Law Review* 9 (Dec. 1910): 102–25, (Feb. 1911): 283–316.

Crosskey, William Winslow. *Politics and the Constitution in the History of the United States.* 3 vols. Chicago: University of Chicago Press, 1953, 1980.

Curtis, Henry B. "Early Judges, Courts, and Members of the Bar." In *Bench and Bar of Ohio*, ed. George Irving Reed. 2 vols. Chicago: Century Pub. and Eng. Co., 1897.

Dictionary of American Biography. Ed. Dumas Malone. 20 vols. New York: Scribner's Sons, 1928–1936.

Dills, R. S. *History of Greene County*. Dayton: Odell & Meyer, 1881.

Documentary History of the Supreme Court of the United States. Ed. Maeve Marcus and James R. Perry. 5 vols. New York: Columbia University Press, 1985–1995.

Dobie, Armistead M. "A Private Law School in Old Virginia." *Virginia Law Review* 16 (June 1930): 815–18.

Ellis, Richard E. *The Jeffersonian Crisis: Courts and Politics in the Young Republic*. New York: Oxford University Press, 1971.

Engdahl, David E. "John Marshall's 'Jeffersonian' Concept of Judicial Review." *Duke Law Journal* 42 (Nov. 1992): 279–339.

Evans, Nelson W., and Emmons Stivers. *A History of Adams County, Ohio*. West Union, Ohio: E. B. Stivers, 1900.

Everts, L. H. & Co. *Combination Atlas Map of Greene County, Ohio*. Chicago: L. H. Everts & Co., 1874.

Fisher, Samuel H. *The Litchfield Law School, 1774–1833*. New Haven: Yale University Press, 1933.

———. *Litchfield Law School: Biographical Catalogue of Students*. New Haven: Yale University Press, 1946.

Garry, Patrick M. *Scrambling for Protection: The New Media and the First Amendment*. Pittsburgh: University of Pittsburgh Press, 1994.

Gilkey, Elliot Howard. *The Ohio Hundred Year Book*. Columbus: F. J. Heer, 1901.

Goebel, Julius, Jr. *Antecedents and Beginnings to 1801*. Vol. 1 of *History of the Supreme Court of the United States*. New York: Macmillan, 1971– .

Greene County, 1803–1908. Ed. Committee of Homecoming Association. Xenia: Aldine Pub. House, 1908.

Gutgesell, Stephen. *Guide to Ohio Newspapers, 1793–1973*. Columbus: Ohio Historical Society, 1974.

Hall, Kermit L. "The Judiciary on Trial: State Constitutional Reform and the Rise of an Elected Judiciary." *Historian* 45 (May 1983): 337–54.

Hamilton, Alexander, et al. *The Federalist*. New York: A. & J. McLean, 1788.

Haskins, George Lee. *Foundations of Power: John Marshall, 1801–15*. Part I of *History of the Supreme Court of the United States*. New York: Macmillan Pub. Co., 1981.

Hawley, Zerah. *A Tour Through Connecticut, Massachusetts, New York, the North Part of Pennsylvania, and Ohio*. New Haven: S. Converse, 1822.

[Higgins, Jesse.] *Sermon Against the Philistines*. 2d ed. Philadelphia: n.p., 1805.

Hitchcock, Walter Theodore. *Timothy Walker, Antebellum Lawyer*. New York: Garland, 1990.

Hoffer, Peter Charles, and N. E. H. Hull. *Impeachment in America, 1635–1805*. New Haven: Yale University Press, 1984.

Holmes, Oliver Wendell, Jr. *Collected Legal Papers*. New York: Harcourt, Brace & Howe, 1920.

Howe, Henry. *Historical Collections of Ohio*. Centennial Edition, 2 vols. Columbus: State of Ohio, 1900.

Hurst, James Willard. *The Growth of American Law, The Law Makers*. Boston: Little, Brown and Co., 1950.

Jefferson, Thomas. *Notes on the State of Virginia*. Ed. William Peden. Chapel Hill: University of North Carolina Press, 1954.

Kent, James. "An Introductory Lecture to a Course of Lectures, Delivered November 17, 1794." Reprinted as "Kent's Introductory Lecture." *Columbia Law Review* 3 (May 1903): 330–43.

Klunder, Willard Carl. *Lewis Cass and the Politics of Moderation*. Kent, Ohio: Kent State University Press, 1996.

Kramer, Larry D. "The Supreme Court, 2000 Term, Foreward: We the Court." *Harvard Law Review* 115 (Nov. 2001): 4–169.

Looper, Austin. *Two Centuries of Brothersvalley Church of the Brethren, 1762–1962*. N.p, privately printed, 1962.

Madison, James. "Report of 1800." Reprinted in *Languages of Power: A Source Book of Early American Constitutional History*, ed. Jefferson Powell, 139–47. Durham, N.C.: Carolina Academic Press, 1991.

Mann, Mary Tyler. *Life of Horace Mann*. 2d ed. Boston: Walker, Fuller & Co., 1865.

Marshall, Carrington T. *A History of the Courts and Lawyers of Ohio*. 4 vols. New York: American Historical Society, 1934.

Massie, David M. *Nathaniel Massie: A Pioneer of Ohio: A Sketch of His Life and Selections from His Correspondence*. Cincinnati: R. Clarke & Co., 1896.

Mayer, David N. *The Constitutional Thought of Thomas Jefferson*. Charlottesville: University Press of Virginia, 1994.

McKenna, Marian C. *Tapping Reeve and the Litchfield Law School*. New York: Oceana, 1986.

Meese, Edwin, III. "The Law of the Constitution." *Tulane Law Review* 61 (Apr. 1987): 979–990.

Melhorn, Donald F., Jr. "The First Trial in Ohio that Lasted More than a Day." *Ohio Lawyer* 9 (July–Aug. 1995): 16–17, 31.

———. "A Moot Court Exercise: Debating Judicial Review Prior to *Marbury v. Madison*." *Constitutional Commentary* 12 (winter 1995): 327–54.

Mendelson, Wallace. "Jefferson on Judicial Review: Consistency Through Change." *University of Chicago Law Review* 29 (winter 1962): 327–37.

Metcalf, Henry Harrison, ed. *Laws of New Hampshire*. 10 vols. Concord, N.H.: Rumford Press, 1904–1922.

Morgan, Edmund S. *The Gentle Puritan, A Life of Ezra Stiles, 1727–1795*. New Haven: Yale University Press, 1962.

Moyer, Thomas J., Chief Justice of Ohio. "State of the Judiciary" Report to the Ohio General Assembly, Mar. 20, 2001. 91 Ohio St. 3d cxxxii–cxlvii.

Neff, William B. *Bench and Bar of Northern Ohio*. Cleveland: Historical Publishing Co., 1921.

Nelson, Caleb. "A Re-Evaluation of Scholarly Explanations for the Rise of the Elective Judiciary in Antebellum America." *American Journal of Legal History* 37 (Apr., 1993): 190–224.

Nelson, Larry L. *Men of Patriotism, Courage & Enterprise!: Fort Meigs in the War of 1812*. Canton, Ohio: Daring Books, 1985.

Nelson, William E. *Marbury v. Madison: The Origins and Legacy of Judicial Review*. Lawrence: University Press of Kansas, 2000.

———. "Changing Conceptions of Judicial Review: The Evolution of Constitutional Theory in the States, 1790–1860." *University of Pennsylvania Law Review* 120 (May 1972): 1166–85.

Ohio State Bar Association. *Proceedings of the Annual Session of the Association*. Columbus: Ohio State Bar Association, 1880– .

Parrish, John C. *Robert Lucas.* Iowa Biographical Series, ed. Benjamin F. Shambaugh. Iowa City: State Historical Society of Iowa, 1907.

Pollack, Ervin H. *Ohio Unreported Decisions Prior to 1823.* Indianapolis: Allen Smith Co., 1952.

Potter, David. *Debating in the Colonial Chartered Colleges: An Historical Survey, 1642 to 1900.* New York: Columbia University, 1944.

———. "The Literary Society." In *History of Speech Education in America: Background Studies,* ed. Karl Wallace. New York: Appleton-Century-Crofts, 1954.

Powell, Esther W. *Tombstone Inscriptions and Family Records of Jefferson County, Ohio.* Akron: n.p., 1968.

Rakove, Jack N. "Constitutional Problematics, Circa 1787." In *Constitutional Culture and Democratic Rule,* ed. John Ferejohn et al., 41–70. New York: Cambridge University Press, 2001.

Ratcliffe, Donald J. *Party Spirit in a Frontier Republic: Democratic Politics in Ohio, 1793–1821.* Columbus: Ohio State University Press, 1998.

Reed, George Irving. *The Bench and Bar of Ohio, A Compendium of History and Biography.* 2 vols. Chicago: Century Pub. & Engraving Co. 1897.

Reed, M. C. "History of the Ohio Judiciary." In Ohio State Bar Association, *Reports—Proceedings of the Annual Meeting* 9 (1888): 206–70.

Reid, John Phillip. *Law for the Elephant: Property and Social Behavior on the Overland Trail.* San Marino, Calif.: Huntington Library, 1980.

Ritz, Wilfred J. "United States v. Yale Todd (U.S. 1794)." *Washington & Lee Law Review* 15 (fall 1958): 220–31.

Robinson, George F. *History of Greene County, Ohio.* Chicago: S. J. Clarke Pub. Co., 1902.

Schwartz, Bernard, ed. *The Bill of Rights, A Documentary History.* 2 vols. New York: Chelsea House Publishers, 1971.

Sears, Alfred Byron. *Thomas Worthington, Father of Ohio Statehood.* Columbus: Ohio State University Press, 1958.

Sherman, Gordon E. "The Case of John Chandler v. The Secretary of War." *Yale Law Journal* 14 (June 1905): 431–51.

Siegel, Andrew M. "'To Learn and Make Respectable Hereafter': The Litchfield Law School in Cultural Context." *New York University Law Review* 73 (Dec. 1998): 1978–2028.

Skemer, Don C. "The *Institutio Legalis* and Legal Education in New Jersey: 1783–1817." *New Jersey History* 96 (autumn/winter 1978): 123–33.

Smith, James Morton. *Freedom's Fetters: The Alien and Sedition Law and American Civil Liberties.* Ithaca: Cornell University Press, 1956.

Sosin, J. M. *The Aristocracy of the Long Robe: The Origins of Judicial Review in America.* New York: Greenwood Press, 1989.

Stickles, Arndt M. *The Critical Court Struggle in Kentucky, 1819–1829.* Bloomington: Graduate Council, Indiana University, 1929.

Stiles, Ezra. *The Literary Diary of Ezra Stiles.* Ed. Franklin Bowditch Dexter. New York: C. Scribner's Sons, 1901.

Swift, Zephaniah. *A System of the Laws of the State of Connecticut.* 1795, repr. New York: Arno Press, 1972.

Tappan, Benjamin. "The Autobiography of Benjamin Tappan." Ed. Donald J. Ratcliffe. *Ohio History* 85 (spring 1976): 107–57.

———. *Cases Decided in the Court of Common Pleas of the Fifth Circuit of the State of Ohio.* Steubenville, Ohio: J. Wilson, 1831.

Taylor, Creed. *Journal of the Law School and of the Moot Court Attached to It, at Needham, in Virginia.* Richmond: J. & G. Cochran, 1822.

Tocqueville, Alexis de. *Democracy in America.* Ed. Phillips Bradley. New York: A. A. Knopf, 1945.

Tod, John. *Some Account of the History of the Tod Family and Connections.* N.p., privately printed, 1917.

Utter, William T. "Judicial Review in Early Ohio." *Mississippi Valley Historical Review* 14 (June 1927): 3–24.

———. "St. Tammany in Ohio: A Study in Frontier Politics." *Mississippi Valley Historical Review* 15 (Dec. 1928): 321–40.

———. "Ohio and the English Common Law." *Mississippi Valley Historical Review* 16 (Dec. 1929): 321–33.

Varnum, James. *The Case, Trevett Against Weeden.* Providence: John Carter, 1787.

Walker, Timothy. *Introduction to American Law.* Philadelphia: P. H. Nicklin & T. Johnson, 1837.

———. "Letters from Ohio." No. I. *New England Magazine* 1 (July 1831): 30–34; No. II. *New England Magazine* 1 (Nov. 1831): 381–84.

Warren, Charles. *The Supreme Court in United States History.* 3 vols. Boston: Little, Brown & Co., 1922.

Weisenberger, Francis P. "A Life of Charles Hammond, the First Great Journalist of the Old Northwest." *Ohio Archaeological and Historical Society Publications [Ohio History]* 43 (Oct. 1934): 337–427.

———. *The Life of John McLean.* Columbus: Ohio State University Press, 1937.

Wickham, John. *The Substance of an Argument in the Case of the Carriage Duties, Delivered before the Circuit Court of the United States, In Virginia, May Term, 1795.* Richmond: Augustine Davis, 1795.

Unpublished Dissertations and Papers

Cable, Jonathan H. "Two Hundred Years of the Cable Family and the Legal Profession." Seminar paper, University of Toledo College of Law, 2001.

Utter, William Thomas. "Ohio Politics and Politicians, 1802–1815." Ph.D dissertation, University of Chicago, 1929.

Index

Abbot, David, 112
Adams, Abigail, 3
Adams, John, 13
Adams, John Quincy, 18
Addison, Alexander, 15
Ames, James Barr, 47
Anti-Federalists, 9
appeals, early nineteenth century, 23. *See also* *certiorari*
Associate Judges. *See* common Pleas Courts, Ohio
Aurora, 61, 69

bar, admission to, Ohio and Northwest Territory, 39, 44
Bayard v. Singleton, 55. *See also* Spaight, Richard
Beckett, William, 89, 91
Belt, Levin, 36, 133, 189
Berger, Raoul, 179
Bigger, John, 108, 113, 120
Binney, Horace, 113, 188
Blackstone, William, 11
Borders, Peter, 149–50
Browder v. Mendenhall, 154, 155, 157
Brown, Ethan Allen, 101, 133–34, 183
Brush, Henry, 89, 98, 102, 110, 115–16, 142, 144, 146
Bull, Epaphras, 50
Burnet, Jacob, 40, 44
    assault on Cincinnati newspaperman, 62
    "Examiner" letter, 99–101, 180
    impeachment counsel for Tod, 98, 102
Burr, Aaron, 47, 49, 98

Cabell, Philip, 27, 29–30. *See also Rutherford v. M'Faddon*
Caldwell, James, 146, 171
Calhoun, John C., 49–50
Campbell, Alexander
    impeachment prosecutions, Tod and Pease, 99, 110, 111, 116
    Ohio House, 1807–08, opposition to judicial review, 72, 73, 77, 79
Cass, Lewis
    impeachment counsel for Tod, 98–99, 111
    Lawyers' Circular Letter, 115
Cayton, Andrew R. L., xiv, 1, 135
certiorari, 23, 26
Chase, Samuel, 13, 16–17
Chillicothe, city of. *See under* Ohio state capital
Chillicothe *Independent Republican*
    denounces *Scioto Gazette*, 142–43
    support of judicial independence as voice of moderate Republicans, 135
    Sweeping Resolution and Ohio Supreme Court, 139–41
    Tammany Society, 147
Chillicothe *Scioto Gazette*
    Cost Award Cases, 19
    Lawyers' Circular Letter, 127
    legislative elections, 126, 142
    Morris rape charge, 124
    Rutherford v. M'Faddon, 46
    Sweeping Resolution, 138–39
Chillicothe *Supporter*
    judicial elections, 123
    Morris rape charge, 124–25

Sweeping Resolution, 123, 134

Tod, Pease impeachment trials, 108–111, 121–23

Chipman, Daniel, 11–12

Cincinnati, city of. *See under* Ohio state capital

Circular Letter, Members of Ohio Bar, January, 1809, 115, 127, 180

college literary societies, 52–53. *See also* Phi Beta Kappa

Collett, Joshua, 124, 154–55

Collier, James, 159, 160

Columbus, city of. *See under* Ohio state capital

common law, 88–89, 152

common pleas courts, Ohio, 22, 24, 26, 27, 75 (*see also under* county names)
>> Associate Judges, 24–26
>> incumbents and the Sweeping Resolution, 148 (*see also under* individual names)
>> Presiding Judges, 24–25

concurrent review, 3

Congress, U.S., Ohio seats, 169, 172, 175

Constitutions, U. S., Ohio, constitutional conventions. *See* Ohio Constitution, 1802, *id.* 1851; U.S. Constitution

Cost Award Cases
>> first published Ohio decision, 19
>> issues in, opinions, 28–30
>> proceedings in Jefferson County Court of Common Pleas, 27–28

Couch, Jessup, 115

courthouses, Ohio counties, 26, 30, 149–52

courts, other states:
>> judicial review, 7, 32–33, 55–56, 112–13, 188
>> Kentucky Supreme Court schism, 1823–1826, 140–41
>> New Hampshire, 32–33
>> Pennsylvania (*see* impeachment trials, Pennsylvania judges; *Emerick v. Harris*)

Creighton, William, Jr.
>> defense counsel in *State v. Beckett*, 89

impeachment counsel for Pease, 115–16

impeachment counsel for Tod, 98, 102, 107, 110

Lawyers' Circular Letter, 115

Ohio House, 1810–1811, 144, 146, 170

Ohio secretary of state, expiration of term as, 129

Tammany Society, opposition to, 164

Crosskey, William, 7

Davis, Owen, 150

Dayton *Ohio Centinel*
>> Greene County Court of Common Pleas, 153–54, 159–60
>> Morris, Thomas, 141
>> Sweeping Resolution, 142, 157–58

debating in American colleges, 52–53. *See also* Phi Beta Kappa

Dred Scott v. Sandford, 18, 161

Duane, William, 61

Dunlavy, Francis, 91, 133, 149, 152–54, 159–61, 176. *See also* Greene County Court of Common Pleas

Eakin v. Raub, 13–13

Edwards, Abraham, 171–72

Edwards, John Starke, 50, 57, 59

elections, Ohio, governor and legislators. *See also* judicial elections and appointments
>> 1807: Worthington, Meigs, Massie, Kirker, 70–71
>> 1808: Worthington, Kirker, Huntington, judiciary principal issue, 76, 92–94, 99 (*see also* Chillicothe *Scioto Gazette* and Steubenville *Western Herald*)
>> 1809: House and Senate elections, impeachment verdict, 126–28 (*see also* Chillicothe *Scioto Gazette*, Chillicothe *Supporter*)
>> 1810: Worthington, Meigs, Sweeping Resolution, 141–45, 151
>> 1811: House and Senate elections, Ross, Greene county contests, 170

1814, 1820: "no party" gubernatorial elections, Worthington, Brown, 183
Elliott, Thomas, 116
Emerick v. Harris, 33, 56, 112–13, 188
en banc sessions. *See under* Supreme Court, Ohio
Engdahl, David, 7
Ewing, Thomas, 186

Fearing, Paul, 36, 41, 110, 111, 117
federal judiciary, Republicans' mistrust of, 12–14
Federalist, The, No. 78, 9–12, 15, 187
Federalists, Federalist Party
    U.S., 2, 3, 12, 17
    Ohio, 40–41, 98, 172
Fifty Dollar Act, 21, 23–26, 45, 70–73, 76, 77–78, 91, 93–95, 100–02, 108, 112–16, 125–26, 135, 142–43, 180. *See also* Seventy Dollar Act; Three Hundred Dollar Act
Finlay, David, 166, 176
Fisher, Samuel H., 47
Fourth of July, Cincinnati celebrations, 1808, 76
Fulton, Jesse, 166, 176

Gazlay, James, 25
General Assembly, Ohio
    elections of judicial, executive branch officers, 24–25
    legislative sessions, 36–37
Gibson, John, 187
Giles, William Branch, 17–18, 32
Goebel, Julius, 54
Greene County Court of Common Pleas
    court sessions (terms): August, 1803: Borders cabin, 149–50; May, 1810: Huston, Snowden refusals to serve under Sweeping Resolution, Browder, Richards, Cottrell trials, 153–55; May, 1811: Snowden's violent ouster, McLean's resignation, 159–61; September, 1812: normal function restored, 163

judges, 1809–1811, 152–53, 157, 162–63, 176 (*see also* individual names); petition campaigns for successor associate judge's appointment, 162–63
Greene County, Ohio. *See also* Greene County Court of Common Pleas; Xenia, Ohio
    formation in 1803, 149
    representatives in Ohio General Assembly, 153–54, 157, 163
Griffin, David, 163

Haines, Jacob, 162–63, 176
Hamilton, Alexander, 7, 9–12, 15, 25, 55–57, 64, 102
Hamm, John, 133, 171
Hammond, Charles
    Cost Award Cases, 28
    journalist, career as, 167
    Lawyers' Circular Letter, 115
    reporter, Ohio Supreme Court decisions, 184, 186
    Rights of the Judiciary, 81–87
    Rutherford v. M'Faddon, 27–28, 44–45
    Sweeping Resolution, 166–69
Harrison, William Henry, 170, 183
Harvard Law School, 47–48
Hitchcock, Peter, 182, 187
Holmes, Oliver Wendell, Jr., 8
Hough, Benjamin, 26–27, 33, 44–45, 71, 107, 112, 145. *See also Rutherford v. M'Faddon*
House of Representatives, Ohio
    1806–07 session: *Cost Award Cases,* Lewis Committee report, 33–34
    1807–08 session: *Rutherford v. M'Faddon,* Worthington Committee report, Campbell, Sloane debates, 71–73, 77–80
    Greene County judicial impasse, 156
    impeachment proceedings, Tod and Pease, 94–99, 102–05, 114 (*see also* impeachment trial, Tod; *id.,* Pease)
    Morris's challenge to ouster, 144–45
    Sweeping Resolution, repeal, 146, 171–72, 174
Hubbard, Elijah, 57, 59

Huntington, Samuel. *See also Rutherford v. M'Faddon*
  advocate of statehood, 41
  as Governor, avoidance of issues re judiciary, 94–95, 137
  chief judge, Ohio Supreme Court, 36, 41–43, 46, 76, 88–89
  common law, durability of, 88
  Connecticut background, 37, 39
  delegate, 1802 Ohio constitutional convention, 41
  gubernatorial election, 1808, 76, 92–94
  impeachment charges avoided, 94
  opinion in *Rutherford v. M'Faddon*, 45–46, 63–66, 68–69, 93, 181, 186
  recommendations re Ohio Supreme Court judgeships, 119–20
  State v. Beckett, 89–91
  Sweeping Resolution, 129, 131, 137, 148, 153, 170–72, 175
Hurst, Willard, 189
Huston, David. *See also* Greene County Court of Common Pleas
  associate judge, Greene County Court of Common Pleas, 152–53, 155
  refusal to accept re-election pursuant to Sweeping Resolution, 153–54
  resigned to break impasse, 157

impeachment. *See also* impeachment trial(s), [name]
  grounds for, 16–17, 32, 113
  other states' judges threatened with, in re judicial review, 32–33
  vehicle for testing judicial review's legitimacy, 32
impeachment trial, Samuel Chase, 16–17
impeachment trial, William Irwin [sometimes "Irvin"], 32
impeachment trial, Calvin Pease, 95–98, 106, 115–117
impeachment trials, Pennsylvania judges, 15–17, 33, 113
impeachment trial, John Pickering, 16

impeachment trial, Robert F. Slaughter, 31–32
impeachment trial, George Tod
  aftermath of frustration, disquiet, 114–15, 117
  answer, Tod's, 102–04, "stability and value" conclusion, 105, 191
  arguments, 110–12
  charges, 95–96
  counsel, 98–99, 107
  defense strategy, 99, 101
  Elliott, Thomas, previous support of judicial review, 110–11
  evidence, 107–08
  "Examiner" letter, 99–101
  Managers' Replication, 104–05
  newspaper coverage (*see under* Chillicothe *Supporter*)
  process and procedure, 96–98, 106
  trial proceedings, verdict, 107–14
Independent Republican. See Chillicothe Independent Republican
"independent Republicans." *See* Republicans, Republican Party, Ohio
Institutio Legalis. See moot courts
Iredell, James, 55
Ireland, Mary, 124–25
Irwin, Thomas, 117, 172
Irwin, William, 71–72, 133, 156–57
  controversy over Sweeping Resolution, 137–38, 156–57, 167–69
Irwin, William [sometimes "Irvin"], 32

Jay, John, 7, 9
Jefferson, Thomas
  advice re study of law, 51
  concurrent review, 3–5, 118
  Jewett letter, 1, 2, 118
  judiciary an "effectual check," 3
  Notes on the State of Virginia, 3, 79
  Sedition Act, 3, 13–14
  separation of powers, 3, 79
Jefferson County Court of Common Pleas, 2–8
  Cost Award Cases, 19, 27–30
  Rutherford v. M'Faddon, 26–27

Jennings [sometimes "Jenings"], Obadiah, 28, 44, 70

Jewett, Leonard, 1, 132
    letter to Jefferson, 1–2

judicial branch, as best suited to decide constitutional questions, 10, 11, 56

judicial elections and appointments
    election by popular vote, 1851 constitution, 11, 181
    Ohio common pleas courts: presiding judges: 24–25; associate judges: 24–26; threat to block 1812 elections: 172, 175
    Ohio Supreme Court: Tod, 1806 and 1807, 37, 42; Sprigg and Meigs, "fourth" seat, 1808, 76; Scott and Morris, unknowable successor to "fourth" seat, 1809, 119–20, 123, 131–32; Scott, Irwin, and Brown elected, Tod, Sprigg, and Morris ousted, 133–34

judicial independence, 88, 135

judicial office, 24–26. *See also* common pleas courts, Ohio; Supreme Court, Ohio; judicial elections and appointments;
Greene County Court of Common Pleas
    commissions for, 129–32, 148, 153, 171–74
    oath required, 63–64, 78, 86, 148, 153

judicial opinions
    early Ohio cases, 62–63
    "opinions of the court," Ohio and U.S. Supreme Courts, 186
    regular reporting of, 19

judicial review. *See also* concurrent review, judicial supremacy
    arguments Ohio disputants failed to meet, 180
    arguments *contra*: Zephaniah Swift, 11, 65
    arguments *pro*: Hamilton, Marshall, 9–10, 15, 65
    debated in letters published in Ohio newspapers:
        "A Back-Woodsman," *Scioto Gazette*, 1810, 142

        "Agricola," *Western Herald*, 1807, 69–70
        "Agrippina," *Western Herald*, 1808, 93
        Captain Hare's militia muster, *Scioto Gazette*, 1810, 142
        "Examiner," *Scioto Gazette*, 1808, 99–101, 180
        "Farmer," *Western Herald*, 1807, 69
        "Gaius Graccus," *Western Herald*, 1808, 93
        "Horatius," *Scioto Gazette*, 1808, 93–94
        "Justice," *Scioto Gazette*, 1810, 139
        "Mechanic," *Western Herald*, 1807, 69
        "Old Jowler," *Supporter*, 1809, 127
        "One of the People," *Scioto Gazette*, 1809, 127
        "Plain Farmer," *Scioto Gazette*, 1808, 93
        "Seventy Six," *Supporter*, 1809, 128
    debated in Ohio General Assembly (*see under* House of Representatives, Ohio)
    defended by Charles Hammond (*see Rights of the Judiciary*)
    established in Ohio constitutional law, 181–83, 189–91
    formerly a Republican doctrine, 128
    Greene County citizens' resolution, 127
    impeachment threats to other states' judges, for claiming power, 32
    legislature's popular mandate, as constitutional limitation on, 187
    not contemplated under early state constitutions, 11–12
    Ohio cases recognizing power, post-1820, 182
    rejected in circuit decision of Scott and Sprigg, 1809 (*see Reed v. Moore*)
    seldom argued as issue in judicial proceedings, 54
    upheld by Jefferson County Court of Common Pleas, 1806 (*see Cost Award Cases*)

upheld by Ohio Supreme Court, 1807
(*see Rutherford v. M'Faddon*)
judicial supremacy
distinguished from judicial review, 9,
179
rejected as doctrine of Ohio constitutional law, 118
Judiciary Acts (U.S.), 1789, 15, 67; 1801, 14
jury nullification, 13
Justices of the Peace, 19–22
number who were legislators, 21
practice before, pettifoggers, 22
small claims jurisdiction, 21 (*see also*
Fifty Dollar Act)

Kentucky Supreme Court. *See* courts, other
states
Kinney, Lewis, 116
Kirker, Thomas, 71, 92, 94, 174–75
Kramer, Larry D., 8, 11, 12
Kyle, Samuel, 153–55, 159

lawyers
change in public attitude toward,
188
described by Tocqueville, 188
education, competence, 37–38, 40
preference for common pleas in small
claims cases, 22
professional fellowship, circuit bench
and bar, 189
"Lest We Again Be Marshall'd," vii, 76
"Letters from Ohio," 20–21
Lewis, Philip, 33
Ohio House committee, chaired by,
33–34, 108, 186
Linonia Society, 52–53
Litchfield Law School, 37–38, 47–50. *See also*
Tod, George
moot court, organization and procedure, 53
argument over judicial review, 1797:
framed as "one issue" case, 53–54;
counsel, 54; setting, 56–57; record,
57; formalistic arguments superseded, 56; Twining, for affirmative,

57–58; Tod and Williams, contra,
58–59; judges' opinions, 59–60
Looker, Othniel, 96, 110
Lucas, Robert, 99
Ludlow, William, 171–72
Lyon, Matthew, 13

Madison, James, 3, 6–7, 9, 13–14, 61, 79,
80–81, 170, 189
Mann, Horace, 49–51
Marbury v. Madison, 1–2, 7–10, 17–18, 32,
53–55, 63–67
Marbury, William, 14–15
Marietta *Western Spectator*
Morris speech, Ohio House, 145
Marshall, John, 7, 10, 12, 14–15, 17–18, 53, 55,
63–66, 186. *See also Marbury v. Madison*
"Marshall'd," vii, 76
Martin, Jacob, 27, 29
Massie, Nathaniel, 71, 135, 164
McArthur, Duncan, 135, 169–70, 172
McConnell, Robert, 172
McCormick v. Alexander, 187
M'Faddon, Daniel, 26. *See also Rutherford v.*
M'Faddon
spelling variants: "M'Fadden,"
"McFaddon," etc., 27
McKean, Thomas, 61
McLean, John
confused with U. S. Supreme Court
Justice John McLean, 161
Greene County Associate Judge, 157,
159–61
McLene, Jeremiah, 171
Meigs, Return Jonathan, Jr., 36, 70–71, 76,
143–44
Greene County judicial impasse,
156–58, 162–63
Monnett, Samuel, 94, 96, 110, 164–65,
170
moot courts, 51. *See also* Litchfield Law
School
Morris, Thomas
defeated for reelection to Ohio
Supreme Court, 1810, 133–34; im-
possibility of

identifying successor incumbent, 131
(*see also* Sweeping Resolution, Morris unintended victim)
efforts to regain his seat, 1810–11, 139, 141
election to Ohio Supreme Court, 1809, 120–23, 125, 128
member, Ohio House, 1810–1812, 141, 146, 171–72, 174; self-initiated challenge of qualifications to serve, 144–45
prosecutor, Tod, Pease impeachment trials, 96, 99, 107, 110–12, 114, (*see also* Chillicothe *Supporter*, Tod, Pease impeachment trials)
rape, accused of, by Mary Ireland, 124–25 (*see also* Chillicothe *Supporter*, Morris rape charge)
Morrow, James, 147, 157, 159, 163

Nelson, William E., 2, 67, 82, 187
New Lisbon *Ohio Patriot*
Tod and Sprigg's condemnation of Sweeping Resolution, 137
New Philadelphia, Ohio, 150
newspapers, Ohio, 19, 61–63. *See also* individual names
Northwest Ordinance, 40–41, 85, 101
Northwest Territory, 21, 30, 39, 44, 83, 109, 153
Norton, Carlos, 145–46, 175
Norton v. McLeary, 188
Notes on the State of Virginia, 3, 79

Ohio Centinel. See Dayton *Ohio Centinel*
Ohio Constitution, 1802. *See also Rights of the Judiciary*
"inviolate" right of jury trial, 22–23
judicial office: qualifications, election, interim appointment, 24–25
process for amending, 114
term of office, successor holders, 129, 130–31
Ohio Constitution, 1851
Convention deliberations, supreme court circuit sessions, 191

"inviolate" right of jury trial, 188
popularly elected judiciary, 11, 181
Ohio Hundred Year Book, 125
Ohio Patriot. See New Lisbon *Ohio Patriot*
Ohio state capital
Chillicothe, 19, 41, 109, 169
Cincinnati, 41
Columbus, 176
Zanesville, 133, 169
Ohio Supreme Court. *See* Supreme Court, Ohio
"opinions of the court." *See under* judicial opinions

Patten, Thomas, 27, 29
Pease, Calvin, 30–31, 37, 133, 143
impeachment trial, 1809 (*see* impeachment trial, Calvin Pease)
investigation of rulings, Ohio House, 1807, 31–33
Judge, Ohio Supreme Court, 1816–30, 183–86
judicial review, 93 (*see also Cost Award Cases; Rutherford v. M'Faddon*)
War of 1812 service, 183
Pennsylvania judges, impeachment trials, 15–17, 33, 113
Pension Act Cases (U.S.), 55, 67
pettifoggers, practice in justices' courts, 22
Phi Beta Kappa, Yale Chapter, 38–39, 40, 52
Pickering, John, 16–17
Pierce, Sarah, Female Academy, Litchfield, 57
Pollock, John, 175
Pritchard, James, 96
Purviance, David, 146, 165, 172, 175

"Quids," 61

Rakove, Jack, 11
Ranney, Rufus, 181, 191
Ratcliffe, Donald J., 1, 135, 144, 161
Reed v. Moore, 125
Reeve, Tapping. *See* Litchfield Law School
Rehnquist, William H., 17

Reporter, Ohio Supreme Court decisions.
See Supreme Court, Ohio, reporter
Republicans, Republican Party
   U.S.: "moderate," "old," "radical" Re-
      publicans, 12–13; mistrust of feder-
      al judiciary, 12, 14; repeal of 1801
      Judiciary Act, 14; radicals favored
      greater jurisdiction for lay magis-
      trates, 12; advocated broad scope
      for impeachment power, 16–17
   Ohio: efforts to gain statehood,
      40–41; radical faction referred to
      by historians as "regular" or "radi-
      cal" Republicans, by themselves as
      "democratic Republicans" or "De-
      mocrats," 135; their leader Wor-
      thington, platform of opposition
      to judicial review and judicial inde-
      pendence, 71; their success in 1810
      judicial elections as victory over
      "insidiousness of Quiddism,
      wickedness of Federalism," 133;
      "moderates" or "independents"
      supported judiciary, along with
      Federalists, 76, 144; their leaders:
      Massie, McArthur, Creighton, edi-
      torial voice: Chillicothe *Independent
      Republican*, 135; their gains in 1810–11
      House of Representatives, 144; at-
      tacked as "quids," "lordly aristo-
      crats," "high court party," 135;
      "quid" as a name, 61; "ticket vot-
      ing," 144
Resnick, Alice Robie, 180–81
Rights of the Judiciary, The, 80–87. *See also* judi-
   cial review
   examples of unconstitutional laws:
      denying entitlement to bail, 85; au-
      thorizing forced removal of immi-
      grant negroes, 85–86; landowner
      prosecutions for resisting irregular
      public takings, 82, 84–85
   Ohio constitution, 1802: rights of po-
      litical minorities, 82; already being
      cited and applied in Ohio courts,
      82

Ruggles, Benjamin, 133
Rutherford, Benjamin, 26–27, 107, 112
Rutherford v. M'Faddon
   cited in *State ex rel. Academy of Trial
      Lawyers v. Sheward*, 180–81
   debated in letters published in Ohio
      newspapers (*see under* judicial re-
      view)
   disregarded as precedent for invalidat-
      ing Fifty Dollar Act, 117–18, 121,
      125; overruled *sub silentio* in *Norton v.
      McLeary*, 188
   Huntington's opinion, 63–66, 68;
      avoidance of pivotal issue, 65–66;
      reference to other decisions, 66; his
      ruling Fifty Dollar Act unconstitu-
      tional, 68
   Jefferson County common pleas
      court, proceedings in, 27
   Justice of the Peace Benjamin Hough,
      proceedings before, 26–27, 44, 107
   "M'Faddon" spelling, 27
   Ohio House Lewis Committee's
      awareness of, 33
   Ohio Supreme Court, proceedings in,
      44–45; opinions: distinctive fea-
      tures, first publication, 62–63
   political campaign issue, 76, 92–94,
      99, 142
   Tod's contribution to judicial review's
      acceptance, 191
   Tod's opinion, 66–68; judicial review:
      grounded on Ohio constitution's
      grant of "judicial power," 66; pro-
      tects individual rights, 67; Ohio
      constitution's "open courts" provi-
      sion, 67; rhetorical features, 67; his
      ruling Fifty Dollar Act unconstitu-
      tional, 68; threat to disqualify Jus-
      tices of the Peace from serving in
      legislature, 68

Scioto Gazette. See Chillicothe *Scioto Gazette*
Scott, Jessup W., 49
Scott, Thomas, 120–21, 123, 125–26, 131–33,
   136–38, 143, 145, 155, 167–69. *See also*

Sweeping Resolution, *Browder v. Mendenhall*

Sedition Act (U.S.), 3, 13–14, 128
  conduct of federal judges in trials under, 13
  Virginia and Kentucky resolutions, 13

Senate, Ohio. *See also* judicial elections and appointments; impeachment trials
  passage of Fifty Dollar Act, 108, 113
  repeal of Sweeping Resolution:
    1810–11 session, 146; 1811–12 session, 172–75

separation of powers, 3, 181

Seventh Amendment. *See* U.S. Constitution

Seventy Dollar Act, 117, 142, 180

Sharp, Joseph, 94, 96

Silliman, Benjamin, 175

Silliman, Wyllys, 34, 179

Slaughter, Robert F., 31

Sloane [also "Sloan"], John
  gubernatorial election, 1808, 92
  opposed judicial review, Ohio House, 73, 77–81, 99, 180
  "Sloan" spelling variant, 77
  temporizing remedies, as alternative to judicial review, 79, 105, 179, 180

Smith, Jacob, 153–54, 157–58, 163, 175

Snowden, James, 152–54, 157–60, 166, 169, 176, 191. *See also* Sweeping Resolution; Greene County Court of Common Pleas; judicial elections and appointments

Society of St. Tammany. *See* Tammany Society

Sosin, J. M., 7, 10

Spaight, Richard, 55–56

Sprigg, William, 36, 76, 89–90, 95, 126. *See also* Sweeping Resolution
  attempts to reclaim seat, 136–41
  ouster from Ohio Supreme Court, 1810, 130, 133

"Squirrel Law," 74

St. Clair, Arthur, 20, 40–41, 98

St. Clair, Arthur, Jr., 98, 102

St. Clairsville *Ohio Federalist*, 167. *See also* Hammond, Charles

State of Ohio
  admission to statehood, 40–41
  population increase, 1810 census, 169 (*see also* Congress, U.S., Ohio seats)
  state capitals: Chillicothe, 96; Zanesville, 133, 169; Columbus, 176, 184

State ex rel. Academy of Trial Lawyers v. Sheward, 181

State v. Beckett, 89–91

State v. Cottrell, 155. *See also* Greene County Court of Common Pleas

State v. Richards, 155. *See also* Greene County Court of Common Pleas

State v. Zane, 84–85, 180

Sterett, John, 157, 162–63

Steubenville *Western Herald*
  Campbell speech opposing judicial review, 77
  powers, independence of judiciary as electoral issue, 70, 72, 92–93
  Rutherford v. M'Faddon, 45–46, 63, 69–70
  "Squirrel Law," 74

Stiles, Ezra, 51

Story, Joseph, 48

Sullivan, Samuel, 166

Supporter. See Chillicothe *Supporter*

Supreme Court, Ohio
  circuits, judges' pairings, 42, 75, 121, 125
  en banc (full bench) hearings, 42, 75–76, 89–91, 120–21, 132, 182, 184
  "fourth" judgeship, 74–75, 119–20, 131–32, 136, 145, 168–69
  Greene County session, 1810. *See Browder v. Mendenhall*
  judges' length of service, 183–84
  jurisdiction, 35–36, 75
  members' titles as "judge," "chief judge," 35
  post-1820s judicial review cases, 182–83
  quorum of judges, 35
  reporter, 184 (*see also* Hammond, Charles)
  sessions, 35

Sweeping Resolution, proceedings re, 137, 139, 141, 155–56, 167
    Sprigg proposal for schismatic court, 136–40
transformation into modern appellate tribunal, 75, 184
Swan, Cyrus, 57, 59–60
"Sweeping Resolution," 129–33. *See also* House of Representatives, Ohio; and Senate, Ohio
    Associate Judges, unintended consequences for, 147–48
    debated in letters published in Ohio newspapers:
        "Backwoodsman," *Scioto Gazette*, 1810, 142
        "Calpurnius" [Charles Hammond], *Supporter*, 1811, 166–69
        "Farmer," *Scioto Gazette*, 1810, 142
        Hare, Captain, Militia Muster, report of, *Scioto Gazette*, 1810, 142
        "Justice," *Scioto Gazette*, 1810, 139
        "Lawyer," *Supporter*, 1810, 134–35, 165–66
        "Logan," *Scioto Gazette*, 1810, 139
        "Lover of Good Government," *Ohio Centinel*, 1810, 142
        McArthur, Duncan, *Scioto Gazette*, 1811, 169
        "Ploughman" [Charles Hammond], *Independent Republican*, 1811, 166–67
    effect on Scott, Morris seats unascertainable, 131
    issue in election campaigns (*see* elections, Ohio, Governor and Legislators)
    Morris unintended victim, 133–34; speech in Ohio House, 1811, 144–45
    Ohio Supreme Court, proceedings concerning, 137, 139, 141, 155–56, 167
    related legislative actions: abolishing "fourth" judgeship, 132; repealing provisions for two supreme court circuits and *en banc* proceedings, 132; amendment to Commissioning Act, 132, 171, 173–74
    repeal, 146, 163, 171–75
    Tappan, Benjamin, advocated adoption, 130–31, 165
    Tod, Sprigg casualties of, 130, 133; efforts to retain their seats, 136–41
Swift, Zephaniah, 11, 57, 65
Symmes, Daniel, 36, 42–43, 45, 76, 119, 130–31

Taft, William Howard, 47
Taggart v. Carothers, 82
Tammany Society, 135, 143–44, 146–47, 157–58, 162–66, 175–76
    1810 election; "ticket voting," 144
    Chillicothe "Wigwam No. 1," 143–44, 163, 165; Tiffin's "Long Talk," 164
    members in Ohio General Assembly, 147
    opposed, ridiculed, 147, 157, 162–63, 164–65
    support for Sweeping Resolution, 165
    Xenia "Wigwam No. 4," 158–59; campaign for Haines appointment, 162–63
Tappan, Benjamin, 25, 73, 92, 130–31, 133–4, 150–51, 165
Tecumseh (Shawnee chief), 170
Thompson, John, 133
Three Hundred Dollar Act, 188
Thurman, Allen G., 186
Tiffin, Edward, 34, 36, 70, 88, 130, 143–44, 157, 164
    Sweeping Resolution, promoted, 130, 133, 169
Tippecanoe, battle, 170
Tocqueville, Alexis de, 182
Tod, George. See also *Rutherford v. M'Faddon*, Sweeping Resolution
    appointed, then elected to Ohio Supreme Court, 37
    contribution to judicial review's acceptance (*see under* judicial review)
    family life, 37, 39, 176–77
    Fifty Dollar Act, opposed adoption as legislator, 42
    impeachment (*see* impeachment trial, Tod)

Litchfield Law School, 37, 50; moot
court, 53; argument of judicial review, 54–60, 180
Ohio Senate, 1810–1812, 141, 146, 170,
172–74
opinion in *Rutherford v. M'Faddon (see
under Rutherford v. M'Faddon)*
ouster from Ohio Supreme Court,
1810, 129–30, 133, 136–41
pioneer settler, Western Reserve,
37–40
presiding judge, common pleas circuit, 1816–30, 183
statehood, opposition to, 41
Sweeping Resolution, repeal, 170,
172–74
War of 1812 service, 177–78, 183
Yale College, 37; student debating,
51–53
Torrance, W. H., 4
Trevett v. Weeden, 55
Tucker, St. George, 48
Turner, George, 20
Twining, Stephen, 54, 57–58

U.S. Constitution
Article III, "judicial power," 7
Constitutional Convention, 1787, 7–8,
52, 55
Seventh, Fourteenth Amendments, 22
United States v. Hylton, 54–55
Utter, William T., 1–2, 61

Van Horne, Isaac, 171–72
Varnum, James, 55

Walker, Timothy
Cincinnati College of Law, 49
collection practices in Justices' courts,
20–21
egalitarianism in frontier Ohio as to
educational qualification, 38
judicial review, approval of, 181–82
"Letters from Ohio," 20–21, 38
War of 1812, 170, 177, 183. *See also* Harrison,
William Henry; Tod, George; Pease,
Calvin

Western Herald. See Steubenville *Western Her-
ald*
Western Reserve, 39–40
Western Spectator. See Marietta Western Spectator
Whittlesey, Elisha, 116
Wickam, John, 54
Williams, Thomas Scott, 54, 58–59, 104, 180
Wilson, John, 162–63
Wood, Stephen, 101–02
Woodbridge, William, 110–11, 114–15, 117
Lawyers' Circular Letter, 115
Worthington, Thomas
Adams, John Quincy, described by, 18
gubernatorial candidate
defeated 1808, 76, 92, 94; 1810, 143–44,
161–62
elected 1814, 1816, 183
impeachment trials, Tod and Pease,
122–23
judicial elections: 1809, 123, 128; 1810,
134
judicial independence, 18
judicial review, opposition to, 34,
71–73, 86, 91
Ohio statehood, 18, 40–41
Republican political leader, 40–41,
70–71, 98, 135, 169
Tammany Society, 143
Tod, George, army commission, personal feelings toward, 177–78
Sweeping Resolution, 146, 165, 171–72,
175, 179
U. S. Senate, 18, 170, 177–78
Wright, Samuel, 151
writ of error, 23
Wythe, George, 48

Xenia, Ohio, 127, 144, 150–52, 158–59

Yale College, student debating, 51, 53
Yates, Robert, 9
Yeates, Jasper, 113

Zane, Isaac, 84, 180
Zanesville, city of. *See under* Ohio state capital

Series on Law, Politics, and Society

Lichfield
THE U.S. ARMY ON TRIAL
Jack Gieck

Murder, Culture, and Injustice
FOUR SENSATIONAL CASES IN AMERICAN HISTORY
Walter Hixson

Superintending Democracy
THE COURTS AND THE POLITICAL PROCESS
Christopher P. Banks and John C. Green, eds.